CAMBRIDGE GREEK AND LATIN CLASSICS

GENERAL EDITORS

P. E. EASTERLING
Regius Professor Emeritus of Greek, University of Cambridge

PHILIP HARDIE
Senior Research Fellow, Trinity College, and Honorary Professor of Latin, University of Cambridge

NEIL HOPKINSON
Fellow, Trinity College, University of Cambridge

RICHARD HUNTER
Regius Professor of Greek, University of Cambridge

E. J. KENNEY
Kennedy Professor Emeritus of Latin, University of Cambridge

S. P. OAKLEY
Kennedy Professor of Latin, University of Cambridge

GREEK ELEGY AND IAMBUS

A SELECTION

EDITED BY

WILLIAM ALLAN

McConnell Laing Fellow and Tutor in Classics
University College, Oxford

CAMBRIDGE
UNIVERSITY PRESS

University Printing House, Cambridge CB2 8BS, United Kingdom

One Liberty Plaza, 20th Floor, New York, NY 10006, USA

477 Williamstown Road, Port Melbourne, VIC 3207, Australia

314-321, 3rd Floor, Plot 3, Splendor Forum, Jasola District Centre, New Delhi - 110025, India

79 Anson Road, #06-04/06, Singapore 079906

Cambridge University Press is part of the University of Cambridge.

It furthers the University's mission by disseminating knowledge in the pursuit of education, learning and research at the highest international levels of excellence.

www.cambridge.org
Information on this title: www.cambridge.org/9781107122994
DOI: 10.1017/9781316403341

© Cambridge University Press 2019

This publication is in copyright. Subject to statutory exception and to the provisions of relevant collective licensing agreements, no reproduction of any part may take place without the written permission of Cambridge University Press.

First published 2019

A catalogue record for this publication is available from the British Library

Library of Congress Cataloging in Publication data
NAMES: Allan, William, 1970– editor.
TITLE: Greek elegy and iambus : a selection / edited by William Allan.
DESCRIPTION: Cambridge : Cambridge University Press, 2019. | Includes bibliographical references and index.
IDENTIFIERS: LCCN 2019011498 | ISBN 9781107122994 (alk. paper)
SUBJECTS: LCSH: Elegiac poetry, Greek. | Iambic poetry, Greek. | Iambic poetry, Greek – History and criticism. | Elegiac poetry, Greek – History and criticism.
CLASSIFICATION: LCC PA3445.E6 G74 2019 | DDC 881/.01–dc23
LC record available at https://lccn.loc.gov/2019011498

ISBN 978-1-107-12299-4 Hardback
ISBN 978-1-107-55997-4 Paperback

Cambridge University Press has no responsibility for the persistence or accuracy of URLs for external or third-party internet websites referred to in this publication, and does not guarantee that any content on such websites is, or will remain, accurate or appropriate.

TO LAURA, IONA, AND XANTHE
Till a' the seas gang dry

CONTENTS

Preface	*Page* ix
Notes on the Text	x
List of Abbreviations	xi
Map	xiv
Introduction	1
1. Elegy and Iambus as Poetic Forms	1
2. Performance and Mobility	6
3. Poets and Personae	9
4. Society and Culture	11
5. Language, Style, Metre	14
6. Transmission of the Text	18
GREEK ELEGY AND IAMBUS: A SELECTION	21
Archilochus	23
Semonides	29
Callinus	33
Tyrtaeus	33
Mimnermus	36
Solon	37
Theognis	43
Xenophanes	47
Hipponax	49
Simonides	53
Commentary	57
Works Cited	237
Index	251

PREFACE

Elegy and iambus are major forms of Greek literature and are crucial to understanding the Archaic and early Classical periods in particular. Yet in literary courses students often jump from reading Homer to fifth-century literature, especially tragedy, and so miss the important role played by Archaic poetry other than epic. Moreover, elegy and iambus are not all that difficult linguistically or metrically and are therefore highly suitable texts to study. The publication of this volume, together with one on early Greek lyric in this series, will, one hopes, promote their wider use in teaching. The selection aims to give a representative sample of each poet's surviving work, while also highlighting their variety – alas, only one substantial piece of Callinus survives. I aimed to select around 1,000 lines of Greek – a little under the average length of a Greek tragedy – so as to leave enough space for linguistic, literary, and cultural commentary. The selection covers ten poets, two iambic (Semonides and Hipponax), six elegiac (Callinus, Tyrtaeus, Mimnermus, Theognis, Xenophanes, and Simonides), and two writing in both forms (Archilochus and Solon, who accordingly get more space). Also included are Hipponax's parodic hexameters (fr. 128) and Xenophanes' combination of iambic trimeter and hexameter (fr. B 14). I have relied on the standard editions in creating my own text and apparatus, and have inspected the papyri where possible and used photographs where not. The apparatus has been kept as succinct as possible, and thorny issues are discussed in the notes.

I would like to thank the staff of the British Library, the Oxyrhynchus Papyri, and the Institut für Altertumskunde (Papyrologie) in Cologne. I am immensely grateful to Pat Easterling, Neil Hopkinson, and Richard Hunter, general editors of the series, whose wise and penetrating comments led to numerous improvements, and to Michael Sharp, Lisa Sinclair, and Sophie Taylor at Cambridge University Press for their expertise and care in the production of the book. I owe particular thanks to John Jacobs for his learned and meticulous copy-editing.

My greatest debt, expressed in the dedication, is to my wife Laura Swift and our wonderful daughters. They have improved the book, and my life, in innumerable ways.

W. R. A.
Oxford
September 2018

NOTES ON THE TEXT

1. An asterisk following a reference (e.g. Archil. 1* or fr. 1*) means that the poem or fragment is included in this selection.
2. 'Fr.' and 'frr.' are generally omitted where this creates no ambiguity. Thus Archil. 196a* = Archil. fr. 196a W.
3. The numbering of West 1989–92 is used throughout, with the addition of Archil. 17a Swift and Xenoph. B 14 DK (= D12 Laks–Most).
4. The Greek text features the following conventions:

    ] left-hand limit of the papyrus

    [right-hand limit of the papyrus

    [α] letter supplied by editor (gap in the papyrus)

    <α> letter inserted by editor (no gap in papyrus or manuscript)

    α̣ letter cannot be identified with certainty

ABBREVIATIONS

The poets edited in this volume are abbreviated as follows:

Archil., Semon., Callin., Tyrt., Mimn., Sol., Thgn., Xenoph., Hippon., Simon.

Abbreviations of other ancient authors and texts generally follow those used in the *Oxford Classical Dictionary* (4th ed., 2012). Note also:

Bernabé	A. Bernabé, *Poetarum epicorum Graecorum: testimonia et fragmenta, Pars I*, 2nd ed., Stuttgart 1996
CEG	P. A. Hansen, *Carmina epigraphica Graeca*, 2 vols, Berlin 1983–9
CGCG	E. van Emde Boas et al., *The Cambridge grammar of Classical Greek*, Cambridge 2019
DK	H. Diels and W. Kranz, *Die Fragmente der Vorsokratiker*, 3 vols, 6th ed., Berlin 1951–2
Fowler	R. L. Fowler, *Early Greek mythography*, 2 vols, Oxford 2000–13
FGrH	F. Jacoby, *Die Fragmente der griechischen Historiker*, Berlin/Leiden 1923–
Goodwin	W. W. Goodwin, *Syntax of the moods and tenses of the Greek verb*, 2nd ed., London 1889
GP	J. D. Denniston, *The Greek particles*, 2nd ed. revised by K. J. Dover, Oxford 1950
IEG^2	see W below
Laks–Most	A. Laks and G. W. Most, *Early Greek philosophy*, 9 vols, Cambridge, MA 2016
LIMC	*Lexicon iconographicum mythologiae classicae*, 18 vols, Zurich 1981–97
LSJ	H. G. Liddell and R. Scott, revised by H. S. Jones, *A Greek–English lexicon*, 9th ed. with supplement, Oxford 1996
MW	R. Merkelbach and M. L. West, *Fragmenta Hesiodea*, Oxford 1967
P. Argent.	*Strasbourg Papyri* (1912–)
P. Colon.	*Kölner Papyri* (1976–)
P. Oxy.	*Oxyrhynchus Papyri* (1898–)
PSI	*Papiri greci e latini* (Pubblicazioni della Società Italiana per la ricerca dei papiri greci e latini in Egitto), Florence 1912–
Page	D. L. Page, *Epigrammata graeca*, Oxford 1975

PMG	D. L. Page, *Poetae melici Graeci*, Oxford 1962
PMGF	M. Davies, *Poetarum melicorum Graecorum fragmenta, vol 1: Alcman, Stesichorus, Ibycus*, Oxford 1991
SEG	*Supplementum epigraphicum Graecum*, Leiden 1923–
Smyth	H. W. Smyth, *Greek grammar*, Cambridge, MA 1920
W	M. L. West, *Iambi et elegi Graeci ante Alexandrum cantati*, 2 vols, 2nd ed., Oxford 1989–92

MAP

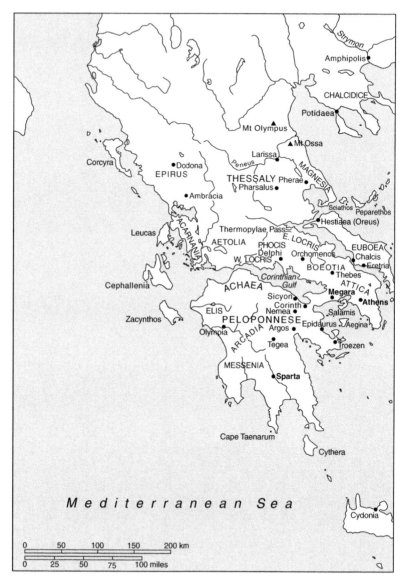

Map 1 Greece and the Aegean, including the birthplaces of Archilochus (Paros), Semonides (Samos), Callinus and Hipponax (Ephesus), Tyrtaeus (Sparta), Mimnermus (Smyrna), Solon (Athens), Theognis (Megara), Xenophanes (Colophon), and Simonides (Ceos).

MAP

INTRODUCTION

1 ELEGY AND IAMBUS AS POETIC FORMS

By the time elegy and iambus become visible to us in the mid-seventh century BC they are well-established poetic forms with a long history, though these pre-literary traditions are obscure. The Spartan Tyrtaeus, one of the first poets whose work has survived, composed his elegies with Doric speakers in mind but wrote in the Ionic dialect, since this was already a traditional feature of elegy (see §5 below). In general, the technical mastery of the earliest seventh-century authors (Archilochus, Semonides, Callinus, Tyrtaeus, Mimnermus) indicates that elegy and iambus had been flourishing for some time, and not only in Ionia. Both forms are strikingly diverse in their subject-matter and tone, and the poets, often using the first person (see §3 below), speak directly about fundamental human concerns.[1]

Elegy. Though elegy is easy to define formally as poetry composed in elegiac couplets (see §5), this uniformity should not be allowed to obscure the breadth of its content and style, ranging from poetry about grief (e.g. Archil. 13*) and erotic desire (Mimn. 1*) to mythological narrative (Archil. 17a*) and political or military exhortation (Callin. 1*).[2] The flexibility of elegy made it one of the most widely used poetic forms throughout antiquity, and we can see its variety reflected in the largest surviving corpus of early elegy, the 'Theognidea', which blends political and social commentary with sympotic banter and homoerotic song.[3] Moreover, the vagaries of transmission and the stereotyping of particular authors in antiquity mean that we have only a partial view of these poets: Tyrtaeus, for example, tended to be quoted for his rousing war poetry (12*) and Mimnermus for his reflections on youth and old age (2*), but the selection process does not give us a representative picture of their

---

[1] A similar diversity and personal perspective are evident in Archaic and Classical lyric poetry. Despite the modern (Romantic-period) idea of 'lyric' as a single form encompassing lyric (both solo and choral), elegy, and iambus, it makes sense to see them as distinct genres, even if the boundaries between them are fluid. On definitions of 'lyric', ancient and modern, see Budelmann 2018: 2–4.

[2] On various aspects of elegy, see West 1974: 1–21, Adkins 1985, Herington 1985: 192–3, Bowie 1986, 1990, 2016b, Fowler 1987: 86–103, Bartol 1993: 18–30, 46–60, Gerber 1997b, Kurke 2000: 54–7, Irwin 2005: 19–111, Aloni and Iannucci 2007: 3–108, Faraone 2008, Garner 2011, Lulli 2011, Budelmann and Power 2013, Swift and Carey 2016.

[3] See the headnote to Theognis in the commentary.

work (for the former's historical elegy, see Tyrt. 5–7*; for the latter's mythological narrative, see Mimn. 12*). The variety of early elegy is potentially further obscured by the form's association with mourning and lamentation. By the late fifth century the term ἔλεγος was used to describe songs of mourning (e.g. Eur. *Tro.* 119, *Hel.* 185, *IT* 146), and later writers frequently connected elegy with grief or claimed that elegy originated in lament (e.g. Hor. *Ars P.* 75 *uersibus impariter iunctis querimonia primum*). However, the surviving examples of Archaic elegy tell a different story, since only a few have anything to do with mourning (e.g. Archil. 13*, Simonides' Plataea Elegy*). So unless a whole foundational tradition of lamentatory elegy has vanished without trace,[4] the particular association of elegy with mourning is likely to be due to a later narrowing of the genre, akin to the narrowing definition of iambus as invective poetry evident from the fifth century onwards (see below). Although elegy was deployed for laments and funerary epitaphs in the Archaic period, this was only one aspect of its use. But it is the later sense of elegy as intrinsincally mournful, and especially the tendency to compose epitaphs in elegiacs, which has shaped the modern notion of 'elegy' and 'elegiac', even though this was a relatively minor feature of a highly flexible form.

Most surviving elegy was performed at *symposia* (see §2), with pieces ranging from single couplets to 100 lines (cf. Solon 1–3*),[5] but the elegies performed at public festivals (e.g. Tyrt. 4*, Simon.10–16*) could be much longer, some of them well over a thousand lines.[6] In these the poet or speaker addresses the entire city or community, while elegies performed at *symposia* typically have a narrower audience in mind and may be addressed to a particular friend or political faction (e.g. Thgn. 39–52*; see §4). Public elegy tends to take a wider view of history, stretching back to the foundations of cities or their colonies,[7] while sympotic elegy is more focused on the here and now – for example, in reflecting on the proper conduct of the *symposion* itself (Xenoph. 1*) or foregrounding the speaker's erotic desires, friendships, and political allegiances – but there is no need to posit a rigid division between the two occasions or their functions, since sympotic elegy can also take the long view, especially in its liking for philosophical reflection (e.g. Sol. 13*), and both types can deploy narrative

---

[4] An unlikely scenario: see Bowie 1986: 22–7, contra Page 1936; cf. Harvey 1955: 170–1, Nobili 2011.
[5] See Bowie 2016a. The longest extant elegy is Solon 13*, which is 76 lines.
[6] Bowie 1986: 30–4. On public elegy, see further §2.
[7] See Dougherty 1994.

and heroic myth, as do Archilochus' Telephus and Simonides' Plataea poems (Archil. 17a*, Simon. 10–16*).⁸ Elegy was sung to the accompaniment of *auloi* (reed pipes, usually played as a pair; cf. Thgn. 239–43*), but here too one must allow for variation: if no aulete was available to play for a drinking-party, or a particular symposiast simply could not sing, a more recitative-like chant could be used, without melodic accompaniment.⁹ More formal public occasions would feature well-rehearsed auletes and singers, but the repeated and relatively simple elegiac metre presumably entailed fairly straightfoward tunes, so that even the amateur sympotic performer of elegy might feel less daunted than he would by the more complex melodies of lyric poetry; in addition, he did not have to accompany himself (as in lyric) but had a professional aulete to guide his voice.

Elegy's metrical similarity to the hexameter of heroic epic and didactic not only enabled it to incorporate and adapt their formulae, themes, and tone, but is also likely to have shaped its development.¹⁰ Elegy's perceived closeness to these serious genres discouraged the use of scurrilous or obscene language and subject-matter, whose absence perhaps constitutes elegy's most marked difference from iambus. Elegy's engagement with the genres of Archaic Greece extended well beyond epic to all varieties of lyric poetry, from erotic song to religious hymns. Flexible in both length and theme, elegy was the most adaptable form of Greek verse, and it continued to flourish well after Simonides (the latest poet, for reasons of space, in this selection). The songful *symposion* flourished throughout the fourth century and beyond, shaping the development of elegy, which remained a highly malleable form, used for consolatory tales of unhappy love (Antimachus' *Lyde*), learned aetiology (Callimachus' *Aetia*), mimetic hymns (Callim. *Bath of Pallas*), didactic (Nicander's *Cynegetica*), and much else besides, including countless epigrams.¹¹

Iambus. Like elegy, iambus can be defined metrically, as poetry composed in iambic trimeters and other closely associated forms: trochaic

---

⁸ On narrative elegy, see Bowie 2001a, 2001b, Lulli 2011.
⁹ For elegy sung to *auloi*, see Bowie 1986: 14, Bartol 1993: 46–51. Budelmann and Power 2013 stress variation in performance.
¹⁰ For elegy and epic, see Archil. 1*, 2*, 5*, 17a*, Callin. 1*, Tyrt. 12*, Mimn. 14*, Sol. 1–3*, 4*, 5*, 13*, Thgn. 237–54*, Xenoph. 1*, Simon. 11*, and Garner 2011: 19–38 on the adaptation of epic formulae. On elegy and didactic, see Semon. 1*, 7*, Sol. 4*, 13*, Thgn. 19–26*, 27–30*, 53–68*, 1197–202*, Xenoph. 1*, and Hunter 2014: 123–66 on Hesiod and the *symposion*.
¹¹ On expansion of the genre in post-Classical Greek elegy, see Lightfoot 2009: x. Cameron 1995: 70–90 outlines the creation of new sympotic poetry (especially elegiac epigram) in the Hellenistic period.

tetrameters, choliambics, and epodes (see §5).[12] Although some scholars have argued that it is more accurate to understand *iambos* as a term referring to poetry with a particular content (especially invective, vulgarity, and sex), of which the iambic rhythm was characteristic,[13] there is no need to prioritize content over metre, since ancient authors use *iambos* to refer to both features (metrical and generic), and rhythm is perceived as part of its meaning from the seventh century onwards (cf. Archil. 215).[14] In addition, much early iambic poetry contained none of the abusive or low material allegedly typical of the genre (cf. Semon. 1*, Sol. 36*).

Of course, this is not to deny that invective, vulgarity, and sexual exuberance are important aspects. And although attacks against enemies or expressions of erotic desire are found in all types of early Greek poetry (e.g. Sappho 31, Alc. 129), they generally avoid the vulgar language, reference to body parts, and obscene content of iambus (e.g. Archil. 42*, Hippon. 92*).[15] The association of iambus with mockery is seen in the figure of Iambe, a female servant in the house of Celeus at Eleusis, whose jokes and teasing cheer up the grieving Demeter (*HHDem.* 202–4). But whereas Iambe's mockery is gentle and beneficial, that of the iambic poets is much more caustic, and they attack their enemies in various ways and for a variety of reasons: Archilochus, for example, uses the fable of the fox and the eagle to expose Lycambes' treachery in breaking his promise to betroth one of his daughters (172–81*); in revenge he seduces his former fiancée's younger sister and destroys the entire family's reputation (196a*). Similarly, Hipponax has illicit sex with the mistress of his enemy Bupalus (16–17*, 84). These iambic attacks are intended to be entertaining and are often humorous, but they also communicate serious ideas: conventional morality is implicitly affirmed, as the poet's public display of his enemy's crimes reinforces a variety of social norms (oath-keeping, for example, or guarding unmarried daughters).[16]

But there is much more to iambic poetry than invective and vulgar humour: it can be moralizing (e.g. Archil. 19*, Semon. 7*, Hippon. 115*), philosophical (Semon. 1*), or political (Archil. 114*, Sol. 36*).

---

[12] On iambus, see West 1974: 22–39, Bartol 1993: 30–41, 61–74, Brown 1997, Kurke 2000: 51–4, Steinrück 2000, 2009, Bowie 2001b, 2002, Kantzios 2005, Hedreen 2006, Rosen 2007a, Carey 2009, Lennartz 2010, Rotstein 2010, Swift and Carey 2016.
[13] E.g. West 1974: 22.
[14] Bartol 1993: 32–4, Rotstein 2010: 224–5; for metrical versus content-based conceptions of iambus, see Lennartz 2010: 86–100.
[15] In lyric Alcaeus' 'potbelly' (φύσγων), applied to Pittacus, is about as rude as it gets (129.21). Homeric insults can be vigorous (e.g. *Il.* 1.225 οἰνοβαρές, κυνὸς ὄμματ' ἔχων, κραδίην δ' ἐλάφοιο), but are never obscene.
[16] See Brown 1997: 41–2.

1 ELEGY AND IAMBUS AS POETIC FORMS 5

Like elegy, iambus is a wide-ranging and flexible form: it uses narrative (much of it apparently autobiographical: see §3), embedded speech (Archil. 196a*), fables (Archil. 172–81*, Semon. 7*), parody (Hippon. 3a*, 32* 34*), and many other literary devices. And far from being sealed off from other genres, it constantly interacts with them, sometimes parodically (as in the mock-epic language and mock-didactic tone of Semon. 7*), sometimes seriously (as when Solon's iambics echo the political *paraenesis* of elegy: 36*). Each poet had a distinctive style and persona(e): Hipponax, for example, plays up the low-class nature of his character and actions – as a thief (3a*) or a pauper begging Hermes for wealth (32*, 34*, 36*) – and goes further than his iambic predecessors in situating himself on the margins of respectable society (see 92*). Unfortunately, much of this variety of tone and subject-matter was lost in the course of transmission, especially when invective came to be seen (from the Hellenistic period onwards) as the defining feature, narrowing the genre and obscuring the range of Archaic and Classical iambus.[17]

Like most small-scale early Greek poetry, iambus was primarily performed at the *symposion*,[18] but it could also be performed at musical contests (μουσικοὶ ἀγῶνες)[19] and civic religious festivals,[20] though few now believe that its performance was tied to fertility cults of Demeter and Dionysus.[21] Its mode of performance was no less flexible: ancient sources speak of spoken, recited, and sung iambics (to the accompaniment of *auloi* or stringed intstruments).[22] As with elegy, it is best to allow for variation, depending on the performer's ability, the availability of musicians, and the formality of the occasion. Iambic poetry continued to

---

[17] See Rotstein 2010: 319–46, 2016.
[18] Cf. e.g. Archil. 173*, where the speaker says to Lycambes 'you turned your back on the great oath sworn by salt and table', constructing himself as a fellow symposiast whose enemy has violated the bonds of the sympotic *hetaireia*.
[19] Cf. Heraclit. B 42 DK (= D21 Laks–Most) τόν τε Ὅμηρον ἔφασκεν ἄξιον ἐκ τῶν ἀγώνων ἐκβάλλεσθαι καὶ ῥαπίζεσθαι καὶ Ἀρχίλοχον ὁμοίως. On iambus at *mousikoi agônes*, see Rotstein 2010: 256–60.
[20] For iambic poetry at public gatherings and the *symposion*, see Bartol 1993: 65–70, Bowie 2001a: 61–2, 2002: 38, Kantzios 2005: 1–33, Rotstein 2010: 253–78.
[21] The evidence for the ritual origins of iambus in cultic mockery and bawdiness (cf. West 1974: 23–7, 1997: 496) is tenuous: see Rotstein 2010: 180–2 (on the story of Iambe). In any case, the scope of surviving iambic poetry shows that by the seventh century the genre had developed well beyond its cultic origins (if it had any) to embrace a variety of themes and purposes.
[22] Bartol 1993: 61–5. One cannot be certain, but it seems plausible that trimeters tended to be spoken or recited, epodes and trochaic tetrameters sung: see Dale 1963: 46–8, West 1974: 33, Lloyd-Jones 1975: 13, Bartol 1993: 63–4, Rotstein 2010: 229–52.

be written throughout antiquity,[23] though the Alexandrian canonization of Archilochus, Semonides, and Hipponax (as counterparts to the nine lyric poets), together with an increasing focus on invective (see above), influenced the subsequent perception of its range and character.[24]

2 PERFORMANCE AND MOBILITY

The predominantly oral culture of Archaic Greece offered a variety of occasions for the performance and enjoyment of elegiac and iambic poetry, but the most important venues were *symposia* and festivals. Discussions of the *symposion* tend to retroject the model of Classical Athens back on other cities and earlier periods; we have little hard evidence for the *symposion* on (for example) seventh-century Paros, beyond the clues given in Archilochus' surviving poetry. Nonetheless, the frequent references to the *symposion* in elegy and iambus, including 'rules' for its proper conduct (see Xenoph. 1*), allow us to piece together a more or less consistent picture of aristocratic entertainment and male bonding.[25] Archaeological evidence suggests drinking groups of around fourteen to thirty men, reclining in pairs on couches arranged around the edge of the men's banqueting-hall (or ἀνδρών). This relatively small-scale and exclusive environment encouraged poetry purportedly directed at the poet's friends (as when Archilochus addresses Glaucus, or Theognis his beloved Cyrnus), but this intimacy is in part a fictional ploy which fosters the bonding of each sympotic group that performs and enjoys the poetry,[26] while the tone of the poetry itself can range from shockingly flippant (Archil. 5*) to solemn and moralizing (e.g. Semon. 1*).

In an important strand of sympotic poetry, typified by the elegies of Theognis, the sympotic group identify themselves as ἀγαθοί (e.g. Thgn. 31–2*, 37*), members of a social elite whose proper behaviour and civilized values complement their noble birth. No longer able to rely on

---

[23] On 'minor' iambic poets through to the late fourth century BC, see Carey 2016.
[24] Hipponax was particularly influential in the Hellenistic period: Callimachus' book of *Iamboi* opened with Hipponax returning from the Underworld (fr. 191 Pf.), while Herodas used choliambics to depict low-class urban life in his dramatic *Mimiamboi* (monologues and dialogues): Kerkhecker 1999, Acosta-Hughes 2002, Zanker 2009. For the variety of post-Classical iambus, see Cavarzere *et al.* 2001, Nesselrath 2007, Rosen 2007b.
[25] On various aspects of the *symposion*, see Murray 1990, 2018, Lissarrague 1991, Stehle 1997: 213–61, Slings 2000, Catoni 2010, Hobden 2013, Węcowski 2014, Cazzato *et al.* 2016.
[26] Even if we assume that Theognis' Cyrnus was a real person (unlikely: see on Thgn. 19–20*), most performances of the poetry about him will have been by amateur symposiasts rather than by the famous poet himself.

their wealth or status to mark themselves as a superior class, many aristocrats of the Archaic and Classical period appreciated the exclusivity of the *symposion* and the kind of poetry in which aristocratic manners and ideology were inculcated. When the drinking session was over, a rowdy procession (κῶμος) through the streets would further cement the cohesion of the all-male group. But there is much more to sympotic poetry than confirmation of group identity and the symposiasts' sense of belonging to an elite,[27] and poets explore all manner of topics, including sex (e.g. Archil. 42–3*, 196a*), gender stereotypes (Semon. 7*, Hippon. 68*), youth, maturity, and old age (Mimn. 1*, Sol. 27*), soldiering (Archil. 2*, 5*), military defeat (Archil. 17a*), patriotism (Callin. 1*, Tyrt. 12*, Sol. 1–3*), the mutability of fortune (Semon. 1*, Mimn. 2*, Sol. 13*), grief (Archil. 13*), the corruption of wealth (Sol. 4*), contentment with one's lot (Archil. 19*), and the value of poetry itself (Archil. 1*, Thgn. 237–54*, Xenoph. 2*).

Several Greek festivals featured competitions in music and poetry (μουσικοὶ ἀγῶνες).[28] An agonistic context has been suggested for Simonides' Plataea Elegy*, but it is much likelier to have been commissioned for a Panhellenic festival within a few years of the battle.[29] Similarly, the focus on foundations, victories, and historical and mythological narrative throughout public elegy (cf. Tyrt. 4–7*, Mimn. 14*, Xenoph. 3*) supports its performance and reperformance at civic festivals, with no need for poetic competitions to motivate its composition. Civic festivals may also have been the venue for Solon's political iambus (36*) and Archilochus' Lycambes poems (see on 172–81*).

Different performance contexts are reflected in the poetry, especially in the sphere of politics: whereas the *symposion* fosters poetry aimed at men who think themselves (or who aspire to be) the community's ἀγαθοί, the poetry performed at public festivals is addressed to the whole community and so tends to display more egalitarian values. Thus, Solon foregrounds his initiative in calling a public meeting to resolve the political crisis facing Athens, an imaginary gathering mirrored in the festival audience listening to his poem (36.1–2*). So skilful is Solon's evocation of civil strife and public exhortation that later tradition pictured him rushing into the agora to perform his poem on

---

[27] In any case, larger and more inclusive civic banquets (see Schmitt Pantel 1992) will have encouraged poetry with a broader appeal: cf. e.g. Solon's attempts to reconcile the aristocratic elite and the discontented δῆμος (5–6*, 36*).

[28] See Herington 1985: 161–6; also n. 19 above.

[29] See the headnote to Simonides. Though not a funeral, this festival will have focused on commemorating the war dead. As it happens, our earliest reference to a poetic contest is connected to a funeral: Hesiod boasts that he won first prize with a hymn at the funeral games of Alcidamas in Chalcis (*WD* 654–7).

Salamis (Plut. *Sol.* 8.1–2). The 'agora' probably stems from a misunderstanding of the poem's opening lines (see on 1.2*), though *Salamis* is likely to have been composed for a public occasion such as a civic festival. A related misunderstanding is present in the idea that some martial elegy (including Tyrt. 12*, but excluding sympotic poems like Callin. 1* and Mimn. 14*) was composed for recitation during military campaigns as a parade-ground performance to prepare the soldiers for imminent battle. There were, however, *symposion*-like gatherings both at Sparta itself (in *syssitia*, communal meals of citizen-soldiers) and on campaign (in the king's tent, among a select group of commanders), and these smaller, select groups, in part akin to the aristocratic *symposia* of Ionian communities, probably formed the original audiences of Tyrtaeus' martial elegies.[30]

Finally, it is important to bear in mind that poems could migrate from one performance context to another and that this would affect how they were received. And since poets were no doubt aware of this, they may have composed some works with different venues in mind. Thus Semonides' so-called 'Satire on Women' (7*) is well suited to performance at the all-male *symposion*, but it would be no less effective in the mixed setting of a public festival, where it could provoke mutual teasing between the sexes. A similar move between *symposion* and more public performance may inform Solon's political elegies, in which Solon seeks to persuade the Athenians in general and not (unlike Theognis) a narrow elite (cf. Sol. 4–6*, 9–11*). Conversely, poems such as Simonides' Plataea Elegy*, composed for first performance at a large-scale festival, could be reperformed at any Greek *symposion*, where a tale of heroic excellence and Panhellenic valour would be well received. Moreover, the poets themselves were part of Panhellenic cultural networks that encouraged travel in search of new engagements and commissions: Xenophanes of Colophon is said to have worked in Zancle, Catana, and Elea in Sicily, for example, while Simonides of Ceos plied his trade all over the Greek world (including Andros, Athens, Sicily, and Thessaly).[31] Thus poets had an interest in ensuring their work had broad appeal and could be performed on a range of occasions.[32]

---

[30] Cf. Bowie 1990: 224–9. By contrast, Tyrtaeus' political elegies, including his *Eunomia* ('Good Government'), were written for public festivals: see on Tyrt. 4*.

[31] On Panhellenic networks and poets' travels, see Stewart 2017a: 33–64.

[32] Tyrtaeus, Solon, and Theognis, whose poetry is closely tied to a particular city, nonetheless address contemporary problems of political and social turmoil that have purchase well beyond their notional audience of Spartans, Athenians, and Megarians. Similarly, some poets create a strong sense of local identity (especially Tyrtaeus and Solon; cf. D'Alessio 2009), but this is compatible with performance elsewhere.

3 POETS AND PERSONAE

What unites the various forms of Greek personal poetry (iambic and elegiac as well as lyric) is their basis in the world of the speaker (the 'I' of the poem), whose ideas and experiences come to the fore. Whereas genres like epic and tragedy typically focus on the mythical past, and the 'I' of the poet is foregrounded only occasionally (as in epic) or not at all (as in tragedy), much of this poetry appears to spring from the speaker's feelings and responses in the here and now. At first sight this kind of poetry seems highly familiar to us. The Enlightenment's emphasis on the individual as socially, politically, and artistically determinative culminated in the Romantic idea that spontaneous, genuine feeling is the basis of the best or truest poetry. Wordsworth's famous definition of poetry, in the Preface to his *Lyrical Ballads* (1802), as 'the spontaneous overflow of powerful feelings', encapsulates a conception of the art, as founded on the poet's personal emotional response to the world, which remains influential. However, while ancient personal poetry purports to express the speaker's response to the world, and while it no doubt draws on the poet's (and audience's) personal experiences, the goal of the ancient poet is not to reflect on his own experience, but to construct a persona which the audience will find both credible and engaging.[33]

In other words, poets are performers too and their goal is not unmediated self-expression, but the creation of a persona suited to the conventions of their chosen poetic form, the occasion of its performance, and the purpose for which they have composed the work.[34] There is no sharp dichotomy of real (or autobiographical) versus fictional, but a spectrum of possibilities, with different degrees of fictionalizing, and every poet is free to move along this continuum as s/he sees fit. So, for example, we have evidence that Glaucus (addressed by Archilochus) and Bupalus and

---

[33] On persona in Archaic poetry, see Slings 1990, Morrison 2007: 45–57. The tendency to read the poems (auto)biographically, ignoring the centrality of persona, began in antiquity: cf. e.g. the fifth-century author Critias' tirade against Archilochus as slavish, poor, abusive, adulterous, lecherous, arrogant, and a military deserter (Archil. 295). The ancient lives of the poets are largely based on the same approach: see Lefkowitz 2012.

[34] Thus we should beware of the idea that because much of this poetry is (or purports to be) 'personal', it is somehow less traditional or less concerned to interact with earlier literary works. Again this is a modern notion: the philosopher Immanuel Kant, for example, claimed, 'Among all the arts poetry holds the highest rank. It owes its origins almost entirely to genius and is least open to guidance by precept or examples' (*Critique of Judgement*), expressing a conception of poetry as the pure expression of the individual, not subject to literary tropes and traditions – the very opposite of ancient poets, lyric or otherwise, who are always aware of what genre they are writing in and its history.

Athenis (addressed by Hipponax) were real people.³⁵ But even if the poets are making some of their narrators engage with historical figures, this does not mean we can equate a poem's narrator with the historical author or overlook the fact that figures like Glaucus and Bupalus are made part of a fictional world.³⁶ An additional complication is the difficulty of saying who the speaker actually is: it is clear that the narrator of Alcaeus fr. 10, 'me, a pitiable woman', is not the poet himself but a female persona, but unless Aristotle had told us that the speaker of Archil. 19* was Charon the carpenter (*Rh.* 3.17.1418b28), we might have assumed it was Archilochus himself advocating a life of contentment with one's lot.

We may see real human lives as having a narrative structure, but there the story is lived before it is told – fiction (including poetry) is different, since the poet can construct a story without having lived it. Narrative, including personal narrative, is often taken to be a defining feature of iambus,³⁷ but it is no less important to elegy (as in Theognis' tales of social upheaval, told by an embittered aristocrat) and other forms of early Greek poetry (as when Hesiod creates the personae of cantankerous farmer and wastrel brother to suit the needs of his didactic *Works and Days*). Personae and their stories abound in Greek poetry, not least because poets and their audiences enjoy the spectacle and experience of *mimêsis* (pretending to be someone else), seen by Aristotle as not only a defining human characteristic but also a fundamental part of poetry and music (*Poet.* 4.1448b3–23). The poets create identities which later performers will enjoy, and learn from, adopting.

A single poet can deploy a variety of personae: Archilochus and Hipponax, for example, both act as guardians of morality, preaching the importance of keeping oaths (Archil. 172–81*, Hippon. 115*), but Archilochus can also play the part of unscrupulous seducer (196a*) and Hipponax the roles of beggar and thief (3a*, 32*, 34*). Just as the *symposion* and festival context reassert traditional social hierarchies,³⁸ so many poems transmit cultural roles and expectations – for example, what it is to be a proper aristocrat (Thgn. 53–68*, 183–92*), a good soldier (Archil. 17a*, 114*) and patriot (Callin. 1*, Tyrt. 12*, Mimn. 14*, Sol. 1–3*), or a virtuous woman (Semon. 7*, Thgn. 1225–6*, Hippon. 68*) – but also play with these social roles, exploiting the audience's expectations for

---

³⁵ See the headnotes to Archilochus and Hipponax.
³⁶ So with Solon, a poet with a significant role in Archaic history, we need to distinguish between the historical author and the various personae he creates, even if the overlap between the two is unusually large in his case.
³⁷ See Bowie 2001b; also Bowie 2002: 40 'telling stories is an important generic mark of *iambos*'.
³⁸ On 'role ascription' (division by age, gender, social status, etc.) at festivals, see Parker 2011: 217–18.

poetic effect (e.g. Archil. 5* on putting personal survival above honour on the battlefield). In conclusion, the poetic 'I' and its persona always track the needs of genre and occasion and are constructed to make the most compelling appeal to the audience, whether the goal of the narrator is to conduct the ideal *symposion* (Xenoph. 1*), act as a reconciler between warring political factions (Sol. 4–6*, 36*), or ruminate on the best approach to life (Semon. 1*, Mimn. 1–2*).

4 SOCIETY AND CULTURE

Elegy and iambus are valuable historical sources for Archaic Greece, not least because little prose literature of the period has survived.[39] Of course it is important not to be misled by the conventional label 'Archaic' into thinking that the poetry of this period is somehow primitive or simple – on the contrary, it is among the most impressive and sophisticated ever written. Similarly, in historical terms the Archaic age is one of great expansion and experimentation. This section will briefly consider how some of its most distinctive aspects are reflected in elegiac and iambic poetry.

Expansion and contact with foreign cultures. The growth of colonization and trade led to increasing familiarity with non-Greek cultures and encouraged the mobility of the poets themselves.[40] Various factors encouraged colonization and emigration, from a growing Greek population in need of new land to the desire for personal profit.[41] Archilochus is said to have joined the Parian colonization of Thasos (see 2.1–2*, 5.1*, 17a*; cf. frr. 21–2, 102, 228), Semonides to have led a group of Samian colonists to Amorgos, and Hipponax's attack on a treacherous friend reflects Greek trade and colonization around the Black Sea coastline and inland Thrace (115*). Growing awareness of other cultures also contributes to Hipponax's parodic treatment of Lydian language and religion (Hippon. 3*, 3a*, 32*, 92*). This mockery is a reminder that interaction with foreigners not only enhanced a growing sense of Greekness,[42] but also led to xenophobia: Archilochus (19*) and Xenophanes (3*) reject Lydian luxury as decadent excess. Since Greek elites of the period increasingly adopted eastern clothing, hairstyles, jewellery, and perfume, these poetic attacks on luxury lifestyles have a political as well as a racial edge.

---

[39] See Fowler 2000 and 2013 on early prose mythography. For the influence of elegy and iambus on the development of historiography, see Bowie 2001a: 62–6.
[40] Archil. 1* asserts the speaker's role as both soldier and poet. For a soldier's pride in his profession, see also Archil. 2*.
[41] See Graham 1983, Dougherty 1993, Boardman 1999.
[42] Cf. e.g. Archil. 102, where the poet describes his fellow settlers in the northern Aegean as Πανέλληνες.

Foreign states expanded too, leading to conflict with Greek communities, especially in Asia Minor: Mimnermus' *Smyrneis* celebrated the Smyrnaeans' victory over Lydian invaders under Gyges in the 660s, and fr. 14* contrasts such glory with the feebleness of the poet's contemporaries faced with a similar threat. On a larger scale, Simonides' Plataea Elegy* celebrates a united Greek victory over the expanding Persian empire (10–16*). But it was not only foreigners who threatened Greeks; fellow Hellenes could be no less lethal. Sparta's annexation of neighbouring Messenia and the enslavement of its population (as helots) are praised by Tyrtaeus, who sees their forced labour as essential to Sparta's prosperity and the maintenance of its increasingly militarized society (5–7*), a hierarchical system which he celebrates as embodying 'good order' (or *Eunomia*: 4*).

Contact with other cultures also fuelled the intellectual revolution of sixth-century Ionia, as seen, for example, in Xenophanes' critique of anthropomorphic religion (B 14*). Many concepts of rational thinking, philosophy, and science had long been in use in neighbouring cultures, and these ideas will have passed along trade routes to Greek cities like Xenophanes' Colophon from (for example) Egypt and Babylonia.[43]

Social and political revolution. The rise in trade and commercial success led to the emergence of new wealthy individuals and families, who increasingly demanded a role in the running of their communities.[44] For some members of the elite, the granting of political rights to the *nouveaux riches* was unacceptable: Theognis laments that the common herd are now considered the city's ἀγαθοί (53–68*) and that once pure bloodlines are now spoiled by intermarriage with inferior but newly rich stock (183–92*). Class distinctions are being eroded, Theognis claims, and the rightful elite (such as himself) are robbed of their land or forced into exile (1197–202*). As hereditary aristocracies clung to power, popular discontent often led to the emergence of tyrants, whose power threatened both rich and poor.[45] Thus Theognis fears that the corrupt behaviour of his city's leaders will result in civil war and the rise of a tyrant (39–52*). Though he and the proto-democratic Solon have very different political

---

[43] For early Greek philosophy's debt to various Near Eastern cultures, see e.g. West 1971, Hussey 1972: 28–31, Burkert 1992: 128–9.
[44] On the various conceptions of citizenship in Archaic Greece, involving not only membership of a community but also participation in its social and political life, see Duplouy and Brock 2018. Yoffee 2005: 5–6 outlines the multiplicity found in the earliest states across many cultures. On non-aristocratic elements in Archaic poetry, see Griffiths 1995.
[45] For Greek thinking about tyranny (the word is first attested in Archil. 19*), see Morgan 2003.

values, Theognis echoes the Athenian's diagnosis of civic degeneration, where the elite ruin their city for the sake of personal gain (Thgn. 46*, Sol. 4.11*), sparking factional strife (Thgn. 51*, Sol. 4.19*) and a descent into one-man rule (Thgn. 52*, Sol. 9*, 11*).

Solon is aware of the risks of giving the δῆμος too much power (4.5–6*, 5.1–2*, 6*, 36.20–2*), but his poetry reflects the increasingly influential idea that the good of the community as a whole should be the primary goal of the state. He boasts of reforming the Athenian legal system: 'I wrote laws for the lower and upper classes alike, creating a fair legal process for each man' (36.18–20*). The principle that all citizens are equal before the law (ἰσονομία) became the foundation of later democratic ideology. Solon similarly defends his policies as being in the best interests of all Athenians and presents his unbiased reforms as having prevented civil war (36.22–5*). This focus on impartial justice, equality, and the dignity of ordinary people is one of the most influential political ideas to emerge from the development of Archaic *poleis*. Related communal values are to be detected in the group mentality of phalanx warfare throughout the Greek world (cf. Archil. 114.3–4*, Callin. 1.20–1*, Tyrt. 12.16–22*, Sol. 5.5–6*).

Sexuality and gender. One of the most distinctive aspects of the small-scale personal poetry of the period is the way it deals with love and sex, especially (in contrast to epic) homoeroticism. The idea that it was acceptable for an adult man to desire and court an adolescent youth, who was meant to modestly resist full penetration (anal or oral), became part of the social structure of upper-class life in many Greek *poleis*.[46] Mimnermus observes that one of the disadvantages of getting old is that one becomes ugly and 'hated by boys' (1.9*).

There is a striking contrast between homoerotic fantasy – which portrays the lover's desire as pure and honourable – and the graphic, often shaming depiction of heterosexual sex. Thus Solon longs to 'fall in love with a boy in the lovely flower of youth, yearning for thighs and a sweet mouth' (fr. 25), and Theognis complains that his beloved Cyrnus has withheld the sexual favours owed to him, but avoids explicit language and speaks of the 'respect' (αἰδώς) due to him from his young lover (253–4*; cf. Thgn. 1353–5*). In contrast to the homoerotic fantasy-building of

---

[46] For homosexuality (male and female) in the Archaic period, see Dover 1978: 194–6. On Greek constructions of male sexuality and masculinity, see Halperin 1990, Foxhall and Salmon 1998. Davidson 2007 argues that the age of the boyfriend (or *erômenos*) should be raised to eighteen and that pederasty was practised at all levels of society, but the literary and artistic evidence (for the latter, see Dover 1978: 4–9, Kilmer 1997, Lear and Cantarella 2008) does not support either claim. Cohen 2015: 81–5 discusses the use of male prostitutes in elite homoerotic culture.

sympotic elegy, iambus portrays heterosexual sex in all its exuberant variety, yet the spectacle of female sexual pleasure is shocking as well as titillating for the male audience (see Archil. 42*). Moreover, women are frequently shamed by their portrayal as sexual beings, as when Hipponax has sex with his enemy's mistress (or even perhaps wife: 15–17*), and Archilochus destroys the reputation of Lycambes and his daughters by advertising the fact that he successfully seduced Neoboule and her younger sister (196a*).

The ideal woman (of patriarchal ideology) is illustrated by Semonides' bee-woman, who is a paragon of industry, affection, motherhood, and fidelity (7.83–93*). Here female sexuality is chanelled 'properly' (7.90–1*), and the bee-woman is the only one of the poem's ten female types who is presented as having children (7.87*), emphasizing her status as the ideal wife. Yet there is a sting in the tail for the male audience, as the poem's ending reveals all men to be naïve and deluded, for every man thinks his wife to be a bee-woman (7.112–14*) and no one can escape the misogynist's dilemma of actually needing a wife (7.115–16*). Nonetheless, although the speaker cleverly undercuts his audience's smugness, there is no serious challenge to patriarchy, and the dehumanizing of women ultimately reinforces male superiority and solidarity.

5 LANGUAGE, STYLE, METRE

Elegy and iambus originated in Ionia and were composed in the Ionic dialect, regardless of the poet's provenance.[47] Thus elegists from mainland Greece like Tyrtaeus, Solon, and Theognis follow the Ionian tradition, even if features of their local dialects occasionally come through (e.g. Thgn. 299 λῆι, a Doric equivalent of θέλει, Sol. 13.50* Attic χειροῖν, Sol. 4.35* αὐαίνει).[48] In contrast to iambus, elegiac language is decorous (though not as elevated as lyric) and free of colloquialisms. Its generally serious tone and subject-matter were influenced by the presence of the hexameter line in the elegiac couplet, which encouraged the use of epic forms and formulae (e.g. Archil. 1.1* Ἐνυαλίοιο ἄνακτος, Mimn. 14.7* αἱματόεν<τος ἐν> ὑσμίνηι πολέμοιο, Simon. 11.18* ἡμ]ιθέων ὠκύμορον γενεή[ν), shaping the development of the genre.[49] However, elegists always

---

[47] Similarly, the influence of genre and tradition can be seen in the Doric forms used in choral lyric composed by Ionic- or Aeolic-speaking poets; cf. Budelmann 2018: 24–5.
[48] On the literary dialects of elegy and iambus, see Palmer 1980: 105–13, Tribulato 2010: 390–2, Horrocks 2010: 49–50. West 1974: 77–117 discusses numerous features of language and metre.
[49] For epic formulae in elegy, see Garner 2011: 19–38, 95–108.

use epic language and imagery for their own ends, as when Archilochus and Solon, for example, enhance a particular aspect of their persona, the former by abandoning his shield on the battlefield (5*), the latter by protecting both sides with his (5*). Iambus too borrows from epic tradition (e.g. Semon. 1.1* Ζεὺς . . . βαρύκτυπος, 1.14* μελαίνης Ἀίδης ὑπὸ χθονός), often parodically (e.g. Semon. 7.105* ἐς μάχην κορύσσεται), but makes greater use of colloquial language (e.g. Hippon. 32.2–3* κάρτα γὰρ κακῶς ῥιγῶ | καὶ βαμβαλύζω), and deploys a degree of coarseness and obscenity unknown to elegy and most lyric (cf. Archil. 42–3*, Hippon. 17*, 92*).

It can be difficult to describe the style of fragmentary authors and unwise to generalize too readily about them; nonetheless, the texts that survive show each poet developing a distinctive voice, bolstered by a range of poetic techniques.[50] Similes are used for a variety of ends, depicting a man's remarkable ejaculation (Archil. 43*), the hardships of slavery (Tyrt. 6.1*), human ephemerality (Mimn. 2.1–5*), a swarm of dung-beetles (Hippon. 92.10–15*), and much else besides.[51] Metaphors illuminate grief (Archil. 13.4–5*, 13.8*), wealth (19.4*), guilt (181.9*), sex (196a.20–4*), hope (Semon. 1.6*), and blame (7.84*).[52] The poets use enjambment to enhance a speaker's outrage (Archil. 172.2–3*) and to emphasize the glory and risks of battle (Callin. 1.8–9*) or the pleasures of love (Mimn. 1.4–5*).[53] Alliteration and assonance are used to mimic the chewing of dense bread (Archil. 2.1*) and a beggar's shivering (Hippon. 32.2–3*), and to underscore a particularly ludicrous technique for the curing of male impotence (Hippon. 92.2*).[54] Chiasmus underlines a speaker's dual identity as soldier and poet (Archil. 1*),[55] and lengthy priamels emphasize the importance of martial courage (Tyrt. 12.1–12*) or

---

[50] For details of how the following poetic figures work in context, see the relevant sections of the commentary.
[51] Cf. Semon. 7.37–42*, Sol. 13.14–15*, 13.17–25*, 36.26–7*, Thgn. 55–6*, 254*, Simon. 11.1–3*.
[52] Cf. Callin. 1.4*, 1.11*, 1.15*, 1.20*, Tyrt. 12.22*, Mimn. 1.1*, Sol. 4.19*, 4.35–7*, 5.5–6*, 6.3*, 36.3*, 36.20–2*, Thgn. 39*, 237–9*, 247–50*, Xenoph. 1.22*, Hippon. 16.2*, Simon. 11.21*, 14.9*. On metaphor and simile in early Greek poetry, see Silk 1974 and (with a focus on Solon's particularly creative use of these figures to make abstract political ideas easier to understand) Noussia-Fantuzzi 2010: 67–77.
[53] Cf. Semon. 1.15–17*, 7.63–4*, 7.67–8*, 7.96–7*, Callin. 1.14–15*, Tyrt. 12.21–2*, Mimn. 1.5–6*, Sol. 3*, 4.5–6*, 4.7–8*, 4.12–13*, 13.3–4*, 13.7–8*, 13.43–5*, Thgn. 51–2*, 64–5*, 183–4*, 237–9*, 239–40*, Xenoph. 7–7a.4–5*.
[54] Cf. Semon. 7.28*, Mimn. 2.1*, 14.4*, Sol. 10.1*, Thgn. 39*, 45–6*, Xenoph. 1.11*, Hippon. 117.11*. For other sound effects, see Archil. 13.3*, where the Homeric formula πολυφλοίσβοιο θαλάσσης mimics the sound of the sea and glorifies those who have died, and Hippon. 13.2*, where κατήραξε recreates the sound of a shattered cup; cf. Thgn. 23–4*, Hippon. 128.1*.
[55] Cf. Semon. 7.67–8*, Sol. 4.34*, 4.36–7*, 13.5–6*, 13.7–8*, 27.5–6*.

take issue with the fetishizing of physical strength and celebrate brain power instead (Xenoph. 2.1–12*).[56] Ring composition rounds off sections (Semon. 1.1–5*, Tyrt. 4.10*) or scenes (Sol. 13.18–24*) and enhances the sense of closure (Semon. 7.115*, Sol. 4.39*, 13.71–6*, 27.18*, 36.26*, Thgn. 37–8*), while proverbial wisdom is deployed for a great variety of ends, from rationalizing defeat (Archil. 17a.4* φεύγ[ειν δέ τις ὥρη) to justifying an entire political philosophy (Sol. 6.3* τίκτει γὰρ κόρος ὕβριν).[57]

The elegiac couplet was the most common and adaptable verse form in antiquity.[58] The metrical pattern is

$$-\overline{\smile\smile}-\overline{\smile\smile}-\overline{\smile\smile}-\overline{\smile\smile}-\overline{\smile\smile}-\times\|$$
$$-\overline{\smile\smile}-\overline{\smile\smile}-\,|\,-\smile\smile-\smile\smile\times\|$$

The hexameter has caesura (or word-end) either in the third foot (called a 'feminine' caesura if after the first short, 'masculine' if after the first long) or much less frequently in the fourth foot after the first long (less than 1% of lines: cf. Thgn. 123*, Xenoph. 1.15*, 7a.1*).[59] In the pentameter the position of the caesura is fixed and the second hemiepes (−∪∪−∪∪−) must be dactylic. Moral and aesthetic qualities were ascribed to different metres, and elegy's closeness to the epic hexameter, as discussed above, helped ensure its dignity.[60] Moreover, the higher the proportion of long to short syllables, the grander and more solemn the rhythm was felt to be. So elegiac couplets with a majority of spondees may enhance the seriousness of the verse, as when Callinus begins two consecutive distichs with five long syllables in each line, enhancing his description of the hero who dies while fighting for his people (1.18–21*).[61] Similarly, where lines

---

[56] Cf. Sol. 9.1–4*. On the priamel, see Race 1982.
[57] E.g. Archil. 173.2*, 178*, 196a.39–41*, Semon. 1.1–5*, 7.7–8*, 7.33–4*, 7.73*, Mimn. 2.9–10*, Sol. 11.5–6*, 13.27–8*, 13.35–6*, 13.63–4*, Thgn. 25–6*, 55–6*, 1225–6*, Hippon. 115.8*, Simon. 16.2*.
[58] The elegiac distich, as it is sometimes called, is (strictly speaking) not stichic verse (with repeated lines, like the iambic trimeter or trochaic tetrameter) but an epodic strophe consisting of a dactylic hexameter followed by a pentameter. West 1982: 44–6, 157–9, 181–2, Adkins 1985: 1–19, van Raalte 1988, Barnes 1995, and Faraone 2008 discuss the structure, development, and popularity of the elegiac couplet. For the musical accompaniment to elegy and iambus (including instruments and tempos), see West 1992: 25, 137–40, 152, 335.
[59] The ratio of feminine to masculine caesurae in the hexameter in Archilochus, Semonides, Callinus, Tyrtaeus, and Mimnermus is around 2:1; in Solon, Theognis, and Xenophanes it is a little lower at around 4:3.
[60] This is seen most clearly where elegy overlaps in subject-matter with iambus: erotic desire, for example, is handled more delicately, and paraenetic elegy gives firm advice, but avoids iambic abuse.
[61] Spondaic fifth feet in the hexameter are rare. At Sol. 13.71* I prefer ἀνδράσι κεῖται to ἀνθρώποισι, avoiding the spondee.

5 LANGUAGE, STYLE, METRE

are highly or completely dactylic, the faster pace can underline the sense, as in Callinus' appeal to charge straight ahead with spear at the ready (1.10*, completely dacylic).

The stichic metres used in Archaic iambus are the iambic trimeter and the trochaic tetrameter catalectic.[62] The schemes are

Iambic trimeter   x⏓⏑⏓x ⦂ ⏓⏑⦂⏓x–⏑x ‖
Trochaic tetrameter catalectic   ⏓⏑⏓x⏓⏑⏓x | ⏓⏑⏓x–⏑x ‖

The tetrameter is longer by three positions at the start, but the rhythms are basically the same, with coinciding word end (usually after the fifth element in the trimeter, always after the eighth in the tetrameter) and identical endings.[63] A distinctive version of these metres is used by Hipponax, called scazon ('limping') or choliambic ('lame iambs'), in which the penultimate element is long instead of short. The three long syllables at the end have a dragging and intentionally clumsy effect, accentuating the humour of the poetry (for parodic hexameters, see Hippon. 128*). The epodes of Archilochus and Hipponax are strophic forms of two or three periods, usually an iambic trimeter or hexameter followed by shorter iambic or dactylic cola, which allow for a greater degree of metrical creativity than the stichic iambic metres.[64] Since the iambic metre was felt to resemble more closely than others the rhythm of ordinary speech (cf. Arist. *Poet.* 4.1449a19–28, *Rh.* 3.1408b24–6), it suited the earthy qualities of much iambus (especially its focus on sex and invective), but it was not *per se* an undignified metre, and its closeness to everyday speech made it an ideal medium for Semonides' philosophizing (1*) and Solon's political manifesto (36*). Trochaics too are used for moralizing (Archil. 128, 130–1, 133) and statements from an Everyman persona (114*). The epodes are richer linguistically as well as metrically, with denser use of imagery and metaphor and language of a higher register (on the whole): the erotic language and imagery of Archilochus' Cologne Epodes (188–91, 196a*), for

---

[62] Formed from the iamb (⏑–) or its inversion the trochee (–⏑). On the metres of Archaic iambus, see West 1982: 39–44, Lennartz 2000, Rotstein 2010: vi, 32.
[63] The caesura in the trimeter comes after the seventh element in about 25% of lines; cf. e.g. Semon. 1.20*, Semon. 7.15*, Hippon. 14.2*, 115.9*.
[64] Archil. 172–81* alternate iambic trimeter and dimeter, 196a* iambic trimeter, hemiepes, and iambic dimeter, Hippon. 115* and 117* iambic trimeter and hemiepes. Xenophanes combines iambic trimeter and hexameter in his critique of conventional religion (fr. B 14*), using the same parodic metre as the contemporary mock epic *Margites*. On epodic metres, see West 1974: 10, 1982: 43–4, Itsumi 2007: 322–5.

example, are more delicate and indirect than those of his graphic iambics (e.g. 42–3*).⁶⁵

6 TRANSMISSION OF THE TEXT

The texts included in this selected edition have survived a long and hazardous journey from the time of their composition and first performance.⁶⁶ In the Archaic period itself poems circulated primarily in performance, especially at *symposia*. Since elegy and iambus were less demanding to compose and perform than monodic or choral lyric, they continued to be newly created well into the fourth century and were better suited to amateur reperformance.⁶⁷ Small-scale song was more suitable for sympotic performance than large-scale public elegy (which was often tied to a particular place and occasion: see Simonides' Plataea Elegy*), and so small-scale pieces were likelier to survive.⁶⁸ Moreover, we can see from Aristophanes' quotation of lyric, elegiac, and iambic poetry that already in the fifth century the songs sung at *symposia* tended to be established 'classics'. In *Peace*, for example, Trygaeus asks the son of Cleonymus to sing for him; the boy chooses Archil. 5*, in which the narrator recalls that he abandoned his shield in battle, the very act that got Cleonymus himself branded a disgraceful coward (1295–1301). The humour relies on the audience knowing the shocking tone of this classic sympotic piece, which makes it particularly shaming for Cleonymus.

But for all the importance of (re)performance, elegy and iambus, like lyric and epic poetry, owe their survival to the invention of writing and the spread of literacy and texts.⁶⁹ Some poets may have composed with the aid of writing; some may have kept written copies of their works; and popular pieces may have been copied and acquired by performers, patrons, and teachers. Theognis' famous *sphragis* or 'seal', for example, is intended to ward off those who would meddle with the written text (19–26*).⁷⁰

---

⁶⁵ Archil. 189, attacking a former lover's promiscuity, is a partial exception: 'and you took in many blind eels'. The image is graphic, albeit metaphorical.

⁶⁶ On the circulation and survival of Greek texts until the invention of printing, see Irigoin 2003, Reynolds and Wilson 2013. West 1973 outlines the editing process; on the possibilities for progress in new editions, see Tarrant 2016: 145–56.

⁶⁷ For the importance of reperformance, see Herington 1985: 48–50. On new elegy and iambus in the fifth and fourth centuries, see Carey 2016: 137–9. For the continuity of elegy, see also n. 11 above.

⁶⁸ See Bowie 1986: 35.

⁶⁹ On the use of written texts alongside performance, see Herington 1985: 45–7, 201–6, Thomas 1992, Gerber 1997a: 2–4, Ford 2003. The growth of literacy meant that later elegy and iambus were written with reading as much as performance in mind.

⁷⁰ See Lane Fox 2000: 45.

6 TRANSMISSION OF THE TEXT

A systematic attempt to gather and edit the lyric, iambic, and elegiac poets of early Greece was undertaken in the Hellenistic period,[71] but with the exception of the Theognidea and Pindar's epinicians, none of these editions survived to have their own medieval manuscript tradition. For all other texts we rely on two modes of transmission: papyrus finds ('direct' transmission) and quotations embedded in later (mainly prose) writers ('indirect' transmission).

In addition to the twelve passages of Theognis, there are 71 pieces in this edition, 14 of which are preserved on papyri, the other 57 in quotations. The papyri range in size from substantial pieces (e.g. Simon. 11*), containing probably complete (Sol. 36*) or almost complete poems (Archil. 17a*, 196a*), to scraps of a few lines (Archil. 175*, 181*, Simon. 10*).[72] The 57 quotations date from the fourth century BC (Demosthenes and the author of the Aristotelian *Athenian Constitution*: Sol. 4*, 5–6*, 36*) through to late antiquity. By far the most salient sources are Athenaeus' fifteen-book *Scholars at Dinner*, composed around AD 200, in which learned banqueters discuss various aspects of literature and culture (and especially eating and drinking), citing much poetry to illustrate their points (over 10,000 lines of verse from around 1,250 authors), and Stobaeus' four-book *Anthology* of excerpts from poetry and prose, assembled in the early fifth century AD. Athenaeus supplies ten and Stobaeus eleven of our 57 quoted pieces.[73] Other sources are scholia or commentaries (e.g. Archil. 180*, Hippon. 3*), metrical and grammatical handbooks (e.g. Hippon. 16*), and lexica (e.g. Archil. 43*).[74]

Thus, with the exception of Theognis, most surviving elegiac and iambic poetry has been cited to suit the particular focus and aims of an individual anthologist, metrician, or scholar, giving us a selective and biased picture of these genres. Stobaeus, for example, sought out morally edifying passages for the education of his son, and thus many surviving pieces are full of gnomic passages. The process of selection can affect our perception of individual poets too: most of Mimnermus' larger pieces are cited by Stobaeus (1*, 2*, 14*), but if we had more of his work, it is likely that Mimnermus would appear less gnomic and sententious, just as

---

[71] See Pfeiffer 1968, Montana 2015.
[72] On the discovery and editing of papyrus rolls, see Turner 1980, and for their impact on our knowledge of Greek literature, Parsons 2007: 137–58.
[73] For Athenaeus' knowledge and use of elegiac and iambic poetry, see Bowie 2000; for Stobaeus', see Campbell 1984 and Bowie 2010. On 'quotation culture' in Classical literature, see Wright (forthcoming).
[74] See Dickey 2007, esp. 42–3; for the Roman tradition, see Zetzel 2018.

all poets would emerge as much less obsessed with food and drink than Athenaeus' selection might suggest.[75]

It is estimated that the Alexandrians had access to around 100,000–150,000 lines of early Greek lyric, elegiac, and iambic poetry, but only a fraction has survived.[76] The number of complete poems (leaving aside Pindar's epinicians) is small, though far from negligible; of the 83 pieces included here a case can be made for 22 complete poems.[77] The survival of Classical literature is the story of a long and gradual process of selection and narrowing, as fewer and fewer texts were read and recopied. A number of factors contributed to this process, some deliberate, some accidental. Among the former, one of the most important was selection for use in the school curriculum: if a text was deemed, for example, too difficult linguistically or too naughty, it was in trouble, and the salaciousness of much iambic poetry in particular damaged its chances of survival.[78] It is not a coincidence that only the frequently didactic and moralistic Theognidea reached the Middle Ages intact. But although the threads connecting us to early Greek elegy and iambus are tenuous, some of the accidents of history are happy ones: new elegiac and iambic texts are still being discovered and published, and highly accomplished poems such as Simonides' Plataea Elegy (10–16*) or Archilochus' Telephus Elegy (17a*) and Cologne Epode (196a*) show that new discoveries continue to enrich our view of early Greek poetry.[79]

---

[75] On the role of gnomic sayings and anthologies in ancient education, see Morgan 1998: 120–51.
[76] See Gerber 1997a: 2–4.
[77] See Archil. 1*, 2*, 5*, 13*, 114*, Semon. 1*, 7*, Callin 1*, Tyrt. 12*, Mimn. 1*, 2*, Sol. 4*, 13*, 27*, 36*, Thgn. 39–52*, 183–92*, 237–54*, Xenoph. 1*, 2*, Hippon. 32+34*, 128*.
[78] Bloomer 2013 discusses the role of Archaic literary texts as 'cultural icons' (p. 458), some of which continued to be read in schools despite their difficulty. On tensions between Christianity and Classical literature, see e.g. Marrou 1958: 314–29; for selections made in the Byzantine school curriculum, see Nelson 2010.
[79] First published in 1974 (Cologne Epode), 1992 (Plataea Elegy), and 2005 (Telephus Elegy).

GREEK ELEGY AND IAMBUS

A SELECTION

ARCHILOCHUS 1

εἰμὶ δ' ἐγὼ θεράπων μὲν Ἐνυαλίοιο ἄνακτος
καὶ Μουσέων ἐρατὸν δῶρον ἐπιστάμενος.

ARCHILOCHUS 2

ἐν δορὶ μέν μοι μᾶζα μεμαγμένη, ἐν δορὶ δ' οἶνος
Ἰσμαρικός· πίνω δ' ἐν δορὶ κεκλιμένος.

ARCHILOCHUS 5

ἀσπίδι μὲν Σαΐων τις ἀγάλλεται, ἣν παρὰ θάμνωι,
ἔντος ἀμώμητον, κάλλιπον οὐκ ἐθέλων·
αὐτὸν δ' ἐξεσάωσα. τί μοι μέλει ἀσπὶς ἐκείνη;
ἐρρέτω· ἐξαῦτις κτήσομαι οὐ κακίω.

ARCHILOCHUS 13

κήδεα μὲν στονόεντα, Περίκλεες, οὔτέ τις ἀστῶν
μεμφόμενος θαλίηις τέρψεται οὐδὲ πόλις·
τοίους γὰρ κατὰ κῦμα πολυφλοίσβοιο θαλάσσης
ἔκλυσεν, οἰδαλέους δ' ἀμφ' ὀδύνηις ἔχομεν
πνεύμονας. ἀλλὰ θεοὶ γὰρ ἀνηκέστοισι κακοῖσιν,   5
ὦ φίλ', ἐπὶ κρατερὴν τλημοσύνην ἔθεσαν
φάρμακον. ἄλλοτε ἄλλος ἔχει τόδε· νῦν μὲν ἐς ἡμέας
ἐτράπεθ', αἱματόεν δ' ἕλκος ἀναστένομεν,
ἐξαῦτις δ' ἑτέρους ἐπαμείψεται. ἀλλὰ τάχιστα
τλῆτε, γυναικεῖον πένθος ἀπωσάμενοι.   10

Archil. 2 1 μοι Synes. : τοι *Suda* : om. Athen.
Archil. 5 3 αὐτὸν δ' Hoffmann : αὐτόν μ' Elias : ψυχὴν δ' Ar. : αὐτὸς δ' ἐξέφυγον θανάτου τέλος Sext.
Archil. 13 4 ἔκλυσεν Par. 1985 (s. xv) : ἔκλαυσεν S   ἀμφ' ὀδύνηις ἔχομεν Gaisford : ἀμφ' ὀδύνη ἴσχομεν S   9 ἑτέρους Frobenius : ἑταίρους S

ARCHILOCHUS 17A SWIFT

]ι ῥ[ο]ῆι[ς
εἰ δὲ] . [. . . .] . [.] . . θεοῦ κρατερῆ[ς ὑπ' ἀνάγκης,
οὐ δεῖ ἀν]αλ[κείη]ν καὶ κακότητα λέγει[ν.
]ημ. . . [. . εἴμ]εθ' ἄρ[η]α φυγεῖν· φεύγ[ειν δέ τις ὥρη·
κα̣ὶ̣ ποτ̣[ε μ]οῦνος ἐὼν Τήλεφος Ἀρκα̣[σίδης   5
Ἀργείων ἐφόβησε πολὺν στρατ̣[όν,] ο̣[ὐ̣δ̣' ἔτι μεῖναν
ἄλκιμ̣[οι,] – ἦ τόσα δὴ μοῖρα θεῶν ἐφόβει̣ –
αἰχμηταί̣ περ ἐόντε[ς.] ἐΰρρείτης δὲ Κ[άϊκος
π]ιπ̣τ̣όντων νεκύων στείνετο καὶ [πεδίον
Μ̣ύ̣σ̣ι̣ο̣ν̣, οἱ δ' ἐπὶ θῖ̣ν̣α̣ πολυφλοίσβοι[ο θαλάσσης   10
χέρσ'] ὑπ' ἀμειλίκτου φωτὸς ἐναιρό[μενοι
προ]τ̣ροπάδην ἀπέκλινον ἐϋκνήμ[ιδες Ἀχαιοί·
ἀ]σ̣πάσιοι δ' ἐς νέας ὠ̣[κ]υπόρ[ο]υ̣ς̣ [ἔφυγον
παῖδές τ̣ ἀ̣θανάτων κα̣ὶ̣ ἀδελφεοί̣, [οὓς Ἀγαμέμνων
Ἴλιον εἰς ἱερὴν ἦγε μαχησομένο̣[υς·   15
ο̣]ἰ̣ δὲ τότ̣ε̣ βλαφθέντες ὁδοῦ παρὰ θ[ῖν' ἀφίκοντο,
Τε]ύθραντος δ' ἐρατὴν πρὸς πόλιν [εἰσανέβαν,
ἔ]νθα [μ]ένος πνείοντες ὅμως αὐτο̣[ί τε δάμησαν
κἀ]φρ[αδί]ηι μεγάλως θυμὸν ἀκηχέ[δατο·
φ]άν̣[το] γὰρ ὑψίπυλον Τρώων πόλιν εἰσ[αναβαίνειν   20
αὐ]τ̣ίκ̣[α]· γῆν δ' ἐπάτευν Μυσίδα πυροφόρο̣[ν.
Ἡρακλ]έ̣ης δ' ἤντησ[ε], βοῶν ταλ[α]κάρδιον [υἱόν,
οὖ]ρον ἀμ̣[ε]ί̣λ̣ι̣κ̣[τον] δηΐωι ἐν [πολ]έ̣μ̣[ωι,
Τ]ήλεφον, ὃς Δαναοῖσι κακὴν [τ]ό̣[τε φύζαν ἐνόρσας
ἤ]ρ̣ειδε [πρό]μαχος, πατρὶ χαριζό̣μ̣[ενος.   25
. . .] . . . . [.] . . . . . [
. . .] . [.] . . . [. . . . . .] . . [
. . .] . . . . [. . . . . .] . θα . [

Archil. 17A   suppl. Obbink exceptis quae infra memorantur   1]ι ῥ[ο]ῆι[ς Swift   2 εἰ δὲ] West   κρατερῆ[ς ὑπ' ἀνάγκης Henry   3 οὐ δεῖ ἀν]αλ[κείη]ν West   4 West   5 κα̣ὶ̣ ποτ̣[ε μ]οῦνος ἐὼν West   6 ο̣[ὐ̣δ̣' ἔτι μεῖναν Magnelli   8 αἰχμηταί̣ et ἐόντε[ς.] Parsons   περ Janko   9 [πεδίον West   10 Μ̣ύ̣σ̣ι̣ο̣ν̣ West   11 χέρσ'] West   13 [ἔφυγον West   16 θ[ῖν' ἀφίκοντο Janko   17 [εἰσανέβαν West   18 ἔ]νθα Janko   αὐτο̣[ί τε δάμησαν D'Alessio   19 κἀ]φρ[αδί]ηι D'Alessio   20 φ]άν̣[το] West   21 αὐ]τ̣ίκ̣[α]· γ̣ῆν Burzacchini   22 ἤντησ[ε] West   23 οὖ]ρον ἀμ̣[ε]ί̣λ̣ι̣κ̣[τον] West   24 ὃς Δαναοῖσι Janko   [τ]ό̣[τε φύζαν ἐνόρσας West   25 ἤ]ρ̣ειδε [πρό]μαχος D'Alessio

ARCHILOCHUS 19

"οὔ μοι τὰ Γύγεω τοῦ πολυχρύσου μέλει,
οὐδ' εἷλέ πώ με ζῆλος, οὐδ' ἀγαίομαι
θεῶν ἔργα, μεγάλης δ' οὐκ ἐρέω τυραννίδος·
ἀπόπροθεν γάρ ἐστιν ὀφθαλμῶν ἐμῶν."

ARCHILOCHUS 42

ὥσπερ αὐλῶι βρῦτον ἢ Θρέϊξ ἀνὴρ
ἢ Φρὺξ ἔμυζε· κύβδα δ' ἦν πονεομένη.

ARCHILOCHUS 43

ἡ δέ οἱ σάθη
x – ◡ – x ὥστ' ὄνου Πριηνέως
κήλωνος ἐπλήμυρεν ὀτρυγηφάγου.

ARCHILOCHUS 114

οὐ φιλέω μέγαν στρατηγὸν οὐδὲ διαπεπλιγμένον
οὐδὲ βοστρύχοισι γαῦρον οὐδ' ὑπεξυρημένον,
ἀλλά μοι σμικρός τις εἴη καὶ περὶ κνήμας ἰδεῖν
ῥοικός, ἀσφαλέως βεβηκὼς ποσσί, καρδίης πλέως.

ARCHILOCHUS 172

πάτερ Λυκάμβα, ποῖον ἐφράσω τόδε;
τίς σὰς παρήειρε φρένας
ἧις τὸ πρὶν ἠρήρεισθα; νῦν δὲ δὴ πολὺς
ἀστοῖσι φαίνεαι γέλως.

ARCHILOCHUS 173

ὅρκον δ' ἐνοσφίσθης μέγαν
ἅλας τε καὶ τράπεζαν.

Archil. 42 2 ἔμυζε Wilamowitz : ἔβρυζε cod.
Archil. 43 1 ἡ δέ οἱ Schneidewin : οἱ δέ οἱ *Et. Gud.* 3 ἐπλήμυρεν Bergk : ἐπλήμυρον Eust.
Archil. 114 1 διαπεπλιγμένον Hemsterhuys : -πεπλεγμένον Dio : -πεπηγμένον Gal.

ARCHILOCHUS 174

αἶνός τις ἀνθρώπων ὅδε,
ὡς ἄρ' ἀλώπηξ καἰετὸς ξυνεωνίην
ἔμειξαν ...

ARCHILOCHUS 175

× – ⏑ ἐς παῖ]δας φέρων
   δαῖ]τα δ' οὐ καλὴν ἐπ[ὶ
ὥρμησαν ἀπτ]ῆνες δύο
× – ⏑ – ×]. γῆ[ς] ἐφ' ὑψηλῶι π[άγωι
× – ⏑ –]νεοσσιῆι   5
× – ⏑ –]προύθηκε, τὴν δ[' ἀλώπεκα
× – ⏑ –].εχο.[⏑ –
× – ⏑ –]αδε..[⏑ – × – ⏑ –
× – ⏑ – ×]φωλά[δ –

ARCHILOCHUS 176

ὁρᾶις ἵν' ἐστὶ κεῖνος ὑψηλὸς πάγος,
τρηχύς τε καὶ παλίγκοτος;
ἐν τῶι κάθηται, σὴν ἐλαφρίζων μάχην.

ARCHILOCHUS 177

ὦ Ζεῦ, πάτερ Ζεῦ, σὸν μὲν οὐρανοῦ κράτος,
σὺ δ' ἔργ' ἐπ' ἀνθρώπων ὁρᾶις
λεωργὰ καὶ θεμιστά, σοὶ δὲ θηρίων
ὕβρις τε καὶ δίκη μέλει.

ARCHILOCHUS 178

μή τευ μελαμπύγου τύχηις.

ARCHILOCHUS 179

προύθηκε παισὶ δεῖπνον αἰηνὲς φέρων.

Archil. **175** suppl. Lobel   1 Lasserre   2 δαῖ]τα Lasserre   3 ὥρμησαν West ἀπτ]ῆνες Lobel   6 δ[' ἀλώπεκα West   9 φωλά[δ West
Archil. **177**   3 καὶ θεμιστά Matthiae : κἀθέμιστα fere test.

ARCHILOCHUS 180

πυρὸς δ' ἐν αὐτῶι φεψάλυξ.

ARCHILOCHUS 181

].ω[
]ηρκ[
].τάτην[
μ]έγ' ἠείδει κακ[όν
φ]ρέ[ν]ας   5
].δ' ἀμήχανον τ.[
]ακον·
].ανων μεμνημένος[
].ην κλύσας
κέ]λευθον ὠκέως δι' αἰθέρος[10
λαιψηρὰ κυ]κλώσας πτερά
]ν ἠσ..· σὸς δὲ θυμὸς ἔλπεται

ARCHILOCHUS 196A

πάμπαν ἀποσχόμενος
ἶσον δὲ τόλμ[
εἰ δ' ὦν ἐπείγεαι καί σε θυμὸς ἰθύει,
ἔστιν ἐν ἡμετέρου
ἣ νῦν μέγ' ἱμείρε[ι   5
καλὴ τέρεινα παρθένος· δοκέω δέ μι[ν
εἶδος ἄμωμον ἔχειν·
τὴν δὴ σὺ ποίη[σαι φίλην."
τοσαῦτ' ἐφώνει· τὴν δ' ἐγὼνταμει[βόμην·
"Ἀμφιμεδοῦς θύγατερ,   10
ἐσθλῆς τε καὶ[
γυναικός, ἣν νῦν γῆ κατ' εὐρώεσσ' ἔ[χει,
τ]έρψιές εἰσι θεῆς
πολλαὶ νέοισιν ἀνδ[ράσιν

Archil. 180   δ' ἐν Schneidewin : δὲ ἦν codd.
Archil. 181   suppl. Lobel   4 μ]έγ' Lasserre   κακ[όν Peek   8 ὀρ]φανῶν Lobel
10 init., de τάμνων cogitavit Lobel   11 cf. Attici fr. 2 λαιψηρὰ κυκλῶσαι πτερά
Archil. 196A   suppl. Merkelbach–West   1 ανασχ sscr. πο   2 τόλμ[ησον Snell
8 Ebert–Luppe

παρὲξ τὸ θεῖον χρῆμα· τῶν τις ἀρκέσε[ι. 15
τ]αῦτα δ' ἐφ' ἡσυχίης
εὖτ' ἂν μελανθῆ[
ἐ]γώ τε καὶ σὺ σὺν θεῶι βουλεύσομεν.
π]είσομαι ὥς με κέλεαι·
πολλόν μ' ε[20
θρ]ιγκοῦ δ' ἔνερθε καὶ πυλέων ὑποφ[
μ]ή τι μέγαιρε φίλη·
σχήσω γὰρ ἐς ποη[φόρους
κ]ήπους. τὸ δὴ νῦν γνῶθι· Νεοβούλη[ν
ἄ]λλος ἀνὴρ ἐχέτω· 25
αἰαῖ, πέπειρα, δὶς τόση,
ἄν]θος δ' ἀπερρύηκε παρθενήϊον
κ]αὶ χάρις ἢ πρὶν ἐπῆν·
κόρον γὰρ οὐκ[
ἄτ]ης δὲ μέτρ' ἔφηνε μαινόλις γυνή· 30
ἐς] κόρακας ἄπεχε·
μὴ τοῦτ' ἐφ.ιτ' αν[
ὅ]πως ἐγὼ γυναῖκα τ[ο]ιαύτην ἔχων
γεί]τοσι χάρμ' ἔσομαι·
πολλὸν σὲ βούλο[μαι πάρος· 35
σὺ] μὲν γὰρ οὔτ' ἄπιστος οὔτε διπλόη,
ἡ δ]ὲ μάλ' ὀξυτέρη,
πολλοὺς δὲ ποιεῖτα[ι φίλους·
δέ]δοιχ' ὅπως μὴ τυφλὰ κἀλιτήμερα
σπ]ουδῆι ἐπειγόμενος 40
τὼς ὥσπερ ἡ κ[ύων τέκω."
τοσ]αῦτ' ἐφώνεον· παρθένον δ' ἐν ἄνθε[σιν
τηλ]εθάεσσι λαβὼν
ἔκλινα, μαλθακῆι δ[έ μιν
χλαί]νηι καλύψας, αὐχέν' ἀγκάληις ἔχω[ν, 45
δεί]ματι παυ[σ]αμένην
τὼς ὥστε νέβρ[
μαζ]ῶν τε χερσὶν ἠπίως ἐφηψάμην
ἧιπε]ρ ἔφαινε νέον

29 κ[ατέσχε πω M.–W.   30 ἄτ]ης Snell   46 δεί]ματι West   47 νέβρ[ιον τρέμειν Gronewald   48 μαζ]ῶν West : μηρ]ῶν Merkelbach   49 ἧιπε]ρ Page

ἥβης ἐπήλυσιν χρόα 50
ἅπαν τ]ε σῶμα καλὸν ἀμφαφώμενος
λευκ]ὸν ἀφῆκα μένος
ξανθῆς ἐπιψαύ[ων τριχός.

SEMONIDES 1

ὦ παῖ, τέλος μὲν Ζεὺς ἔχει βαρύκτυπος
πάντων ὅσ' ἐστὶ καὶ τίθησ' ὅκηι θέλει,
νοῦς δ' οὐκ ἐπ' ἀνθρώποισιν, ἀλλ' ἐπήμεροι
ἃ δὴ βοτὰ ζόουσιν, οὐδὲν εἰδότες
ὅκως ἕκαστον ἐκτελευτήσει θεός. 5
ἐλπὶς δὲ πάντας κἀπιπειθείη τρέφει
ἄπρηκτον ὁρμαίνοντας· οἱ μὲν ἡμέρην
μένουσιν ἐλθεῖν, οἱ δ' ἐτέων περιτροπάς·
νέωτα δ' οὐδεὶς ὅστις οὐ δοκεῖ βροτῶν
Πλούτωι τε κἀγαθοῖσιν ἵξεσθαι φίλος. 10
φθάνει δὲ τὸν μὲν γῆρας ἄζηλον λαβὸν
πρὶν τέρμ' ἵκηται, τοὺς δὲ δύστηνοι βροτῶν
φθείρουσι νοῦσοι, τοὺς δ' Ἄρει δεδμημένους
πέμπει μελαίνης Ἀΐδης ὑπὸ χθονός·
οἱ δ' ἐν θαλάσσηι λαίλαπι κλονεόμενοι 15
καὶ κύμασιν πολλοῖσι πορφυρῆς ἁλὸς
θνήσκουσιν, εὖτ' ἂν μὴ δυνήσωνται ζόειν·
οἱ δ' ἀγχόνην ἅψαντο δυστήνωι μόρωι
καὐτάγρετοι λείπουσιν ἡλίου φάος.
οὕτω κακῶν ἄπ' οὐδέν, ἀλλὰ μυρίαι 20
βροτοῖσι κῆρες κἀνεπίφραστοι δύαι
καὶ πήματ' ἐστίν. εἰ δ' ἐμοὶ πιθοίατο,
οὐκ ἂν κακῶν ἐρῶιμεν, οὐδ' ἐπ' ἄλγεσιν
κακοῖς ἔχοντες θυμὸν αἰκιζοίμεθα.

SEMONIDES 7

χωρὶς γυναικὸς θεὸς ἐποίησεν νόον
τὰ πρῶτα. τὴν μὲν ἐξ ὑὸς τανύτριχος,
τῆι πάντ' ἀν' οἶκον βορβόρωι πεφυρμένα

51 ἅπαν τ]ε West 52 λευκ]ὸν Merkelbach : θερμ]ὸν West
Semon. 1 4 ἃ δὴ βοτὰ ζώουσιν Ahrens (ζό- West) : δὴ βροτοὶ ζώομεν codd. 12–13
Ahrens : νόσοι φθείρουσι θνητῶν codd. SM : ν. φθ. βροτῶν θνητῶν cod. A

30   SEMONIDES 7

ἄκοσμα κεῖται καὶ κυλίνδεται χαμαί·
αὐτὴ δ' ἄλουτος ἀπλύτοις ἐν εἵμασιν   5
ἐν κοπρίηισιν ἡμένη πιαίνεται.
   τὴν δ' ἐξ ἀλιτρῆς θεὸς ἔθηκ' ἀλώπεκος
γυναῖκα πάντων ἴδριν· οὐδέ μιν κακῶν
λέληθεν οὐδὲν οὐδὲ τῶν ἀμεινόνων·
τὸ μὲν γὰρ αὐτῶν εἶπε πολλάκις κακόν,   10
τὸ δ' ἐσθλόν· ὀργὴν δ' ἄλλοτ' ἀλλοίην ἔχει.
   τὴν δ' ἐκ κυνός, λιτοργόν, αὐτομήτορα,
ἣ πάντ' ἀκοῦσαι, πάντα δ' εἰδέναι θέλει,
πάντηι δὲ παπταίνουσα καὶ πλανωμένη
λέληκεν, ἢν καὶ μηδέν' ἀνθρώπων ὁρᾶι.   15
παύσειε δ' ἄν μιν οὔτ' ἀπειλήσας ἀνήρ,
οὐδ' εἰ χολωθεὶς ἐξαράξειεν λίθωι
ὀδόντας, οὐδ' ἄν μειλίχως μυθεόμενος,
οὐδ' εἰ παρὰ ξείνοισιν ἡμένη τύχηι,
ἀλλ' ἐμπέδως ἄπρηκτον αὐονὴν ἔχει.   20
   τὴν δὲ πλάσαντες γηΐνην Ὀλύμπιοι
ἔδωκαν ἀνδρὶ πηρόν· οὔτε γὰρ κακὸν
οὔτ' ἐσθλὸν οὐδὲν οἶδε τοιαύτη γυνή·
ἔργων δὲ μοῦνον ἐσθίειν ἐπίσταται.
κὤταν κακὸν χειμῶνα ποιήσηι θεός,   25
ῥιγῶσα δίφρον ἆσσον ἕλκεται πυρός.
   τὴν δ' ἐκ θαλάσσης, ἣ δύ' ἐν φρεσὶν νοεῖ·
τὴν μὲν γελᾶι τε καὶ γέγηθεν ἡμέρην·
ἐπαινέσει μιν ξεῖνος ἐν δόμοις ἰδών·
"οὐκ ἔστιν ἄλλη τῆσδε λωΐων γυνὴ   30
ἐν πᾶσιν ἀνθρώποισιν οὐδὲ καλλίων"·
τὴν δ' οὐκ ἀνεκτὸς οὐδ' ἐν ὀφθαλμοῖς ἰδεῖν
οὔτ' ἆσσον ἐλθεῖν, ἀλλὰ μαίνεται τότε
ἄπλητον ὥσπερ ἀμφὶ τέκνοισιν κύων,
ἀμείλιχος δὲ πᾶσι κἀποθυμίη   35
ἐχθροῖσιν ἶσα καὶ φίλοισι γίνεται·
ὥσπερ θάλασσα πολλάκις μὲν ἀτρεμὴς
ἕστηκ', ἀπήμων, χάρμα ναύτηισιν μέγα,
θέρεος ἐν ὥρηι, πολλάκις δὲ μαίνεται
βαρυκτύποισι κύμασιν φορεομένη.   40

Semon. 7   20 αὐονὴν West   25 κὤταν Ahrens : χ' οταν cod. S : κοὔτ' ἂν codd. MA
29 μιν Valckenaer : μὲν codd.

ταύτηι μάλιστ' ἔοικε τοιαύτη γυνὴ
ὀργήν· φυὴν δὲ πόντος ἀλλοίην ἔχει.
  τὴν δ' ἐκ σποδιῆς τε καὶ παλιντριβέος ὄνου,
ἣ σύν τ' ἀνάγκηι σύν τ' ἐνιπῆισιν μόγις
ἔστερξεν ὦν ἅπαντα κἀπονήσατο   45
ἀρεστά· τόφρα δ' ἐσθίει μὲν ἐν μυχῶι
προνὺξ προῆμαρ, ἐσθίει δ' ἐπ' ἐσχάρηι.
ὁμῶς δὲ καὶ πρὸς ἔργον ἀφροδίσιον
ἐλθόντ' ἑταῖρον ὁντινῶν ἐδέξατο.
  τὴν δ' ἐκ γαλῆς, δύστηνον οἰζυρὸν γένος·   50
κείνηι γὰρ οὔ τι καλὸν οὐδ' ἐπίμερον
πρόσεστιν οὐδὲ τερπνὸν οὐδ' ἐράσμιον.
εὐνῆς δ' ἀληνής ἐστιν ἀφροδισίης,
τὸν δ' ἄνδρα τὸν παρεόντα ναυσίηι διδοῖ.
κλέπτουσα δ' ἔρδει πολλὰ γείτονας κακά,   55
ἄθυστα δ' ἱρὰ πολλάκις κατεσθίει.
  τὴν δ' ἵππος ἁβρὴ χαιτέεσσ' ἐγείνατο,
ἣ δούλι' ἔργα καὶ δύην περιτρέπει,
κοὔτ' ἂν μύλης ψαύσειεν, οὔτε κόσκινον
ἄρειεν, οὔτε κόπρον ἐξ οἴκου βάλοι,   60
οὔτε πρὸς ἰπνὸν ἀσβόλην ἀλεομένη
ἵζοιτ'. ἀνάγκηι δ' ἄνδρα ποιεῖται φίλον·
λοῦται δὲ πάσης ἡμέρης ἄπο ῥύπον
δίς, ἄλλοτε τρίς, καὶ μύροις ἀλείφεται,
αἰεὶ δὲ χαίτην ἐκτενισμένην φορεῖ   65
βαθεῖαν, ἀνθέμοισιν ἐσκιασμένην.
καλὸν μὲν ὦν θέημα τοιαύτη γυνὴ
ἄλλοισι, τῶι δ' ἔχοντι γίνεται κακόν,
ἢν μή τις ἢ τύραννος ἢ σκηπτοῦχος ἦι,
ὅστις τοιούτοις θυμὸν ἀγλαΐζεται.   70
  τὴν δ' ἐκ πιθήκου· τοῦτο δὴ διακριδὸν
Ζεὺς ἀνδράσιν μέγιστον ὤπασεν κακόν.
αἴσχιστα μὲν πρόσωπα· τοιαύτη γυνὴ
εἶσιν δι' ἄστεος πᾶσιν ἀνθρώποις γέλως·
ἐπ' αὐχένα βραχεῖα· κινεῖται μόγις·   75
ἄπυγος, αὐτόκωλος. ἆ τάλας ἀνὴρ
ὅστις κακὸν τοιοῦτον ἀγκαλίζεται.
δήνεα δὲ πάντα καὶ τρόπους ἐπίσταται

43 σποδιῆς τε Brunck : τε σποδιῆς codd.   67 ὦν Brunck : οὖν codd.

32   SEMONIDES 7

ὥσπερ πίθηκος· οὐδέ οἱ γέλως μέλει·
οὐδ' ἄν τιν' εὖ ἔρξειεν, ἀλλὰ τοῦτ' ὁρᾶι   80
καὶ τοῦτο πᾶσαν ἡμέρην βουλεύεται,
ὅκως τι κὼς μέγιστον ἔρξειεν κακόν.
τὴν δ' ἐκ μελίσσης· τήν τις εὐτυχεῖ λαβών·
κείνηι γὰρ οἴηι μῶμος οὐ προσιζάνει,
θάλλει δ' ὑπ' αὐτῆς κἀπαέξεται βίος,   85
φίλη δὲ σὺν φιλέοντι γηράσκει πόσει
τεκοῦσα καλὸν κὠνομάκλυτον γένος.
κἀριπρεπὴς μὲν ἐν γυναιξὶ γίνεται
πάσηισι, θείη δ' ἀμφιδέδρομεν χάρις.
οὐδ' ἐν γυναιξὶν ἥδεται καθημένη   90
ὅκου λέγουσιν ἀφροδισίους λόγους.
τοίας γυναῖκας ἀνδράσιν χαρίζεται
Ζεὺς τὰς ἀρίστας καὶ πολυφραδεστάτας.
τὰ δ' ἄλλα φῦλα ταῦτα μηχανῆι Διὸς
ἔστιν τε πάντα καὶ παρ' ἀνδράσιν μένει.   95
Ζεὺς γὰρ μέγιστον τοῦτ' ἐποίησεν κακόν,
γυναῖκας· ἤν τι καὶ δοκέωσιν ὠφελεῖν
ἔχοντι, τῶι μάλιστα γίνεται κακόν·
οὐ γάρ κοτ' εὔφρων ἡμέρην διέρχεται
ἅπασαν, ὅστις σὺν γυναικὶ ναιετᾶι,   100
οὐδ' αἶψα Λιμὸν οἰκίης ἀπώσεται,
ἐχθρὸν συνοικητῆρα, δυσμενέα θεῶν.
ἀνὴρ δ' ὅταν μάλιστα θυμηδεῖν δοκῆι
κατ' οἶκον, ἢ θεοῦ μοῖραν ἢ ἀνθρώπου χάριν,
εὑροῦσα μῶμον ἐς μάχην κορύσσεται.   105
ὅκου γυνὴ γάρ ἐστιν οὐδ' ἐς οἰκίην
ξεῖνον μολόντα προφρόνως δεκοίατο.
ἥτις δέ τοι μάλιστα σωφρονεῖν δοκεῖ,
αὕτη μέγιστα τυγχάνει λωβωμένη·
κεχηνότος γὰρ ἀνδρός, οἱ δὲ γείτονες   110
χαίρουσ' ὁρῶντες καὶ τόν, ὡς ἁμαρτάνει.
τὴν ἣν δ' ἕκαστος αἰνέσει μεμνημένος
γυναῖκα, τὴν δὲ τοὐτέρου μωμήσεται·
ἴσην δ' ἔχοντες μοῖραν οὐ γινώσκομεν.

82 τι κὼς West : τί χ' ὠσ fere codd.   100 ναιετᾶι Wilhelm : πέλεται codd.   102 θεόν Grotius

SEMONIDES 7 : CALLINUS 1 : TYRTAEUS 4 33

Ζεὺς γὰρ μέγιστον τοῦτ' ἐποίησεν κακόν, 115
καὶ δεσμὸν ἀμφέθηκεν ἄρρηκτον πέδην,
ἐξ οὗ τε τοὺς μὲν Ἀΐδης ἐδέξατο
γυναικὸς εἵνεκ' ἀμφιδηριωμένους.

CALLINUS 1

μέχρις τέο κατάκεισθε; κότ' ἄλκιμον ἕξετε θυμόν,
ὦ νέοι; οὐδ' αἰδεῖσθ' ἀμφιπερικτίονας
ὧδε λίην μεθιέντες; ἐν εἰρήνηι δὲ δοκεῖτε
ἧσθαι, ἀτὰρ πόλεμος γαῖαν ἅπασαν ἔχει
  .   .   .   .
καί τις ἀποθνήσκων ὕστατ' ἀκοντισάτω. 5
τιμῆέν τε γάρ ἐστι καὶ ἀγλαὸν ἀνδρὶ μάχεσθαι
γῆς πέρι καὶ παίδων κουριδίης τ' ἀλόχου
δυσμενέσιν· θάνατος δὲ τότ' ἔσσεται, ὁππότε κεν δὴ
Μοῖραι ἐπικλώσωσ'. ἀλλά τις ἰθὺς ἴτω
ἔγχος ἀνασχόμενος καὶ ὑπ' ἀσπίδος ἄλκιμον ἦτορ 10
ἔλσας, τὸ πρῶτον μειγνυμένου πολέμου.
οὐ γάρ κως θάνατόν γε φυγεῖν εἱμαρμένον ἐστὶν
ἄνδρ', οὐδ' εἰ προγόνων ἧι γένος ἀθανάτων.
πολλάκι δηϊοτῆτα φυγὼν καὶ δοῦπον ἀκόντων
ἔρχεται, ἐν δ' οἴκωι μοῖρα κίχεν θανάτου, 15
ἀλλ' ὁ μὲν οὐκ ἔμπης δήμωι φίλος οὐδὲ ποθεινός·
τὸν δ' ὀλίγος στενάχει καὶ μέγας ἤν τι πάθηι·
λαῶι γὰρ σύμπαντι πόθος κρατερόφρονος ἀνδρὸς
θνήσκοντος, ζώων δ' ἄξιος ἡμιθέων·
ὥσπερ γάρ μιν πύργον ἐν ὀφθαλμοῖσιν ὁρῶσιν· 20
ἔρδει γὰρ πολλῶν ἄξια μοῦνος ἐών.

TYRTAEUS 4

Φοίβου ἀκούσαντες Πυθωνόθεν οἴκαδ' ἔνεικαν
μαντείας τε θεοῦ καὶ τελέεντ' ἔπεα·
ἄρχειν μὲν βουλῆς θεοτιμήτους βασιλῆας,
οἷσι μέλει Σπάρτης ἱμερόεσσα πόλις,
πρεσβυγενέας τε γέροντας· ἔπειτα δὲ δημότας ἄνδρας 5

116 πέδην Crusius : πέδη(ι) codd.
Callin. 1 1 τέο Fick : τεῦ codd.
Tyrt. 4 1 οἴκαδ' ἔνεικαν Amyot : οἳ τάδε νικᾶν codd.

TYRTAEUS 4-7, 12

εὐθείαις ῥήτραις ἀνταπαμειβομένους
μυθεῖσθαί τε τὰ καλὰ καὶ ἔρδειν πάντα δίκαια,
μηδέ τι βουλεύειν τῆιδε πόλει ⟨σκολιόν⟩·
δήμου τε πλήθει νίκην καὶ κάρτος ἕπεσθαι.
Φοῖβος γὰρ περὶ τῶν ὧδ' ἀνέφηνε πόλει.   10

TYRTAEUS 5

ἡμετέρωι βασιλῆϊ, θεοῖσι φίλωι Θεοπόμπωι,
ὃν διὰ Μεσσήνην εἵλομεν εὐρύχορον,
Μεσσήνην ἀγαθὸν μὲν ἀροῦν, ἀγαθὸν δὲ φυτεύειν·
ἀμφ' αὐτὴν δ' ἐμάχοντ' ἐννέα καὶ δέκ' ἔτη
νωλεμέως αἰεὶ ταλασίφρονα θυμὸν ἔχοντες   5
αἰχμηταὶ πατέρων ἡμετέρων πατέρες·
εἰκοστῶι δ' οἱ μὲν κατὰ πίονα ἔργα λιπόντες
φεῦγον Ἰθωμαίων ἐκ μεγάλων ὀρέων.

TYRTAEUS 6

ὥσπερ ὄνοι μεγάλοις ἄχθεσι τειρόμενοι,
δεσποσύνοισι φέροντες ἀναγκαίης ὕπο λυγρῆς
ἥμισυ πάνθ' ὅσσων καρπὸν ἄρουρα φέρει.

TYRTAEUS 7

δεσπότας οἰμώζοντες, ὁμῶς ἄλοχοί τε καὶ αὐτοί,
εὖτέ τιν' οὐλομένη μοῖρα κίχοι θανάτου.

TYRTAEUS 12

οὔτ' ἂν μνησαίμην οὔτ' ἐν λόγωι ἄνδρα τιθείην
οὔτε ποδῶν ἀρετῆς οὔτε παλαιμοσύνης,
οὐδ' εἰ Κυκλώπων μὲν ἔχοι μέγεθός τε βίην τε,
νικώιη δὲ θέων Θρηΐκιον Βορέην,
οὐδ' εἰ Τιθωνοῖο φυὴν χαριέστερος εἴη,   5
πλουτοίη δὲ Μίδεω καὶ Κινύρεω μάλιον,
οὐδ' εἰ Ταντάλιδεω Πέλοπος βασιλεύτερος εἴη,
γλῶσσαν δ' Ἀδρήστου μειλιχόγηρυν ἔχοι,

8 βουλεύειν Bach : ἐπιβουλεύειν V   σκολιόν add. Bach
Tyrt. 12   6 Κινύρεω μάλιον M. Schmidt : κινυρέοιο μᾶλλον codd.

TYRTAEUS 12

οὐδ' εἰ πᾶσαν ἔχοι δόξαν πλὴν θούριδος ἀλκῆς·
οὐ γὰρ ἀνὴρ ἀγαθὸς γίνεται ἐν πολέμωι 10
εἰ μὴ τετλαίη μὲν ὁρῶν φόνον αἱματόεντα,
καὶ δηίων ὀρέγοιτ' ἐγγύθεν ἱστάμενος.
ἥδ' ἀρετή, τόδ' ἄεθλον ἐν ἀνθρώποισιν ἄριστον
κάλλιστόν τε φέρειν γίνεται ἀνδρὶ νέωι.
ξυνὸν δ' ἐσθλὸν τοῦτο πόληΐ τε παντί τε δήμωι, 15
ὅστις ἀνὴρ διαβὰς ἐν προμάχοισι μένηι
νωλεμέως, αἰσχρῆς δὲ φυγῆς ἐπὶ πάγχυ λάθηται,
ψυχὴν καὶ θυμὸν τλήμονα παρθέμενος,
θαρσύνηι δ' ἔπεσιν τὸν πλησίον ἄνδρα παρεστώς·
οὗτος ἀνὴρ ἀγαθὸς γίνεται ἐν πολέμωι. 20
αἶψα δὲ δυσμενέων ἀνδρῶν ἔτρεψε φάλαγγας
τρηχείας, σπουδῆι δ' ἔσχεθε κῦμα μάχης.
αὐτὸς δ' ἐν προμάχοισι πεσὼν φίλον ὤλεσε θυμόν,
ἄστυ τε καὶ λαοὺς καὶ πατέρ' εὐκλεΐσας,
πολλὰ διὰ στέρνοιο καὶ ἀσπίδος ὀμφαλοέσσης 25
καὶ διὰ θώρηκος πρόσθεν ἐληλαμένος.
τὸν δ' ὀλοφύρονται μὲν ὁμῶς νέοι ἠδὲ γέροντες,
ἀργαλέωι δὲ πόθωι πᾶσα κέκηδε πόλις,
καὶ τύμβος καὶ παῖδες ἐν ἀνθρώποις ἀρίσημοι
καὶ παίδων παῖδες καὶ γένος ἐξοπίσω· 30
οὐδέ ποτε κλέος ἐσθλὸν ἀπόλλυται οὐδ' ὄνομ' αὐτοῦ,
ἀλλ' ὑπὸ γῆς περ ἐὼν γίνεται ἀθάνατος,
ὅντιν' ἀριστεύοντα μένοντά τε μαρνάμενόν τε
γῆς πέρι καὶ παίδων θοῦρος Ἄρης ὀλέσηι.
εἰ δὲ φύγηι μὲν κῆρα τανηλεγέος θανάτοιο, 35
νικήσας δ' αἰχμῆς ἀγλαὸν εὖχος ἕληι,
πάντες μιν τιμῶσιν, ὁμῶς νέοι ἠδὲ παλαιοί,
πολλὰ δὲ τερπνὰ παθὼν ἔρχεται εἰς Ἀΐδην,
γηράσκων δ' ἀστοῖσι μεταπρέπει, οὐδέ τις αὐτὸν
βλάπτειν οὔτ' αἰδοῦς οὔτε δίκης ἐθέλει, 40
πάντες δ' ἐν θώκοισιν ὁμῶς νέοι οἵ τε κατ' αὐτὸν
εἴκουσ' ἐκ χώρης οἵ τε παλαιότεροι.
ταύτης νῦν τις ἀνὴρ ἀρετῆς εἰς ἄκρον ἱκέσθαι
πειράσθω θυμῶι μὴ μεθιεὶς πολέμου.

11 ὁρᾶν Pl. *Leg.* 629e   19 δ' ἔπεσιν Par. 2092 (s. xvi) : δὲ πεσεῖν codd.

MIMNERMUS 1

τίς δὲ βίος, τί δὲ τερπνὸν ἄτερ χρυσῆς Ἀφροδίτης;
τεθναίην, ὅτε μοι μηκέτι ταῦτα μέλοι,
κρυπταδίη φιλότης καὶ μείλιχα δῶρα καὶ εὐνή,
οἷ' ἥβης ἄνθεα γίνεται ἁρπαλέα
ἀνδράσιν ἠδὲ γυναιξίν· ἐπεὶ δ' ὀδυνηρὸν ἐπέλθηι 5
γῆρας, ὅ τ' αἰσχρὸν ὁμῶς καὶ κακὸν ἄνδρα τιθεῖ,
αἰεί μιν φρένας ἀμφὶ κακαὶ τείρουσι μέριμναι,
οὐδ' αὐγὰς προσορῶν τέρπεται ἠελίου,
ἀλλ' ἐχθρὸς μὲν παισίν, ἀτίμαστος δὲ γυναιξίν·
οὕτως ἀργαλέον γῆρας ἔθηκε θεός. 10

MIMNERMUS 2

ἡμεῖς δ', οἷά τε φύλλα φύει πολυάνθεμος ὥρη
ἔαρος, ὅτ' αἶψ' αὐγῆις αὔξεται ἠελίου,
τοῖς ἴκελοι πήχυιον ἐπὶ χρόνον ἄνθεσιν ἥβης
τερπόμεθα, πρὸς θεῶν εἰδότες οὔτε κακὸν
οὔτ' ἀγαθόν· Κῆρες δὲ παρεστήκασι μέλαιναι, 5
ἡ μὲν ἔχουσα τέλος γήραος ἀργαλέου,
ἡ δ' ἑτέρη θανάτοιο· μίνυνθα δὲ γίνεται ἥβης
καρπός, ὅσον τ' ἐπὶ γῆν κίδναται ἠέλιος.
αὐτὰρ ἐπὴν δὴ τοῦτο τέλος παραμείψεται ὥρης,
αὐτίκα δὴ τεθνάναι βέλτιον ἢ βίοτος· 10
πολλὰ γὰρ ἐν θυμῶι κακὰ γίνεται· ἄλλοτε οἶκος
τρυχοῦται, πενίης δ' ἔργ' ὀδυνηρὰ πέλει·
ἄλλος δ' αὖ παίδων ἐπιδεύεται, ὧν τε μάλιστα
ἱμείρων κατὰ γῆς ἔρχεται εἰς Ἀίδην·
ἄλλος νοῦσον ἔχει θυμοφθόρον· οὐδέ τίς ἐστιν 15
ἀνθρώπων ὧι Ζεὺς μὴ κακὰ πολλὰ διδοῖ.

MIMNERMUS 12

Ἠέλιος μὲν γὰρ ἔλαχεν πόνον ἤματα πάντα,
οὐδέ ποτ' ἄμπαυσις γίνεται οὐδεμία

Mimn. 1 4 οἷ' Ahrens : οἱ M : εἰ A   6 κακὸν Hermann : καλὸν codd.   7 μιν Bergk : μὲν codd.
Mimn. 2 2 αὐγῆις Schneidewin : αὐγὴ codd.   16 διδοῖ Par. 1985 et fort. S a.c. : διδῶ S p.c., MA

ἵπποισίν τε καὶ αὐτῶι, ἐπὴν ῥοδοδάκτυλος Ἠώς
Ὠκεανὸν προλιποῦσ᾽ οὐρανὸν εἰσαναβῆι.
τὸν μὲν γὰρ διὰ κῦμα φέρει πολυήρατος εὐνή,   5
κοίλη, Ἡφαίστου χερσὶν ἐληλαμένη,
χρυσοῦ τιμήεντος, ὑπόπτερος, ἄκρον ἐφ᾽ ὕδωρ
εὕδονθ᾽ ἁρπαλέως χώρου ἀφ᾽ Ἑσπερίδων
γαῖαν ἐς Αἰθιόπων, ἵνα δὴ θοὸν ἅρμα καὶ ἵπποι
ἑστᾶσ᾽, ὄφρ᾽ Ἠὼς ἠριγένεια μόληι·   10
ἔνθ᾽ ἐπέβη ἑτέρων ὀχέων Ὑπερίονος υἱός.

MIMNERMUS 14

οὐ μὲν δὴ κείνου γε μένος καὶ ἀγήνορα θυμὸν
τοῖον ἐμέο προτέρων πεύθομαι, οἵ μιν ἴδον
Λυδῶν ἱππομάχων πυκινὰς κλονέοντα φάλαγγας
Ἕρμιον ἂμ πεδίον, φῶτα φερεμμελίην·
τοῦ μὲν ἄρ᾽ οὔ ποτε πάμπαν ἐμέμψατο Παλλὰς Ἀθήνη   5
δριμὺ μένος κραδίης, εὖθ᾽ ὅ γ᾽ ἀνὰ προμάχους
σεύαιθ᾽ αἱματόεν⟨τος ἐν⟩ ὑσμίνηι πολέμοιο,
πικρὰ βιαζόμενος δυσμενέων βέλεα·
οὐ γάρ τις κείνου δηίων ἔτ᾽ ἀμεινότερος φὼς
ἔσκεν ἐποίχεσθαι φυλόπιδος κρατερῆς   10
ἔργον, ὅτ᾽ αὐγῆισιν φέρετ᾽ ὠκέος ἠελίοιο

SOLON 1

αὐτὸς κῆρυξ ἦλθον ἀφ᾽ ἱμερτῆς Σαλαμῖνος,
κόσμον ἐπέων ὠιδὴν ἀντ᾽ ἀγορῆς θέμενος.

SOLON 2

εἴην δὴ τότ᾽ ἐγὼ Φολεγάνδριος ἢ Σικινήτης
ἀντί γ᾽ Ἀθηναίου πατρίδ᾽ ἀμειψάμενος·
αἶψα γὰρ ἂν φάτις ἥδε μετ᾽ ἀνθρώποισι γένοιτο·
"Ἀττικὸς οὗτος ἀνήρ, τῶν Σαλαμιναφετέων".

Mimn. 12 6 κοίλη Meineke : κοίλη codd.   8 εὕδονθ᾽ Musurus : εὕδονθ᾽ ὅθ᾽ A χώρου Musurus : χοροῦ A   9 ἵνα δὴ θοὸν Meineke : ἵν᾽ ἀληθοον A
Mimn. 14 2 ἐμέο West : ἐμεῦ codd.   6 ὅ γ᾽ Schneidewin : ὅτ᾽ codd.   7 σεύαιθ᾽ Schneidewin : σεύηθ᾽ A, σεῦ᾽ ἤθ᾽ M   αἱματόεν suppl. Gesner
Sol. 2 4 Σαλαμιναφετέων Renner : σαλαμίναφετων B

SOLON 3

ἴομεν ἐς Σαλαμῖνα μαχησόμενοι περὶ νήσου
ἱμερτῆς χαλεπόν τ' αἶσχος ἀπωσόμενοι.

SOLON 4

ἡμετέρη δὲ πόλις κατὰ μὲν Διὸς οὔποτ' ὀλεῖται
αἶσαν καὶ μακάρων θεῶν φρένας ἀθανάτων·
τοίη γὰρ μεγάθυμος ἐπίσκοπος ὀβριμοπάτρη
Παλλὰς Ἀθηναίη χεῖρας ὕπερθεν ἔχει·
αὐτοὶ δὲ φθείρειν μεγάλην πόλιν ἀφραδίηισιν 5
ἀστοὶ βούλονται χρήμασι πειθόμενοι,
δήμου θ' ἡγεμόνων ἄδικος νόος, οἷσιν ἑτοῖμον
ὕβριος ἐκ μεγάλης ἄλγεα πολλὰ παθεῖν·
οὐ γὰρ ἐπίστανται κατέχειν κόρον οὐδὲ παρούσας
εὐφροσύνας κοσμεῖν δαιτὸς ἐν ἡσυχίηι 10
. . . .
πλουτέουσιν δ' ἀδίκοις ἔργμασι πειθόμενοι
. . . .
οὔθ' ἱερῶν κτεάνων οὔτε τι δημοσίων
φειδόμενοι κλέπτουσιν ἀφαρπαγῆι ἄλλοθεν ἄλλος,
οὐδὲ φυλάσσονται σεμνὰ Δίκης θέμεθλα,
ἣ σιγῶσα σύνοιδε τὰ γιγνόμενα πρό τ' ἐόντα, 15
τῶι δὲ χρόνωι πάντως ἦλθ' ἀποτεισομένη,
τοῦτ' ἤδη πάσηι πόλει ἔρχεται ἕλκος ἄφυκτον,
ἐς δὲ κακὴν ταχέως ἤλυθε δουλοσύνην,
ἣ στάσιν ἔμφυλον πόλεμόν θ' εὕδοντ' ἐπεγείρει,
ὃς πολλῶν ἐρατὴν ὤλεσεν ἡλικίην· 20
ἐκ γὰρ δυσμενέων ταχέως πολυήρατον ἄστυ
τρύχεται ἐν συνόδοις τοῖς ἀδικέουσι φίλους.
ταῦτα μὲν ἐν δήμωι στρέφεται κακά· τῶν δὲ πενιχρῶν
ἱκνέονται πολλοὶ γαῖαν ἐς ἀλλοδαπὴν
πραθέντες δεσμοῖσί τ' ἀεικελίοισι δεθέντες 25
. . . .
οὕτω δημόσιον κακὸν ἔρχεται οἴκαδ' ἑκάστωι,
αὔλειοι δ' ἔτ' ἔχειν οὐκ ἐθέλουσι θύραι,
ὑψηλὸν δ' ὑπὲρ ἕρκος ὑπέρθορεν, εὗρε δὲ πάντως,
εἰ καί τις φεύγων ἐν μυχῶι ἦι θαλάμου.

Sol. 4   16 ἀποτεισομένη Hiller : ἀποτισομένη B p.c.   22 φίλους F p.c. : φίλοις cett.
29 ἦι θαλάμου Schneidewin : ἢ θαλάμωι codd.

SOLON 4–6, 9   39

ταῦτα διδάξαι θυμὸς Ἀθηναίους με κελεύει,   30
ὡς κακὰ πλεῖστα πόλει Δυσνομίη παρέχει·
Εὐνομίη δ' εὔκοσμα καὶ ἄρτια πάντ' ἀποφαίνει,
καὶ θαμὰ τοῖς ἀδίκοις ἀμφιτίθησι πέδας·
τραχέα λειαίνει, παύει κόρον, ὕβριν ἀμαυροῖ,
αὐαίνει δ' ἄτης ἄνθεα φυόμενα,   35
εὐθύνει δὲ δίκας σκολιάς, ὑπερήφανά τ' ἔργα
πραΰνει· παύει δ' ἔργα διχοστασίης,
παύει δ' ἀργαλέης ἔριδος χόλον, ἔστι δ' ὑπ' αὐτῆς
πάντα κατ' ἀνθρώπους ἄρτια καὶ πινυτά.

SOLON 5

δήμωι μὲν γὰρ ἔδωκα τόσον γέρας ὅσσον ἀπαρκεῖ,
τιμῆς οὔτ' ἀφελὼν οὔτ' ἐπορεξάμενος·
οἳ δ' εἶχον δύναμιν καὶ χρήμασιν ἦσαν ἀγητοί,
καὶ τοῖς ἐφρασάμην μηδὲν ἀεικὲς ἔχειν·
ἔστην δ' ἀμφιβαλὼν κρατερὸν σάκος ἀμφοτέροισι,   5
νικᾶν δ' οὐκ εἴασ' οὐδετέρους ἀδίκως.

SOLON 6

δῆμος δ' ὧδ' ἂν ἄριστα σὺν ἡγεμόνεσσιν ἕποιτο,
μήτε λίην ἀνεθεὶς μήτε βιαζόμενος·
τίκτει γὰρ κόρος ὕβριν, ὅταν πολὺς ὄλβος ἕπηται
ἀνθρώποις ὁπόσοις μὴ νόος ἄρτιος ἦι.

SOLON 9

ἐκ νεφέλης πέλεται χιόνος μένος ἠδὲ χαλάζης,
βροντὴ δ' ἐκ λαμπρῆς γίγνεται ἀστεροπῆς·
ἀνδρῶν δ' ἐκ μεγάλων πόλις ὄλλυται, ἐς δὲ μονάρχου
δῆμος ἀϊδρίηι δουλοσύνην ἔπεσεν.
λίην δ' ἐξάραντ' ⟨οὐ⟩ ῥάιδιόν ἐστι κατασχεῖν   5
ὕστερον, ἀλλ' ἤδη χρὴ ⟨καλὰ⟩ πάντα νοεῖν.

Sol. 5   1 γέρας codd. : κράτος Plut.   ἀπαρκεῖ pap. Arist. : ἐπαρκεῖ Plut.
Sol. 9   3 τυράννου Diod.   5 λίην δ' ἐξάραντ' Schneidewin : λείης δ' ἐξέραντα Diod.
οὐ add. L. Dindorf   6 καλὰ add. West

SOLON 10

δείξει δὴ μανίην μὲν ἐμὴν βαιὸς χρόνος ἀστοῖς,
δείξει ἀληθείης ἐς μέσον ἐρχομένης.

SOLON 11

εἰ δὲ πεπόνθατε λυγρὰ δι' ὑμετέρην κακότητα,
μὴ θεοῖσιν τούτων μοῖραν ἐπαμφέρετε·
αὐτοὶ γὰρ τούτους ηὐξήσατε ῥύματα δόντες,
καὶ διὰ ταῦτα κακὴν ἔσχετε δουλοσύνην.
ὑμέων δ' εἷς μὲν ἕκαστος ἀλώπεκος ἴχνεσι βαίνει, 5
σύμπασιν δ' ὑμῖν χαῦνος ἔνεστι νόος·
ἐς γὰρ γλῶσσαν ὁρᾶτε καὶ εἰς ἔπη αἱμύλου ἀνδρός,
εἰς ἔργον δ' οὐδὲν γιγνόμενον βλέπετε.

SOLON 13

Μνημοσύνης καὶ Ζηνὸς Ὀλυμπίου ἀγλαὰ τέκνα,
Μοῦσαι Πιερίδες, κλῦτέ μοι εὐχομένωι·
ὄλβον μοι πρὸς θεῶν μακάρων δότε, καὶ πρὸς ἁπάντων
ἀνθρώπων αἰεὶ δόξαν ἔχειν ἀγαθήν·
εἶναι δὲ γλυκὺν ὧδε φίλοις, ἐχθροῖσι δὲ πικρόν, 5
τοῖσι μὲν αἰδοῖον, τοῖσι δὲ δεινὸν ἰδεῖν.
χρήματα δ' ἱμείρω μὲν ἔχειν, ἀδίκως δὲ πεπᾶσθαι
οὐκ ἐθέλω· πάντως ὕστερον ἦλθε δίκη.
πλοῦτον δ' ὃν μὲν δῶσι θεοί, παραγίγνεται ἀνδρὶ
ἔμπεδος ἐκ νεάτου πυθμένος ἐς κορυφήν· 10
ὃν δ' ἄνδρες τιμῶσιν ὑφ' ὕβριος, οὐ κατὰ κόσμον
ἔρχεται, ἀλλ' ἀδίκοις ἔργμασι πειθόμενος
οὐκ ἐθέλων ἕπεται, ταχέως δ' ἀναμίσγεται ἄτηι·
ἀρχῆς δ' ἐξ ὀλίγης γίγνεται ὥστε πυρός,
φλαύρη μὲν τὸ πρῶτον, ἀνιηρὴ δὲ τελευτᾶι· 15
οὐ γὰρ δὴν θνητοῖς ὕβριος ἔργα πέλει,
ἀλλὰ Ζεὺς πάντων ἐφορᾶι τέλος, ἐξαπίνης δὲ
ὥστ' ἄνεμος νεφέλας αἶψα διεσκέδασεν

Sol. 11   3 ῥύσια Diog.   6 χαῦνος Plut. : κοῦφος Diod., Diog.   7 ἔπη αἱμύλου Plut. : ἔπος αἱόλον Diod., Diog.
Sol. 13   14 ἀρχῆς δ' ἐξ ὀλίγης West : ἀρχὴ δ' ἐξ ὀλίγου S   16 δὴν Gesner et Par. 1985 : δὴ S

SOLON 13

ἠρινός, ὃς πόντου πολυκύμονος ἀτρυγέτοιο
πυθμένα κινήσας, γῆν κάτα πυροφόρον   20
δηιώσας καλὰ ἔργα θεῶν ἕδος αἰπὺν ἱκάνει
οὐρανόν, αἰθρίην δ' αὖτις ἔθηκεν ἰδεῖν,
λάμπει δ' ἠελίοιο μένος κατὰ πίονα γαῖαν
καλόν, ἀτὰρ νεφέων οὐδ' ἓν ἔτ' ἐστὶν ἰδεῖν.
τοιαύτη Ζηνὸς πέλεται τίσις· οὐδ' ἐφ' ἑκάστωι   25
ὥσπερ θνητὸς ἀνὴρ γίγνεται ὀξύχολος,
αἰεὶ δ' οὔ ἑ λέληθε διαμπερές, ὅστις ἀλιτρὸν
θυμὸν ἔχει, πάντως δ' ἐς τέλος ἐξεφάνη·
ἀλλ' ὁ μὲν αὐτίκ' ἔτεισεν, ὁ δ' ὕστερον· οἳ δὲ φύγωσιν
αὐτοί, μηδὲ θεῶν μοῖρ' ἐπιοῦσα κίχηι,   30
ἤλυθε πάντως αὖτις· ἀναίτιοι ἔργα τίνουσιν
ἢ παῖδες τούτων ἢ γένος ἐξοπίσω.
θνητοὶ δ' ὧδε νοέομεν ὁμῶς ἀγαθός τε κακός τε,
εὖ ῥεῖν ἣν αὐτὸς δόξαν ἕκαστος ἔχει,
πρίν τι παθεῖν· τότε δ' αὖτις ὀδύρεται· ἄχρι δὲ τούτου   35
χάσκοντες κούφαις ἐλπίσι τερπόμεθα.
χὤστις μὲν νούσοισιν ὑπ' ἀργαλέηισι πιεσθῆι,
ὡς ὑγιὴς ἔσται, τοῦτο κατεφράσατο·
ἄλλος δειλὸς ἐὼν ἀγαθὸς δοκεῖ ἔμμεναι ἀνήρ,
καὶ καλὸς μορφὴν οὐ χαρίεσσαν ἔχων·   40
εἰ δέ τις ἀχρήμων, πενίης δέ μιν ἔργα βιᾶται,
κτήσασθαι πάντως χρήματα πολλὰ δοκεῖ.
σπεύδει δ' ἄλλοθεν ἄλλος· ὁ μὲν κατὰ πόντον ἀλᾶται
ἐν νηυσὶν χρήιζων οἴκαδε κέρδος ἄγειν
ἰχθυόεντ' ἀνέμοισι φορεόμενος ἀργαλέοισιν,   45
φειδωλὴν ψυχῆς οὐδεμίαν θέμενος·
ἄλλος γῆν τέμνων πολυδένδρεον εἰς ἐνιαυτὸν
λατρεύει, τοῖσιν καμπύλ' ἄροτρα μέλει·
ἄλλος Ἀθηναίης τε καὶ Ἡφαίστου πολυτέχνεω
ἔργα δαεὶς χειροῖν ξυλλέγεται βίοτον,   50
ἄλλος Ὀλυμπιάδων Μουσέων πάρα δῶρα διδαχθείς,
ἱμερτῆς σοφίης μέτρον ἐπιστάμενος·
ἄλλον μάντιν ἔθηκεν ἄναξ ἑκάεργος Ἀπόλλων,
ἔγνω δ' ἀνδρὶ κακὸν τηλόθεν ἐρχόμενον,
ὧι συνομαρτήσωσι θεοί· τὰ δὲ μόρσιμα πάντως   55
οὔτε τις οἰωνὸς ῥύσεται οὔθ' ἱερά·

34 εὖ ῥεῖν ἣν Büchner et Theiler : ἐνδηνην S   48 μέλει Gesner : μένει S   50 ἔργα δαεὶς
Par. 1985 m² : ἔργλα εἰσ S

ἄλλοι Παιῶνος πολυφαρμάκου ἔργον ἔχοντες
ἰητροί· καὶ τοῖς οὐδὲν ἔπεστι τέλος·
πολλάκι δ' ἐξ ὀλίγης ὀδύνης μέγα γίγνεται ἄλγος,
κοὐκ ἄν τις λύσαιτ' ἤπια φάρμακα δούς·   60
τὸν δὲ κακαῖς νούσοισι κυκώμενον ἀργαλέαις τε
ἁψάμενος χειροῖν αἶψα τίθησ' ὑγιῆ.
Μοῖρα δέ τοι θνητοῖσι κακὸν φέρει ἠδὲ καὶ ἐσθλόν,
δῶρα δ' ἄφυκτα θεῶν γίγνεται ἀθανάτων.
πᾶσι δέ τοι κίνδυνος ἐπ' ἔργμασιν, οὐδέ τις οἶδεν   65
πῆι μέλλει σχήσειν χρήματος ἀρχομένου·
ἀλλ' ὁ μὲν εὖ ἔρδειν πειρώμενος οὐ προνοήσας
ἐς μεγάλην ἄτην καὶ χαλεπὴν ἔπεσεν,
τῶι δὲ κακῶς ἔρδοντι θεὸς περὶ πάντα δίδωσιν
συντυχίην ἀγαθήν, ἔκλυσιν ἀφροσύνης.   70
πλούτου δ' οὐδὲν τέρμα πεφασμένον ἀνδράσι κεῖται·
οἳ γὰρ νῦν ἡμέων πλεῖστον ἔχουσι βίον,
διπλάσιον σπεύδουσι· τίς ἂν κορέσειεν ἅπαντας;
κέρδεά τοι θνητοῖς ὤπασαν ἀθάνατοι,
ἄτη δ' ἐξ αὐτῶν ἀναφαίνεται, ἣν ὁπότε Ζεὺς   75
πέμψηι τεισομένην, ἄλλοτε ἄλλος ἔχει.

SOLON 27

παῖς μὲν ἄνηβος ἐὼν ἔτι νήπιος ἕρκος ὀδόντων
φύσας ἐκβάλλει πρῶτον ἐν ἕπτ' ἔτεσιν.
τοὺς δ' ἑτέρους ὅτε δὴ τελέσηι θεὸς ἕπτ' ἐνιαυτούς,
ἥβης ἐκφαίνει σήματα γεινομένης.
τῆι τριτάτηι δὲ γένειον ἀεξομένων ἔτι γυίων   5
λαχνοῦται, χροιῆς ἄνθος ἀμειβομένης.
τῆι δὲ τετάρτηι πᾶς τις ἐν ἑβδομάδι μέγ' ἄριστος
ἰσχύν, ἧι τ' ἄνδρες πείρατ' ἔχουσ' ἀρετῆς.
πέμπτηι δ' ὥριον ἄνδρα γάμου μεμνημένον εἶναι
καὶ παίδων ζητεῖν εἰσοπίσω γενεήν.   10
τῆι δ' ἕκτηι περὶ πάντα καταρτύεται νόος ἀνδρός,
οὐδ' ἔρδειν ἔθ' ὁμῶς ἔργ' ἀπάλαμνα θέλει.
ἑπτὰ δὲ νοῦν καὶ γλῶσσαν ἐν ἑβδομάσιν μέγ' ἄριστος
ὀκτώ τ'· ἀμφοτέρων τέσσαρα καὶ δέκ' ἔτη.

61 κυκώμενον Gesner : κακώμενον S   71 ἀνδράσι κεῖται S, Arist., Basil. : ἀνθρώποισι Thgn., Plut.
Sol. 27   8 πείρατ' Stadtmüller : σήματ' vel μνήματ' codd.

SOLON 27, 36 : THEOGNIS 19-26   43

τῆι δ' ἐνάτηι ἔτι μὲν δύναται, μαλακώτερα δ' αὐτοῦ   15
πρὸς μεγάλην ἀρετὴν γλῶσσά τε καὶ σοφίη.
τὴν δεκάτην δ' εἴ τις τελέσας κατὰ μέτρον ἵκοιτο,
οὐκ ἂν ἄωρος ἐὼν μοῖραν ἔχοι θανάτου.

SOLON 36

ἐγὼ δὲ τῶν μὲν οὕνεκα ξυνήγαγον
δῆμον, τί τούτων πρὶν τυχεῖν ἐπαυσάμην;
συμμαρτυροίη ταῦτ' ἂν ἐν δίκηι Χρόνου
μήτηρ μεγίστη δαιμόνων Ὀλυμπίων
ἄριστα, Γῆ μέλαινα, τῆς ἐγώ ποτε   5
ὅρους ἀνεῖλον πολλαχῆι πεπηγότας,
πρόσθεν δὲ δουλεύουσα, νῦν ἐλευθέρη.
πολλοὺς δ' Ἀθήνας πατρίδ' ἐς θεόκτιτον
ἀνήγαγον πραθέντας, ἄλλον ἐκδίκως,
ἄλλον δικαίως, τοὺς δ' ἀναγκαίης ὑπὸ   10
χρειοῦς φυγόντας, γλῶσσαν οὐκέτ' Ἀττικὴν
ἱέντας, ὡς δὴ πολλαχῆι πλανωμένους·
τοὺς δ' ἐνθάδ' αὐτοῦ δουλίην ἀεικέα
ἔχοντας, ἤθη δεσποτέων τρομεομένους,
ἐλευθέρους ἔθηκα. ταῦτα μὲν κράτει   15
ὁμοῦ βίην τε καὶ δίκην ξυναρμόσας
ἔρεξα, καὶ διῆλθον ὡς ὑπεσχόμην·
θεσμοὺς δ' ὁμοίως τῶι κακῶι τε κἀγαθῶι
εὐθεῖαν εἰς ἕκαστον ἁρμόσας δίκην
ἔγραψα. κέντρον δ' ἄλλος ὡς ἐγὼ λαβών,   20
κακοφραδής τε καὶ φιλοκτήμων ἀνήρ,
οὐκ ἂν κατέσχε δῆμον· εἰ γὰρ ἤθελον
ἃ τοῖς ἐναντίοισιν ἥνδανεν τότε,
αὖτις δ' ἃ τοῖσιν οὕτεροι φρασαίατο,
πολλῶν ἂν ἀνδρῶν ἥδ' ἐχηρώθη πόλις.   25
τῶν οὕνεκ' ἀλκὴν πάντοθεν ποιεόμενος
ὡς ἐν κυσὶν πολλῆισιν ἐστράφην λύκος.

THEOGNIS 19-26

Κύρνε, σοφιζομένωι μὲν ἐμοὶ σφρηγὶς ἐπικείσθω
τοῖσδ' ἔπεσιν – λήσει δ' οὔποτε κλεπτόμενα,   20

Sol. 36   12 δὴ West : ἂν pap. et codd.

οὐδέ τις ἀλλάξει κάκιον τοὐσθλοῦ παρεόντος,
ὧδε δὲ πᾶς τις ἐρεῖ· "Θεύγνιδός ἐστιν ἔπη
τοῦ Μεγαρέως· πάντας δὲ κατ' ἀνθρώπους ὀνομαστός"·
ἀστοῖσιν δ' οὔπω πᾶσιν ἁδεῖν δύναμαι.
οὐδὲν θαυμαστόν, Πολυπαΐδη· οὐδὲ γὰρ οὖν Ζεὺς   25
οὔθ' ὕων πάντεσσ' ἁνδάνει οὔτ' ἀνέχων.

THEOGNIS 27–30

σοὶ δ' ἐγὼ εὖ φρονέων ὑποθήσομαι, οἷάπερ αὐτός,
Κύρν', ἀπὸ τῶν ἀγαθῶν παῖς ἔτ' ἐὼν ἔμαθον.
πέπνυσο, μηδ' αἰσχροῖσιν ἐπ' ἔργμασι μηδ' ἀδίκοισιν
τιμὰς μηδ' ἀρετὰς ἕλκεο μηδ' ἄφενος.   30

THEOGNIS 31–8

ταῦτα μὲν οὕτως ἴσθι· κακοῖσι δὲ μὴ προσομίλει
ἀνδράσιν, ἀλλ' αἰεὶ τῶν ἀγαθῶν ἔχεο·
καὶ μετὰ τοῖσιν πῖνε καὶ ἔσθιε, καὶ μετὰ τοῖσιν
ἵζε, καὶ ἅνδανε τοῖς, ὧν μεγάλη δύναμις.
ἐσθλῶν μὲν γὰρ ἄπ' ἐσθλὰ μαθήσεαι· ἢν δὲ κακοῖσι   35
συμμίσγηις, ἀπολεῖς καὶ τὸν ἐόντα νόον.
ταῦτα μαθὼν ἀγαθοῖσιν ὁμίλει, καί ποτε φήσεις
εὖ συμβουλεύειν τοῖσι φίλοισιν ἐμέ.

THEOGNIS 39–52

Κύρνε, κύει πόλις ἥδε, δέδοικα δὲ μὴ τέκηι ἄνδρα
εὐθυντῆρα κακῆς ὕβριος ἡμετέρης.   40
ἀστοὶ μὲν γὰρ ἔθ' οἵδε σαόφρονες, ἡγεμόνες δὲ
τετράφαται πολλὴν εἰς κακότητα πεσεῖν.
οὐδεμίαν πω, Κύρν', ἀγαθοὶ πόλιν ὤλεσαν ἄνδρες·
ἀλλ' ὅταν ὑβρίζειν τοῖσι κακοῖσιν ἅδηι,
δῆμόν τε φθείρωσι δίκας τ' ἀδίκοισι διδῶσιν   45
οἰκείων κερδέων εἵνεκα καὶ κράτεος,
ἔλπεο μὴ δηρὸν κείνην πόλιν ἀτρεμίεσθαι,
μηδ' εἰ νῦν κεῖται πολλῆι ἐν ἡσυχίηι,

---

25 οὖν ostr. (*P. Berol.* 12319) : ὁ codd.
47 ἀτρεμίεσθαι Wackernagel : ἀτρεμέεσθαι codd.

εὖτ' ἂν τοῖσι κακοῖσι φίλ' ἀνδράσι ταῦτα γένηται,
κέρδεα δημοσίωι σὺν κακῶι ἐρχόμενα.   50
ἐκ τῶν γὰρ στάσιές τε καὶ ἔμφυλοι φόνοι ἀνδρῶν
μούναρχοί τε· πόλει μήποτε τῆιδε ἄδοι.

THEOGNIS 53–68

Κύρνε, πόλις μὲν ἔθ' ἥδε πόλις, λαοὶ δὲ δὴ ἄλλοι,
οἳ πρόσθ' οὔτε δίκας ἤιδεσαν οὔτε νόμους,
ἀλλ' ἀμφὶ πλευραῖσι δορὰς αἰγῶν κατέτριβον,   55
ἔξω δ' ὥστ' ἔλαφοι τῆσδ' ἐνέμοντο πόλεος.
καὶ νῦν εἰσ' ἀγαθοί, Πολυπαΐδη· οἱ δὲ πρὶν ἐσθλοὶ
νῦν δειλοί. τίς κεν ταῦτ' ἀνέχοιτ' ἐσορῶν;
ἀλλήλους δ' ἀπατῶσιν ἐπ' ἀλλήλοισι γελῶντες,
οὔτε κακῶν γνώμας εἰδότες οὔτ' ἀγαθῶν.   60
μηδένα τῶνδε φίλον ποιεῦ, Πολυπαΐδη, ἀστῶν
ἐκ θυμοῦ χρείης οὕνεκα μηδεμιῆς·
ἀλλὰ δόκει μὲν πᾶσιν ἀπὸ γλώσσης φίλος εἶναι,
χρῆμα δὲ συμμείξηις μηδενὶ μηδ' ὁτιοῦν
σπουδαῖον· γνώσηι γὰρ ὀιζυρῶν φρένας ἀνδρῶν,   65
ὥς σφιν ἐπ' ἔργοισιν πίστις ἔπ' οὐδεμία,
ἀλλὰ δόλους ἀπάτας τε πολυπλοκίας τ' ἐφίλησαν
οὕτως ὡς ἄνδρες μηκέτι σωιζόμενοι.

THEOGNIS 119–28

χρυσοῦ κιβδήλοιο καὶ ἀργύρου ἀνσχετὸς ἄτη,
Κύρνε, καὶ ἐξευρεῖν ῥάιδιον ἀνδρὶ σοφῶι·   120
εἰ δὲ φίλου νόος ἀνδρὸς ἐνὶ στήθεσσι λελήθηι
ψυδρὸς ἐών, δόλιον δ' ἐν φρεσὶν ἦτορ ἔχηι,
τοῦτο θεὸς κιβδηλότατον ποίησε βροτοῖσιν,
καὶ γνῶναι πάντων τοῦτ' ἀνιηρότατον.
οὐδὲ γὰρ εἰδείης ἀνδρὸς νόον οὐδὲ γυναικός,   125
πρὶν πειρηθείης ὥσπερ ὑποζυγίου,
οὐδέ κεν εἰκάσσαις ὥσπερ ποτ' ἐς ὥριον ἐλθών·
πολλάκι γὰρ γνώμην ἐξαπατῶσ' ἰδέαι.

THEOGNIS 183–92

κριοὺς μὲν καὶ ὄνους διζήμεθα, Κύρνε, καὶ ἵππους
εὐγενέας, καί τις βούλεται ἐξ ἀγαθῶν

52 τε Leutsch : δὲ codd.
119 ἀνσχετὸς Camerarius : ἄσχετος codd.   127 ὤνιον Camerarius

βήσεσθαι· γῆμαι δὲ κακὴν κακοῦ οὐ μελεδαίνει 185
ἐσθλὸς ἀνήρ, ἤν οἱ χρήματα πολλὰ διδῶι,
οὐδὲ γυνὴ κακοῦ ἀνδρὸς ἀναίνεται εἶναι ἄκοιτις
πλουσίου, ἀλλ' ἀφνεὸν βούλεται ἀντ' ἀγαθοῦ.
χρήματα μὲν τιμῶσι· καὶ ἐκ κακοῦ ἐσθλὸς ἔγημε
καὶ κακὸς ἐξ ἀγαθοῦ· πλοῦτος ἔμειξε γένος.
οὕτω μὴ θαύμαζε γένος, Πολυπαΐδη, ἀστῶν 190
μαυροῦσθαι· σὺν γὰρ μίσγεται ἐσθλὰ κακοῖς.

THEOGNIS 237-54

σοὶ μὲν ἐγὼ πτέρ' ἔδωκα, σὺν οἷσ' ἐπ' ἀπείρονα πόντον
πωτήσηι καὶ γῆν πᾶσαν ἀειρόμενος
ῥηϊδίως· θοίνηις δὲ καὶ εἰλαπίνηισι παρέσσηι
ἐν πάσαις, πολλῶν κείμενος ἐν στόμασιν, 240
καί σε σὺν αὐλίσκοισι λιγυφθόγγοις νέοι ἄνδρες
εὐκόσμως ἐρατοὶ καλά τε καὶ λιγέα
ἄισονται. καὶ ὅταν δνοφερῆς ὑπὸ κεύθεσι γαίης
βῆις πολυκωκύτους εἰς Ἀΐδαο δόμους,
οὐδέποτ' οὐδὲ θανὼν ἀπολεῖς κλέος, ἀλλὰ μελήσεις 245
ἄφθιτον ἀνθρώποις αἰὲν ἔχων ὄνομα,
Κύρνε, καθ' Ἑλλάδα γῆν στρωφώμενος ἠδ' ἀνὰ νήσους
ἰχθυόεντα περῶν πόντον ἐπ' ἀτρύγετον,
οὐχ ἵππων νώτοισιν ἐφήμενος, ἀλλά σε πέμψει
ἀγλαὰ Μουσάων δῶρα ἰοστεφάνων· 250
πᾶσι δ' ὅσοισι μέμηλε καὶ ἐσσομένοισιν ἀοιδὴ
ἔσσηι ὁμῶς, ὄφρ' ἂν γῆ τε καὶ ἥλιος·
αὐτὰρ ἐγὼν ὀλίγης παρὰ σεῦ οὐ τυγχάνω αἰδοῦς,
ἀλλ' ὥσπερ μικρὸν παῖδα λόγοις μ' ἀπατᾶις.

THEOGNIS 337-40

Ζεύς μοι τῶν τε φίλων δοίη τίσιν, οἵ με φιλεῦσιν,
τῶν τ' ἐχθρῶν μεῖζον, Κύρνε, δυνησόμενον.
χοὕτως ἂν δοκέοιμι μετ' ἀνθρώπων θεὸς εἶναι,
εἴ μ' ἀποτεισάμενον μοῖρα κίχηι θανάτου. 340

---

185 κτήσεσθαι Stob.
238 καὶ Bergk : κατὰ codd.   251 πᾶσι δ' ὅσοισι Lachmann : πᾶσι διὸσ οἷσ A :
πᾶσιν οἷσι O : πᾶσι γὰρ οἶσι *p*

THEOGNIS 805-10

τόρνου καὶ στάθμης καὶ γνώμονος ἄνδρα θεωρὸν   805
εὐθύτερον χρὴ ἔμεν, Κύρνε, φυλασσόμενον,
ὧιτινί κεν Πυθῶνι θεοῦ χρήσασ᾽ ἱέρεια
ὀμφὴν σημήνηι πίονος ἐξ ἀδύτου·
οὔτε τι γὰρ προσθεὶς οὐδέν κ᾽ ἔτι φάρμακον εὕροις,
οὐδ᾽ ἀφελὼν πρὸς θεῶν ἀμπλακίην προφύγοις.   810

THEOGNIS 1197-202

ὄρνιθος φωνήν, Πολυπαΐδη, ὀξὺ βοώσης
ἤκουσ᾽, ἥ τε βροτοῖς ἄγγελος ἦλθ᾽ ἀρότου
ὡραίου· καί μοι κραδίην ἐπάταξε μέλαιναν,
ὅττι μοι εὐανθεῖς ἄλλοι ἔχουσιν ἀγρούς,   1200
οὐδέ μοι ἡμίονοι κυφὸν ἕλκουσιν ἄροτρον
†τῆς ἄλλης μνηστῆς† εἵνεκα ναυτιλίης.

THEOGNIS 1225-6

οὐδέν, Κύρν᾽, ἀγαθῆς γλυκερώτερόν ἐστι γυναικός·   1225
μάρτυς ἐγώ, σὺ δ᾽ ἐμοὶ γίνου ἀληθοσύνης.

XENOPHANES 1

νῦν γὰρ δὴ ζάπεδον καθαρὸν καὶ χεῖρες ἁπάντων
καὶ κύλικες· πλεκτοὺς δ᾽ ἀμφιτιθεῖ στεφάνους,
ἄλλος δ᾽ εὐῶδες μύρον ἐν φιάληι παρατείνει·
κρητὴρ δ᾽ ἕστηκεν μεστὸς ἐϋφροσύνης·
ἄλλος δ᾽ οἶνος ἑτοῖμος, ὃς οὔποτέ φησι προδώσειν,   5
μείλιχος ἐν κεράμοις, ἄνθεος ὀζόμενος·
ἐν δὲ μέσοις ἁγνὴν ὀδμὴν λιβανωτὸς ἵησιν,
ψυχρὸν δ᾽ ἐστὶν ὕδωρ καὶ γλυκὺ καὶ καθαρόν·
παρκέαται δ᾽ ἄρτοι ξανθοὶ γεραρή τε τράπεζα
τυροῦ καὶ μέλιτος πίονος ἀχθομένη·   10
βωμὸς δ᾽ ἄνθεσιν ἂν τὸ μέσον πάντηι πεπύκασται,
μολπὴ δ᾽ ἀμφὶς ἔχει δώματα καὶ θαλίη.

805 θεωρὸν Vinetus : θεωρῶν codd.   806 χρὴ ἔμεν Ahrens : χρὴ μὲν codd.
1202 μάλα μισητῆς Hertzberg et Crusius
Xenoph. 1   9 παρκέαται Wackernagel : πάρκεινται codd.

XENOPHANES 1-2

χρὴ δὲ πρῶτον μὲν θεὸν ὑμνεῖν εὔφρονας ἄνδρας
εὐφήμοις μύθοις καὶ καθαροῖσι λόγοις,
σπείσαντάς τε καὶ εὐξαμένους τὰ δίκαια δύνασθαι   15
πρήσσειν· ταῦτα γὰρ ὦν ἐστι προχειρότερον,
οὐχ ὕβρεις· πίνειν δ' ὁπόσον κεν ἔχων ἀφίκοιο
οἴκαδ' ἄνευ προπόλου μὴ πάνυ γηραλέος·
ἀνδρῶν δ' αἰνεῖν τοῦτον ὃς ἐσθλὰ πιὼν ἀναφαίνει,
ὡς ἧι μνημοσύνη καὶ τόνος ἀμφ' ἀρετῆς,   20
οὔ τι μάχας διέπειν Τιτήνων οὐδὲ Γιγάντων
οὐδέ ⟨τι⟩ Κενταύρων, πλάσματα τῶν προτέρων,
ἢ στάσιας σφεδανάς· τοῖς οὐδὲν χρηστὸν ἔνεστιν·
θεῶν ⟨δὲ⟩ προμηθείην αἰὲν ἔχειν ἀγαθήν.

XENOPHANES 2

ἀλλ' εἰ μὲν ταχυτῆτι ποδῶν νίκην τις ἄροιτο
ἢ πενταθλεύων, ἔνθα Διὸς τέμενος
πὰρ Πίσαο ῥοῆις ἐν Ὀλυμπίηι, εἴτε παλαίων
ἢ καὶ πυκτοσύνην ἀλγινόεσσαν ἔχων
εἴτε τὸ δεινὸν ἄεθλον ὃ παγκράτιον καλέουσιν,   5
ἀστοῖσίν κ' εἴη κυδρότερος προσορᾶν,
καί κε προεδρίην φανερὴν ἐν ἀγῶσιν ἄροιτο,
καί κεν σῖτ' εἴη δημοσίων κτεάνων
ἐκ πόλεως, καὶ δῶρον ὅ οἱ κειμήλιον εἴη—
εἴτε καὶ ἵπποισιν· ταῦτά κε πάντα λάχοι,   10
οὐκ ἐὼν ἄξιος ὥσπερ ἐγώ· ῥώμης γὰρ ἀμείνων
ἀνδρῶν ἠδ' ἵππων ἡμετέρη σοφίη.
ἀλλ' εἰκῆι μάλα τοῦτο νομίζεται, οὐδὲ δίκαιον
προκρίνειν ῥώμην τῆς ἀγαθῆς σοφίης·
οὔτε γὰρ εἰ πύκτης ἀγαθὸς λαοῖσι μετείη   15
οὔτ' εἰ πενταθλεῖν οὔτε παλαισμοσύνην,
οὐδὲ μὲν εἰ ταχυτῆτι ποδῶν, τόπερ ἐστὶ πρότιμον,
ῥώμης ὅσσ' ἀνδρῶν ἔργ' ἐν ἀγῶνι πέλει,

20 ἧι Ahrens : η A, ἡ epit.   τόνος Koraes : τὸν ὃς codd.   22 τι add. Meineke
πλάσματα Schweighäuser : πλασμάτων codd.   23 σφεδανάς Osann : φενδόνας A
24 δὲ add. Camerarius
Xenoph. 2   5 εἴτε τὸ Wakefield : εἴτέτι cod.   6 προσορᾶν Jacobs : προσεραν cod.
10 κε πάντα Schweighäuser : κ'εἰπάντα cod.   15 λαοῖσι μετείη Stephanus : λαοῖσιν
ἔτ' εἴη cod.

τοὔνεκεν ἂν δὴ μᾶλλον ἐν εὐνομίηι πόλις εἴη·
σμικρὸν δ᾽ ἄν τι πόλει χάρμα γένοιτ᾽ ἐπὶ τῶι, 20
εἴ τις ἀεθλεύων νικῶι Πίσαο παρ᾽ ὄχθας·
οὐ γὰρ πιαίνει ταῦτα μυχοὺς πόλεως.

XENOPHANES 3

ἁβροσύνας δὲ μαθόντες ἀνωφελέας παρὰ Λυδῶν,
ὄφρα τυραννίης ἦσαν ἄνευ στυγερῆς,
ἤιεσαν εἰς ἀγορὴν παναλουργέα φάρε᾽ ἔχοντες,
οὐ μείους ὥσπερ χείλιοι ὡς ἐπίπαν,
αὐχαλέοι, χαίτηισιν ἀγαλλόμενοι εὐπρεπέεσσιν, 5
ἀσκητοῖς ὀδμὴν χρίμασι δευόμενοι.

XENOPHANES 7–7A

νῦν αὖτ᾽ ἄλλον ἔπειμι λόγον, δείξω δὲ κέλευθον.
. . . . . .
καί ποτέ μιν στυφελιζομένου σκύλακος παριόντα
φασὶν ἐποικτῖραι καὶ τόδε φάσθαι ἔπος·
"παῦσαι, μηδὲ ῥάπιζ᾽, ἐπεὶ ἦ φίλου ἀνέρος ἐστὶν
ψυχή, τὴν ἔγνων φθεγξαμένης ἀϊών".

XENOPHANES B 14 DK

ἀλλ᾽ οἱ βροτοὶ δοκέουσι γεννᾶσθαι θεούς,
τὴν σφετέρην δ᾽ ἐσθῆτα ἔχειν φωνήν τε δέμας τε.

HIPPONAX 3

ἔβωσε Μαίης παῖδα, Κυλλήνης πάλμυν.

HIPPONAX 3A

Ἑρμῆ κυνάγχα, Μηιονιστὶ Κανδαῦλα,
φωρῶν ἑταῖρε, δεῦρό μοι σκαπαρδεῦσαι.

Xenoph. 3 1 ἁβροσύνας Schneider : ἀφροσύνας cod. 4 ὡς Schweighäuser : εἰς cod. 5 ἀγαλλόμενοι Heitsch : ἀγαλλομεν cod. 6 χρίμασι Musurus : χρήμασι cod.
Xenoph. 7–7a 1 νῦν αὖτ᾽ Stephanus : νῦν οὖν τ᾽ codd.
Hippon. 3 ἔβωσε W. Dindorf : ἐβόησε codd.
Hippon. 3a 2 μοι Dübner : τί μοι codd.

HIPPONAX 12

τούτοισι θηπέων τοὺς Ἐρυθραίων παῖδας
ὁ μητροκοίτης Βούπαλος σὺν Ἀρήτηι
καὶ <μὴν> ὑφέλξων τὸν δυσώνυμον δαρτόν

HIPPONAX 13

ἐκ πελλίδος πίνοντες· οὐ γὰρ ἦν αὐτῆι
κύλιξ, ὁ παῖς γὰρ ἐμπεσὼν κατήραξε.

HIPPONAX 14

ἐκ δὲ τῆς πέλλης
ἔπινον· ἄλλοτ' αὐτός, ἄλλοτ' Ἀρήτη
προὔπινεν.

HIPPONAX 15

τί τῶι τάλαντι Βουπάλωι συνοίκησας;

HIPPONAX 16

ἐγὼ δὲ δεξιῶι παρ' Ἀρήτην
κνεφαῖος ἐλθὼν 'ρωιδιῶι κατηυλίσθην.

HIPPONAX 17

κύψασα γάρ μοι πρὸς τὸ λύχνον Ἀρήτη

HIPPONAX 32

Ἑρμῆ, φίλ' Ἑρμῆ, Μαιαδεῦ, Κυλλήνιε,
ἐπεύχομαί τοι, κάρτα γὰρ κακῶς ῥιγῶ
καὶ βαμβαλύζω . . .
δὸς χλαῖναν Ἱππώνακτι καὶ κυπασσίσκον
καὶ σαμβαλίσκα κἀσκερίσκα καὶ χρυσοῦ   5
στατῆρας ἑξήκοντα τοὐτέρου τοίχου.

Hippon. 12   1 θηπέων ten Brink : θήπων codd.   3 μὴν add. Ebert   δαρτόν Masson : ἄρτον codd.
Hippon. 15 συνοίκησας Bergk : -ώικησας NC, -οικήσας V
Hippon. 16   1 παρ' Ἀρήτην Schneidewin : παρὰ ῥητῆρ cod.
Hippon. 32   1 Ἑρμῆ, φίλ' Prisc. : ὦ φίλ' Tzetz.   3 βαμβαλύζω Schneidewin : βαμβακύζω codd. Plut.

HIPPONAX 34

ἐμοὶ γὰρ οὐκ ἔδωκας οὔτέ κω χλαῖναν
δασεῖαν ἐν χειμῶνι φάρμακον ῥίγεος,
οὔτ' ἀσκέρηισι τοὺς πόδας δασείηισι
ἔκρυψας, ὥς μοι μὴ χίμετλα ῥήγνυται.

HIPPONAX 36

ἐμοὶ δὲ Πλοῦτος — ἔστι γὰρ λίην τυφλός —
ἐς τὠικί' ἐλθὼν οὐδάμ' εἶπεν "Ἱππῶναξ,
δίδωμί τοι μνέας ἀργύρου τριήκοντα
καὶ πόλλ' ἔτ' ἄλλα"· δείλαιος γὰρ τὰς φρένας.

HIPPONAX 68

δύ' ἡμέραι γυναικός εἰσιν ἥδισται,
ὅταν γαμῆι τις κἀκφέρηι τεθνηκυῖαν.

HIPPONAX 92

ηὔδα δὲ Λυδίζουσα· "βασκι...κρολεα".
πυγιστί· "τὸν πυγεῶνα παρ[".
καί μοι τὸν ὄρχιν τῆς φαλ[
κ]ράδηι συνηλοίησεν ὥσπ[ερ φαρμακῶι
.].τοις διοζίοισιν ἐμπεδ[5
καὶ δὴ δυοῖσιν ἐν πόνοισ[ι
ἥ τε κράδη με τοὐτέρωθ[εν
ἄνωθεν ἐμπίπτουσα, κ[
παραψιδάζων βολβίτωι[
ὦζεν δὲ λαύρη· κάνθαροι δὲ ῥοιζέοντες   10
ἦλθον κατ' ὀδμὴν πλέονες ἢ πεντήκοντα·
τῶν οἱ μὲν ἐμπίπτοντε[ς
κατέβαλον, οἱ δὲ τοὺς οδ..[
οἱ δ' ἐμπεσόντες τὰς θύρα[ς
τοῦ Πυγέλησι[.....].[15
..]ρυσσον οἱα[....]αροιμο[
..]ω δ' ἐς υμν[.....]...[
   ]εντ[......]..[

Hippon. 34 1 κω χλαῖναν Schneidewin : χωλεύαν, χωδαῖνε, χλαῖναν, τὴν χλαῖναν codd. 4 μοι μὴ Hartung : μή μοι codd.
Hippon. 92 suppl. Coppola 3 e.g. φαλ[ῆς παρ-/προσέλκουσα Allan 5 ἐμπεδ[ωθέντι Knox 6 πόνοισ[ιν εἰχόμην Bossi, πόνοισ[ιν ἡγρεύμην Knox 7 ἔκνιζεν Coppola, ἤλγυνεν Knox 8 κ[ἄνθεν ὁ πρωκτός Latte 13 ὀδό[ντας ὤξυνον Knox 14 marg. θ, i.e. versus DCCC

HIPPONAX 115

.[
η[
π.[   ]ν[. . .]. . . .[
κύμ[ατι] πλα[ζόμ]ενος·
κἂν Σαλμυδ[ησσ]ῷι γυμνὸν εὔφρονε.[5
Θρήϊκες ἀκρό[κ]ομοι
λάβοιεν — ἔνθα πόλλ' ἀναπλήσει κακὰ
δούλιον ἄρτον ἔδων —
ρίγει πεπηγότ' αὐτόν· ἐκ δὲ τοῦ χνόου
φυκία πόλλ' ἐπιχ⟨έ⟩οι,   10
κροτέοι δ' ὀδόντας, ὡς [κ]ύ̣ων ἐπὶ στόμα
κείμενος ἀκρασίηι
ἄκρον παρὰ ρηγμῖνα κυμα. . . .δο̣υ·
ταῦτ' ἐθέλοιμ' ἂν ἰδεῖν,
ὅς μ' ἠδίκησε, λ[ὰ]ξ δ' ἐπ' ὁρκίοις ἔβη,   15
τὸ πρὶν ἑταῖρος [ἐ]ών.

HIPPONAX 117

]. .[.]. .[
ἡ χλαῖν[α . . . . . .]ασ̣τ̣ινη[
κυρτον ε[. . . . . .]φιλεῖς
ἀγχοῦ καθῆσ̣θ̣αι· ταῦτα δ' Ἱππῶνα[ξ ⏑—
ο]ἶδεν ἄριστα βροτῶν,   5
οἶ]δ̣ε̣ν δὲ κἀρίφαντος· ἃ μάκαρ ὅτ[ις
μηδαμά κώ σ' ἔϊδε
.]ρ̣[. .]ου π̣νέοντα φῶρα. τῶι χυτρεῖ [δὲ νῦν
Αἰσχυλίδηι πολέμει·
ἐκεῖνος ἤμερσέ[ν σε τῆς ἀπαρτί]ης,   10
πᾶς δὲ πέφηνε δό[λος.
]. .[

Hippon. 115 suppl. Reitzenstein 4 κύμ[ασι] Cantarella πλα[ζόμ]ενος Keil 5 εὐφρονέσ[τατα] Diels 7 ἀναπλήσει Reitzenstein : ἐνθαναπλησει pap. 9 χνόου Masson : χνου pap. 10 ἐπιχ⟨έ⟩οι Masson : επιχοι pap. 15 εφορκίοις pap., sscr. επιορκιοις : ἐπ' Blass
Hippon. 117 suppl. Reitzenstein 4 -α]κτίδης Maas 6 Wilamowitz 7 μηδαμά Blass 8 τ]ρ[άγ]ου Diehl 10 -έ[ν σε Blass τῆς ἀπαρτί]ης West 11 Diels

HIPPONAX 128

Μοῦσά μοι Εὐρυμεδοντιάδεα τὴν ποντοχάρυβδιν,
τὴν ἐν γαστρὶ μάχαιραν, ὃς ἐσθίει οὐ κατὰ κόσμον,
ἔννεφ', ὅπως ψηφῖδι < > κακὸν οἶτον ὀλεῖται
βουλῆι δημοσίηι παρὰ θῖν' ἁλὸς ἀτρυγέτοιο.

SIMONIDES 10

]υχν[
..... πατὴ]ρ προπάτω[ρ τε
.........] . θωνην σ[
...... μελε]τῶν ὑπὲρ ἡμ[ετέρων
κούρης εἰν]α̣λίης ἀγλαόφη[με πάϊ   5
....]ησι̣[

SIMONIDES 11

π̣αι̣[..]σ̣ . [
ἢ πίτυν ἐν βήσ[σαις
ὑλοτόμοι τάμ[νωσι
πολλὸν δ' †ἤρῶσ[
ἣ μέγα πένθ]ος λαὸν [ἐπέλλαβε· πολλὰ δ' ἐτίμων,   5
καὶ μετὰ Πατρ]όκλου σ' ἄ[γγεϊ κρύψαν ἐνί.
οὐ δή τίς σ' ἐδ]άμασσεν ἐφ[ημέριος βροτὸς αὐτός,
ἀλλ' ὑπ' Ἀπόλλ]ωνος χειρὶ [τυπεὶς ἐδάμης.
Παλλὰς δ' ἐγγὺ]ς ἐοῦσα πε[ρικλεὲς ἄ]στ[υ καθεῖλεν,
σὺν δ' Ἥρη, Πρ]ιάμου παισὶ χ[αλεπτ]όμ̣[εναι   10
εἵνεκ' Ἀλεξά]νδροιο κακόφρ[ονο]ς, ὥσ σ̣ [
       ] . θείης ἅρμα καθεῖλε δίκ̣[ης.
τοὶ δὲ πόλι]ν πέρσαντες ἀοίδιμον [οἴκαδ' ἵ]κοντο
       ]ωων ἀγέμαχοι Δαναοί[,

Hippon. 128 2 τὴν ἐν γαστρὶ μάχαιραν West : ἐγγαστριμάχαιραν codd., Hsch.
3 <κακῆι> Musurus : <κακὸς> Cobet : <κακῶς> Kalinka   ὀλεῖται Cobet : ὄληται codd.
Simon. 10 suppl. West
Simon. 11 suppl. Parsons vel West exceptis quae infra memorantur   1 παῖ[σέ]
σ̣ [West   4 ἡρώησ[ε Danielewicz   14 φέρτατοι ἡρ]ώων Parsons

54 SIMONIDES 11

οἷσιν ἐπ' ἀθά]νατον κέχυται κλέος ἀν[δρὸς] ἕκητι   15
ὃς παρ' ἰοπ]λοκάμων δέξατο Πιερίδ[ων
πᾶσαν ἀλη]θείην, καὶ ἐπώνυμον ὁπ[λοτέρ]οισιν
ποίησ' ἡμ]ιθέων ὠκύμορον γενεή[ν.
ἀλλὰ σὺ μὲ]ν νῦν χαῖρε, θεᾶς ἐρικυ[δέος υἱέ
κούρης εἰν]αλίου Νηρέος· αὐτὰρ ἐγώ[20
κικλήισκω] σ' ἐπίκουρον ἐμοί, π[ολυώνυμ]ε Μοῦσα,
εἴ πέρ γ' ἀν]θρώπων εὐχομένω[ν μέλεαι·
ἔντυνο]ν καὶ τόνδ[ε μελ]ίφρονα κ[όσμον ἀο]ιδῆς
ἡμετ]έρης, ἵνα τις [μνή]σεται υ[
ἀνδρῶ]ν, οἳ Σπάρτ[ηι τε καὶ Ἑλλάδι δούλιον ἦμ]αρ   25
ἔσχον] ἀμυνόμ[ενοι μή τιν' ἰδεῖν φανερ]ῷ[ς
οὐδ' ἀρε]τῆς ἐλάθ[οντο φάτις δ' ἔχε]ν οὐρανομ[ήκ]ης,
καὶ κλέος ἀ]νθρώπων [ἔσσετ]αι ἀθάνατο⟨ν⟩.
οἳ μὲν ἄρ' Εὐ]ρώταν κα[ὶ Σπάρτη]ς ἄστυ λιπόντ[ες
ὥρμησαν] Ζηνὸς παισὶ σὺν ἱπποδάμοις   30
Τυνδαρίδα]ις ἥρωσι καὶ εὐρυβίηι Μενελάω[ι
. . . . . πατ]ρώιης ἡγεμόνες π[ό]λεος,
τοὺς δ' υἱὸς θείοιο Κλεο]μβ[ρ]ότου ἔξ[α]γ' ἄριστ[ος
                         ]αγ . Παυσανίης.
                         ] . καὶ ἐπικλέα ἔργα Κορίν[θ]ου   35
                         ] Τανταλίδεω Πέλοπος
                         Ν]ίσου πόλιν, ἔνθά περ ὥ[λλοι
                         ] φῦλα περικτιόνων
. . . . . θεῶν τεράε]σσι πεποιθότες, οἳ δὲ συν[
ἷκον Ἐλευσῖνος γῆς ἐ]ρατὸν πεδίον   40
Παν]δίονος ἐξε[λάσα]ντες
Κέκρ]οπος ἀντιθέου[
                         ] . ς δαμάσαντ[
                         ] . ι εἴδομεν[
                         ὠ]νυμον α . [45

17 ὁπ[λοτέρ]οισιν Hutchinson   19 ἐρικυ[δέος υἱέ Lobel   20 Lobel   24 ὕ[στερον
αὖ West   27 οὐρανομ[ήκ]ης I. C. Rutherford   32 ἐσθλοὶ West : κλεινοὶ Parsons
35 αἶψα δ' ἵκοντ' Ἰσθμὸ]ν West   36 νήσου τ' ἐσχατιήν] West : νῆσον δ' ἐξέλιπον]
Parsons   37 καὶ Μέγαρ' ἀρχαίην West   39 σύν[οπλοι Parsons : σὺν [αὐτοῖς
West   42 Κέκρ]οπος Parsons : μάν]τιος West   44 εἴδομεν[Allan : εἰδομεν[West
45 εὐώ]νυμον Fowler

SIMONIDES 13

```
              ]θεα[
              ]ρεμ[
              ]πτο[
              ]ετερη[
              ]κουφ[
   θ[      ]πτολε[μ
τα. [    ]αρα[
ὄφρ' ἀπὸ μὲν Μήδ[ων
καὶ Περσῶν, Δώρου δ[ὲ
παισὶ καὶ Ἡρακλέος [
οἳ] δ' ἐπεὶ ἐς πεδίον [
εἰ]σ̣ωποὶ δ' ἔφ[α]νεν[
       ]ρεστε[ . ]ο̣ντ̣[
```

SIMONIDES 14

```
] . [ ] . . . [ ] . . . . [
          ]α̣δον βαλλομε[ν
λ]έγω ποταμοῦ λα̣[
          ]ρψαι πρῶτα β[ι]η[
δεινὸν ἀμαι]μάκετόν τε κακ̣[όν· μίμνουσι δ' ἔσεσθαι
νίκην, ἧς μνή]μην ἤματα πάντ[α μενεῖν.
ἐξ Ἀ]σ̣ί[η]ς ἐλάσει, νεύσαντο[ς
          ]νην συμμα[χ]ίην φιλέω[ν
] . νωι γὰρ̣ [ὑ]π̣[ὸ κ]ρηπῖδα τ̣[
          ]επα̣[ . . . . . . ]ορίην β[
]ν̣δε[          ]ει ποτεφ[
                    ]π̣ολω̣[
                    ]ωστ[
                    ]     [
                    ]λ̣υων[
                         ]χεκ[
                         ]ιν̣[
```

Simon. 13 suppl. West 6 μενε]πτόλε[μ- Gentili–Prato 8 λαὸν ἅπαντ' ἐλάσαι West 11 οἳ] Lobel [Βοιώτιον εὐρὺ κατῆλθον West
Simon. 14 suppl. West 2 ὅμ]αδον βαλλομέ[νων σακέων West 3–4 προλ] ἔγω ποταμοῦ λα̣[οῖς ἐθέλουσιν | ὅττι πέρην μά]ρψαι πρῶτα β[ι]η[σαμένοις West 8 και]νὴν West

SIMONIDES 15

μέσσοις δ' οἵ τ' Ἐφύρην πολυπίδακα ναιετάοντες,
παντοίης ἀρετῆς ἴδριες ἐν πολέμωι,
οἵ τε πόλιν Γλαύκοιο Κορίνθιον ἄστυ νέμοντες·

SIMONIDES 16

κάλλιστον μάρτυν ἔθεντο πόνων,
χρυσοῦ τιμήεντος ἐ]ν αἰθέρι[· καί σφιν ἀέξει
αὐτῶν τ' εὐρεῖαν κλ]ηδόν]α καὶ πατέρων
                        ]πολυ[

Simon. 15   1 μέσσοις West : μέσσοισι codd.   τ' Ἐφύραν Reiske (-ρην Schneidewin) : γέφυραν vel γ' ἔφυραν codd.   3 νέμοντες Ald. : νέμονται codd.

COMMENTARY

ARCHILOCHUS

Archilochus of Paros was active in the middle of the seventh century. A variety of factors point to this period: for example, the colonization of Thasos (e.g. frr. 21–2, 102, 228; cf. Owen 2003), the Lydian king Gyges who died *c.* 652 (see 19*), and a solar eclipse probably of 6 April 648 (122.1–4). External evidence includes a late seventh-century inscription commemorating Archilochus' friend Glaucus (*SEG* 14.565), who is addressed in several poems (15, 48, 105, 117, 131).

Given Archilochus' reputation as one of the foremost poets of the Archaic period, ranked and performed alongside Homer and Hesiod (cf. Heraclit. fr. B 42 DK = D21 Laks–Most, Pl. *Ion* 531a), it is no surprise that a rich biographical tradition developed around him. This was based partly on local Parian pride (see below) but mostly on the poetry itself, with no regard to the poet's various personae. Thus, for example, Archilochus was said to be the son of a slave woman called Enipo, 'Blame' (fr. 295), but the description 'son of blame' will have derived from his talent for invective and may well have been a persona adopted in a poem now lost. Similarly, the story of his betrothal to Neoboule, which ended with her, her sister, and her father Lycambes all hanging themselves, was not autobiography, but part of a fictional song cycle that embodied the always popular themes of betrayal and revenge, seduction and sex (see 172–81*, 196a*). Archilochus may at times be talking of real people (such as Glaucus) or places (most often Paros and Thasos), but they are all made part of a fictionalized imaginative world (compare, for example, Hipponax's use of the possibly historical Bupalus and Athenis: Hippon. 12–17*), and like any other lyric, elegiac, or iambic poet he is always role-playing, developing a character or persona which cannot be equated with the poet himself (cf. Introduction §3).

The Parians' pride in their most famous cultural export eventually led to Archilochus becoming a figure of cult worship on the island. A formal hero-cult with shrine and sacrifices, the Archilocheion, is first attested in the third century BC on the so-called Mnesiepes inscription (*SEG* 15.517), but it is likely that Archilochus was honoured as a poet (if not as a hero) from the Archaic period onwards (cf. Clay 2004). Archilochus' surviving work, despite its fragmentary state, illustrates more clearly than any other Archaic poet's the sheer variety of iambus and elegy in both tone and subject-matter. Unfortunately, the tendency to focus on Archilochus as primarily a blame poet (which began in antiquity: cf. Rotstein 2010: 281–318) has obscured the range of his iambic poetry in particular, which runs from explicit sex (e.g. 42–3*, contrast the non-explicit 196a*) to didactic and political advice (19*, 114*). Archilochus engages repeatedly with the language and values of heroic epic (see 1*, 2*, 13*, 17a*, 114*), sometimes flippantly (5*), and a similar mixture of seriousness and parody can be seen in his deployment of the tropes of wisdom poetry (13*, 122, 196a*) and animal fable (172–81*). For a detailed discussion of all aspects of Archilochus' poetry, see Swift (2019).

Archilochus 1

Source: Athenaeus, *Scholars at Dinner* 14.627c.

Archilochus asserts his role as both soldier and poet. Though Homeric epic compares its central heroes, Achilles and Odysseus, to bards (cf. *Il.* 9.189, *Od.* 13.1–2, 21.404–11), it nonetheless maintains a clear distinction between the professions of singer (ἀοιδός) and warrior (ἥρως), hence Archilochus' pride in his ability to excel as both. Like an epic fighter, Archilochus is 'the servant of Lord Enyalios', and like an epic bard he has poetic power derived from the Muses (Μουσέων ... ἐπιστάμενος). Thus the couplet (which may be a stand-alone piece) redeploys epic language and convention to boost the speaker's status and stress how unusually talented he is.

1 εἰμὶ δ' ἐγώ: the emphatic first-person opening expresses the speaker's pride in his achievements (cf. *HHAp.* 480 εἰμὶ δ' ἐγὼ Διὸς υἱός, Ἀπόλλων δ' εὔχομαι εἶναι). **θεράπων ... ἄνακτος** combines the epic formulae θεράποντες Ἄρηος, 'attendants of Ares' (e.g. *Il.* 6.67 ὦ φίλοι ἥρωες Δαναοὶ, θεράποντες Ἄρηος), and Ἐνυαλίοιο ἄνακτος ([Hes.] *Shield of Heracles* 371). Enyalios may have been a separate deity in Mycenaean times, but by Archilochus' day he was fully identified with Ares (cf. *Il.* 18.309 ξυνὸς Ἐνυάλιος, Archil. 110 ἐτήτυμον γὰρ ξυνὸς ἀνθρώποις Ἄρης). As a symbol of fighting power (e.g. *Il.* 22.132, where Achilles approaches Hector, ἶσος Ἐνυαλίωι), he enhances Archilochus' claim to prowess. Poets, including epic singers, are not usually noted for their fighting skills (compare the bard Phemius' claim that he was overpowered by the suitors: *Od.* 22.344–53); by beginning a self-defining poem with his role as a soldier, Archilochus stresses his unusual range of abilities.

2 The line creates a chiasmus, with ἐπιστάμενος complementing θεράπων, and poetry (Μουσέων ἐρατὸν δῶρον) balancing war (Ἐνυαλίοιο ἄνακτος). The a-b-b-a pattern underlines how intertwined the two aspects of Archilochus' identity are. **μὲν ... | καί** articulate his twin abilities: 'I am both the servant of ... and an expert in ....' **Μουσέων ... δῶρον** links Archilochus to an age-old tradition of poetic inspiration. For poetry as the gift of the Muses, cf. e.g. Hes. *Theog.* 93 τοίη Μουσάων ἱερὴ δόσις ἀνθρώποισιν, 103 δῶρα θεάων. ἐρατόν, 'lovely', contrasts with the world of war and further stresses the range of Archilochus' skills. ἐπιστάμενος: present participle used adjectivally with εἰμί; this periphrasis is used 'to describe or characterize the subject like an adjective, i.e. the subject has a quality which it may display in action' (Smyth §1857; cf. CGCG §52.51). The word proudly asserts the poet's expertise even as he acknowledges the gift of the gods, a form of double motivation well known from epic, as when Phemius declares, 'I am self-taught, and god has planted in my mind various paths of song' (Od. 22.347–8); cf. Sol. 13.51–2* ἄλλος Ὀλυμπιάδων Μουσέων πάρα δῶρα διδαχθείς, | ἱμερτῆς σοφίης μέτρον ἐπιστάμενος. Similarly, the final word contrasts with the chiastic θεράπων in stressing that the poet is more than a servant of the Muses (cf. Hes. Theog. 99–100 ἀοιδὸς | Μουσάων θεράπων): his verses are divinely inspired, but he is an expert creator in his own right.

Archilochus 2

Source: Athenaeus, Scholars at Dinner 1.30f.

The couplet (which could be a stand-alone piece) is built around the triple repetition of ἐν δορί, the first two occurrences highlighting the advantages of being a soldier and the speaker's pride in his profession, the last changing tack to emphasize the constraints of military life. The soldier's dependence on his spear permeates his world and unifies the poem.

1 ἐν δορὶ ... μεμαγμένη 'in my spear is my daily bread', lit. 'my kneaded barley bread', a staple of the soldier's diet. The speaker's food and livelihood are 'in' his spear in the sense that they come from his soldier's pay. **μέν μοι μᾶζα μεμαγμένη**: alliteration and assonance mimic the chewing of the dense dough. The fact that this is basic unbaked bread is underlined by the figura etymologica (both words from the same *μασ- root, μάσσω/ μαγῆναι, 'knead'). The simple rations suggest the speaker's pride in his ability to endure such a rugged lifestyle.

1–2 ἐν δορὶ ... | Ἰσμαρικός 'and in my spear Ismarian wine': wine from Ismarus on the Thracian coast was considered particularly fine (cf. Od. 9.196–211). Archilochus is said to have fought on behalf of the Parian colonists on Thasos, not far from Ismarus, against the indigenous Thracians (cf. 5*).

2 πίνω ... κεκλιμένος: the final ἐν δορί takes the listener by surprise, since it differs in meaning from the first two (where ἐν is instrumental) and means 'under arms' (i.e. 'with my spear ready for use', locatival ἐν). The difference marks the speaker's striking switch from the benefits to the drawbacks of warfare. The idea is that even when he relaxes to enjoy a drink (πίνω ... κεκλιμένος), the soldier must be ready to react (ἐν δορί). **κεκλιμένος** encourages the listener to picture the soldier 'reclining' at a *symposion* (mirroring the performance setting of the poem itself), only to point his inability to do so while on active service. The soldier, unable to truly unwind, can only rest against his spear, an idea evoked at the same time by ἐν δορὶ κεκλιμένος (cf. *Il.* 3.135 ἀσπίσι κεκλιμένοι).

Archilochus 5

Source: Plutarch, *Ancient Customs of the Spartans* 34.239b (1–4); Aristophanes, *Peace* 1298–1301 (1–3); Sextus Empiricus, *Outlines of Pyrrhonism* 3.216 (1–3); Strabo 10.2.17, 12.3.20 (1–2); Olympiodorus on Pl. *Gorg.* p. 141.1 (Westerink), Elias *proleg. philos.* 8 (*Comm. in Arist. Graeca* xviii.22.21), Ps.-Elias on Porph. *Isagoge* (Westerink) 12.19 (3–4).

As the number of quotations suggests, this was one of Archilochus' most popular (and most notorious) poems. Reading biographically, ancient writers criticized him for his rejection of martial values. Plutarch, for example, claimed that he was expelled from Sparta for composing it. However, it is more than a travesty or subversion of heroic values, since the narrator is hardly free from blame, and the poem's exploration of the complexity of heroism (when is it legitimate to make a tactical battlefield retreat?) is in itself Homeric (e.g. *Il.* 8.139–56). The narrator's shamefully casual attitude to the loss of his shield reminds the audience of the 'right' thing to do: never retreat. But for all his flippancy, the narrator's decision reflects a genuine battlefield dilemma, where the demand to hold one's ground may be overcome by a pragmatic need to back off.

Like Sappho's claim that the 'finest thing' is not an array of cavalry or infantry or ships, but 'whatever one loves' (16.1–4), Archilochus' poem creates a distinctive persona (one of symposiastic insouciance) by setting itself against a particular aspect of heroic values, namely the pressure not to retreat or abandon one's weapons. The fact that similar pressures remained a part of Greek popular morality throughout antiquity made the poem's flippant attitude seem particularly outrageous, and contributed to its perennial popularity (for similarly shocking deployment of the *rhipsaspia* motif, cf. Alc. fr. 401B 'Alcaeus is safe, but his fine armour and shield the Athenians have hung up in the shrine of the gleaming-eyed goddess', Anac. fr. 381 *PMG* 'throwing away my shield by the banks of a fair-flowing river', Hor. *Odes* 2.7.10 *relicta non bene parmula*). The epic language of the first couplet (ἀγάλλεται, ἔντος ἀμώμητον) clashes with its unheroic content, while the short clauses, asyndeton, and first-person forms (αὐτὸν δ' ἐξεσάωσα, τί μοι μέλει, κτήσομαι) of the second couplet underline the speaker's absolute focus on saving himself and his defiance of public disapproval.

The poem is likely to be complete.

1 ἀσπίδι ... ἀγάλλεται 'my shield some Saian now glories in'. ἀσπίδι: the first word introduces the central contrast of the poem. Σαΐων τις is dismissive, an attempt to downplay the event and the humiliation that goes with it. But if his opponent was a nobody, the speaker's flight was all the more shameful. The Saians were a Thracian tribe, and the imagined scene could be a battle for the Parian colony on Thasos (see on Archil. 1.1–2*) or on behalf of Thasian colonists in Thrace (attested there by the second half of the seventh century: Tiverios 2008: 79). ἀγάλλεται links the Saian to the epic motif of a warrior exulting in the capture of his enemy's weapons (the word is used twice in the *Iliad* to describe Hector's joy at the capture of Achilles' arms: 17.473, 18.132). The narrator is trying to mock his enemy's excessive triumphalism, but his word choice reminds us that he, unlike (for example) Patroclus facing Hector, did not stand firm and fight to the death, but abandoned his shield and ran away. παρὰ θάμνωι, 'by a bush', deflates the speaker's pretensions to epic grandeur (see next line) and underlines his sudden flight and cowardice. Contrast *Il.* 10.465–8, where Odysseus hangs the spoils taken from Dolon (including his spear) in a tamarisk bush, marking the spot so that he and Diomedes can pick them up on their return.

2 ἔντος ἀμώμητον, 'the blameless armour', uses epic language to mock-heroic effect, as the narrator aggrandizes his shield, yet is content to dump it by a bush. Moreover, by calling the shield 'blameless', he draws attention to his own culpability and shame. The rare singular ἔντος (Homer always uses the plural ἔντεα of armour) serves to draw attention to the disputed item. κάλλιπον = κατέλιπον, aor. of the epic form καλλείπω, 'leave behind'. οὐκ ἐθέλων, 'against my will', placed as if it were the final word on the matter, stresses that he did not really want to abandon his shield and run away, but in fact the phrase makes us wonder who was responsible if he was not, and so highlights the lack of any real excuse for his behaviour.

3–4 The second couplet undercuts the first with a sudden change of attitude, especially clear after οὐκ ἐθέλων, as the speaker moves (via μέν ... δέ) from regretting the loss of his shield to dismissing it as of no importance at all. The couplet's plainer language and colloquial style underline the speaker's off-hand rejection of criticism, guiding us to question his casual attitude to blame and disgrace.

3 αὐτόν ... ἐξεσάωσα 'but I saved myself': αὐτόν in first position contrasts emphatically with ἀσπίδι (1) and heralds the second couplet's focus on self-preservation over honour. Similarly, ἐξεσάωσα echoes Σαΐων (1), but points the difference: the enemy is welcome to his glory as long as the speaker gets away alive. τί ... ἐκείνη 'what do I care about that shield?': a defiant question, with dismissive ἐκείνη implying that there are plenty

more shields where 'that' one came from, an idea made explicit in the following line (ἐξαῦτις κτήσομαι, 'I'll get one another time').

4 ἐρρέτω, 'to hell with it!', expresses anger and contempt, as if the shield itself were responsible for being left behind. The humorous contrast with his earlier description of it as 'blameless' undermines his final dismissal of the shield and the values it embodies. **οὐ κακίω** 'just as good' (lit. 'no worse', fem. acc. sg.): the narrator is focused on the purely material quality of the shield, but κακός is a standard word for 'coward' (especially in epic: cf. LSJ I 3): κακίω reminds us that this soldier has failed to perform on the battlefield, endangering his comrades and falling short of the expectations of his community.

Archilochus 13

Source: Stobaeus 4.56.30.

This poem (probably complete) is the only substantial piece among several elegiac fragments on shipwreck and grief for those who have drowned (8–13). Plutarch quotes 9 and 11 as coming from a lament by Archilochus for his sister's husband who had died at sea (*How to Study Poetry* 6.23b, 12.33a–b), but 13* need not be referring to the same disaster. In any case, it concerns the loss of many men (τοίους, 3), not one, and is focused on shared rather than individual grief. The speaker addresses and advises a fellow mourner, his friend Pericles (not his sister, as one might expect if the shipwreck had claimed her husband). Pericles may have existed (he also appears in frr. 16, 124a–b), but a real person can be transformed into a fictional persona (as with Archilochus' friend Glaucus: see the introduction above), and the shipwreck itself may be completely imaginary.

The poem is not a lament but a rejection of lamentation (for the later connection between elegy and lamentation, see Introduction §1). The speaker offers consolation to Pericles and their wider circle, who appear in the second-person plurals of the final line (τλῆτε . . . ἀπωσάμενοι, 10), and urges them to endure. Its themes of human vicissitude, grief, and endurance are highly traditional (see on Sol. 13.63–70*). Archilochus makes skilful use of epic language (e.g. 1 κήδεα . . . στονόεντα, 3 κῦμα πολυφλοίσβοιο θαλάσσης, 5–6 θεοὶ . . . ἐπὶ κρατερὴν τλημοσύνην ἔθεσαν) and physical imagery (e.g. 4–5 οἰδαλέους . . . πνεύμονας, 8 αἱματόεν δ' ἕλκος) to bring home both the painful, irreparable loss of those who have died and the necessity of living on as best one can. The poem is clearly structured. The speaker begins by reassuring Pericles and ends with exhortation: our mourning will incur no blame, so fine were the men we have lost (1–4); our grief is painful, but the gods have given us endurance (4–7); it is now our turn to suffer, but the suffering must be endured (7–10).

COMMENTARY: ARCHILOCHUS 13   63

1-2 κήδεα ... | ... πόλις 'none of the citizens will criticize our mournful laments, Pericles, as he enjoys the festivities, nor will the city': the negatives οὔτε and οὐδέ govern the participle μεμφόμενος, but not the verb τέρψεται, since 'none of the citizens will criticize our mourning or enjoy the festivities' would spoil the contrast between the mourners' grief and the wider community's pleasure, i.e. their ability to get on with their lives, which is a central idea of the poem. **κήδεα ... στονόεντα** is used by Odysseus to describe his own sufferings (*Od.* 9.12). But whereas Odysseus resists talking about his grief in case it spoils the party mood among the Phaeacians, Archilochus stresses the co-existence of mourning and pleasure, since the happy citizens may not share their grief, but they can understand it and empathize. **οὔτέ τις ἀστῶν | ... οὐδὲ πόλις** enhances the general validity of the statement by specifying both the individual citizen and the city as a whole. **θαλίης** = θαλίαις (dative with τέρπομαι, 'delight in').

3-4 τοίους is placed first for emphasis, 'such fine men did the surge of the much-resounding sea wash over'. **κατά ... ἔκλυσεν:** epic tmesis, as also in line 6 ἐπί ... ἔθεσαν. **πολυφλοίσβοιο θαλάσσης:** the Homeric formula mimics the sound of the sea and elevates the status of those who died.

4-5 οἰδαλέους ... πνεύμονας, 'and our lungs are swollen with pain', captures the mourners' convulsive weeping, but also assimilates them to their loved ones, whose lungs will have been swollen with water as they drowned.

5-7 For endurance (τλημοσύνη) as a remedy given by the gods, cf. e.g. *Il.* 24.49 (where Apollo complains that Achilles cannot control his grief) τλητὸν γὰρ Μοῖραι θυμὸν θέσαν ἀνθρώποισιν. **ἀνηκέστοισι ... | ... φάρμακον:** medical language highlights the uncanny strength of 'powerful endurance' (κρατερὴν τλημοσύνην), which serves as a 'palliative' (φάρμακον) for 'incurable woes' (ἀνηκέστοισι κακοῖσιν), i.e. the inevitability of death), a striking oxymoron. The gods themselves, like a good doctor, ἐπί ... ἔθεσαν | φάρμακον: cf. *Il.* 4.190-1 (Agamemnon to the wounded Menelaus) ἕλκος δ' ἰητὴρ ἐπιμάσσεται ἠδ' ἐπιθήσει | φάρμαχ', ἅ κεν παύσησι μελαινάων ὀδυνάων. **κρατερήν:** κρατ- (or καρτ-) words often connote endurance, e.g. κρατερῶς, καρτερεῖν.

7 ἄλλοτε ... τόδε 'now one, now another has this woe'. **ἄλλοτε ἄλλος** is often used to express the alternation of human fortune, e.g. *Od.* 4.236-7 ἀτὰρ θεὸς ἄλλοτε ἄλλωι | Ζεὺς ἀγαθόν τε κακόν τε διδοῖ. For hiatus in this phrase, cf. Hes. *WD* 713, Mimn. 2.11*, Sol. 13.76*. **τόδε** refers back to κακά in line 5.

7-9 νῦν μέν, balanced by ἐξαῦτις δ', and the verbs of turning (ἐτράπεθ') and passing (ἐπαμείψεται), all articulate the inescapability of suffering; for a classic treatment of the idea, see *Il.* 24.524–51 (the two jars of Zeus; cf. on Mimn. 2.15–16*).

8 αἱματόεν . . . **ἀναστένομεν** 'and we groan over our bleeding wound': as in the image of 'swollen lungs' (4–5), the ἕλκος metaphor depicts grief in strongly physical terms, underlining the mourners' pain.

10 τλῆτε . . . ἀπωσάμενοι: the speaker turns from Pericles (1 Περίκλεες, 6 ὦ φίλ') to the wider community of the bereaved. **τλῆτε**, placed emphatically at the start of the line, picks up τλημοσύνην and reinforces its necessity. **γυναικεῖον . . . ἀπωσάμενοι** 'thrusting aside womanly lament': a strongly gendered rejection, exploiting the audience's ideology of male/ female = strong/weak, so that γυναικεῖον πένθος is denigrated as inferior to κρατερὴν τλημοσύνην ('powerful endurance', 6). For women's essential role in lamentation and other mourning rituals, see Dillon 2002: 268–92. Excessive grief is often rejected as futile: cf. *Il.* 24.549–51 ἄνσχεο, μὴ δ' ἀλίαστον ὀδύρεο σὸν κατὰ θυμόν· | οὐ γάρ τι πρήξεις ἀκαχήμενος υἷος ἑῆος, | οὐδέ μιν ἀνστήσεις.

Archilochus *17a* (Swift)

Source: *P. Oxy.* 4708 fr. 1.

First published in 2005, the so-called Telephus Elegy is one of the most significant discoveries of recent years, and it greatly expands our view of Archilochus' elegiac poetry (cf. Obbink 2005, 2006, West 2006, Aloni and Iannucci 2007: 205–37, Nicolosi 2013: 123–48, 2016, Swift 2012, 2014, 2019). The surviving portion of the poem (twenty-four lines are restorable) is by far the longest piece of Archilochean elegy we have. Moreover, it is the only surviving poem of Archilochus that tells a story drawn from heroic myth; and it is the earliest known example of mythological narrative in elegiacs (cf. Lulli 2011: 87–105). It treats the Achaeans' defeat at the hands of Heracles' son Telephus when they landed by mistake on the Mysian, rather than the Trojan, plain (cf. 9–10 καὶ [πεδίον | Μύσι̣ο̣ν̣, 21 γῆν δ' ἐπάτευν Μυσίδα πυροφόρο[ν).

Archilochus' handling of the episode shows that both he and his audience were well versed in the wider mythology of the Trojan War, just as Homer exploited his audience's knowledge of events outside the temporal frame of his narrative (e.g. the initial Judgement of Paris: *Il.* 24.25–30). The Telephus incident itself is not covered by Homer but featured in the later *Cypria*, which told of events before the *Iliad*, including Telephus' wounding by Achilles and his eventual guiding of the Achaeans to Troy in return for being healed (fr. 20 Bernabé). Not only is Archilochus aware of the wider epic tradition, but his description of the river Caicus suggests he may be exploiting his audience's knowledge of the *Iliad* (see on lines 8–9 below). Along with heroic myth Archilochus deploys epic language: e.g. μοῖρα θεῶν (7), ἐπὶ θῖνα πολυφλοίσβοι[ο θαλάσσης (10), ἐϋκνήμ[ιδες Ἀχαιοί (12). The strong epic colouring enhances the multiple ironies that pervade the poem: these Greek heroes are fighting the wrong war (15), in the wrong country (16–17, 20–1), and against a fellow Greek (5, 22).

It is tempting to see a contemporary resonance here, with Archilochus reflecting on a recent military defeat suffered by his community, perhaps by Parian colonists on Thasos (cf. 2.1–2*, 5.1*) or in their struggle against Naxos (treated in frr. 89, 94). If so, it is important that his portrayal of the defeated Achaeans mixes mitigation (sometimes it is better to retreat: cf. 5*) with criticism (defeat is shameful). Thus the fragment begins 'one need not call it weakness and cowardice, having to retreat, if it is under the compulsion of a god' (2–3), and goes on to insist 'so greatly did the doom of the gods frighten them' (7), mitigating the shame of the Achaeans' withdrawal. On the other hand, by emphasizing Telephus' triumphant victory (e.g. 5–6 μ]οῦνος ἐὼν ... | ... ἐφόβησε πολὺν στρατ[όν, 24 κακὴν [τ]ό[τε φύζαν ἐνόρσας), it reminds the audience of the cost of defeat (see Swift 2012). However, even if there is no contemporary Parian reference, the poem's consideration of justifiable battlefield conduct would be of intrinsic interest to any Archaic audience, not least because such audiences were largely composed of citizen-soldiers (see Introduction §4).

The surviving narrative begins with the point of comparison, flight from battle (1–4), then tells the story of Telephus' victory (5–15, 22–5), pausing to explain how the Achaeans ended up in Mysia in the first place (16–21). The poem's focus on a defeated and fleeing army makes it less likely that it was written for civic performance, since large-scale public elegies normally celebrate victories (cf. Tyrtaeus 4*, Simonides' Plataea Elegy 10–16*; for a counter-view, see Bowie 2016b: 17–25, who argues for original performance in the Heracleion of Thasos). With its potential criticism of a recent military campaign, the poem would be less controversial if it were performed before a group of sympotic *hetairoi*, while its partly consolatory effect (we had no choice but to flee, the gods were against us, etc.) would help offset the disgrace of defeat.

1–4 introduce the paradigmatic idea that to retreat is not necessarily an act of cowardice. The question when it is legitimate to make a tactical withdrawal is often debated in epic (e.g. *Il*. 8.139–56).

1]ι ῥ[ο]ῆι[ς, 'streams', may refer to the site of a recent battle fought by the Parians (see the introduction above), creating a correspondence with the battle fought by the Achaeans beside the river Caicus.

2–3 εἰ δέ]... | ... λέγει[ν 'but if [an army is driven back by] the powerful compulsion of a god, there is no need to call it weakness and cowardice'. **θεοῦ ... ἀνάγκης:** the epic formula κρατερῆ[ς ὑπ' ἀνάγκης is strengthened by the addition of θεοῦ. **ἀν]αλ[κείη]ν ... κακότητα:** Nestor reassures Diomedes that retreat is acceptable, εἴ περ γάρ σ' Ἕκτωρ γε κακὸν καὶ ἀνάλκιδα φήσει (*Il.* 8.153).

4 εἴμ]εθ' ... φυγεῖν 'we hastened to flee the fighting'. For ἄρ[η]α used of combat, cf. μίμνομεν ὀξὺν ἄρηα παρ' ἀλλήλοισι μένοντες (*Il.* 17.721). **φεύγ[ειν ... ὥρη** 'but there is a time for fleeing': gnomic moralizing and the repetition φυγεῖν· φεύγ[ειν reveal the speaker's attempt to rationalize the disaster.

5 μ]οῦνος ἐών, placed at the start of the mythological battle narrative and in opposition to πολὺν στρατ[όν], likens Telephus to a Homeric warrior engaged in an *aristeia*. **Ἀρκα[σίδης** 'the descendant of Arcas': Telephus was related via his mother Auge to Arcas, founder of Arcadia; cf. [Hes.] *Catalogue of Women* fr. 165.8 Τήλεφον Ἀρκασίδην. The juxtaposition Ἀρκα[σίδης | Ἀργείων (5–6) underlines the Argives' mistaken attack on a fellow Greek.

6–8 ο[ὐδ' ἔτι... | ... περ ἐόντε[ς.] 'nor did those powerful men stand firm ... warriors though they were': the Achaeans' failure is mitigated by the parenthetic phrase ἦ ... ἐφόβει, 'so greatly did the doom of the gods frighten them'. **μοῖρα θεῶν**, an epic phrase combining the pressure of fate as well as the gods, repeats the double causation of θεοῦ κρατερῆ[ς ὑπ' ἀνάγκης (2).

8–9 ἐϋρρείτης ... | ... στείνετο 'the Caicus with its beautiful streams was stuffed with corpses as they fell'. Archilochus' use of the phrase νεκύων στείνετο may evoke the Iliadic scene where the river Scamander asks Achilles to kill the Trojans on the plain since he is στεινόμενος νεκύεσσι (21.220). Such a link between Telephus and Achilles would enhance our sense of the Achaeans' mistake in attacking a fellow Greek rather than the Trojans.

9–10 καὶ ... | Μύσιον, 'and so was the Mysian plain': Mysian, placed first, points the fundamental idea: they are in the wrong place.

10–15 describe the headlong flight of the Achaeans back to their ships. **10 θῖνα ... θαλάσσης:** Homeric formula (e.g. *Il.* 1.34), as with ἐϋκνήμ[ιδες Ἀχαιοί (12), highlights their unheroic behaviour.

11 χέρσ']... ἐναιρό[μενοι 'slaughtered at the hands of a pitiless man'. **ἀμειλίκτου** presents Telephus as the Achaeans see him (so too in line 23) and encourages our sympathy as they are killed by an implacable enemy.

12 προ]τροπάδην 'headlong': an apt word for a rout; cf. *Il.* 16.303–4 οὐ γάρ πώ τι Τρῶες ἀρηϊφίλων ὑπ' Ἀχαιῶν | προτροπάδην φοβέοντο μελαινάων ἀπὸ νηῶν. **ἀπέκλινον** 'turned away', i.e. 'fled'.

13 ἀ]σπάσιοι, placed first, stresses the Achaeans' joy at escaping from Telephus.
14 παῖδές ... ἀδελφεοί 'the sons and brothers of immortals': the Achaean heroes' semi-divine status (cf. Simon. 11.17–18*) magnifies Telephus' victory.
14–15 [οὓς ... | ... μαχησομένο[υς, 'whom Agamemnon was leading to holy Ilios to wage war', takes us back to the origins (and goal) of the campaign, preparing for the account of their wayward journey (16–21).
16–21 describe how the Achaeans ended up in Mysia, foregrounding their folly and dejection.
16 βλαφθέντες ὁδοῦ: lit. 'impaired in their journey' (for the construction, cf. *Od.* 1.195 τόν γε θεοὶ βλάπτουσι κελεύθου). The passive βλαφθέντες may imply divine influence; cf. 1 θεοῦ κρατερῆ[ς ὑπ' ἀνάγκης, 7 μοῖρα θεῶν. θ[ῖν' evokes Troy (cf. θῖνα πολυφλοίσβοι[ο θαλάσσης, 10), highlighting this as the wrong beach.
17 Τε]ύθραντος: Teuthras, king of Mysia, had adopted Auge when she was exiled to Mysia, where she bore Telephus to Heracles; cf. [Hes.] *Catalogue of Women* fr. 165.6–7. ἐρατὴν ... πόλιν, 'the lovely city', reminds us of the Mysians' blamelessness and the Achaeans' confusion. [εἰσανέβαν: for the hostile sense, cf. ὅτε Ἴλιον εἰσανέβαινον | Ἀργεῖοι (*Od.* 2.172–3 *et al.*).
18 ἔ]νθα ... δάμησαν 'and there, though breathing might, they were themselves defeated'. [μ]ένος πνείοντες: the epic formula (*Il.* 3.8 *et al.*) captures their mistaken self-confidence, which is immediately overturned (αὐτο[ί τε δάμησαν).
19 κὰ]ϕρ[αδίη]ηι ... ἀκηχέ[δατο, 'and in their folly were greatly dejected in their hearts', combines the Achaeans' error and their reaction to defeat. ἀκηχέ[δατο: 3rd pl. pluperfect of ἀκαχίζομαι, 'to be troubled' (cf. *Il.* 17.637 οἵ που δεῦρ' ὁρόωντες ἀκηχέδατ').
20–1 φ]ὰν[το] ... | αὐ]τίκ[α] 'for they thought they were attacking the high-gated city of the Trojans right away'. εἰσ[αναβαίνειν | αὐ]τίκ[α]: the repeated verb ([εἰσανέβαν, 17) marks the Achaeans' deluded assault, αὐ] τίκ[α] their disastrous haste. γῆν ... πυροφόρο[ν 'but the land they were treading was that of wheat-bearing Mysia'. ἐπάτευν: 3rd pl. imperfect of πατέω. πυροφόρο[ν contrasts with ὑψίπυλον (20), opposing the war-mongering Achaeans to the peaceful and innocent Mysians.
22–5 return to the battle, describing Heracles' epiphany in support of his son Telephus.
22 ἤντησ[ε] 'came to face them', 3rd sg. aor. of ἀντάω.
23 οὖ]ρον ... [πολ]έμ[ωι 'a pitiless guardian in the carnage of war'. Epic οὖρος (cf. οὖρος Ἀχαιῶν, applied to Nestor, *Il.* 8.80 *et al.*) enhances Telephus' prowess, while ἀμ[ε]ίλικ[τον], as in line 11, presents the Achaeans' view of their rampaging enemy.

24–5 ὅς ... | ... [πρό]μαχος 'who, arousing cowardly flight in the Danaans, pressed on in the front ranks'. **Δαναοῖσι:** the use of all three Homeric terms, Ἀργεῖοι (6), Ἀχαιοί (12), and Δαναοί, intensifies the epic atmosphere, underlining Telephus' heroism and the Achaeans' potentially shameful retreat (κακὴν ... φύζαν, 24). [πρό]μαχος, like μοῦνος (5), singles out Telephus' unique courage. πατρὶ χαριζόμ[ενος 'pleasing his father': Heracles' pleasure in the Achaeans' defeat highlights once again their deluded attack on a fellow Greek (cf. Ἀρκα[σίδης | Ἀργείων, 5–6).

Archilochus 19

Source: Plutarch, *On Tranquillity of Mind* 10.470b–c.

Plutarch cites these lines to support the idea that tranquillity comes from not desiring things that are beyond one's status. According to Aristotle, the lines were spoken by a figure called Charon the carpenter (*Rh.* 3.17.1418b28). This detail is valuable, since it reminds us not to read the 'I' here, with its strongly worded preferences, as expressing the views of Archilochus himself (see Introduction §3). Nonetheless, Aristotle's claim that Archilochus attributed these lines to someone else because he wanted to avoid being seen as 'insulting or rude' makes little sense in view of Archilochus' reputation as a blame-poet and his readiness to use invective elsewhere. On the contrary, by putting the rejection of Gyges' wealth and power into the mouth of a carpenter, an archetypal 'common man' (whose name Charon is attested throughout the Greek world), the speaker's endorsement of the simple life and contentment with one's lot becomes more plausible and persuasive. Charon's rejection of Lydian gold and absolute power is indicative of Greek views of Near Eastern culture. Foreign luxury, elitism, monarchy, and ambition are opposed to Greek moderation and honest toil (cf. Xenoph. 3*, Thgn. 51–2*). Of course, we do not know the fragment's wider context, and it is possible that Charon's rhetoric of simplicity was undermined by subsequent remarks (Aristotle says this was the beginning of the poem), whether by Charon himself or by a narrator. For this technique, compare Horace's second *Epode*, where the overblown praise of the simple country life turns out to have been spoken by the usurer Alfius, who never becomes a rustic but returns to his questionable city trade. Charon may have emerged as equally sanctimonious.

1 οὔ μοι: the opening words set the tone for a strongly negative and personal statement (οὔ ... οὐδ' ... οὐδ' ... οὐκ; μοι ... με ... ἀγαίομαι ... ἐρέω ... ὀφθαλμῶν ἐμῶν). **τὰ Γύγεω** is dismissive, 'Gyges' stuff'. **πολυχρύσου:** Gyges' wealth was in large part due to the gold carried down from Mt Tmolus by the river Pactolus (cf. Hdt. 1.93.1). Herodotus describes the huge amount of gold and silver offerings he sent to Delphi (1.14). For Archilochus and his audience Gyges is evidently a byword for luxury and power, though the poem could have been composed after his reign (*c.* 687–652), since Gyges endured in the Greek imagination as an archetypal foreign autocrat. For Greek rejection of Lydian luxury, see on Xenoph. 3.1* ἁβροσύνας δὲ μαθόντες ἀνωφελέας παρὰ Λυδῶν.

2 οὐδ'... ζῆλος 'nor has envy ever seized me': the physical jolt of εἷλε acknowledges the real temptations of wealth and power. For the absolute ruler as an enviable figure, cf. e.g. Archil. 23.20–1 κείνης ἄνασσε καὶ τ[υραν]νίην ἔχε· | π[ο]λ̣[λοῖ]σ̣[ί θ]η[ν ζ]ηλωτὸς ἀ[νθρ]ώπων ἔσεαι. Solon, a champion of moderate rule (Sol. 6.3–4*, 9*, 11*, 36.20–2*), rejects the temptations of 'tyranny' (32–3).

2–3 οὐδ'... ἔργα, 'nor am I jealous of divine favour', acknowledges the role played by divine assistance in human success, but θεῶν ἔργα also implies that such favour may be withdrawn, with dangerous consequences for the mortal who enjoys it.

3 μεγάλης... τυραννίδος 'and I don't desire great power': τυραννίς is first attested here (τύραννος at Semon. 7.69*). The sense is 'dominion' or 'sole power' rather than 'tyranny' (i.e. despotic rule), since the speaker is rejecting the *benefits* enjoyed by Gyges. Nonetheless, a Greek audience would be aware of the dangers of absolute power, so that the word comes freighted with negative possibility, especially when applied to a foreign king.

4 ἀπόπροθεν... ἐμῶν: lit. 'for [such things] are far from my eyes', i.e. 'for these are far beyond the sights of such as me'. The metaphor distances Charon the carpenter from the world of Gyges, highlighting his contentment with his humble lifestyle.

Archilochus 42–3

Archilochus' iambic poetry presents a variety of erotic scenes, especially in the trimeters, where the description of sex organs and sex acts is particularly graphic, ranging from aroused vaginas (fr. 40) and penises (66) to oral sex (42*, 44) and ejaculation (43*, 45); contrast the artful seduction and veiled language of the Cologne Epode (196a*). For the strikingly crude treatment of sex possible in iambus, see Introduction §1.

Archilochus 42

Source: Athenaeus, *Scholars at Dinner* 10.447b.

A woman performs fellatio while being penetrated from behind. This was a popular scene in Greek erotic art (see Kilmer 1993: 55, 114–17, 156–7). Drinking beer was considered characteristic of barbarians (cf. Aesch. *Suppl.* 952–3, where Pelasgus, king of Argos, calls the Egyptians effeminate for that reason), and here Archilochus gives the image 'barbarian sucking beer through a straw' a characteristically lewd twist. Archilochus' erotic scenes often portray all parties (male and female) apparently enjoying exuberant sex: in fr. 41, for example, a woman bounces up and down 'like a kingfisher flapping its wings on a protruding rock'. By contrast, the erotic fragments that recall sex with Lycambes' daughters are intended to shame the women involved (188–91, 196a*). Here the possibility that the woman is a prostitute (see below) will affect our interpretation of the scene.

1–2 ὥσπερ ... ἔμυζε 'she was sucking like a Thracian or Phrygian man [drinking] beer through a tube'. αὐλῶι likens the straw to the equally phallic tube of an *aulos*, but since female *aulos*-players at *symposia* might also be prostitutes (cf. Goldman 2015), the word enhances the innuendo. **βρῦτον:** usually brewed from malted barley, beer was widely consumed throughout the ancient world, but largely disdained in wine-growing Greece and Italy. **ἔμυζε:** Xenophon reports seeing beer being sucked (μύζειν) through straws in Armenia: τούτους [i.e. τοὺς καλάμους] ἔδει ὁπότε τις διψώιη λαβόντα εἰς τὸ στόμα μύζειν (*An.* 4.5.26–7).
2 κύβδα ... πονεομένη: lit. 'she was bent forward and working hard'. **κύβδα** is attested only in sexual contexts and always describes penetration from behind (e.g. Ar. *Thesm.* 489), so the sense is 'she was hard at it, engaged from behind as well'. **ἦν πονεομένη** = ἐπονεῖτο; for the periphrasis, see Archil. 1* εἰμί ... ἐπιστάμενος. **πονεομένη** has a sexual connotation too: as in English, 'working girl' is a Greek euphemism for a prostitute (cf. Archil. fr. 208, where Neobule is described as an ἐργάτις). The context will have made it clear whether the woman is in fact a prostitute or is being represented as willing to perform like one; the latter seems likelier, since it is both more shocking and more titillating to a Greek male audience.

Archilochus 43

Source: *Etymologicum Gudianum* i.230.15 de Stefani (1–3); Eustathius on Hom. *Od.* 8.335 (p. 1597.28) (2–3).

This fragment is formed from two overlapping quotations focusing on ὀτρυγηφάγου ('grain-fed') and κήλων ('stud') respectively (cf. West 1974: 124–5). Whereas epic typically uses animal similes to reflect heroic prowess, iambus often develops a cruder point of comparison, ranging from the scatological (cf. Hippon. 92.10–15*) to the explicitly sexual. So here the narrator compares a man's remarkable ejaculation to that of a donkey kept for breeding. For the depiction of donkeys in Greek culture, including their reputation for lust, see Semonides' 'donkey-woman' (7.43–9*).

1 ἡ δέ οἱ σάθη 'his cock': σάθη is a colloquial word, found elsewhere in Archilochus (25.3, 82.4) and in Aristophanes (*Lys.* 1119); σάθων was a pet-name for baby boys.

COMMENTARY: ARCHILOCHUS 43, 114   71

2–3 ὥστ' ... | ... ὀτρυγηφάγου, 'flooded over like that of a Prienian donkey, a stud fed on grain', combines several vivid details. ὄνου Πριηνέως: Priene, north of Miletus in Ionia, was presumably well known for its prized breeding stock. κήλωνος (gen. of κήλων, a breeding donkey or stallion) stresses the animal's (and the man's) exceptional potency. ἐπλήμυρεν (from πλημυρέω, 'to be in flood, in full spate') likens the ejaculation to a raging river or deluge, a humorous exaggeration characteristic of male bragging. ὀτρυγηφάγου suggests the prized animal's superior diet. Male breeding donkeys (or 'jacks') fetched high prices (cf. Griffith 2006: 222–4).

Archilochus 114

Source: Dio Chrysostom, *Discourses* 33.17 (1–4); Galen on Hippocrates, *On Joints*, xviii (I) 604 Kühn (1 + 3–4), p. 537 (3–4); Pollux, *Vocabulary* 2.192 (4).

As in 5*, which dealt with glory versus self-preservation, this poem continues a debate already present in epic, namely how to distinguish true heroic courage or moral worth from superficial appearance: cf. e.g. *Il.* 3.43–5 (Hector to Paris) 'The long-haired Achaeans must be laughing out loud, saying that with us a chieftain becomes a champion only for his good looks, when there is no strength or courage in his heart'; *Od.* 8.176–7 (Odysseus to Euryalus) 'So it is with you: you have outstanding looks – not even a god could make them better – but an empty mind.' So here the iambic idea of mockery as something that gets under the surface of things to reveal the truth is turned against the tall, well-groomed general, who merely looks the part. The narrator sides with the physically unimpressive, but brave and reliable, general instead. A similar distinction between physical appearance and true courage in battle is made by Tyrtaeus (12.1–12*). Archilochus also pokes fun at the aristocratic ideal of the 'beautiful and good' man (καλοκἄγαθος), an ideology in which beauty, nobility, and excellence go together. The poem is carefully structured and self-contained; it may be complete. The dashing but useless general is described purely in physical terms – height, gait, hairstyle, and beard (1–2). The description of the second rebuts these apparent advantages by distinguishing between mere appearance and actual ability: let him be small and bandy-legged so long as he has courage (3–4). The trochaic metre promotes the creation of a popular Everyman persona (see Introduction §5).

1–2 οὐ ... οὐδὲ ... | οὐδὲ ... οὐδ': the series of negatives underlines the speaker's rejection of external features and the dandy general's reliance upon them. οὐ φιλέω, placed first, draws attention to his personal evaluation. διαπεπλιγμένον, 'who struts around' (perf. part. of διαπλίσσομαι, 'to

stand or walk with legs apart' (LSJ)), contrasts with ἀσφαλέως βεβηκώς ποσσί (4). **βοστρύχοισι γαῦρον** 'proud of his curls': cf. Eur. *Or.* 1532 (Orestes on Menelaus) ἀλλ' ἴτω ξανθοῖς ἐπ' ὤμων βοστρύχοις γαυρούμενος. **ὑπεξυρημένον**, 'partly shaven' (perf. part. pass. of ὑποξυράω), suggests a dainty beard of some kind. The description has moved from the man's size (μέγαν) and stride (διαπεπλιγμένον), which are at least potentially useful in battle, to his hair and beard, which are purely symbols of his vanity.
3 σμικρός: cf. *Il.* 5.801 (Athena rebukes Diomedes) Τυδεύς τοι μικρὸς μὲν ἔην δέμας, ἀλλὰ μαχητής.
3–4 περὶ . . . | ῥοικός 'bandy-legged to look at round the shins': Galen quotes these lines (see above) to illustrate the point that people who are bandy-legged are harder to knock over, an attribute illustrated here by ἀσφαλέως βεβηκώς ποσσί. **ἰδεῖν** underlines the gap between appearance and reality. **ἀσφαλέως . . . ποσσί** 'standing firm on his feet': a soldier's ability to stand firm in battle was crucial to the group mentality and collective ethics of phalanx warfare, and is regularly extolled in martial elegy: cf. Callin. 1.20–1*, Tyrt. 11.21–2, 12.16–22*. The short general's stability implies a commitment to the common good, in contrast to the tall general's self-obsession and preening. **καρδίης πλέως** 'full of guts': the final phrase seals the short general's superiority and reinforces the poem's fundamental distinction between real merit and external show.

Archilochus 172–81

This epode, composed in alternating iambic trimeters and dimeters, used the fable of the fox and the eagle to demonstrate the treachery of Lycambes, who had broken a promise to give one of his daughters in marriage to Archilochus (for their fictional feud, see the introduction above). The surviving fragments suggest that Archilochus' version of the fable was close to that found in the later Aesopic collection (*Fab.* 1 Perry). In this a (female) fox and (male) eagle became friends. One day when the fox was away, the eagle carried off the fox-cubs to feed his chicks. Unable to reach the eagle's nest and avenge her young, the fox cursed the eagle. Soon afterwards the eagle snatched a piece of burnt offering from an altar and brought it back, unaware that the meat contained a spark, which set fire to the nest, killing his chicks. They fell to the ground and the fox devoured them as the eagle looked on.

Archilochus specifies that there are two eaglets (175*), corresponding to the two daughters of Lycambes, making it clear that Lycambes' betrayal will have disastrous consequences for him and his family. The fox's appeal to Zeus for justice (177*) guides us to sympathize with Archilochus' undeserved suffering. The killing of the fox-cubs (175*)

symbolizes Lycambes' destruction of the marriage agreement (173*), while the death of the eagle's chicks (179–80*) looks forward to the suicide of Lycambes' daughters (cf. Archil. fr. 45, P. Dublin inv. 193a). The audience, aware of the wider Lycambid song cycle (cf. 33, 38, 48, 54, 60, 71, 118, 196a*, 197), will have appreciated Archilochus' skilled use of the fable to explore important ethical issues, especially the abuse of friendship and the betrayal of oaths. Similar themes are explored in the story of the eagle and the snake in *Etana*, an Akkadian poem whose oldest version dates to the seventeenth century BC; there too the eagle breaks a vow of friendship, devours the snake's young, and is punished after an appeal for divine vengeance (for its possible influence on the Greek fable of the eagle and the fox, see West 1997: 502–5, Corrêa 2007: 104–5).

Archilochus often exploits his audience's knowledge of animals to produce allusive and compressed imagery: 'The fox knows many tricks, the hedgehog only one – but it's a big one' (fr. 201). Here, as in the Fox and Eagle Epode, Archilochus identifies himself with the apparently weaker animal who ends up besting his enemy. The hedgehog's 'one big thing' is to curl up into a spiky ball, and the parallel with the narrator is made explicit elsewhere: 'But one big thing I know: to pay back with terrible harm the one who harms me' (fr. 126). The message is clear: if anyone tries to hurt Archilochus, not only can he protect himself, but he can do so (like the hedgehog) in a way that will cause his enemy pain – including, it is implied, by producing abusive poetry about him. Thus in the Fox and Eagle Epode the poem itself becomes a means of revenge, exacted through the offender's children. The epode simultaneously shames the oath-breaker Lycambes and presents Archilochus' attack as morally justified. Whether performed at the *symposion* or in a more public (e.g. festival) context, Archilochus' poems about the Lycambids presented an evolving and engaging drama of sex and seduction, betrayal and revenge, and were able to explore a wide variety of social norms and ethical values (cf. Carey 1986).

Archilochus 172

Source: Scholiast on Hermogenes, *Rhetores Graeci* vii.820.17 Walz (1–4); Hephaestion, *On Poems* 7.2 (1–2).

This was probably the beginning of the poem; together with 173* it outlines Lycambes' offence, which motivates the telling of the fable (begun in 174*).

1 πάτερ ... τόδε 'Father Lycambes, what on earth did you mean by this?' The vocative and direct question create urgency and drama, casting the audience into the midst of the feud. πάτερ: the opening word introduces

one of the epode's central themes, Lycambes' failure as both a father and prospective father-in-law. What is usually a term of respect and endearment becomes here a rebuke. ποῖον expresses surprise and indignation, as in various epic formulae, e.g. ποῖον τὸν μῦθον ἔειπες; (addressed six times by Hera to Zeus in the *Iliad*). ἐφράσω: 2nd sg. aor. of φράζομαι, 'think, intend'.

2–3 τίς . . . | . . . ἠρήρεισθα 'who has unhinged your wits, once so sound?' Enjambment enhances the speaker's tone of outraged disbelief. The assonance of παρήειρε (3rd sg. aor. of παραείρω) and ἠρήρεισθα (2nd sg. pluperf. of ἀραρίσκω, lit. 'with which you had been fixed in place') stresses the idea of things coming apart. Lycambes' folly ends up destroying his daughters, just as the eagle's destroys his chicks (179–80*). ἧις (Ionic) = αἷς.

3–4 νῦν . . . | . . . γέλως 'now you turn out to be a big laughing-stock for the townsfolk': public mockery isolates Lycambes from the wider community (ἀστοῖσι), who implicitly share Archilochus' evaluation. **νῦν δέ** contrasts with τὸ πρίν. **φαίνεαι**, lit. 'you are seen to be', emphasizes Lycambes' exposure. **γέλως**: the final word seals Lycambes' humiliation; for the power of public ridicule, cf. Archil. 196a.34* γεί]τοσι χάρμ' ἔσομαι, Semon. 7.73–4* τοιαύτη γυνὴ | εἶσιν δι' ἄστεος πᾶσιν ἀνθρώποις γέλως.

Archilochus 173

Source: Origen, *Against Celsus* 2.21.

Archilochus continues to address Lycambes, making it clear why he has become an object of ridicule (γέλως, 172.4*). By exposing his oath-breaking (ὅρκον . . . μέγαν) and his abuse of the bonds of commensality (ἅλας . . . τράπεζαν), Archilochus emphasizes Lycambes' contempt for the community's fundamental moral principles.

1 ὅρκον . . . μέγαν 'you turned your back on the great oath': the epic phrase 'great oath' (e.g. *Il.* 9.132 ἐπὶ δὲ μέγαν ὅρκον ὀμοῦμαι) elevates the seriousness of the broken betrothal. As Swift 2019 notes ad loc., the word order is significant, since the verb expressing Lycambes' dishonesty (ἐνοσφίσθης) comes between ὅρκον and μέγαν and breaks the 'great oath' apart. **ἅλας . . . τράπεζαν**, 'sworn by salt and table' (lit. 'and on salt and table'), refers to the bonds of friendship created by shared sympotic dining. In other words, the father and prospective son-in-law's marriage agreement was also a sympotic alliance, and Lycambes' perjury has destroyed the harmony of the *hetaireia* (cf. Gagné 2009). **ἅλας:** acc. of ἅλας, ατος, τό, = ἅλς. 'Salt and table' became proverbial for the social bonds of shared meals: cf. Dem. 19.189 ποῦ δ' ἅλες; ποῦ τράπεζα; ποῦ σπονδαί;

Archilochus 174

Source: Herennius Philo, *On the Different Meanings of Words* 32 (p. 142 Palmieri).

With Lycambes' treachery laid bare (172–3*), Archilochus begins the fable of the fox and the eagle.

1 αἶνός ... ὅδε 'there is a fable men tell': αἶνος ('tale') is used of stories that have an implicit message for the addressee (e.g. *Il.* 23.652 ἐπεὶ πάντ' αἶνον ἐπέκλυε Νηλεΐδαο, where Nestor's account of his youthful victories confirms Achilles' gift of a prize). It is particularly associated with animal fable: Hesiod introduces his fable of the hawk and the nightingale νῦν δ' αἶνον βασιλεῦσιν ἐρέω φρονέουσι καὶ αὐτοῖς (*WD* 202), and Archilochus his fable of the fox and the monkey ἐρέω τιν' ὕμιν αἶνον, ὦ Κηρυκίδη (fr. 185). **αἶνος ... ἀνθρώπων** is nicely ambiguous, since what follows is not only a tale 'told by men', but also 'about men', as fable uses its animal characters to explore human behaviour and morality (cf. 177.4* ὕβρις τε καὶ δίκη).

2–3 ὡς ... | ἔμειξαν 'of how a fox and an eagle joined in partnership': the language emphasizes fellowship (ξυνεωνίην) and unity (ἔμειξαν), underlining the eagle's (and Lycambes') betrayal of friendship. **καἰετός** (crasis) = καὶ αἰετός. **ξυνεωνίην** (= Attic κοινωνίαν), attested only here; the importance of partnership is echoed in Aristophanes' account of the fable, which also stresses its disastrous results: ὅρα νυν, ὡς ἐν Αἰσώπου λόγοις | ἐστὶν λεγόμενον δή τι, τὴν ἀλώπεχ', ὡς | φλαύρως ἐκοινώνησεν αἰετῶι ποτέ (*Birds* 651–3). The phrase ξυνεωνίην ἔμειξαν also has connotations of marriage and sexuality (cf. LSJ κοινωνία and μείγνυμι), suggesting the marriage agreement sworn and subsequently broken by Lycambes, to the detriment of his daughters (see 196a*).

Archilochus 175

Source: P. Oxy. 2315 fr. 1.

This fragment describes the eagle's return to his eyrie, carrying the fox-cubs, whom he feeds to his chicks. The repeated emphasis on the eagle's young (1 παῖ]δας, 3 ἀπτ]ῆνες, 5 νεοσσιῆι) foreshadows the ruin of his (and Lycambes') own family.

1–3 ἐς ... | ... δύο 'bringing to his children ... and the two fledglings fell upon an unlovely feast': παῖ]δας and δαῖ]τα are usually applied to humans and their meals, not animals, and their likely use here highlights both the anthropomorphic nature of the animals themselves and the fable's applicability to Archilochus' and Lycambes' human situation. **ἀπτ]ῆνες**, lit. 'without wings', stresses the chicks' dependence on their parents: cf. *Il.* 9.323–4 ὡς δ' ὄρνις ἀπτῆσι νεοσσοῖσι προφέρηισι | μάστακ' ἐπεί κε λάβηισι, κακῶς δ' ἄρα οἱ πέλει αὐτῆι. **δύο** is an important detail (not present in the Aesopic version), since it corresponds to the two daughters who will suffer as a result of their father's treachery (see the introduction to 172–81*).

4–5 γῆ[ς] . . . | . . . νεοσσιῆι 'on the land's high crag [where they had their] nest': their location explains why the fox was unable to reach the eagles and get her revenge. (The Aesopic version has a very tall tree.) **ὑψηλῶι π[άγωι:** a likely restoration based on 176.1* κεῖνος ὑψηλὸς πάγος. **νεοσσιῆι:** lit. 'a nest of young birds'.

6 προύθηκε, 'he set before', probably refers to the meal being served to the eaglets.

6–9 τὴν δ[' ἀλώπεκα . . . φωλά[δ: if West's supplement and restoration are right, the focus now turns to the fox's reaction as she realizes her cubs have been snatched from the 'fox-hole' (φωλά[δ).

Archilochus 176

Source: Atticus fr. 2 (p. 41 des Places).

The fox soliloquizes, expressing her frustration at not being able to reach the eagle's nest. Some (e.g. Campbell 1982 ad loc.) think these words spoken by a third animal to the fox, but there is no trace of such a figure in the fable, and it would muddy the clear analogy between fox/eagle and Archilochus/Lycambes.

1 κεῖνος . . . πάγος, 'that high crag', stresses once again the inaccessibility of the nest (cf. 175.4* ὑψηλῶι π[άγωι).

2 τρηχύς . . . παλίγκοτος, 'rough and hostile', personifies the crag as harshly opposed to the fox's revenge plans.

3 ἐν . . . μάχην 'there he sits, mocking your assault'. **ἐλαφρίζων** ('making light of, scorning') expresses the eagle's cruel contempt for the fox's plight, as he thinks himself safe from punishment.

Archilochus 177

Source: Stobaeus 1.3.34.

Powerless to avenge herself, the fox prays to Zeus for justice. Whereas Hesiod presents justice as unique to humans and given to them by Zeus to distinguish them from animals (*WD* 276–90), Archilochus deploys the fable's conventional moral parallelism between human and animal worlds. The fox's solemn prayer makes clear that δίκη is something animals should respect, and presents Zeus as the guardian of moral order for humans and animals alike. The fox's language aligns her with traditional piety, preparing for the eagle's punishment, which he brings upon himself by an act of sacrilege (see fr. 179–80*).

1 ὦ Ζεῦ, πάτερ Ζεῦ: the repeated vocatives are characteristic of urgent prayers (compare Hipponax's parodic fr. 38, 'O Zeus, father Zeus ... why have you not given me lots of money?'), while πάτερ echoes the opening address to πάτερ Λυκάμβα (172.1*), foreshadowing Zeus's punishment of the eagle/Lycambes.

1–3 σὸν ... | σὺ ... | ... σοί: polyptoton underlines Zeus's supreme power and the certainty of his justice. The effect is enhanced by splitting Zeus's domain into the separate levels of gods (οὐρανοῦ κράτος, 1), humans (ἐπ' ἀνθρώπων, 2), and animals (θηρίων, 3).

2 ἐπ' ... ὁρᾶις, 'you oversee' (tmesis), emphasizes Zeus's omniscience and concern for justice; ἐφοράω is often used in contexts where transgressions are punished: cf. *Od.* 13.213–14 Ζεύς σφεας τείσαιτο ἱκετήσιος, ὅς τε καὶ ἄλλους | ἀνθρώπους ἐφορᾶι καὶ τείνυται, ὅς τις ἁμάρτηι, 17.485–7 καί τε θεοὶ ... | ... ἀνθρώπων ὕβριν τε καὶ εὐνομίην ἐφορῶντες.

3–4 λεωργὰ καὶ θεμιστά ... ὕβρις τε καὶ δίκη: the 'wicked and lawful' deeds of humans are balanced by the 'violence and justice' of animals, stressing the moral equivalence between the two worlds and justifying the fox's appeal for the eagle's punishment (and, by implication, Archilochus' prediction of Lycambes' destruction).

Archilochus 178

Source: Porphyry on Homer, *Iliad* 24.315.

The phrase μή τευ μελαμπύγου τύχηις ('in case you encounter one that is black-rumped') is quoted as a proverb meaning 'watch out you don't encounter someone strong and powerful' (Hesych. μ 1277, II.664 Latte), and this would suit a scene where the fox warns the eagle that he is not immune from retribution.

τευ: Ionic gen. = τινος. μελαμπύγου: black-rumped eagles were thought fiercer than the white-rumped variety (cf. Ar. *Lys.* 802–3 μελάμπυ- | γός τε τοῖς ἐχθροῖς ἅπασιν): the fox is warning the eagle that he may meet with someone stronger who will in turn destroy him. The eagle is the bird most closely associated with Zeus (cf. Aesch. *Ag.* 114–15, οἰωνῶν βασιλεὺς βασιλεῦσι νε- | ῶν, ὁ κελαινὸς ὅ τ' ἐξόπιν ἀργᾶς, where both the black- and white-tailed eagle symbolize Zeus's punishment of Troy), and so it is appropriate that Zeus turns out to be 'the black-rumped one' who exacts the fox's revenge.

Archilochus 179

Source: *Etymologicum Genuinum* α 187 (cod. B), *Symeonis* α 256, *Magnum* α 462.

The fragment describes a second meal brought by the eagle to his children (cf. 175*), but this one is αἰηνές, 'grievous, harmful', because it will set fire to the nest and kill the chicks.

προύθηκε ... φέρων: the verbs deliberately echo the earlier meal (175.1–6* φέρων ... προύθηκε), where the eagle served up the fox-cubs for dinner, making clear the moral symmetry involved in the subsequent destruction of the eagle's children. παισὶ δεῖπνον: the anthropomorphic language (cf. 175.1–2* ἐς παῖ]δας ... | ... δαῖ]τα) underlines the relevance of the scene to the human behaviour it reflects (i.e. the treachery of Lycambes).

Archilochus 180

Source: Scholiast on Aristophanes, *Acharnians* 279.

The fragment refers to a piece of meat which the eagle has stolen from a sacrifice (for the full Aesopic narrative, see the introduction to 172–81*). The theft confirms the eagle's contempt for piety and morality (compare the wicked weasel-woman of Semon. 7.56* ἄθυστα δ' ἱρὰ πολλάκις κατεσθίει), while the fact that the death of the eagle's chicks springs from a religious ceremony frames the eagle's punishment as a response to the fox's prayer (fr. 177*) and underscores the gods' role in ensuring justice.

πυρός ... φεψάλυξ '(there was) a spark of fire in it'.

Archilochus 181

Source: P. Oxy. 2316.

This fragment describes the reaction of the fox to the killing of her cubs, and so belongs near 176* and 177* (very likely between them, before the fox's prayer in 177*: see on lines 4–6 and 12 below). West (1974) 134 takes it to portray the eagle's reaction to the burning nest, but this goes against the account of Atticus, who quotes 176* and paraphrases 181.11* λαιψηρὰ κυ]κλώσας πτερά ('circling on nimble wings') in the context of the fox's inability to fly up to the nest to take her revenge.

4–6 μ]έγ' ... | ... ἀμήχανον, 'recognized the great disaster ... [in her/my] heart ... helpless', emphasizes the fox's frustration at not being able to reach the high crag (the focus of 176*). ᾐείδει: the subject could be the fox or perhaps (in preparation for 177*) Zeus.

8–11 μεμνημένος ... | ... κλύσας ... | ... κυ]κλώσας: the masculine participles must refer to the eagle, so the fox is most likely speaking again (cf. 176–7*), complaining of the eagle's betrayal. μεμνημένος, 'mindful', may recall the eagle's failure to be 'mindful' of their alliance (ξυνεωνίην, 174.2*). κλύσας (aor. part. of κλύζω, 'wash away, purge'), is metaphorical (cf. Eur. *IT* 1193 θάλασσα κλύζει πάντα τἀνθρώπων κακά), emphasizing the impossibility of the eagle 'washing away' his guilt. κέ]λευθον ... | ... πτερά, 'a path swiftly through the air, circling on nimble wings', laments the eagle's escape.

12 σός... ἔλπεται 'but your heart expects': the likeliest sense is 'but you expect to get away unpunished', a dramatic direct address to the eagle, leading neatly into the fox's prayer for justice (177*).

Archilochus 196a

Source: P. Colon. 58.1–35 (= Kölner Papyri inv. 7511).

One of the most important papyrological finds of the last century, first published in 1974, the so-called (first) Cologne Epode is the longest surviving fragment of Archilochus' poetry (cf. Merkelbach and West 1974, Campbell 1976, Henderson 1976, Rösler 1976, Slings 1987, Latacz 1992, Hedreen 2006: 295–8, Nicolosi 2007, Eckerman 2011, Swift 2015a). It dramatizes a significant moment in his relationship with the family of Lycambes (for this song cycle, see the introduction above). Whereas the Fox and the Eagle Epode attacked Lycambes for his betrayal of the marriage contract (173*), presenting him as 'a big laughing-stock for the townsfolk' (172.3–4*), the Cologne Epode exacts revenge by having the narrator claim to have had sex with both Lycambes' daughters, destroying the family's reputation completely. Archilochus rejects his former fiancée, Neoboule, as 'overripe' (26) and promiscuous ('she makes friends with many men', 38) and seduces her younger sister instead.

The poem is both shocking and titillating: not only does the young woman try to pimp her elder sister (3–8), but she also betrays her by having sex with her former fiancé, while the male narrator gets his way and achieves sexual climax with the desirable and virginal young girl (παρθένον, 42). As in Archil. 5*, where the narrator throws away his shield, here the poetic persona acts in a disgraceful manner, negotiating extra-marital sex with a free-born girl. The end of the poem is simultaneously explicit and ambiguous: 'I released my white force, touching her blonde hair' (52–3). This creates suspense and interest among the audience (tipsy men at drinking parties, or boisterous festival crowds), who are encouraged not only to speculate among themselves as to exactly what happened, but also to look forward to the next raunchy instalment in the tale of Lycambes and his daughters. However, such iambic invective is not merely titillating, for it also encodes basic moral values for an Archaic Greek audience – as here concerning the keeping of promises, the importance of policing the chastity of unmarried girls, and the value of sexual restraint (mainly for women, of course, to suit the double standards of a patriarchal society). The audience can enjoy the *frisson* of shocking behaviour while disapproving the violation of sexual norms.

The structure of the encounter (the female at first resists, a compromise is agreed, sex takes place) is similar to that found in other seduction scenes, most famously the so-called 'Deception of Zeus' in the *Iliad*, where Hera acts coy while in fact provoking Zeus to have sex with her right away (14.313–51). The adaptability of this 'type scene' in early epic is shown, for example, by *Od.* 6.149–85, where Odysseus defuses the sexual threat he poses to Nausicaa and looks forward to her happy marriage to another man, and *HHAphr.* 81–167, where Aphrodite poses as a demure young virgin in order to seduce a wary Anchises; cf. Forsyth 1979, Faulkner 2008: 161–234, Swift 2015a: 3–10. Like Homer and the poet of the *Hymn to Aphrodite*, Archilochus plays with the conventions of the seduction scene to suit his own ends (especially the disgrace of Lycambes' daughters): rather than being sexually modest the young woman offers her own sister in her place, while the male speaker mixes praise of his would-be conquest with invective against his former lover. The poem's setting, a blossoming meadow, similarly engages with the conventions of Greek erotic poetry, where virginal girls (e.g. Persephone or Europa) are approached while picking flowers. Archilochus uses the conventional fantasy landscape of the fertile meadow to enhance his own skills and success as a seducer (see on 42–4 below).

The fragment begins in the midst of a speech by the young woman in which she deflects the narrator's advances and advertises another woman instead. A clue to what came before this is supplied by fr. 196 ἀλλά μ' ὁ λυσιμελὴς ὦταῖρε δάμναται πόθος ('but limb-loosening desire overpowers me, my friend'). Since this fragment, a hemiepes followed by an iambic dimeter catalectic, overlaps with the metre of fr. 196a* (iambic trimeter alternating with hemiepes and iambic dimeter), it is possible that the poem began with Archilochus addressing a male friend, confessing that he is overcome with desire, then telling a story (196a*) to explain how this condition arose (cf. Bowie 2001b: 17–18). In any case, the surviving lines represent one of the most significant examples of erotic narrative in Greek poetry, with the male speaker flattering the young woman and promising to follow her lead ('I shall do as you bid me', 19) and the audience implicated in a sexual act that is deliberately enigmatic and transgressive (see on 52–3 below).

1–8 The fragment begins during a speech by the young woman in which she rejects and redirects the man's sexual advances. Though only partially preserved, lines 1–2 'holding off completely ... endure just the same' strongly suggest that she began by advising restraint, before then suggesting (3–8) that if he really must have sex right away, she knows of another 'maiden' (παρθένος, 5) who will oblige. The scenario humorously inverts the traditions of didactic poetry, as here the speaker is not an older wise adviser, but a young woman who instructs an older man how to satisfy his lust.

1 ἀποσχόμενος: for the verb used of abstention from sex, cf. *Il.* 14.206–7 (as Hera plots her seduction of Zeus) ἤδη γὰρ δηρὸν χρόνον ἀλλήλων ἀπέχονται | εὐνῆς καὶ φιλότητος, ἐπεὶ χόλος ἔμπεσε θυμῶι.
2 ἶσον δὲ τόλμ[: for endurance in an erotic context, cf. Sapph. 31.17 ἀλλὰ πὰν τόλματον.
3 εἰ ... ἰθύει, 'but if you are in a rush and your heart urges you on', depicts the man as incapable of controlling his desire for sex, a charge which he seeks to defuse in his reply by implying that there are alternative 'pleasures' (13) available and by rejecting 'hasty' sex (40 ἐπειγόμενος ~ 3 ἐπείγεαι) with the girl's sister, Neoboule.
4 ἐν ἡμετέρου (with οἴκωι/δόμωι understood), 'in our house', alerts the audience to the shocking idea that the 'maiden' on offer is the girl's own sister.
5–6 ἥ ... | ... παρθένος, 'a maiden, beautiful and tender, who now greatly desires [a man]', simultaneously advertises the woman's beauty and her sexual appetite. τέρεινα, often used of flowers and leaves (cf. *Il.* 13.180 τέρενα φύλλα, *Od.* 9.449 τέρεν' ἄνθεα ποίης), is the first of many words in the poem that relate the world of nature and natural fertility to female beauty and sexuality (cf. 23–4, 26–7, 39–41, 42–3, 46–7).
6–7 δοκέω ... | ... ἔχειν 'I think she has a faultless figure': the claim will be strongly rebutted by the man (26–8). By insisting on her sister's 'faultless' appearance, the girl prompts the audience to focus on her far from faultless character.
8 τὴν ... φίλην 'make her your friend': as the man points out, however, the problem is that everyone does: 'she makes friends with many men' (38).
9–41 The seducer's speech answers in detail each of the young woman's arguments. Whereas she advised abstinence, he suggests a compromise (13–24); and although she offered her own sister, the man rejects her as not only past her prime but also as morally degraded (24–41).
10–12 Ἀμφιμεδοῦς ... | ... γυναικός 'daughter of Amphimedo, that good and ... lady': women are usually identified via their male relatives ('daughter/sister/wife of *x*'), so the speaker's choice is pointed. By praising the young woman's late mother, the speaker ingratiates himself and links the girl's character to that of her 'good' parent, while the omission of Lycambes reminds the audience of his treachery (frr. 172–81*). ἥν ... ἔ[χει 'whom the mouldering earth now holds'. κατ' ... ἔ[χει (tmesis): from κατέχω, 'hold fast'. εὐρώεσσ', an epic epithet used only of Hades, ties in with the natural imagery used of the female body throughout the poem (e.g. 6 τέρεινα, 23–4 πο̣η[φόρους | κ]ήπους, 26 πέπειρα, 27 ἄν]θος παρθενήϊον) and subtly reminds the addressee of the decay that awaits every human body, thereby encouraging a *carpe diem* approach to sexual pleasure.

13–15 The male speaker reassures the girl that penetrative sex (a certain source of shame and ruin to an unmarried woman) is not the only option. τ]έρψιές ... | ... ἀνδ[ράσιν 'many are the pleasures which the goddess offers young men': the speaker's focus on male pleasure reveals his true motives. θεῆς: Aphrodite, whose domain is sexual desire and pleasure (e.g. *Il.* 14.197–210). παρὲξ ... χρῆμα: lit. 'apart from the divine thing', a striking euphemism for sex, whose use here is meant to communicate the man's delicacy and decency. τὸ θεῖον χρῆμα: Plato's Diotima calls human procreation a θεῖον πρᾶγμα (*Symp.* 206c). τῶν ... ἀρκέσε[ι, 'one of these will suffice', reinforces his attempt to seem moderate and reasonable.

16–18 The speaker looks forward to 'leisurely discussion' (ἐφ' ἡσυχίης ... βουλεύσομεν) of the other options (τ]αῦτα refers back to 13–15) once night has fallen (εὖτ' ἄν μελανθῃ[). The implication is that they should satisfy themselves right away and talk about their relationship later. εὖτ' ἄν μελανθη['when ... grows dark': the likeliest supplement is 'night' or 'sky', e.g. μελανθῇ[ι νύξ, ὁμοῦ (Page), μ. γ' ἕσπερος (Burzacchini), μ. δὴ οὐρανός (Austin); cf. Handley 2007: 97–9. ἐ]γώ τε καὶ σύ unites the two as a couple, suggesting the male speaker's honourable intentions, an effect further enhanced by σὺν θεῶι, 'with god's help'.

19 π]είσομαι ... κέλεαι, 'I shall do as you bid me', reassures the woman that she will remain in control. By presenting himself as subservient to her will, the speaker exerts a subtle pressure, encouraging her to grant his subsequent request for some form of sexual activity (20–4).

20–4 The man's euphemistic and highly metaphorical language – which draws on building (θρ]ιγκοῦ, πυλέων), seafaring (σχήσω), and nature (ποη[φόρους κ]ήπους) – is intended to downplay the indecency of his (extra-marital) acts. θρ]ιγκοῦ ... πυλέων, 'under the coping-stone and the gates', i.e. the pubic bone and vagina, may suggest intercrural sex. θριγκός and πύλη can also refer to the anus (cf. Ar. *Thesm.* 60, *Lys.* 1163), but penetrative sex of any kind seems an unlikely compromise. μ]ή ... φίλη, 'do not begrudge it, my dear', casts the speaker as merely asking for a small favour (τι) in return for his ceding ultimate control to her (19). σχήσω ... | κ]ήπους, 'I shall steer towards the grassy gardens', i.e. towards the pubic hair. Whether he keeps his promise is never made clear: see on 53 below ξανθῆς ἐπιψαύ[ων τριχός ('touching her blonde hair').

24–41 The man's rejection of Neoboule continues the use of nature imagery, but here it is used to attack a woman's sexuality – Neoboule has lost her 'maidenly flower' (27), her children would be 'the bitch's blind and premature babies' (39–41) – rather than to reassure her of her sexual integrity (cf. 21–4).

26 αἰαῖ, πέπειρα 'goodness, she's overripe'. πέπειρα is used of 'ripe' in the sense of 'sexually experienced' women at Ar. *Eccl.* 893–5 εἴ τις ἀγαθὸν βούλεται πα- | θεῖν τι, παρ' ἐμοὶ χρὴ καθεύδειν. | οὐ γὰρ ἐν νέαις τὸ σοφὸν ἔν- |

εστιν, ἀλλ' ἐν ταῖς πεπείροις. Here the sense is 'overripe', implying not only that Neoboule is too old (emphasized by δὶς τόση) and past her prime, but also that she has had too much sexual experience (an idea picked up by ἄν]θος δ' ἀπερρύηκε παρθενήϊον in the next line). δὶς τόση 'twice your age': probably rhetorical exaggeration, though not impossible, given the early age at which girls were married off.

27–8 ἄν]θος . . . παρθενήϊον, 'her maidenly flower has withered', continues the plant imagery and reinforces the accusations of the previous line, i.e. Neoboule is too old (her flower has 'dropped off') and is worn out by sex (the flower symbolizes her virginity). The man thus refutes the positive plant and flower imagery first introduced by the girl's description of Neoboule as καλὴ τέρεινα παρθένος (6). **ἀπερρύηκε:** 3rd sg. perf. ἀπορρέω, 'drop off, perish'. **κ]αὶ . . . ἐπῆν** 'and the charm which she once had': the man acknowledges that Neoboule, his ex-lover, was once desirable. **χάρις:** in erotic contexts the word often implies that sexual 'favours' have been granted (LSJ III 2); cf. MacLachlan 1993: 58–9.

29–30 The man attacks Neoboule for her 'excess' and 'folly', deploying the concepts of κόρος and ἄτη which are fundamental to Archaic Greek thought (cf. Sol. 4.9–10*, 4.34–5*, 6.3–4*, 13.11–13*, 13.71–6*, Thgn. 44–52*). **κόρον . . . οὐκ[:** Merkelbach and West's conjecture οὐ κ[ατέσχε πω gives good sense, 'for she never restrained her excess' (cf. Sol. 4.9* κατέχειν κόρον). **ἄτ]ης . . . γυνή**, 'the crazy woman has shown the limits of her folly', dismisses Neoboule as an irrational and mad woman, a familiar stereotype of Greek gender ideology. **μαινόλις:** cf. Sapph. 1.17–18 κ]ὤττι [μοι μάλιστα θέλω γένεσθαι | μ]αινόλαι [θύμωι.

31 ἐς] . . . ἄπεχε 'to hell with her!' (lit. 'take [her] off to the crows'): a blunt, colloquial phrase, marking the speaker's disgust.

32–4 The man imagines being ridiculed by his neighbours for having such a terrible wife. **ἐφ.ιτ':** West's ἐφοῖτ' (3rd sg. aor. opt. ἐφίημι, 'send upon' (of fate or destiny)) may be right, 'let no one send me this fate'. **γυναῖκα . . . ἔχων:** the implication that the speaker may be interested in marriage acts as a subtle suggestion to the girl that their encounter may lead to something more permanent and respectable. **γεί]τοσι χάρμ':** cf. Semon. 7.73–4* τοιαύτη γυνὴ | εἶσιν δι' ἄστεος πᾶσιν ἀνθρώποις γέλως, 7.110–11* οἱ δὲ γείτονες | χαίρουσ' ὁρῶντες καὶ τόν, ὡς ἁμαρτάνει.

35 πολλὸν . . . πάρος 'I much prefer you': the man sets up the two sisters as rivals, before contrasting their qualities (36–8).

36 σὺ] . . . διπλόη 'since you are neither untrustworthy nor two-faced': the compliment comes with 'unlike your sister' implied. The praise of the girl's character is humorously ironic, since she is after all being asked to have sex with her sister's ex-lover behind her back.

37–8 ἡ . . . ὀξυτέρη, 'she's too keen': the sexual reference is confirmed by πολλοὺς δὲ ποιεῖτα[ι φίλους, 'and she makes friends with many men'.

39–41 expand on the dangers of Neoboule's promiscuity. The speaker moves from plant (26–8) to animal imagery, using the idea of an oversexed bitch who breeds blind and premature puppies. By comparing himself to the bitch (ὥσπερ ἡ κ[ύων τέκω, 41) the speaker foregrounds the consequences for him as husband and father of having such a lustful and untrustworthy wife. **τυφλὰ κἀλιτήμερα** (= καὶ ἀλιτήμερα) 'blind and premature [sc. children]': the idea that the bitch's haste to give birth leads to premature offspring is explored in Aesop's fable of the bitch and the sow (*Fab.* 223 Perry), where the bitch boasts of her frequent and large litters, and the sow retorts that while that may be true, her puppies are born blind. Here the male speaker refers to himself as 'pressing on in haste' (σπ]ουδῆι ἐπειγόμενος, emphatic pleonasm), transferring the idea of haste to give birth into haste to have sex, an idea already associated in Greek thought with the proverbially promiscuous and shameless bitch: cf. Semon. 7.19*, Slings 1976. **σπ]ουδῆι ἐπειγόμενος:** more irony, as he rejects immediate sex with Neoboule while pursuing it with her sister. **τώς** = οὕτως.

42–53 The male narrator's description of the sex scene foregrounds his control (with a string of first-person verbs: e.g. ἔκλινα, ἐφηψάμην, ἀφῆκα), but also stresses his delicacy and concern for the girl's wellbeing (his cloak is 'soft', he touches her breasts 'gently', etc.), using language that avoids any hint of coarseness or vulgarity. The effect is a kind of soft-focus romanticism, whose rhetorical aim is to mask the man's highly disreputable act, the deflowering of a free-born girl (see the introduction above). The account builds vividly to its climax, though its precise details are left deliberately unclear (see on 52–3).

42–4 He lays the girl down. **ἐν ἄνθε[σιν | τηλ]εθάεσσι,** 'in the blossoming flowers', evokes the *locus amoenus* of the fertile meadow, the typical scene of erotic encounters (cf. *Il.* 14.347–9, Hes. *Theog.* 278–9), where virgins are approached while picking flowers (*HHDem.* 1–21, etc.); cf. Calame 1999: 151–74, Heirman 2012: 86–113, Swift 2015a: 10–23. **τηλεθάεσσι** pres. participle act. neut. dat. pl. τηλεθάω, 'to bloom'.

44–5 μαλθακῆι . . . | χλαί]νηι, 'with my soft cloak', underlines his gentleness (see on 42–53 above); so too the gesture αὐχέν' . . . ἔχω[ν ('cradling her neck in my arm'). Yet the act of covering (καλύψας) is also one that veils a girl's modesty and so reminds the audience of the shame brought upon Lycambes' daughter by this sexual encounter.

46–7 The girl stops (παυ[σ]αμένην) doing something in fear (δεί]ματι) just like a fawn (ὥστε νέβρ[), and the likeliest solution is reflected in Gronewald's ὥστε νέβρ[ιον τρέμειν: 'she stopped trembling in fear like a fawn'. Such a description captures well the main themes of the passage: the man's avowed concern for her wellbeing, but also the girl's vulnerability, especially to the loss of honour posed by the sexual predatoriness of such men.

48–53 The narrator caresses her breasts (48–50) and entire body (51) before ejaculating (52–3).

48–50 μαζ]ῶν . . . ἐφηψάμην 'and with my hands I gently took hold of her breasts': μαζ]ῶν is the most explicit word used by the narrator; elsewhere he speaks of the girl's neck (45), body (51), and hair (53), and there is no description of his anatomy, in keeping with the scene's delicate tone (cf. 42–53). **ἥπε]ρ . . . | . . . χρόα**, lit. 'where she revealed her young flesh, the bewitchment of her youth', stresses the narrator's growing excitement. **ἥβης ἐπήλυσιν** stands in apposition to χρόα. ἐπήλυσιν, lit. 'approach, onset', could refer to the onset of her youthful prime (ἥβης), but the word is also glossed by Hesychius as 'bewitchment' (ἐπαγωγή), which would better suit the narrator's increasing focus on her sexual allure.

51 ἀμφαφώμενος 'caressing', lit. 'touching all around'. As Swift 2019 notes (on 42–53), West's supplement ἅπαν 'would allow a listener's mind to move to whatever body-part he wished to imagine'.

52–3 λευκ]όν . . . | . . . τριχός: lit. 'I released my white force, touching her blonde hair'. The narrator's enigmatic climax has exercised the imaginations of scholars, keen to pinpoint the exact nature of the sex act, with suggestions including fellatio, withdrawal/*coitus interruptus*, ejaculation over the girl's pubic hair, masturbation, intercrural sex, premature ejaculation, and full sexual intercourse. However, Archilochus has left the precise details deliberately unclear so as to excite speculation among his audience, who are encouraged not only to use their own erotic imaginations, but also to wonder whether the man has kept his promise to stop short of 'the divine thing' (τὸ θεῖον χρῆμα, 15). Thus the poet's deliberate ambiguity is more effective at involving the audience in the scene than any direct description would be (cf. Swift 2015a: 21–3). **λευκ]όν . . . μένος:** Archilochus adapts the epic phrase μένος ἀφιέναι (used of a god or warrior releasing or checking his might) to suit the erotic context, giving his male narrator a humorous mock-heroic grandeur as he describes his (it is implied) prodigious ejaculation (cf. Archil. fr. 43*). **λευκ]όν:** cf. λευκὸς ἀφρός used of the foam that forms around Ouranos' severed genitals (Hes. *Theog.* 190–1). **ξανθῆς . . . τριχός** makes clear that the narrator touches the girl's hair, but does not specify where the hair is or where his λευκὸν μένος ends up.

SEMONIDES

Semonides, like Archilochus, was active in the early to mid-seventh century BC (cf. Pellizer and Tedeschi 1990: xvii). Just as Archilochus led a colonizing expedition to Thasos, so Semonides is said to have led a group of Samian colonists to Amorgos. Samos had developed wide-ranging trade networks, including Al-Mina in Syria, the Hellespont, and Egypt. Amorgos, though mountainous and agriculturally poor, offered, by virtue of its location in the mid-Aegean among the south eastern Cyclades, a valuable staging-post for Samian trade (cf. Lloyd-Jones 1975: 16–17, Morgan 2005: 73–4). The Suda reports that Semonides wrote 'elegiacs in two books, and iambics' and that his works included an *Archaeology of the Samians*. This account of Samos' foundation and early history may have been in two books (cf. Bowie 1986: 31), but nothing of it or any other elegy survives. The two major extant iambic pieces are included here, and together with the forty or so other fragments, which range from just a couple of words to three lines, they suggest a wide variety of subject-matter and persona, including moralizing reflections on human life (frr. 1–4) and graphic sexual narrative (16–17). Like Archilochus (versus Lycambes) and Hipponax (versus Bupalus), Semonides is said to have attacked a particular personal enemy (called Orodoecides, according to Lucian, *Pseudol.* 2), but again no example of his abuse poetry has survived. In any case, the remaining fragments remind us that iambus was a flexible form, not at all confined to invective or sexual escapades, and that it could be used to reflect on diverse themes in different tones, from morose rumination on life's hardships (1*) to mock-didactic exposition of the nature of women and the relationship between the sexes (7*); cf. Introduction §1.

Semonides 1

Source: Stobaeus 4.34.15.

This poem, probably complete (see 22–4n.), is quoted by the anthologist Stobaeus in a section devoted to melancholy reflections on the miseries of life. The fundamental idea, human ignorance, is presented first (1–5), leading to the vanity of hope and ambition (6–10); such aspirations are undone by the myriad disasters that befall us (11–22). The poem ends by recommending that we avoid dwelling on our wretched condition (22–4). Human vulnerability and the necessity of endurance were staples of the Greek wisdom tradition, whether in the didactic hexameters of Hesiod (*Works and Days*) and Phocylides (frr. 2–16) or the reflective elegies of (for example) Mimnermus (1*, 2*) and Solon (13*); for detailed points of comparison, see below. Here Semonides treats these familiar pessimistic themes of human folly and suffering in moralizing iambics (akin to Archilochus' trochaic tetrameters, especially frr. 128, 130–1, 133), illustrating the form's ability to present serious reflection in appropriately solemn and gnomic terms (cf. Sol. 36*, 37), including the use of epic diction, more familiar in elegiac moralizing (e.g. 1 Ζεὺς … βαρύκτυπος, 14 μελαίνης … χθονός). Although the poem has had many detractors (e.g. Fränkel 1975: 202 'the poem is increasingly dispersed into the lower reaches of banality ... Semonides' outpouring seems feeble and erratic'), it is a neatly constructed meditation on human behaviour, and its unexpected ending offers us a chance to make the most of our 'ephemeral' condition (cf. Carson 1984, who thinks the poem is artfully dull, imitating the lives of those who do not take its advice).

1–5 Zeus's complete knowledge and power (1–2) are contrasted with humans' abject ignorance (3–5).

1–2 ὦ παῖ: Semonides' wisdom is addressed to an anonymous 'boy' (or 'son'), and uses the kind of admonitory persona deployed in Hesiod's advice to his wastrel brother Perses or Theognis' to his younger lover Cyrnus (see on Thgn. 19–20*); numerous pieces in the Theognidea begin ὦ παῖ (1283–94, 1295–8, 1299–1304, etc.). The didactic scenario of older man and younger pupil motivates and justifies the speaker's sententiousness, while the potentially erotic relationship between speaker and addressee gives the poem's ending an added resonance (cf. 22–4n.). Pessimistic reflection on the human condition was a familiar theme of sympotic literature (e.g. Sol. 13*, Thgn. 425–8), and much if not most iambus was, like elegy, performed at *symposia* (cf. Introduction §§1–2). **τέλος . . . | . . . θέλει:** for Zeus's proverbial omnipotence, cf. e.g. Archil. 298 Ζεύς . . . | καὶ τέλος αὐτὸς ἔχει, Sol. 13.17* ἀλλὰ Ζεὺς πάντων ἐφορᾶι τέλος. **βαρύκτυπος:** the epithet ('loud-thundering', 'heavy-booming'), first attested in Hesiod, is particularly characteristic of Zeus (e.g. *Theog.* 388, *WD* 79, *HHDem.* 3), though Hesiod also uses it of Poseidon (*Theog.* 818); cf. Semon. 7.40*. **τίθησ' . . . θέλει:** an ominous idea, since traditionally οὐδέ τίς ἐστιν | ἀνθρώπων ὧι Ζεὺς μὴ κακὰ πολλὰ διδοῖ (Mimn. 2.15–16*). **ὄκηι:** Ionic (= Attic ὅπηι); cf. ὅκως (5).

3–5 νοῦς . . . ἀνθρώποισιν 'mankind possesses no foresight' (lit. 'there is no foresight among humans'): mortal understanding (νοῦς δ(έ)) is contrasted with divine (μὲν Ζεύς, 1), ignorance with omniscience. **ἀλλ' . . . | . . . ζόουσιν** 'but they live like cattle from day to day'. ἐπήμεροι = ἐφήμεροι, with Ionic psilosis, or substitution of plosive for aspirated consonant; the word, first attested here, encapsulates the speaker's complaint: people focus only on the here and now, with no inkling of what the future will bring. **ἃ δή** = οἶα δή, 'like'. For 'depreciatory' δή, see *GP* 219. **βοτά**, cognate with βόσκω ('feed, graze') and βοτάνη ('pasture'), is used of all domestic grazing animals. **ζόουσιν** (Ionic for ζώουσιν): the transmitted ζώομεν is metrically problematic, creating a choriamb (–⏑⏑–) in the second metron (cf. Renehan 1983: 5–11); moreover, the third-person form follows on more naturally from ἀνθρώποισιν in line 2, better suits the speaker's detached observation of human behaviour, and makes the switch from third to first person at 23–4 more striking. οὐδὲν εἰδότες | . . . θεός: human ignorance of what the gods will bring to pass is a topos of gnomic literature: e.g. Thgn. 141–2 ἄνθρωποι δὲ μάταια νομίζομεν εἰδότες οὐδέν· | θεοὶ δὲ κατὰ σφέτερον πάντα τελοῦσι νόον, 1075–8, Mimn. 2.4–5*. ἕκαστον: neuter ('each thing'). ἐκτελευτήσει θεός: ring composition (with τέλος μὲν Ζεὺς ἔχει, 1) rounds off the first section of the poem.

6–10 depict the consequences of human ignorance, as everyone hopes in vain for wealth and success. For mankind's irrepressible, but foolish, optimism, cf. Sol. 13.33–42*.

6–7 ἐλπίς . . . | . . . ὁρμαίνοντας 'yet hope and faith nourish them all as they strive for the impossible'. ἐλπίς denotes the expectation of good things, which sustains and comforts humans. As in Hesiod's myth of Pandora's jar, where Ἐλπίς remains inside the jar as she scatters evils among men (*WD* 94–9), hope here offers some consolation, but it is scant compared with the many ills that beset mankind (11–22); cf. Sol. 13.36* χάσκοντες κούφαις ἐλπίσι τερπόμεθα. κἀπιπειθείη = καὶ ἐπιπειθείη (crasis: cf. 10 κἀγαθοῖσιν, 19 καὐτάγρετοι, 21 κἀνεπίφραστοι): the rare noun, first attested here, refers to people's idle trust in the future. τρέφει: hope is often said to 'nourish' (e.g. Soph. *Ant.* 897 κάρτ' ἐν ἐλπίσιν τρέφω, 1246 ἐλπίσιν δὲ βόσκομαι), but the metaphor also picks up on the image of humans as grazing animals (βοτά, 4).

7–10 οἱ . . . ἐλθεῖν: lit. 'some wait for a day to come'. i.e. expect their hopes will be realized the very next day. οἱ . . . περιτροπάς: lit. 'others for the turnings of years' (cf. *Il.* 2.295 περιτροπέων ἐνιαυτός), which emphasizes their tenacious, but self-deluding, optimism. νέωτα . . . | . . . φίλος 'and every single mortal thinks that next year he will be friends with Wealth and prosperity'. νέωτα is the object of ἵξεσθαι (lit. 'he will reach next year a friend, etc.'). δοκεῖ maintains the idea of (frustrated) 'expectation'. κἀγαθοῖσιν: probably neuter ('good things'), stressing the god's benefits, though 'good people' (masculine) is not impossible ('a friend of Wealth and high society').

11–22 list a series of disasters which come instead of the hoped-for blessings: old age (11–12) and illness (12–13), then death in war (13–14), at sea (15–17), and by suicide (18–19). The catalogue is articulated by an extended μέν . . . δέ construction (τὸν μέν (11) . . . τοὺς δέ (12) . . . τοὺς δ' (13) . . . οἱ δ' (15) . . . οἱ δ' (18) . . .).

11–12 φθάνει . . . | . . . ἵκηται 'one is overtaken by odious old age before he reaches his goal'. ἄζηλον: lit. 'unenviable'; for the miseries of old age, see Mimn. 1.6–10* and 2.9–16*.

12–13 τούς . . . | . . . νοῦσοι 'while others are destroyed by the grim diseases that afflict mortals': cf. Mimn. 2.15* ἄλλος νοῦσον ἔχει θυμοφθόρον.

13–14 Ἄρει δεδμημένους 'slain in war' (lit. 'laid low by Ares', perf. pass. part. δαμάζω). μελαίνης . . . χθονός: epic diction is more easily accommodate within elegy, but it can be deployed in iambus, whether for mock-epic effect (e.g. Semon. 7.105* ἐς μάχην κορύσσεται) or, as here, to suit the serious nature of the poem's reflective style: cf. Ζεύς ... βαρύκτυπος (1), λαίλαπι κλονεόμενοι (15), πορφυρῆς ἁλός (16), λείπουσιν ἠλίου φάος (19), μυρίαι ... κῆρες (20–1), Introduction §5.

15–17 For the risks involved in trying to make a living from the sea, see Sol. 13.43–6*. **λαίλαπι ... | ... ἁλός** 'battered by a gale and the heaving sea's many waves': cf. *Il.* 11.305–6 Ζέφυρος ... | ... βαθείηι λαίλαπι τύπτων, 16.391 ἐς δ' ἅλα πορφυρέην. **κλονεόμενοι:** synizesis of -εο-, scanned as one long syllable (as with -έω- in ἐτέων, 8). **πορφυρῆς:** the epithet can denote movement as well as colour (cf. πορφύρω, 'heave, surge'). **θνήσκουσιν** is emphasized by enjambment. **εὖτ' ... ζόειν** 'when they are unable to make a living', i.e. on land, as the context makes clear, since the sea/land antithesis is proverbial. The idea that only the desperate will resort to seafaring to earn a living is emphatically stated by Hesiod (enhancing his persona as a proud and grouchy farmer): cf. *WD* 236–7 οὐδ' ἐπὶ νηῶν | νίσονται, καρπὸν δὲ φέρει ζείδωρος ἄρουρα, 686–7 χρήματα γὰρ ψυχὴ πέλεται δειλοῖσι βροτοῖσιν. | δεινὸν δ' ἐστὶ θανεῖν μετὰ κύμασιν. **ζόειν:** for the sense, cf. Bacchyl. 1.167 ζώειν τ' ἀπ' οἰκείων ἔχει; for the short vowel, cf. ζόουσιν (4).

18–19 οἵ ... | ... φάος 'and others fasten a noose in a miserable death and leave the sun's light by their own choice': one possible motive is suggested by the wider context, as failure to realize their deluded ambitions (6–10 above) may in itself lead to suicide; cf. Thgn. 173–8, where Theognis recommends that Cyrnus kill himself to escape poverty ('by throwing yourself to the monsters of the deep or down from lofty cliffs', 175–6). **ἅψαντο:** gnomic aorist (the temporal augment is very occasionally omitted in early iambus and elegy: West 1974: 105). **καὐτάγρετοι:** from αὐτός + ἀγρέω ('take, seize'); cf. αὐθαίρετος, also used of suicide (Xen. *Hell.* 6.2.36 αὐθαιρέτωι θανάτωι ἀποθνήισκει). **λείπουσιν ... φάος:** another epic phrase (e.g. *Il.* 18.11 λείψειν φάος ἠελίοιο).

20–2 sum up (cf. οὕτω, 20) the catalogue of miseries (11–19) with a general statement on the inescapability of suffering (cf. Mimn. 2.11–16*). **οὕτω ... οὐδέν** 'so they are spared no calamity', lit. 'thus no evil is missing'; **ἀπ'** = ἄπεστι. **μυρίαι | ... κῆρες** 'countless deaths': cf. *Il.* 12.326–7, where Sarpedon presents the uncertainty of life as a reason for fighting in pursuit of glory, νῦν δ' ἔμπης γὰρ κῆρες ἐφεστᾶσιν θανάτοιο | μυρίαι, ἃς οὐκ ἔστι φυγεῖν βροτὸν οὐδ' ὑπαλύξαι; Mimn. 2.5–7*. **κἀνεπίφραστοι ... | ... πήματ'** 'and unforeseen sorrows and disasters': ἀνεπίφραστος (lit. 'unthought of'), attested only here, underscores once again the theme of human ignorance (cf. 1–5).

22–4 The poem ends by recommending that we *not* do the very thing it has spent so much time doing (dwelling on human misery). The reversal is arresting and encourages a different response to our precarious condition, focused on our opportunities for happiness, however temporary (cf. Gerber 1984: 134–5). πιθοίατο | ... ἐρῷμεν: the change from third to first person ('if they took my advice, we would not, etc.') is sudden and effective, for it not only includes us, the audience or reader, in the poet's analysis of human aspiration, but also expands the dialogue beyond the speaker and his addressee (ὦ παῖ, 1). πιθοίατο: 3rd pl. aor. opt. of πείθομαι (epic–Ionic -ατο for Attic -ντο). οὐκ ... ἐρῷμεν, lit. 'we would not long for evils' (a striking oxymoron), i.e. we would not allow ἐλπίς to give us false hopes of happiness or success (cf. 6–10). οὐδ' ... | ... αἰκιζοίμεθα 'nor would we torment ourselves by dwelling on our evil suffering': i.e. worrying about what might happen to us is useless and damaging, and so (by implication) we should live for the moment; cf. Semon. fr. 3 πολλὸς γάρ ἥμιν ἐστὶ τεθνάναι χρόνος, | ζῶμεν δ' ἀριθμῶι παῦρα <καὶ> κακῶς ἔτεα. The potentially erotic relationship between the speaker and his younger male addressee gives this *carpe diem* motif an added sexual resonance. Though some think the poem incomplete (e.g. Fränkel 1975: 202 'the portion preserved was followed by an injunction to enjoy life and the present moment, that is to say, an invitation to festive drinking'), the speaker's advice, punchily expressed, does not require elaboration. κακῶν ... κακοῖς: polyptoton emphasizes the futility of either attitude. ἐπ' ... θυμόν: for the construction, cf. Hes. *WD* 444–5 ἐπὶ ἔργωι | θυμὸν ἔχων. θυμόν is neatly placed between the two verbs that govern it.

Semonides 7

Source: Stobaeus 4.22.193.

This poem, which is probably complete (see 115–18n.), is quoted by the anthologist Stobaeus in a section dedicated to tirades against women (περὶ γάμου: ψόγος γυναικῶν). At 118 lines it is the longest non-hexameter poem to have survived from before the fifth century. Along with the work of his contemporary Hesiod (esp. *Theog.* 570–612, *WD* 59–99), Semonides' 'Satire on Women' represents the beginning of a long tradition of misogynistic speech in western literature, where a male speaker addresses a (usually) male audience on the subject of women's failings, and where, in contrast to (for example) Archilochus' attacks on specific women (frr. 188–91, 196a*), the speaker takes aim at the whole female sex (cf. Hippon. 68*, Eur. *Hipp.* 616–68, etc). Semonides, like Hesiod, sees women as a necessary evil, since their roles as wives and mothers are essential to the continuity of the (male-dominated) household and descent line (*Theog.* 602–12, Semon. 7.83–7, 115–16; so too Susarion, *IEG*² p. 167). However, in contrast to fr. 6 (γυναικὸς οὐδὲν χρῆμ' ἀνὴρ ληΐζεται | ἐσθλῆς ἄμεινον οὐδὲ ῥίγιον κακῆς), where Semonides reworks Hesiod (οὐ μὲν γάρ τι γυναικὸς ἀνὴρ ληίζετ' ἄμεινον | τῆς ἀγαθῆς, τῆς δ' αὖτε κακῆς οὐ ῥίγιον ἄλλο, *WD* 702–3) in a fairly straightforward manner, this poem plays with the genre of didactic poetry, not only parodying the grand comparisons of the Hesiodic *Catalogue of Women*, but also puncturing the smugness of its male audience, so that it becomes much more than a simple reflection of misogynistic clichés (see further below). On intertextuality between Semonides and Hesiod, cf. Loraux 1993: 72–110, Hunter 2014: 157–66, and, for a more positive view of marital relationships, Thgn. 1225–6*.

The poem's premise is that all women were created from one of eight different animals (sow, vixen, bitch, donkey, weasel, mare, monkey, bee) and two elements (earth and sea), and that they possess their various qualities (mostly bad). Though not strictly speaking a fable itself, the poem draws on the popular traditions of beast fable and proverb, using the natural world to articulate a particular view of human character and society, as Hesiod does with the hawk and the nightingale (*WD* 202–12) or Archilochus with the fox and the eagle (172–81*); for Semonides and the tradition of beast fable, see Brown 2018. Men and women are often compared to animals in early Greek literature, from Homeric similes (where, for example, hunting animals attacking livestock mirror male aggression) to erotic lyric (e.g. Anac. 417, where the male speaker eyes up a 'Thracian filly'), but the idea that women were created from animals goes further and is potentially more negative and dehumanizing. The animals are carefully chosen: they are everyday creatures (sow, bitch, donkey, weasel, mare, bee) or well-known figures of animal fable (fox and monkey: cf. Archil. 185–7). Their familiarity helps the poet create accessible vignettes of female/animal life, while the 'low' nature of women means there is no place for such creatures as the heroic lion of epic.

Moreover, since patriarchal Greek thought framed women as closer to animals and nature than the human ideal of the adult male (cf. Carson 1990, Dean-Jones 1994: 85, King 1998: 11), Semonides' choice of beasts and elements will have itself seemed 'natural', even if the details of each comparison are exaggerated for the sake of entertainment. The speaker's particular bias is evident, not least in the qualities he singles out as most typical of women: gluttony (sow, earth, donkey), cunning (vixen, monkey), changeability (vixen, sea), laziness (donkey, mare), and promiscuity (donkey, weasel). Only the bee-woman, paragon of wifely excellence, escapes censure; only she is presented as having children, thereby fulfilling the ultimate goal of female life (cf. 87n.). Phocylides, writing in hexameters in the mid-sixth century, may be drawing on Semonides (or a shared tradition of animal-to-woman fable) when he presents women as created from four animals, bitch, sow, mare, and bee; he expresses a similar wish to marry the last (fr. 2).

Semonides' poem is composed primarily to entertain and amuse, but its humour has a serious side, since it relies upon a range of gender stereotypes and cultural expectations. Women are presented as fundamentally different from men: both animal and human, wild and (in the case of the bee-woman at least) tamed, with failings that constantly threaten male happiness, prosperity, and esteem, as well as the legitimacy of a man's children. The poem thus tells us much about masculinity and male anxieties, and yet, despite its misogyny, shows the cultural ideal of a fond relationship between husband and wife (86 φίλη δὲ σὺν φιλέοντι γηράσκει πόσει; see 112–14n.). Moreover, there is a sting in the tail for the male audience, as the ending reveals all men to be naïve and deluded, for every man thinks his wife to be a bee-woman (112–14), and no one can escape the misogynist's dilemma of actually needing a wife (115–16). The speaker cleverly undercuts his audience's smugness, but there is no serious challenge to patriarchy, and the dehumanizing of women ultimately reinforces male superiority and solidarity.

The poem is well suited to performance at the all-male *symposion* (cf. Osborne 2001) and may have been composed with such a setting in mind, but its notional audience are men of average wealth and status, not elite aristocrats (see 57–70n.), and it would also work in the mixed setting of (for example) a public festival, provoking mutual teasing between the sexes. (For poems moving from one type of occasion to another, see Introduction §2; nonetheless, performance of Semon. 7 at betrothal or wedding banquets, supported by Schear 1984 and Rotstein 2010: 277, seems an unlikely scenario.) The poem might be received differently in a mixed setting, but its underlying sexist values, which dominated not only the *symposion* but society as a whole, would remain the same.

1–6 A brief statement of female diversity (1–2) leads straight into the first unflattering animal (the sow).

1–2 χωρὶς... | τὰ πρῶτα: 'in the beginning god made woman's mind in different forms'. **χωρίς:** lit. 'separate', i.e. different from each other, rather than different from the mind of man. The latter idea is implicit throughout, but the poem's focus will be the variety of female origins and (mis)conduct, and this is heralded by the word's initial position. Semonides differs in this respect from Hesiod, who presents all women as descended from a single figure, Pandora (*Theog.* 590 ἐκ τῆς γὰρ γένος ἐστὶ γυναικῶν θηλυτεράων), though both agree on the harm they cause men (*Theog.* 592 πῆμα μέγα θνητοῖσι). **θεός:** Zeus; cf. 72, 93, 94, 96, 115. **νόον:** in the sense 'character' (as evidenced by each woman's behaviour) rather than 'intelligence'; cf. *Od.* 1.3 πολλῶν δ' ἀνθρώπων ἴδεν ἄστεα καὶ νόον ἔγνω. In Hesiod Zeus orders Hermes to give Pandora κύνεόν τε νόον καὶ ἐπίκλοπον ἦθος (*WD* 67). **τὰ πρῶτα** (adverbial neuter pl.) 'in the beginning':

COMMENTARY: SEMONIDES 7   93

creation stories are a popular subject for animal fable; cf. Aesop, *Fab.*
240 Perry, 'Following Zeus's orders, Prometheus fashioned humans and
animals. When Zeus saw that the animals far outnumbered the humans,
he ordered Prometheus to reduce the number of the animals by turning
them into people. Prometheus did as he was told, and as a result those
people who were originally animals have a human body but a bestial soul.'

2 τὴν μέν marks the start of the catalogue, with τὴν δέ for each subsequent animal or element (7, 12, etc.) in a simple additive style. Monotony
is avoided by the vivid detail of each scene and the author's ingenuity in
making parallels between the natural and human worlds. **ὑός:** the speaker
begins his 'argument' with perhaps the most familiar animal: pigs were the
main source of meat in ancient Greece, and pig-breeding is described in
detail in the *Odyssey* (e.g. 14.5–20). **τανύτριχος**, 'long-bristled', applied to
a woman, evokes the epic epithet τανύσφυρος ('slender-ankled'); for other
mock-epic phrases, cf. 14 πάντηι παπταίνουσα, 105 ἐς μάχην κορύσσεται.

3–4 τῆι ... | ... χαμαί 'throughout her house everything lies in disorder, smeared with mud, and rolls about on the floor'. **βορβόρωι:** for pigs'
enjoyment of mud, cf. Heraclit. fr. 13 DK (= D80a Laks–Most) ὕες βορβόρωι
ἥδονται μᾶλλον ἢ καθαρῶι ὕδατι. **πεφυρμένα:** cf. LSJ φύρω, 'to mix something
dry with something wet, mostly with a sense of ... to spoil or defile'. Zeus
orders Hephaestus to mix earth with water (*WD* 61 γαῖαν ὕδει φύρειν) to
create Pandora (cf. 21–6n.).

5–6 ἄλουτος ἀπλύτοις: alpha-privates and synonymy ('unwashed, in
unlaundered clothes') emphasize the sow-woman's personal squalor. **ἐν ...
πιαίνεται** 'sits on the dungheap and eats herself fat': a grotesque image,
intensified by the juxtaposition of a word normally used of humans
(ἡμένη) with one normally used of animals (πιαίνεται). Since pigs supplied meat, fattening was important; like them the sow-woman consumes
household scraps, but to no good end, for she simply makes herself ugly
and is a drain on the household. Similar ideas recur in later scenes: e.g.
the earth-woman knows only how to eat (24), the donkey-woman eats all
day and all night (47).

7–8 ἀλιτρῆς ... ἀλώπεκος 'a wicked vixen': foxes stole food of all
kinds, and were hunted as predators and for their meat and fur. Their
cunning was proverbial and often featured in animal fable: e.g. Archil.
185.5–6 (the fox and the monkey) τῶι δ' ἄρ' ἀλώπηξ κερδαλῆ συνήντετο, |
πυκνὸν ἔχουσα νόον; cf. Sol. 11.5* ἀλώπεκος ἴχνεσι βαίνει. **πάντων ἴδριν:** lit.
'who knows everything'; but ἀλιτρῆς and the fox's reputation for cunning
suggest 'knowledgeable in every trick' (cf. Archil. 201 πόλλ' οἶδ' ἀλώπηξ,
ἀλλ' ἐχῖνος ἓν μέγα).

8–9 οὐδέ ... | ... ἀμεινόνων 'nothing bad escapes her nor anything
good': she understands what is good and what is evil, but as the following
phrase makes clear (γάρ, 10), she has no sense of morality.

10–11 τό . . . ἐσθλόν 'for she often calls the good bad and the bad good'. αὐτῶν: i.e. κακὰ καὶ ἀμείνονα, with τὸ μὲν . . . τὸ δέ . . . picking out good and evil in turn. ὀργὴν . . . ἔχει 'she has a different attitude at different times': the vixen-woman has no consistent outlook, but changes to suit the situation and her own advantage; contrast Thgn. 215–18, where the speaker *recommends* the cunning of the octopus (πουλύπου ὀργὴν ἴσχε πολυπλόκου), who takes on the look of the rock he clings to, 'for cleverness beats consistency' (κρέσσων τοι σοφίη γίνεται ἀτροπίης). ἄλλοτ' ἀλλοίην: cf. Hes. *WD* 483 ἄλλοτε δ' ἀλλοῖος Ζηνὸς νόος αἰγιόχοιο.

12–20 The bitch-woman is characterized by nosiness, endless yapping, and shamelessness.

12 λιτοργόν: the first of two disputed *hapax legomena* (λιτοργόν, αὐτομήτορα); the first is probably best understood as the Ionic form of λιτουργόν ('wicked'), which Hesychius glosses as κακοῦργον, i.e. from λιτός ('bad') + ἔργον. Verdenius 1977: 2 takes it to mean 'irascible', from λιτ- ('very') + ὀργή. West translates 'slut', reinforcing his interpretation of αὐτομήτορα (see next note). αὐτομήτορα 'just like her mother'; for the idea 'like mother, like daughter', cf. 57 τὴν δ' ἵππος ἁβρὴ χαιτέεσσ' ἐγείνατο. West 1974: 178 suggests 'it might mean "giving birth without her husband's consent", i.e. promiscuous', but such an interpretation of αὐτός-compounds is unparalleled.

13–14 πάντ' . . . πάντα . . . | πάντηι: the repetition emphasizes her infuriating nosiness. πᾶς words are used rhetorically throughout to stress the women's failings (e.g. 3, 35, 78, 81, 100). πάντηι . . . παπταίνουσα: mock-epic language; cf. *Od*. 12.232–3 (Odysseus looking for Scylla) ἔκαμον δέ μοι ὄσσε | πάντηι παπταίνοντι πρὸς ἠεροειδέα πέτρην.

15 λέληκεν: the perfect (from λάσκω) expresses a continuous state, here the bitch-woman's incessant 'yelping' as she jabbers to herself. ἢν . . . ὁρᾶι, 'even if she sees no human being', likens her to a guard-dog, but points the difference: unlike the barking of a good watch-dog (cf. *Od*. 14.29–31, where Odysseus' arrival is detected by Eumaeus' dogs), hers is pointless and never stops.

16–18 The easy assumption of threats and domestic violence reveals the darkest side of the audience's patriarchal worldview. Significantly, the speaker thinks of using intimidation before resorting to 'gentle words' (μειλίχως μυθεόμενος, 18). Ancient sources (especially oratory) focus on the repercussions of violence between men (cf. Todd 2007: 285–6); domestic violence goes largely unrecorded and unchallenged. ἐξαράξειεν . . . ὀδόντας, 'knock out her teeth with a stone' (3rd sg. aor. opt. of ἐξαράσσω); Eumaeus scatters his dogs with a barrage of stones (*Od*. 14.35–6).

19 παρὰ ξείνοισιν 'among guests': the speaker often exploits his audience's sensitivity to the judgement and potential mockery of others (e.g. 74 πᾶσιν ἀνθρώποις γέλως, 84 κείνηι γὰρ οἴηι μῶμος οὐ προσιζάνει, 110–11 οἱ

COMMENTARY: SEMONIDES 7   95

δὲ γείτονες | χαίρουσ'), including (as here) the reaction of male guests (cf. 29, 107). In the Classical period a woman was not to be present when her husband entertained visitors; Semonides' poem is evidence of a slightly less segregationist (but no less sexist) society. The bitch-woman's indifference to how she is perceived by others is a mark of her shamelessness, a quality often associated with dogs, who perform shameful acts in public: e.g. *Il*. 1.225 κυνῶπα (Achilles to Agamemnon), 3.180 κυνώπιδος (Helen on herself).

20 ἀλλ'... ἔχει 'but ceaselessly she keeps up a yapping which nothing can be done about'. West prints αὐονήν ('dryness, withering') and translates 'all the time he has this hopeless blight', but the transmitted αὐονήν (another *hapax*, from αὔω, 'cry') keeps the focus on the unbearable racket made by the bitch-woman. ἔχει is used in epic of maintaining sound (e.g. *Il*. 18.495 αὐλοὶ φόρμιγγές τε βοὴν ἔχον).

21–42 The only two female types not derived from animals are nonetheless associated with natural elements and given their typical qualities: the earth-woman is stupid and inert, the sea-woman unpredictable and dangerous.

21–6 Pandora, the first woman, is created from earth: αὐτίκα δ' ἐκ γαίης πλάσσε κλυτὸς Ἀμφιγυήεις (Hes. *WD* 70). For women's association with earth, especially dirt, in ancient Greek thought, see Carson 1990: 158–60.

21–2 γηΐνην 'made of earth': the adj. is first attested here. **Ὀλύμπιοι:** a variation on the more prominent figure of Zeus (cf. 1–2n.), though it may be significant that Hesiod presents multiple deities contributing to the creation of Pandora (*WD* 60–82). **πηρόν**, 'feeble-minded', more often refers to physical disability, but is used here of mental incapacity, as the following clause (γάρ, 22) makes clear.

22–3 οὔτε...|... οἶδε: whereas the vixen-woman abuses her knowledge of good and evil (8–11), the earth-woman is ignorant of both.

24 ἔργων... ἐπίσταται 'the only work she understands is eating'; ἔργων suggests the domestic tasks and skills expected of a wife and underlines the earth-woman's uselessness. For eating as a symbol of both gluttony and women's drain on resources, cf. 6 (the sow-woman ἡμένη πιαίνεται), 46–7 (the donkey-woman ἐσθίει μὲν ἐν μυχῶι | προνὺξ προῆμαρ, ἐσθίει δ' ἐπ' ἐσχάρηι).

25–6 κακὸν χειμῶνα 'harsh winter weather'. **ῥιγῶσα... πυρός** 'she shivers and draws her stool closer to the fire', i.e. she just sits there rather than stoking the fire or making herself useful.

27–42 The changeability of the sea (cf. *WD* 663–5, where Hesiod suggests limiting sailing to July and August) and the fickleness of women (Dover 1974: 100) were clichés of Greek popular thought.

27 ἥ... νοεῖ 'who has two moods', which she displays randomly from one day to another: τὴν μὲν... ἡμέρην (28) ... τὴν δ' [sc. ἡμέρην] (32).

28 γελᾶι... γέγηθεν: alliteration emphasizes her smiling, happy demeanour.

29 ἐπαινέσει ... ξεῖνος: for a man's concern with other men's opinion of his wife, cf. 19n.

30–1 λωΐων ... | ... οὐδὲ καλλίων 'better or more beautiful': men evidently took pride in their wives' good looks; cf. 67–8 (the mare-woman is 'a lovely sight for others'), 73–4 (the monkey-woman's ugliness is ridiculed).

32 ἐν ὀφθαλμοῖς ἰδεῖν: an epic phrase, contrasting this encounter with the other (ἰδών, 29).

33–4 ἀλλὰ ... | ... κύων: the bitch's fierce protection of her puppies was proverbial; cf. *Od.* 20.14–15 (a simile describing Odysseus' anger towards the suitors) ὡς δὲ κύων ἀμαλῇσι περὶ σκυλάκεσσι βεβῶσα | ἄνδρ' ἀγνοιήσασ' ὑλάει μέμονέν τε μάχεσθαι. **ἄπλητον** 'unapproachably' (adverbial acc.), a disputed word, probably equivalent here to ἄπλατος ('unapproachable, terrible') rather than ἄπλετος ('boundless, immense').

35–6 ἀμείλιχος ... κἀποθυμίη 'implacable and hateful [= καὶ ἀποθυμίη] to everyone'; ἀμείλιχος, ον, is a two-termination adjective, using the masculine for the feminine. **ἐχθροῖσιν ... φίλοισι** 'enemies and friends alike'; contrast the Homeric ideal of the harmonious married couple who are united in their treatment of enemies and friends, πόλλ' ἄλγεα δυσμενέεσσι, | χάρματα δ' εὐμενέτηισι (*Od.* 6.184–5). **γίνεται** 'shows herself'; cf. 68 τῶι δ' ἔχοντι γίνεται κακόν.

37–42 This description of the sea is the only time the speaker dwells on the substance from which the woman is made and makes an explicit comparison (ὥσπερ ... ταύτηι, similar to the common Homeric simile structure 'as ... so ...'); contrast the much briefer ὥσπερ πίθηκος (79). The sea's two-fold nature is articulated by the balance and contrast of πολλάκις μὲν (37) ... πολλάκις δέ (39), mirroring τὴν μὲν ἡμέρην (28) ... τὴν δ' (32) used of the sea-woman's unpredictable moods.

37–9 ἀτρεμὴς | ... ἀπήμων 'stands motionless and harmless'. For ἀπήμων of the sea, cf. τῆμος δ' [i.e. in the sailing season] εὐκρινέες τ' αὖραι καὶ πόντος ἀπήμων (Hes. *WD* 670). **χάρμα ... μέγα**, 'a great delight to those who sail', stands in apposition to θάλασσα. **θέρεος ... ὥρηι** 'in the summer season', the ideal time for sailing; cf. Hes. *WD* 664–5 ἐς τέλος ἐλθόντος θέρεος ... | ὡραῖος πέλεται θνητοῖς πλόος, 27–42n.

39–40 πολλάκις ... | ... φορεομένη 'but often it rages, tossed about by thunderous waves'. **βαρυκτύποισι:** for the epithet, used of Poseidon as well as Zeus, see on Semon. 1.1–2*.

41–2 The simile concludes by returning to the sea-woman and repeating the point of comparison. Some have found the couplet flat and the use of ἀλλοίην suspicious (e.g. Hordern 2002). However, the meaning is clear (see below), and a 'just so ...' phrase is typical and expected after the initial ὥσπερ. **ταύτηι** refers back to θάλασσα (37). **ὀργήν** 'in her temperament' (acc. of respect). φυήν ... ἔχει 'the sea has a changeable nature': some argue that ἀλλοίην alone cannot mean 'variable' and they point to the description of the equally quixotic vixen-woman, ὀργὴν δ' ἄλλοτ' ἀλλοίην ἔχει (11); cf. e.g. Renehan 1983: 11–12, who suggests deleting ὀργήν in line 42 and reading φυὴν δὲ πόντος <ἄλλοτ'> ἀλλοίην ἔχει. But the idea of different times (ἄλλοτε) is implicit (cf. τὴν μὲν ἡμέρην ... τὴν δ', πολλάκις μέν ... πολλάκις δέ) and ἀλλοῖος can be used on its own with such a sense (cf. LSJ 2 'containing or subject to diversity'), even if its coupling with ἄλλοτε is more common.

43–9 The donkey-woman is work-shy (like the mare-woman: 58–61), gluttonous (like the sow-woman and earth-woman: 6, 24), and promiscuous (like the weasel-woman: 53). Donkeys were indispensable to the ancient economy and daily life (cf. Thgn. 183–5n.), but literary portrayals tend to ignore their good qualities in order to contrast them negatively with horses; on this 'equine hierarchy', see Griffith 2006, Gregory 2007. Here both the donkey and the horse are presented unfavourably, though the lower-class donkey-woman, unlike the pampered mare-woman, cannot escape her domestic duties for ever.

43 ἐκ ... ὄνου 'from an ash-grey donkey that has suffered many blows'. σποδιῆς τε offers the least intrusive correction of the transmitted τὴν δ' ἔκ τε σποδιῆς (which is unmetrical); for other suggestions, e.g. τεφρῆς τε ('ash-grey'), στερεῆς τε ('stubborn'), see Fenno 2005. παλιντριβέος, 'struck repeatedly', marks the donkey's obstinacy, famously depicted in the Homeric simile describing Ajax' reluctant retreat (Il. 11.558–62); but the word also suggests the potential use of violence against the donkey-woman herself (cf. 16–18n.).

44–6 ἀνάγκηι ... ἐνιπῆισιν 'after beatings and curses'. μόγις 'against her will' (lit. 'with difficulty'). ἔστερξεν ... ἄπαντα 'consents to everything': gnomic aor. of στέργω ('acquiesce, endure', LSJ III 2); so too ἐπονήσατο, with crasis. ὦν (Ionic for οὖν), 'after all' (lit. 'in fact'), emphasizes the futility of the donkey-woman's refusal to perform her tasks in 43–4. κἀπονήσατο | ἀρεστά, 'and does her work to an acceptable standard', reveals a typically patronizing view of women's domestic duties.

46–7 The donkey-woman eats throughout the house and all the time (cf. 5–6, 24nn.). Unlike horses, donkeys were often given very basic and minimal feed; if hunger forced them to eat things like thistles, nettles, and twigs, this may have led to a reputation for greediness. τόφρα δ' 'but meanwhile', i.e. while she should be working. ἐν μυχῶι | ... ἐπ' ἐσχάρηι, 'in the back room ... and at the hearth', emphasizes her uncontrollable gluttony, since neither is the proper place for eating; Hesiod's bad wife is called a δειπνολόχος, 'dinner-ambusher' (WD 704). προνὺξ προῆμαρ 'all night, all day': the jingling phrase has a colloquial ring, though both words are attested only here (for consecutive *hapax legomena*, cf.

12) These προ- compounds were probably created by analogy with the Homeric phrase πρόπαν ἦμαρ (*Il.* 1.601, etc.), a strengthened form of πανῆμαρ.

48–9 ὁμῶς δέ 'and likewise': the donkey-woman's insatiable desire for sex matches her appetite for food. The hypersexuality often attributed to male donkeys in early Greek literature and vase-painting (e.g. Archil. 43, Pind. *Pyth.* 10.36; cf. Gregory 2007: 204–5) is here transferred to the female, reflecting the male speaker's anxiety about women's fidelity (cf. 53, 90–1). **ἔργον ἀφροδίσιον:** a variation on the common periphrasis 'the works of Aphrodite' (cf. 'the works of Ares' meaning 'war'); Hesiod, for example, describes a young unmarried girl as οὔ πω ἔργ' εἰδυῖα πολυχρύσου Ἀφροδίτης (*WD* 521). **ἐλθόντ'... ἐδέξατο** 'she welcomes [gnomic aor.] any partner that comes along'. **ἑταῖρον:** for the sense 'sexual partner', cf. Ar. *Eccl.* 912 οὐχ ἥκει μοὐταῖρος. **ὁντινῶν** = ὅντιν' οὖν ('any at all').

50–6 The weasel-woman is repulsive (as is the ugly monkey-woman: 73–7), lascivious (like the donkey-woman: 48–9), and a thief. Weasels were popular domestic animals kept to hunt mice and small snakes (a role gradually taken over by cats), but the speaker predictably ignores their usefulness.

50–2 δύστηνον... γένος 'a miserable, wretched creature', in apposition to τήν. **οὔ τι καλόν... | ... οὐδ' ἐράσμιον:** the barrage of negatives could hardly be more insistent. The weasel-woman's repulsiveness may draw on the animal's proverbially unpleasant smell; e.g. Ar. *Wealth* 693 ὑπὸ τοῦ δέους βδέουσα δριμύτερον γαλῆς ('farting in fear, stinkier than a weasel').

53–4 εὐνῆς... ἀφροδισίης 'she is mad for the bed of love'. **ἀληνής:** a *hapax*, glossed by Hesychius as μαινόμενος. This gives much better sense than Winterton's ἀδηνής, 'inexperienced' (adopted by West). The weasel's sexual appetite features in an Aesopic fable (*Fab.* 50 Perry): a weasel fell in love with a handsome young man and was transformed into a woman by Aphrodite so she could marry him (there is no happy ending); cf. Brown 1997: 73–4. **τὸν... διδοῖ** 'and makes whatever man she is with queasy'. **τὸν παρεόντα:** cf. Thgn. 1367–8 on female infidelity, παιδός τοι χάρις ἐστί· γυναικὶ δὲ πιστὸς ἑταῖρος | οὐδείς, ἀλλ' αἰεὶ τὸν παρεόντα φιλεῖ. **ναυσίηι:** the man is sickened by her generally disgusting presence (see 50–2); but the more literal meaning 'sea-sickness' (Ionic ναυσίη = Attic ναυτία), implying that her partner's nausea is caused by her movements during sex, is also possible.

55–6 The weasel-woman steals not only from her neighbours (γείτονας) but also from the gods. **κλέπτουσα:** Pandora, the first woman, was given a 'thievish character' (ἐπίκλοπον ἦθος, Hes. *WD* 67, 78). **ἄθυστα... κατεσθίει** 'and she often devours unburnt sacrifices', i.e. she steals sacrificial offerings that still await consecration (ἄθυστα = ἄθυτα, 'not successfully offered'); for weasels stealing meat intended for sacrifice, cf. Ar. *Thesm.* 558–9. The verb κατεσθίω is often applied to scavengers or predators (e.g. Hecuba's warning to Hector: ἄνευθε δέ σε μέγα νῶϊν | Ἀργείων παρὰ νηυσὶ κύνες ταχέες κατέδονται, *Il.* 22.88–9); its use here emphasizes the weasel-woman's greed and furtiveness. For more unpleasant eating, cf. 6, 24, 46–7.

57–70 The mare-woman is beautiful but also lazy, luxurious, and vain. While the horse could serve as a positive symbol of female beauty, as in Alcman's maiden-songs (fr. 1.45–59), here the mare-woman's attractiveness comes at too high a price. Such a woman is good for tyrants and kings but not for ordinary people (69–70). Thus her presentation in particular reflects the socio-economic status of the poem's notional audience, who are people of average standing, not great lords. The scene also shows how women's status and role differed according to their own socio-economic position. A wealthy king wants a trophy wife: female beauty and daintiness are desirable for him, and he does not need or indeed want a wife who works. The average man, however, needs a wife who will pull her weight about the house, and beauty is not a priority; tellingly, the ideal bee-woman is not singled out for her looks. Finally, the scene represents a humorous dig at men who are taken in by beauty and end up with a useless wife.

57 ἵππος ἁβρὴ χαιτέεσσ' 'a luxurious, long-maned mare': for similar polemic against 'useless luxury' (ἁβροσύνας . . . ἀνωφελέας), cf. Xenoph. 3.1*. A horse's pride in its mane is used to characterize the self-satisfied Paris, ὑψοῦ δὲ κάρη ἔχει, ἀμφὶ δὲ χαῖται | ὤμοις ἀΐσσονται (*Il.* 6.509–10).

58–62 Whereas the donkey-woman works reluctantly, the mare-woman does no work at all (for the role of social class, see 43–9, 57–70nn.). ἣ . . . περιτρέπει 'who pushes slavish chores and trouble upon others'. δούλι' neatly captures the mare-woman's own view of household tasks. περιτρέπει: the verb ('turn around, divert') is used elsewhere of transferring responsibility; cf. Lys. 6.13 ὑμεῖς οὖν μὴ βούλεσθε εἰς ὑμᾶς τὴν αἰτίαν ταύτην περιτρέψαι. μύλης . . . κόσκινον | . . . κόπρον . . . | . . . ἰπνόν, 'millstone ... sieve ... dung ... oven', are everyday words (so too ἀσβόλη, 'soot') giving a representative sample of a wife's routine duties. Even an upper-class woman, who might not be expected to do these things herself, should at least supervise the slaves who do. **μύλης . . . κόσκινον:** i.e. grinding and sieving corn to make bread, an essential part of daily life. ἄρειεν 'lift', 3rd sg. aor. opt. of ἀείρω. **οὔτε . . . | ἵζοιτ'** 'or sit by the oven, since she avoids soot'.

62 ἀνάγκηι . . . φίλον 'she makes her husband well acquainted with necessity': her poor household management (58–62), coupled with her expensive addiction to hot baths and perfume (63–4), threaten to impoverish her husband: cf. 69–70, 101–2; also Thgn. 351–2 ἆ δειλὴ Πενίη . . . | . . . μὴ δή μ' οὐκ ἐθέλοντα φίλει. Horses were notoriously expensive to keep (e.g. Ar. *Clouds* 83–5), and the same is true of the mare-woman. By contrast, the industrious bee-woman increases her husband's prosperity (85 θάλλει δ' ὑπ' αὐτῆς κἀπαέξεται βίος). Some interpret the line as 'she makes a man her lover by necessity' (i.e. her beauty overpowers a man's disapproval of her behaviour), but her economic rather than erotic impact is more relevant to the context.

63–4 λοῦται . . . ῥύπον 'she washes the dirt off herself every day'. **λοῦται . . . ἄπο** = ἀπολοῦται (tmesis), with a recessive accent on the verbal prefix (ἀπό) when it comes after its verb (anastrophe: Smyth §175, *CGCG* §§24.37, 60.14); ἀπολοῦται implies a full bath in warm water, rather than a quick wash, at considerable expense. For bathing as a symbol of a luxurious lifestyle in general, see Ar. *Clouds* 837–8. (Men had access to bath-houses; women washed at home.) **δίς . . . τρίς** 'twice, sometimes three times': enjambment emphasizes the excess, especially after πάσης ἡμέρης (i.e. once every day would be bad enough). **καὶ . . . ἀλείφεται** 'and anoints herself with perfume': perfumes were expensive and so could be seen (like frequent baths) as luxurious and decadent.

65–6 αἰεὶ . . . | . . . ἐσκιασμένην 'she always wears her lush hair combed out and decked with flowers'. **αἰεί**, i.e. not just for special occasions, stresses the extravagance. **χαίτην** recalls her mother's 'mane' (χαιτέεσσ', 57). **βαθεῖαν** (lit. 'thick') denotes the hair's luxuriant fullness; cf. Ἀρισταῖος βαθυχαίτης (Hes. *Theog.* 977). **ἀνθέμοισιν:** ἄνθεμον (neuter) is a rare poetic equivalent of ἄνθος.

67–8 καλόν . . . | ἄλλοισι, τῶι δ' ἔχοντι . . . κακόν: chiasmus and enjambment underline the contrast ('a lovely sight for others, but ...'). **ὦν** (= οὖν) emphasizes μέν, which is then answered by δέ. **καλὸν . . . θέημα . . . | ἄλλοισι:** despite the positive reaction of others, the mare-woman's husband cannot take pleasure in her good looks (cf. 30–1n.). **τῶι δ' ἔχοντι** '[but evil comes] to the man who has her': cf. LSJ ἔχω A I 4 'have to wife or as husband (usually without γυναῖκα, ἄνδρα)'; ἤν τι καὶ δοκέωσιν ὠφελεῖν | ἔχοντι (97–8).

69–70 ἤν . . . ἧι 'unless he is some tyrant or sceptre-bearing king': only a very wealthy man could afford to maintain such a woman. **τύραννος:** the word is first attested here, though Archilochus has τυραννίς (19.3*) and (probably) τυραννίη (23.20). **σκηπτοῦχος:** a Homeric epithet applied to βασιλεύς (or βασιλῆες), but also used by itself (ὅς τις . . . | σκηπτοῦχός τ' εἴη, *Il.* 14.92–3). **ὅστις . . . ἀγλαΐζεται** 'whose heart delights in such creatures': his expensive and high-maintenance wife serves as a symbol of his own success; see 57–70n. **τοιούτοις:** as often in Ionic the first syllable (usually scanned long: e.g. τοιοῦτον, 77) is shortened before another vowel; cf. Semon. 1.4* ζόουσιν, 1.17* ζόειν, West 1974: 79.

71–82 The monkey-woman is exceptionally ugly, devious, shameless, and malevolent. Archilochus' contemporary fable of the fox and the monkey shows a proud monkey outwitted by an even more cunning opponent (frr. 185–7; see further on 75–6 below). Monkeys were kept

COMMENTARY: SEMONIDES 7   101

as luxury pets or for entertainment, since their talent for imitation was found amusing.

71–2 διακριδὸν | . . . μέγιστον . . . κακόν 'absolutely the biggest evil': the catalogue of bad women culminates in the worst of all, enhancing the contrast with the ideal bee-woman who comes afterwards. **Ζεύς:** cf. 1–2n. **ὤπασεν:** meant ironically, since ὀπάζω, 'bestow', is usually used of giving positive things (e.g. honour, wealth, beauty, etc.); contrast χαρίζεται (92), where Zeus's favour is genuine.

73–7 focus on the monkey-woman's physical repulsiveness, 78–82 on her awful character, and the two sections are linked by μέν (73) . . . δέ (78). For the link between looks and character, cf. e.g. Homer's Thersites (αἴσχιστος δὲ ἀνὴρ ὑπὸ Ἴλιον ἦλθε, *Il.* 2.216) and the disgusting weasel-woman (50–4).

73–4 αἴσχιστα . . . πρόσωπα 'her face is hideous': on the monkey's proverbial ugliness, cf. Pind. *Pyth.* 2.72–3 καλός τοι πίθων παρὰ παισίν, αἰεί | καλός ('Pretty is the monkey in the eyes of children, pretty indeed!'). **ἄστεος . . . γέλως:** public ridicule of the monkey-woman's looks brings shame on her husband too (cf. 30–1, 67–8nn.).

75–6 Asyndeton enhances the punchy list of complaints: 'short neck, moves awkwardly, no bum, all legs'. **κινεῖται μόγις** reflects the monkey's gait when trying to walk on two legs. **ἄπυγος:** lit. 'without buttocks'. Hesiod by contrast warns against the woman who flaunts her attractive behind: μηδὲ γυνή σε νόον πυγοστόλος ἐξαπατάτω (*WD* 373); sex-workers could use padding if they were under-endowed, ὥστε τὴν εὐπυγίαν | ἀναβοᾶν τοὺς εἰσιδόντας (Alexis fr. 103.11–12 K–A; Arnott 1996: 276–7). The monkey's lack of buttocks was felt to be comic. In Archilochus' fable the monkey is trapped with his bum sticking up into the air, and the fox mocks him, τοιήνδε δ', ὦ πίθηκε, τὴν πυγὴν ἔχων (fr. 187); similarly, in the Aesopic version, where the monkey's dancing has won him the title of king of the animals, the fox asks the trapped animal, ὦ πίθηκε, σὺ δὲ τοιαύτην πυγὴν ἔχων τῶν ἀλόγων ζῴων βασιλεύεις; (*Fab.* 81 Perry). A monkey's bum, lacking hair, would be particularly visible, making it a likely subject of mockery. **αὐτόκωλος,** 'all legs', stresses her lack of buttocks.

76–7 ἆ τάλας ἀνήρ 'Ah, poor man': the speaker's seemingly serious language and pitying tone have a comic effect. **ἀγκαλίζεται,** 'embraces', is deliberately placed last, summing up the monkey-woman's physical faults and concluding the section devoted to them (73–7n.).

78–9 δήνεα . . . ἐπίσταται 'she knows all the tricks and schemes': monkeys were proverbially tricky and deceptive (e.g. Ar. *Ach.* 905–7), qualities shared with the vixen-woman (7–11). **ὥσπερ πίθηκος:** 37–42n. **οὐδέ . . . μέλει,** 'nor does she mind being laughed at' (rather than 'she doesn't like a joke' (West)), picks up γέλως (74) and stresses the monkey-woman's shamelessness, a failing also possessed by the bitch-woman (19).

80–2 The monkey-woman's explicit malevolence rounds off the catalogue of bad female types. οὐδ'... ἔρξειεν 'she'd do no one any good' (3rd sg. aor. opt. of ἔρδω). Repetition (τοῦτ'... | καὶ τοῦτο; ὅκως τι κὼς) and synonymy (ὁρᾶι | ... βουλεύεται, 'looks to ... and plans') underline her one and only goal. ἔρξειεν κακόν: the contrast with εὖ ἔρξειεν (80) stresses her constant ill will towards everyone.

83–93 The bee-woman is a paragon of industry, affection, motherhood, and fidelity. Whereas Hesiod compares women to parasitic drones living off the labour of productive 'worker bees', i.e. men (*Theog.* 594–602; cf. *WD* 302–6), Semonides extends the animal's reputation for hard work to the female sex, or at least to one small part of it.

84 κείνηι ... προσιζάνει 'on this woman alone does no blame settle': the verb προσιζάνω is used of insects landing on flowers; the metaphor thus imagines 'blame' as a troublesome insect, flying from woman to woman, but not landing on the bee-woman.

85 θάλλει ... βίος, 'and under her management resources flourish and increase', contrasts the bee-woman's positive effect with the drain on the household represented by other female types (cf. 6, 24, 46–7, 58–66, 101–2). θάλλει continues the flower imagery.

86 φίλη ... φιλέοντι: both elements of this *figura etymologica* are active ('loving'), stressing the mutual affection of wife and husband (for the classic statement of marital 'harmony', see *Od.* 6.180–5). γηράσκει adds the idea of enduring love.

87 τεκοῦσα ... γένος 'having borne beautiful and glorious offspring': significantly, the bee-woman is the only female type who is presented as having children, underlining her status as the ideal wife. Female sexuality is spoken of here in terms of its 'proper' purpose (cf. 90–1), in contrast to the shameful promiscuity of other women (48–9, 53–4). κὠνομάκλυτον = καὶ ὀνομάκλυτον (crasis): the grand epithet exalts the bee-woman's maternal role.

88–9 καριπρεπής: the epic word ἀριπρεπής, 'outstanding', enhances her exceptional status. θείη ... χάρις 'and divine grace surrounds her': a further epic image (cf. e.g. *Od.* 2.12 θεσπεσίην δ' ἄρα τῶι γε χάριν κατέχευεν Ἀθήνη) expresses the bee-woman's miraculous charm. In contrast to the dangerous χάρις of Pandora, a sexual allure which leads men astray (Hes. *WD* 65–6), the bee-woman's 'grace' comes from her success as a wife and mother (see Hunter 2014: 161–2).

90–1 Bees were symbols of chastity and purity, and various goddesses and priestesses were described as 'bees', e.g. Artemis (Ar. *Frogs* 1273–4), Demeter (Callim. *Hymn* 2.110), and the Pythia (Pind. *Pyth.* 4.60). However, unlike (for example) the abnormally asexual Hippolytus, who brings Artemis a garland from 'an untouched meadow' populated by bees (ἀλλ' ἀκήρατον | μέλισσα λειμῶν' ἠρινή διέρχεται, Eur. *Hipp.* 76–7), the bee-woman has the correct attitude to sex, doing her bit for the sake of legitimate children (87) and shunning other women 'when they talk about sex' (91). Greek patriarchal ideology framed women as lascivious and always gossiping about sex (e.g. Ar. *Lys.* 21–5, *Thesm.* 471–519; on the threat posed by such gossip, see McClure 1999: 56–62): the bee-woman's restraint is a sign of her ideal σωφροσύνη (cf. 108 σωφρονεῖν δοκεῖ).

92–3 τοίας γυναῖκας 'women like her'. **ἀνδράσιν ... | Ζεύς** 'which Zeus bestows upon men': though his bad female types outnumber the good (nine to one), the god is responsible for this rare blessing (cf. 1, 72, 94, 96, 115). **πολυφραδεστάτας**, 'most sensible', sums up the bee-woman's combination of intellectual and moral excellence.

94–118 Having described the ten separate types, the poem concludes with general reflection on the evil nature of women.

94–5 τά ... | ... μένει 'but those other breeds, by Zeus's design, all exist and remain with men'. The speaker moves from the admirable bee-woman to general condemnation of women by reminding his audience of the nine bad φῦλα. **ταῦτα** is contemptuous (cf. LSJ οὗτος C I 3). **μένει:** for Zeus has ensured that men cannot do without them; cf. 83–7, 115–16, Hes. *Theog.* 602–12.

96–7 The same idea underlies Hesiod's misogyny: ὡς δ' αὔτως ἀνδρεσσι κακὸν θνητοῖσι γυναῖκας | Ζεὺς ὑψιβρεμέτης θῆκε (*Theog.* 600–1). **γυναῖκας:** emphatic enjambment. The poem's central idea (Ζεύς ... κακόν) is repeated word for word at the end (115); for the phrasing, cf. 71–2.

97–8 emphasize the idea of women merely 'seeming' (δοκέωσιν) to be good (cf. 29–31), which is used to discredit the entire female sex (see 108–11). Deception, a quality typical of the vixen- and monkey-women (10–11, 78–9), is now presented as an inescapable female trait. **ἔχοντι ... κακόν:** cf. 68 τῶι δ' ἔχοντι γίνεται κακόν. The focus is tellingly on the harm done to the man.

99–100 οὐ ... | ἄπασαν 'never gets through a whole day in a good mood': once again the speaker foregrounds (with comic exaggeration) women's negative effect on men. **ὅστις ... ναιετᾶι** 'the man who lives with a woman': the transmitted πέλεται gives good sense, but is unmetrical; the best conjecture is Wilhelm's ναιετᾶι (cf. Hes. *Theog.* 592 on the race of women, πῆμα μέγα θνητοῖσι, σὺν ἀνδράσι ναιετάουσαι).

101–2 οὐδ' ... | ... θεῶν 'nor will he quickly thrust Hunger from his home, a hateful housemate, a hostile deity'. **Λιμόν:** personified Hunger is used by Hesiod to motivate Perses to work: ὄφρα σε Λιμὸς | ἐχθαίρηι, φιλέηι δέ σ' ἐυστέφανος Δημήτηρ | αἰδοίη (*WD* 299–301); but whereas Hunger will 'hate' (ἐχθαίρηι) the industrious Perses and so avoid his home, here it is a hateful (ἐχθρόν) housemate of the unlucky husband. **συνοικητῆρα:** the word (attested only here) imagines Hunger cohabiting with the couple in a miserable *ménage à trois*. For women as a drain on the household's resources, cf. 6, 24, 46–7, 58–66. Hesiod says of the *unmarried* man, ὁ δ' οὐ βιότου γ' ἐπιδευὴς | ζώει (*Theog.* 605–6). θεῶν: some prefer Grotius' θεόν, but the partitive genitive, lit. 'hostile one among the gods', evokes epic – as in, for example, the Homeric δῖα θεάων – and the grander style (cf. 37–40, 66, 88–9, 116–18) suits the baleful image of Hunger.

103–5 ἀνήρ ... | ... οἶκον 'when a man seems to be particularly happy with his household': a man's fun is ruined once again (see on 99–100 above). **μοῖραν ... χάριν**: accusatives in apposition, expanding on θυμηδεῖν, '[to be happy] by god's favour or man's kindness'. **εὑροῦσα ... κορύσσεται** 'she finds some fault and girds herself for battle': mock-epic language (κορύσσω is a Homeric verb of arming) expresses the wife's short temper and hostility.

106–7 restate the idea that bad wives make it difficult to receive guests (cf. 19n.). **γάρ** (delayed to suit the metre) introduces another reason for the statement τῶι μάλιστα γίνεται κακόν (98, with γάρ in 99). **δεκοίατο**: Ionic 3rd pl. present optative (with ἄν omitted), 'they cannot even give a hearty welcome', where 'they' refers to men (i.e. husbands) in general.

108–9 ἥτις ... | ... λωβωμένη 'let me tell you, the one who seems the most respectable, she's the one who in fact commits the greatest outrage'. Some scholars have seen an inconsistency between these lines and the existence of the bee-woman; thus Schear 1984, for example, claims that the bee-woman exists only in her husband's imagination. However, the point is not that the bee-woman does not exist, but that she is a rare exception; and these lines warn men not to assume that a wife who behaves well is in fact a bee-wife. This idea is elaborated in 112–14, where men's tendency to praise their own wives and criticize others' is shown to be mistaken. **τοι** ('I tell you', 'mark my words': cf. *GP* 537 'τοι, strictly speaking, implies an audience') reinforces the didactic relationship between speaker and addressee (see the introduction above). **μάλιστα ... | ... μέγιστα**: the opposing superlatives magnify the extent of the woman's deception. **λωβωμένη** implies shocking mistreatment or insult. Although Semonides allows his audience to imagine the lurid details, σωφρονεῖν (108) is often used of female sexual restraint (e.g. Eur. *Bacchae* 317–18) and leads the listener to think of illicit affairs (among other crimes).

110–11 κεχηνότος ... ἀνδρός 'for while her husband gapes open-mouthed' (genitive absolute): χάσκω (perf. κέχηνα) is used of inattention (e.g. Ar. *Knights* 1032 ὅταν σύ ποι ἄλλοσε χάσκηις) and here marks the man as oblivious to his seemingly virtuous wife's true nature. **οἱ δὲ γείτονες | ... ἁμαρτάνει** 'the neighbours take pleasure in seeing how he too is fooled'. **γείτονες | χαίρουσ'**: according to Hesiod, you should choose a wife carefully, μὴ γείτοσι χάρματα γήμηις (*WD* 701); cf. Archil. 196a.33–4* (of the promiscuous Neoboule) ὅ]πως ἐγὼ γυναῖκα τ[ο]ιαύτην ἔχων | γεί]τοσι χάρμ' ἔσομαι. **καὶ τόν**: i.e. he is not the first man to be duped by his wife. ἁμαρτάνει: lit. 'is mistaken', i.e. is wrong to assume his own wife is exemplary.

112–14 By pointing out that every man tends to believe *mistakenly* that his own wife is the equivalent of the bee-woman, Semonides cleverly punctures his male audience's sense of complacency. The speaker's humour at the audience's expense is unexpected and pointed, but does not in any way challenge the poem's (or the audience's) patriarchal ideology. At the same time, the lines assume that Greek men were proud of their wives, despite the general culture of misogyny; and while they had a negative conception of women in general, they could also admire and love the women they were married to and knew best (cf. 86 φίλη δὲ σὺν φιλέοντι γηράσκει πόσει). τὴν ἥν . . . | γυναῖκα 'his own wife'. αἰνέσει μεμνημένος 'will do all he can to praise': for μιμνήσκομαι in the sense 'take care to', cf. LSJ μιμνήσκω B 4. τὴν . . . μωμήσεται 'and will find fault with the other man's': cf. 84 κείνηι γὰρ οἵηι μῶμος οὐ προσιζάνει. ἴσην .
. . γινώσκομεν 'but we don't realize that we have an equal lot': appropriately, as the poem nears its end (115–18n.), the speaker strikes a strong note of male solidarity. Compensatory lengthening of the syllable before an original postconsonantal digamma is regular in the earlier Ionian poets (ϝίσϝος > epic ἶσος), hence ἴσην rather than ἴσην. However, the short vowel scansion is found at Hes. *WD* 752 ἴσον and Semonides could have used this island Ionic form.

115–18 Most recent editors have judged that the poem is incomplete, arguing that τοὺς μέν (117) was originally answered by a δέ clause containing further mythological examples of evil women. However, emphatic μέν *solitarium* is well attested (see *GP* 359–61), and it makes excellent sense to end such a poem with Helen, the pre-eminent *femme fatale* of Greek myth (see below on 117–18).

115 = 96: the repetition underlines the poem's central theme, while the ring composition enhances the sense of closure.

116 καὶ . . . πέδην: lit. 'and he has placed around [us] a bond, an unbreakable fetter', i.e. 'he has bound us to them with an unbreakable fetter'. The imagery of bonds and fetters emphasizes Zeus's supreme power (e.g. [Aesch.] *Prometheus Bound* 6 δεσμῶν ἐν ἀρρήκτοις πέδαις; Hes. *Theog.* 521–2 δῆσε δ' ἀλυκτοπέδηισι Προμηθέα ποικιλόβουλον, | δεσμοῖς ἀργαλέοισι) and specifically his creation of a world in which men cannot do without women: cf. 83–7, 95, Hes. *Theog.* 602–12.

117–18 ἐξ οὗ is temporal ('from the time when') rather than causal ('because of this [evil]'): the poet is not implying that women did not exist or were not a problem before Helen, but is simply foregrounding the Trojan War as the outstanding symbol of the havoc they cause (naturally, all male responsibility, not least Paris' initial offence, is elided). The major cycles of early Greek epic feature several important and potentially threatening women (e.g. Medea, Althaea, Deianeira), but no event is as far-reaching in its repercussions as the abduction of Helen, and no figure embodies the 'beautiful evil' (καλὸν κακόν, Hes. *Theog.* 585) that is woman to the same degree (see Allan 2008: 10–13). **τούς . . | . . . ἀμφιδηριωμένους** 'Hades received those who fought for the sake of a woman'. **γυναικός:** Helen does not need to be named, so notorious is her part in the suffering of the Trojan War (e.g. *Il.* 2.161–2 Ἀργείην Ἑλένην, ἧς εἵνεκα πολλοὶ Ἀχαιῶν | ἐν Τροίηι ἀπόλοντο), but the refusal to name her is a further sign of the speaker's contemptuous attitude towards women in general (cf. Aesch. *Ag.* 62 πολυάνορος ἀμφὶ γυναικός). **ἀμφιδηριωμένους:** δηριάομαι is a regular epic word (cf. *Il.* 12.421 ὥς τ' ἀμφ' οὔροισι δύ' ἀνέρε δηριάασθον), but the rare compound verb, whose placement necessitates an unusual elision at the caesura, creates a grand (cf. 101–2n.) and sombre ending.

CALLINUS

Callinus of Ephesus is probably to be dated around the middle of the seventh century BC. In fr. 5 'now the cruel Cimmerian horde advances', he refers to a tribe from southern Russia which invaded Asia Minor *c.* 652 BC, sacking Sardis and burning the temple of Artemis in Ephesus. The poem included here (1*), quoted (like Tyrt. 12*) by the anthologist Stobaeus under the heading ἔπαινος τόλμης (4.10.12), is the only piece of any length still extant and may be complete (apart from a brief lacuna after line four). It presents an urgent call to arms, addressed to a group of young men (ὦ νέοι, 2), who are rebuked for lying idle (κατάκεισθε, 1) while their country is under attack. (Who the enemy are is uncertain, though it's tempting to link the poem to the Cimmerian invasion.)

κατάκεισθε can mean 'recline' as well as 'lie idle', implying that the young men are enjoying themselves at a *symposion*, just like the audience of the poem itself. This clever alignment of audiences (internal and external) highlights how the performance of such poetry of martial exhortation (of a type found also in Sparta, in the elegies of Tyrtaeus) shapes and reinforces the community's values: the young men's shameful idleness and their unreadiness for war (1–4) underlines the importance of courage in battle, which is clearest in the soldier's glorious death in defence of his family and people (6–8).

Elegy was the most popular form for these martial themes (besides Tyrtaeus, cf. Archil. 5*, 17a*, Mimn. 14*, Sol. 1–3*), not least because the metre allowed easy adaptation of Homeric formulae: virtually every phrase of Callin. 1 is paralleled in epic (see below and Introduction §§1, 5). Moreover, the appeals to shame and glory used in exhortatory elegy echo those familiar from the *Iliad*, and both epic and elegy stress the individual's service to the community (for the difference made by the development of the city-state, see on Tyrt. 12*). Although it remains a commonplace to stress the difference between Homer and the elegists, on the assumption that Homer was concerned with individual honour and the elegists with collective honour, both forms of poetry make clear that the two are interdependent: Callinus' fighters, too, care about their individual reputation and posthumous glory (cf. 6–8, 16–21, Tyrt. 12.27–42*).

Callinus 1

Source: Stobaeus 4.10.12.

1–3 The text begins with three urgent questions in succession, creating a sense of crisis. **μέχρις τέο** (i.e. τίνος μέχρι χρόνου) 'how long?': τέο is Ionic gen. sg. **κατάκεισθε:** present for future, since the speaker wonders how long their state of idleness will last. On the word's meaning ('lie idle', but also 'recline') and its implications for the audience, see above. This is the earliest reference (in literature or art) to the convention of reclining at the *symposion* (cf. Bowie 1990: 223). **κότ(ε):** Ionic for πότε ('when?'). **ἄλκιμον . . . θυμόν:** cf. Tyrt. 10.17 ἀλλὰ μέγαν ποιεῖτε καὶ ἄλκιμον ἐν φρεσὶ θυμόν. The phrase echoes the Homeric ἄλκιμον ἦτορ, used at line 10 below. **ὦ νέοι:** the men are young, but of fighting age, and should know better; cf. Tyrt. 10.15, 11.10. **οὐδ'** marks the speaker's indignation (*GP* 198). **αἰδεῖσθ' ἀμφιπερικτίονας** 'feel shame before your neighbours' (lit. 'those who dwell all around', with the compound prefix ἀμφιπερι-). For the moral pressure of 'those who dwell round about', cf. Telemachus' unsuccessful attempt to shame the suitors: νεμεσσήθητε καὶ αὐτοί, | ἄλλους τ' αἰδέσθητε περικτίονας ἀνθρώπους, | οἳ περιναιετάουσι (*Od*. 2.64–6). Hortatory appeals to αἰδώς are a staple of martial poetry from the *Iliad* onwards: see Cairns 1993: 160–1. **μεθιέντες:** masc. nom. pl. present active part. of μεθίημι, 'to relax, be at ease'; it is regularly used in Homer of those who 'slack' in battle (e.g. Hector rebuking Paris: ἀλλὰ ἑκὼν μεθιεῖς τε καὶ οὐκ ἐθέλεις, *Il*. 6.523). Unlike the Ephesians (presuming the poem is addressed to them), the neighbouring communities are ready for war.

3–4 The contrast is emphatic: peace (ἐν εἰρήνηι) versus war (πόλεμος), supposition (δοκεῖτε) versus fact (ἀτάρ, with strong adversative force: *GP* 52). ἧσθαι, 'sit around', reinforces the charge of idleness. ἔχει: metaphorical, 'the whole country is in the grip of war'. The switch from the specific situation in 4 to general moralizing in 5 suggests that more than one line is missing, but the lacuna could be as small as three lines (hexameter–pentameter–hexameter). From line 5 onwards the poem focuses on the warrior's glorious death in defence of his community. The tropes of martial exhortation deployed by Callinus (and Tyrtaeus) are familiar from Homer, and their continuing popularity and relevance to audiences throughout Greece is readily understandable, since all able-bodied men were expected to fight (and potentially die) for their community if the need arose. Like other forms of public discourse (e.g. war memorials), these martial texts emphasize the importance of winning glory and averting shame, bolstering the citizen-soldier's resolve in the face of life-threatening violence.

5 τις 'any one', equivalent to 'everyone' in injunctions (cf. 9 ἀλλά τις ἰθὺς ἴτω): 'and let a man hurl his last spear even as he dies'. **ὕστατ' ἀκοντισάτω:** lit. 'let him hurl his spear for the last time'; 3rd sg. aor. imper. of ἀκοντίζω. Seventh-century vases show fighters with two spears (as in Homer), each usable for throwing or thrusting (cf. Anderson 1991: 16–17).

6–8 assert the bonds of family and community that are worth risking one's life for. **τιμῆεν ... ἀγλαόν** 'honourable and glorious': the words (as in epic) stress the warrior's enhanced status. **πέρι:** where the preposition follows its noun, the accent is 'thrown back' (anastrophe: Smyth §175, *CGCG* §§24.37, 60.14). **κουριδίης τ' ἀλόχου:** a Homeric phrase, '(lawfully) wedded wife', as opposed to a concubine. ἄλοχος ('of the same bed') is formed from the so-called copulative alpha + λέχος.

8–13 For the argument (since death is inevitable, let us fight and win glory), found in many traditions of heroic poetry; cf. Sarpedon's account of the hero's privileges and obligations (*Il.* 12.322–8).

8–9 δυσμενέσιν· θάνατος: enjambment and juxtaposition, acknowledging the risk of death at the hands of the enemy, which is then defused by the inevitability of 'fate'. **Μοῖραι:** the Fates (named Clotho, Lachesis, and Atropos by Hes. *Theog.* 905) appoint the time of death when they 'spin' the 'thread' of a person's life at their birth (cf. e.g. *Il.* 24.209–10). **ἐπικλώσωσ':** 3rd pl. aor. act. subjunctive of ἐπικλώθω ('I spin'), with θάνατον understood.

9–11 Having established that fighting is necessary, the speaker explains how it should be done. **ἴτω:** 3rd sg. pres. imperative of εἶμι ('I go'). **ἔγχος ἀνασχόμενος** 'brandishing his spear': aor. middle part. of ἀνέχω; cf. *Il.* 11.594 δούρατ' ἀνασχόμενοι. **ὑπ' ἀσπίδος ... | ἔλσας** 'protecting (lit. covering) his brave heart under his shield': aor. act. part. of εἴλω; cf. *Il.* 13.408 τῆι ὕπο (sc. ἀσπίδι) πᾶς ἐάλη. **μειγνυμένου πολέμου:** gen. absolute; the 'mixing' metaphor (common in Homeric battle narrative) expresses the turbulence and confusion of combat: cf. *Il.* 4.456 ὡς τῶν μισγομένων γένετο ἰαχή τε πόνος τε.

12–13 The idea that even the gods' children (such as Achilles, son of Thetis, or Sarpedon, son of Zeus) cannot escape death is fundamental to the tragic form and impact of the *Iliad*, and hence to all subsequent Greek poetry on the glory and the cost of war. **κως:** Ionic for πως. **εἱμαρμένον ἐστίν** 'it is fated': perf. pass. part. of μείρομαι ('I receive as my portion'), sharing the same root as Μοῖρα (9, 15).

14-21 The remainder of the poem depicts the contrasting fates of the man who flees the battlefield (14-16) and the man who fights bravely (17-21).

14-16 πολλάκι: the asyndeton marks these lines as explaining what has gone before (Smyth §2167b). δηϊοτῆτα... δοῦπον ἀκόντων 'the carnage and the thud of spears': Homeric vocabulary, underlining the shame of flight. φυγών: aor. participle, used substantively and without the article, in an indefinite sense, 'a man who has fled'. ἔρχεται 'returns safely home', emphatic enjambment. ἐν δ' οἴκωι: cf. Sol. 4.28-9* for a similar image of fleeing but finding no escape, even in one's own home. κίχεν: unaugmented gnomic aor. of κιχάνω; the metaphor of being 'overtaken' by death is familiar from epic, e.g. Il. 9.416 (Achilles on his return home) οὐδέ κέ μ' ὦκα τέλος θανάτοιο κιχείη. ὁ μέν: contrasting with the brave man (τὸν δ') in the next line. ἔμπης 'in any case'. δήμωι... οὐδὲ ποθεινός: i.e. shunned by the community, dead or alive.

17-21 The description of the courageous warrior highlights how the individual (τὸν δ'... | ... μοῦνος ἐών) is honoured by the whole community (λαῶι... σύμπαντι), and emphasizes his exalted status alive or dead: universal mourning marks his demise (17-19), while in life he stands out from the crowd (like a tower: πύργον, 20) and is raised to the status of hero (ἄξιος ἡμιθέων, 19). ὀλίγος... καὶ μέγας: the polarity (sc. 'high and low', 'great and small') stresses the grief of all citizens at the brave fighter's death. Tyrtaeus too emphasizes mourning by the whole community (12.27-8*). ἤν τι πάθηι: a familiar euphemism. λαῶι: the word has a strong epic charge, casting the warrior's death in heroic terms. πόθος: in contrast to οὐδὲ ποθεινός (16). κρατερόφρονος ἀνδρός: another Homeric phrase (e.g. Od. 4.333, Menelaus on the 'stout-hearted' Odysseus). θνήσκοντος, ζώων: the juxtaposition is emphatic. The brave man is honoured like a hero while still alive. ἄξιος (+ gen.) 'ranks with' (lit. 'worth as much as'); cf. Agamemnon's complaint, νῦν δ' οὐδ' ἑνὸς ἄξιοί εἰμεν | Ἕκτορος (Il. 8.234-5). ἡμιθέων: the word is used once by Homer looking back from a later period to the men who fought at Troy (Il. 12.23) and by Hesiod of the superior 'heroic race' that preceded his own (WD 160-1). In each case the word marks outstanding qualities and status as much as birth (strictly speaking, only some heroes had a divine parent), and its use here elevates the citizen-soldier to the pinnacle of human achievement and reward. ὥσπερ... πύργον: the metaphor (cf. our 'tower of strength') is regularly used to express an individual's exceptional contribution to the defence of his community, e.g. Odysseus to Ajax in the underworld: τοῖος γάρ σφιν πύργος ἀπώλεο, Od. 11.556. ἐν ὀφθαλμοῖσιν ὁρῶσιν: such pleonasm (with or without ἐν) is characteristic of epic. ἔρδει: another word (poetic and Ionic: ἔρδω, 'I do') typical of epic. πολλῶν ἄξια: echoes ἄξιος ἡμιθέων just above; although just one man (μοῦνος ἐών, epic–Ionic for μόνος ὤν), his deeds are equal to those of many.

TYRTAEUS

The Spartan Tyrtaeus, like the Ionian Callinus, was working around the middle of the seventh century BC, and most of what survives of Tyrtaeus' poetry, including the three longest pieces (10, 11, 12*), deals with martial themes, especially the depiction of the ideal soldier. (On the Homeric background to such exhortatory elegy, see the introduction to Callinus above.) We know from the late seventh-century choral poetry of Alcman, and from archaeological discoveries in local sanctuaries portraying dancers and *aulos*-players, that early Sparta had a rich cultural and musical life, far removed from the stereotypical image of the Spartans as militaristic philistines (for a wide range of sources, including inscriptions and dedications as well as poetry, see Cooley 2017). Even the poetry of Tyrtaeus is not limited to military ideology, since it also responds to contemporary social and political problems (see 4*). Nonetheless, it should not surprise us if most of Tyrtaeus' poetry were martial, as his career coincided with the Second Messenian War, a brutal struggle in which Sparta reasserted its dominance over the Messenians, a neighbouring people whom they had subjugated two generations before (see 5–7*).

The immediacy and realism of Tyrtaeus' martial elegies led some scholars (ancient and modern) to believe they were written for recitation during military campaigns as a kind of parade-ground performance, intended to prepare the soldiers for imminent battle. But there is evidence of *symposion*-like gatherings both at Sparta itself (in *syssitia*, communal meals of citizen-soldiers) and on campaign (in the king's tent, among a select group of commanders), and it is likely that these smaller, select groups, in part akin to the aristocratic *symposia* of Ionian communities, formed the original audiences of Tyrtaeus' martial poetry (see Bowie 1990: 224–9). By contrast, Tyrtaeus' political elegies, including his *Eunomia* ('Good Government', 4*), were written for performance at public festivals (cf. Bowie 1986: 30–1). Although he is the earliest surviving elegist composing with Doric speakers in mind, Tyrtaeus uses (with a few exceptions: cf. on 7.1*) the established Ionic dialect of elegy, thus exploiting his audience's knowledge of Panhellenic tradition and ensuring his work's dissemination and fame beyond the borders of Laconia.

Tyrtaeus 4

Source: Plutarch, *Lycurgus* 6 (1–6); Diodorus Siculus, *Universal History* 7.12.6 (3–10).

This is the most extensive of two surviving fragments of Tyrtaeus' *Eunomia*. We cannot be certain Tyrtaeus himself gave the poem this (or indeed any) title, but it was clearly the traditional name for it by Aristotle's time

(*Pol.* 1306b36). The other fragment, from a papyrus of the late first or early second century AD (*P. Oxy.* 2824), tells how the descendants of Heracles, the mythical ancestors of the Dorians, were granted control of the Peloponnese by Zeus (Tyrt. 2). Tyrt. 4* is concerned more specifically with Spartan history, and reports a Delphic oracle which had decreed the proper roles of kings, elders, and people in the government of the state. According to Aristotle, Tyrtaeus composed the poem in response to factional discord caused by the Second Messenian War (cf. Tyrt. 5–7*), as those hard pressed by the war called for a redistribution of land. The surviving text makes no mention of such a demand, but the emphasis here on the god-given pre-eminence of the kings and council of elders (3–5), together with the warning to the people not to make plans that would damage the state (8), suggests Tyrtaeus' support for the established order, which also includes (he insists) the power of the people to decide the will of the assembly by majority vote (9). In other words, both sides are reminded of the importance of mutual respect. For a similar appeal to all sides aimed at ending factional strife in Athens, cf. Solon's use of Εὐνομίη at 4.32–9*.

1–2 Πυθωνόθεν 'from Delphi' (Πυθῶθεν is also found): for the story of how Apollo gained control over Πυθώ (Delphi), see *HHAp*. 282–374, which spells out the traditional aetiology of the name Pytho (πύθω = 'cause to rot'), the place being named after the rotting corpse of the serpent killed by Apollo. **ἔνεικαν:** 3rd pl. epic–Ionic aor. of φέρω. According to Plutarch (*Lyc.* 6), the oracle was given to the kings Polydorus and Theopompus, who brought it back to Sparta (cf. 1 οἴκαδ'). Polydorus and Theopompus were commanders in the First Messenian War (*c.* 700 BC), recalled in Tyrt. 5–7*. Our other source for Tyrt. 4*, Diodorus Siculus (7.12.6), believed the oracle was given to the legendary Spartan lawgiver Lycurgus, but there is no evidence that Tyrtaeus mentioned him. It was not unusual for Greek states to seek ratification of their political decisions from oracles, especially Apollo's at Delphi (cf. Thuc. 1.118.3 and 3.92.5 for the Spartans doing this before declaring war on Athens in 432 and founding a colony at Heraclea in Trachis in 426), a process which proved highly profitable to the shrines and the surrounding communities (see Parker 2000: 81–2, 85–94). Just as Tyrtaeus evokes the military heroism of past generations which secured victory over the Messenians (cf. 5.6* αἰχμηταὶ πατέρων ἡμετέρων πατέρες), so here he recalls the political wisdom of the same period in order to rally his contemporaries. **τελέεντ':** lit. 'certain to bring fulfilment', i.e. 'certain to be fulfilled'; cf. *Il.* 8.247 αἰετὸν . . . τελειότατον πετεηνῶν, or τέλειος as an epithet of Zeus (e.g. Aesch. *Ag.* 973).

3–9 As is typical of oracles, instructions are given in a series of infinitives (ἄρχειν . . . μυθεῖσθαι . . . ἔρδειν . . . βουλεύειν . . . ἔπεσθαι), standing for imperatives. Oracles were delivered in hexameters, and it has been argued that lines 3, 5, 7, and 9 quote the original oracle, with the pentameters (4, 6, 8) being added by Tyrtaeus (cf. West 1974: 184–5).

3–5 ἄρχειν . . . βουλῆς: the kings and elders are to take the lead in all political discussions. The important word ('rule') is put first. **θεοτιμήτους,** 'honoured by the gods', reinforces the kings' authority. **μέλει:** the word implies that leading the city is the kings' proper concern; cf. *Il.* 6.492–3 (Hector to Andromache) πόλεμος δ' ἄνδρεσσι μελήσει | πᾶσι, μάλιστα δ' ἐμοί. **ἱμερόεσσα:** the epithet is chosen for its appeal to all Spartans; cf. Sol. 1.1*. **πρεσβυγενέας . . . γέροντας:** the Spartan council of elders (*gerousia*) consisted of twenty-eight men over sixty, who were appointed for life, plus the two kings.

5–9 More space is given to defining the power of the *dēmos*, perhaps suggesting that Tyrtaeus is responding to discontent among them (see the introduction above).

6 εὐθείαις ῥήτραις ἀνταπαμειβομένους 'as they respond to (or with) straight proposals': on the first interpretation the authorities' decisions are 'straight' (i.e. correct, and so should be accepted); on the second the people's own response is to be 'straight', i.e. not introduce any 'crooked' alterations (cf. 8 <σκολιόν>) – either way the proposals of the kings and elders are not to be distorted but simply voted on. The use of the word *rhētra* led later writers to see a reference here to the Spartan constitutional agreement known as the 'Great Rhetra', which Plutarch dated to the time of Lycurgus (*Lyc.* 6). However, many later developments were backdated to the legendary Lycurgus, and it is possible that Plutarch's *rhētra* came after Tyrtaeus (cf. van Wees 1999). Nonetheless, it is striking that the *rhētra* recorded by Plutarch gives the people 'the right to speak in opposition and the power' (cf. κάρτος, line 9 below), so it may be that Plutarch's *rhētra* was (like its amendment: see on line 8) a product of the time of Polydorus and Theopompus.

7 ἔρδειν: see on Callin. 1.21*.

8 <σκολιόν>: the supplement gives good sense and is supported by Plutarch's account of the amendment to the *rhētra* made by the kings: 'If the people speak crookedly (σκολιάν), the elders and leaders are to set aside their proposals' (*Lyc.* 6).

9 κάρτος: epic (and Doric) for κράτος. **ἔπεσθαι** 'belong to', lit. 'follow', with dat. (πλήθει).

10 Φοῖβος: ring composition concludes the god's instructions (Φοίβου, 1). **ἀνέφηνε:** 3rd sg. aor. of ἀναφαίνω ('to reveal'), a word suited to oracles (cf. *Il.* 1.87 Δαναοῖσι θεοπροπίας ἀναφαίνεις).

Tyrtaeus 5–7

Tyrtaeus recalls how the Spartans conquered the Messenians two generations before (c. 700 BC) in the so-called First Messenian War, reducing them to the status of helots (see below). It seems likely that these fragments were part of a larger poem in which Tyrtaeus urged the Spartans to emulate their forefathers by crushing the major Messenian revolt of his time. (Bowie 1986: 30 suggested ascribing 5–7* to the *Eunomia* (4*), but our sources for 5–7* indicate a separate poem focused on the Messenians rather than the Spartan constitution.) This conflict, known as the Second Messenian War (c. 640 BC), saw the Spartans emerge victorious, and the Messenians remained under their control (despite further rebellions) until the Theban victory over the Spartans at Leuctra in 371 BC. The fundamental role of the helots (or 'captured people', deriving Εἵλωτες from the passive of *ἕλω = αἱρέω) was to supply their Spartan masters with food, and Tyrt. 6* compares them to toiling donkeys, worn out by their heavy loads and compelled to bring the Spartans half their produce. The helots' forced labour brought great prosperity to Sparta (as seen in seventh-century dedications at local sanctuaries) and also made Sparta's militarized society both possible, since male citizens were freed from work to become full-time soldiers, and necessary, to quell the permanent danger of slave rebellion. Tyrtaeus' surviving poetry is geared to maintaining the helots' subjugation and to reinforcing the increasingly militaristic values of Spartan society during the crisis of the Second Messenian War.

Tyrtaeus 5

Source: Pausanias 4.6.5 (1–2); Schol. Plato, *Laws* 629a (3); Strabo 6.3.3 (4–8).

This piece (which is made up of three separate fragments: 1–2, 3, 4–8) begins in mid-sentence, so we cannot say precisely why Theopompus is in the dative, but Pausanias quotes lines 1–2 as proof that Theopompus 'put an end to the war' (4.6.5), and it seems clear that he is being celebrated for leading the original conquest of Messenia.

1 ἡμετέρωι βασιλῆϊ: Theopompus, who reigned c. 720–670 BC, was a member of the Spartan royal house known as the Eurypontids; for his genealogy, stretching back to Heracles, see Hdt. 8.131. Polydorus, his colleague in the First Messenian War (Paus. 3.3.1, 4.7.7), came from the royal house of the Agiads (cf. Tyrt. 4.1–2*). **θεοῖσι ... Θεοπόμπωι**: the jingle (θεοι- θεο-) and epithet 'dear to the gods' underline the appropriateness of the triumphant king's name.

2 ὅν διά (= δι' ὅν): the postposition of διά puts emphasis upon the relative pronoun and so highlights Theopompus' contribution. **εἵλομεν**:

the first-person plural verb ('we captured'), like ἡμετέρωι (1), stresses the collective achievement of the Messenian conquest, which benefited all Spartans. **εὐρύχορον** 'with broad dancing-places': a common Homeric epithet, denoting a flourishing community, and so marking Messenia's value to her Spartan conquerors. On the importance of choral performance in Greek life, see Swift 2010: 1–5.

3 Μεσσήνην ἀγαθόν: though modifying a feminine noun, ἀγαθός is attracted into the same masc. form as the preceding (two-termination) adjective εὐρύχορος; cf. Hes. *Theog.* 406–8 Λητὼ κυανόπεπλον ... μείλιχον ... ἤπιον ... μείλιχον ... ἀγανώτατον. **ἀγαθὸν ... φυτεύειν** 'good to plough and good to plant': the repetition underlines the fertility of Messenia (cf. πίονα ἔργα, 7), whose produce supported Spartan society and its increasing militarization.

4–8 evoke the twenty years of hard fighting to conquer Messenia. The use of precise numbers (ἐννέα καὶ δέκ' ἔτη, εἰκοστῶι) and temporal adverbs (νωλεμέως αἰεί) stresses the duration of the war and hence the effort invested by the Spartan audience's ancestors, which, Tyrtaeus trusts, will not have been in vain.

4 ἀμφ': strictly 'to secure possession of', but the local sense of ἀμφί is also felt since the fighting took place on Messenian territory.

5 νωλεμέως 'relentlessly'. **ταλασίφρονα:** a Homeric epithet (especially characteristic of Odysseus: 12 of 13 Homeric examples refer to him), further emphasizing the Spartans' heroic endurance.

6 πατέρων ... πατέρες: the original conquest took place two generations ago but already has the exemplary character typical of heroic myth. **ἡμετέρων:** see on εἵλομεν (2).

7 οἱ μέν: i.e. the Messenians. **κατὰ ... λιπόντες** 'leaving behind' (tmesis of καταλείπω). **ἔργα** 'fields' (i.e. earth that has been 'worked'), a standard term for agricultural land: cf. *Il.* 12.283 ἀνδρῶν πίονα ἔργα.

8 Ἰθωμαίων ... ὀρέων 'from Ithome's high peaks': rising to over 800m above the Messenian plain, Mt Ithome was the site of the ancient capital of Messenia and formed a natural refuge and rallying point for the helots (cf. Thuc. 1.101–3 for a lengthy Spartan campaign against rebels there in the 460s–450s BC). In contrast to Tyrtaeus, later accounts of the First Messenian War, written by non-Spartans, and after the liberation of the helots, portray the Messenians' resistance on Mt Ithome in heroic and tragic terms (cf. e.g. Paus. 4.9–13).

Tyrtaeus 6

Source: Pausanias 4.14.5.

Pausanias, our source for 6–7*, thought it was the harsh treatment described here that led the Messenians to revolt, sparking the Second

Messenian War (4.14.6). Tyrtaeus and his Spartan audience will have seen matters differently, of course, and the poem's evocation of the Messenians' misery is likely to have functioned as a further encouragement to the Spartans not to lose this battle, lest they face similar degradation or worse.

1 ὥσπερ ὄνοι: Ajax is compared to an ass at *Il.* 11.558–62 (the word's sole occurrence in Homer), but the simile's point of comparision here is not tenacity (as with Ajax) but grinding physical effort, as in the mule (ἡμίονοι) simile of *Il.* 17.742–6, where Menelaus and Meriones labour to carry the corpse of Patroclus from the battlefield. τειρόμενοι 'oppressed, wearied': the same verb is used in the Homeric mule simile ἐν δέ τε θυμός | τείρεθ' ὁμοῦ καμάτωι τε καὶ ἱδρῶι σπευδόντεσσιν (*Il.* 17.744–5).

2 δεσποσύνοισι 'to their masters': the adjective δεσπόσυνος is here used substantively (= δεσπότης). ἥμισυ: neuter used adverbially, 'to the extent of a half'. The helots' contribution of natural produce helps maintain the system that enslaves them. Assuming that Spartan citizens were better fed than helots, this percentage suggests that the enslaved population outnumbered the free Spartans, adding to Spartan anxiety and reinforcing the militarization of their society.

3 ἄρουρα: a standard poetic word for tilled land (cf. ἀρόω 'I plough').

Tyrtaeus 7

Source: Pausanias 4.14.5.

Pausanias records that following their subjugation the Messenians were forced (among other indignities) to mourn the deaths of Spartan kings and other officials (4.14.4–5). The scenario of fellow Greeks lamenting for their 'masters' will have struck non-Spartan audiences as grotesque, and Herodotus compares the helots' forced participation in the funeral rites to Persian practice when their kings die (6.58).

1 δεσπότας: the acc. pl. ending -ας scanned short (long in Ionic) is a rare Doric feature (cf. 4.5* δημότας). οἰμώζοντες 'wailing for': [Thgn.] 1203–6 attests a natural reluctance to attend the funeral of one's enemy. ὁμῶς ἄλοχοί τε καὶ αὐτοί: all adult Messenians are compelled to participate, marking the humiliation of the entire community.

2 εὖτε 'when': epic–Ionic. οὐλομένη 'accursed': aor. part. of ὄλλυμαι (ὀλόμενος, i.e. that of which one says ὄλοιτο, 'damn it'), with metrical lengthening. μοῖρα ... θανάτου: a formulaic phrase in epic (see Callin. 1.15* for being 'overtaken' by death), casting the deceased Spartans (τιν', 'one of them') in heroic terms.

Tyrtaeus 12

Source: Stobaeus 4.10.1 (1–14), 4.10.6 (15–44).

The three longest extant fragments of Tyrtaeus (10–12), together with Callin. 1*, shape our notion of 'exhortation elegy'. Tyrt. 12* is the most extensive example and is quoted (like Callin. 1*) by the anthologist Stobaeus under the heading ἔπαινος τόλμης. All celebrate the ideal soldier, describing the honour achieved in victory or heroic death on the battlefield, and contrasting it with the shame of defeat or flight. Despite the claims of some modern scholars (discussed by Irwin 2005: 22–9), the development of the city-state (*polis*) did not fundamentally redefine military *aretē* (whose communal aspects are already highlighted in Homeric epic), but it did make the individual's loyalty and obedience to the collective a central tenet of being a good citizen and soldier. This stronger group mentality is seen most clearly in phalanx warfare (cf. Tyrt. 12.15–22*), where there is no place for single combat or a Homeric *aristeia*, and where what matters is sticking together in the line and putting the common good above one's own glory or self-preservation.

Compared with Tyrt. 10–11, 12* is more positive in tenor, emphasizing the benefits (both personal and communal) of martial *aretē* rather than the shame of failure. Luginbill's analysis of 12* as a form of recruitment literature and 'a response to some manpower crisis in the Spartan army' (2002: 413) may be going too far, since its martial sentiments are traditional, but it is certainly true that the demands of the Second Messenian War will have made Tyrtaeus' celebration of military excellence particularly resonant and timely. The regularity of warfare in all city-states (not just in Sparta), and the centrality of fighting prowess to Greek notions of masculinity, make it easy to understand the appeal of exhortation elegy throughout the Greek world: Tyrt. 10, for example, is quoted by the fourth-century Athenian politician Lycurgus to illustrate the importance of patriotism (*Against Leocrates* 107).

The poem falls into two sections and shows every sign of being complete: the first half establishes martial valour as the pre-eminent *aretē*, which serves the common good (1–22); the second depicts the honours given to the soldier who dies in battle (23–34) or returns home victorious (35–42), concluding with a final couplet of explicit exhortation (43–4).

1–12 An elaborate priamel (a list designed to emphasize the final item: see Race 1982) establishes the importance of martial courage. By listing and qualifying several commonly accepted markers of manly excellence (physical strength and beauty, wealth, nobility, and eloquence), all of which are said to be useless in war without courage, Tyrtaeus highlights the supreme value of the brave soldier. The use of repeated negatives

('not for speed or wrestling or ...') to emphasize a speaker's point is a popular rhetorical device: e.g. Archil. 19*, 114*, 122, Semon. 7.16–20*.
1 οὔτ' ἂν μνησαίμην 'I would not recall', i.e. consider him worthy of mention. **οὔτ' ἐν λόγωι ... τιθείην** 'nor would I hold a man of any account'. To focus on a man's value rather than the poet's skill (as does Schwinge 1997, who translates 'nor would I include a man in my poetry') better suits the context, which is entirely concerned with various determinants of 'reputation' (δόξαν, 9). Plato twice quotes the line with the middle optative form τιθείμην, but as West 1974: 187 observes, 'A quotation, especially by Plato, is liable to be less trusty than a direct tradition, and ... τιθείμην was more likely to displace τιθείην after μνησαίμην than vice versa.'
2 ποδῶν ἀρετῆς ... παλαιμοσύνης 'for prowess in running or wrestling': genitive of cause, commonly used in expressions of evaluation ('I praise/blame etc. x (acc.) because of y (gen.)': Smyth §1405, CGCG §30.30). For running and wrestling as markers of male excellence, cf. e.g. Il. 23.700–39 (Ajax and Odysseus' wrestling bout is declared a draw), 740–97 (Odysseus wins the foot-race). Priam's son Polydorus is ποδῶν ἀρετὴν ἀναφαίνων ('displaying his fleetness of foot') when he is killed by Achilles (Il. 20.411).
3 μέγεθός τε βίην τε: an epic phrase, used of the massive Ajax (Il. 7.288). Both in Homer (where they are shepherds) and in Hesiod (where they are craftsmen) the giant one-eyed creatures known as Cyclopes are prone to lawless violence (cf. Od. 9.105–15, Hes. Theog. 139 γείνατο δ' αὖ Κύκλωπας ὑπέρβιον ἦτορ ἔχοντας), so the comparison suggests that mere size and strength are not enough in themselves: what counts is courage in battle (θούριδος ἀλκῆς, 9).
4 θέων: present participle (as indicated by the accent). **Θρηΐκιον Βορέην:** the swiftness of the North Wind in particular, blowing down from Thrace, was proverbial: cf. Hes. Theog. 378–80 Ἀστραίωι δ' Ἠὼς ἀνέμους τέκε καρτεροθύμους, | ἀργεστὴν Ζέφυρον Βορέην τ' αἰψηροκέλευθον | καὶ Νότον.
5 Τιθωνοῖο ... χαριέστερος: Tithonus' exceptional handsomeness led to his abduction by Eos, goddess of the dawn, and to his deathless ageing, when Eos asked Zeus for immortality for him but forgot to ask for eternal youth (e.g. HHAphr. 225, Sapph. 58.19–22). Their son, the Ethiopian king Memnon, is described by Achilles as the handsomest man he ever saw (Od. 11.522).
6 Μίδεω καὶ Κινύρεω: eastern kings who (like Gyges and Croesus) became bywords for wealth. Cinyras of Cyprus gave Agamemnon a richly decorated corslet as a guest-gift (Il. 11.19–28; for his riches, cf. Pind. Nem. 8.18), while Midas, a late eighth-century king of Phrygia, became a popular figure in Graeco-Roman mythology: for the story of how he acquired (to his cost) the 'Midas touch', see Ov. Met. 11.90–193. **μάλιον:** rare Ionic form of the comparative μᾶλλον (with gen.).

7 βασιλεύτερος: Pelops, son of the reprobate eastern king Tantalus (Pind. *Ol.* 1), first gained the kingship of Pisa (the region around Olympia) and then expanded his power to such an extent that the entire Peloponnese was named after him (cf. Thuc. 1.9).

8 Ἀδρήστου: king of Argos, Adrastus was the only commander to survive the expedition launched to restore his son-in-law Polynices to the throne of Thebes. (In Aeschylus, Adrastus leads the expedition, but is not one of the Seven, who all die in the attack: *Seven against Thebes* 575). The myth, known to Homer (e.g. *Il.* 23.346–7), was elaborated in the cyclic epic *Thebais* (which probably postdates Tyrtaeus). **μειλιχόγηρυν:** the epithet ('smooth-voiced') occurs only here. Plato's Socrates speaks of μελίγηρυν Ἄδραστον (*Phdr.* 269a). Despite his reputation for eloquence, Adrastus initially fails to persuade Theseus to help recover the bodies of the Seven, but is later given the task of delivering the funeral speech over the fallen (Eur. *Suppl.* 110–270, 838–917).

9 θούριδος ἀλκῆς: the priamel structure throws particular emphasis on the final words, which encapsulate the poem's central concern. The phrase is a frequent Homeric line-ending (e.g. *Il.* 6.112 ἀνέρες ἔστε, φίλοι, μνήσασθε δὲ θούριδος ἀλκῆς).

10–12 justify (γάρ, 10) the selection of martial courage as the supreme ἀρετή. **εἰ μὴ τετλαίη ... ὁρῶν** 'unless he can bear to see': 3rd sg. perf. optative of τλάω (more often with the infinitive). **φόνον αἱματόεντα** 'bloody slaughter', an epic-sounding phrase (cf. *Il.* 19.214 ἀλλὰ φόνος τε καὶ αἷμα καὶ ἀργαλέος στόνος ἀνδρῶν). **δηίων ὀρέγοιτ'** 'aim at the enemy' (with gen. of the target). **ἐγγύθεν ἱστάμενος:** for skill in close combat, cf. Tyrt. 11.29 ἐγγὺς ἰών, 11.38 πλησίον ἱστάμενοι, 19.13 ἐγγύθεν ἱσ[τάμενοι.

13–20 elaborate upon 10–12, with οὗτος ἀνὴρ ἀγαθὸς γίνεται ἐν πολέμωι (20) echoing οὐ γὰρ ἀνὴρ ἀγαθὸς γίνεται ἐν πολέμωι (10). Tyrtaeus spells out the qualities needed for fighting at close quarters and stresses the warrior's value to the community as a whole.

13–14 ἥδ' ἀρετή, τόδ' ἄεθλον 'this is excellence, this is the best prize ...': the image of 'winning a prize' (ἄεθλον ... | ... φέρειν) recalls the athletic prowess of the priamel's runners and wrestlers, and prepares for the difference (made explicit in 15): the warrior's excellence brings greater benefit to the state. Unlike Xenophanes (2*), however, Tyrtaeus is not criticizing the honour shown to athletes (or those who possess the other qualities included in the priamel), but simply asserting the supreme value of a particular virtue.

15 ξυνὸν δ' ἐσθλόν: the 'common good' achieved by the warrior is a traditional epic idea, but it is given greater prominence in the developed city-state (see the introduction above). **πόληΐ τε παντί τε δήμωι:** the repetition emphasizes the collective benefit; cf. Callin. 1.6–8*, 1.16–21*, Tyrt. 10.2, 10.13, 12.33–4*.

COMMENTARY: TYRTAEUS 12

16–22 encapsulate the military virtues of steadfastness and mutual support and protection.

16 ὅστις: the detailed relative clause clarifies τοῦτο (15). **διαβάς** 'taking a firm stance': aor. part. of διαβαίνω ('stand with legs apart'), a standard military term (e.g. *Il.* 12.458 εὖ διαβάς). **ἐν προμάχοισι:** for valour in the front ranks, cf. Tyrt. 10.1, 10.21, 11.4, 11.12, 12.23*, Mimn. 14.6*.

17 νωλεμέως: cf. Tyrt. 5.5*. **αἰσχρῆς δὲ φυγῆς:** for the shame of flight, cf. Callin. 1.14–16*.

18 ψυχὴν... παρθέμενος 'risking his life and brave heart': aor. middle part. of παρατίθημι ('lay on the line'); cf. *Od.* 2.237–8 σφὰς γὰρ παρθέμενοι | κεφαλὰς κατέδουσι βιαίως | οἶκον Ὀδυσσῆος.

19 θαρσύνηι... παρεστώς: encouragement of one's comrades, especially those adjacent in the ranks, was an important part of maintaining a strong phalanx line.

21–2 sum up the crucial feats of the ideal warrior (20) and lead into the second part of the poem on the honours given to him, dead (23–34) or alive (35–42). **ἔτρεψε:** aor. of repeated action, like the following ἔσχεθε (22). **φάλαγγας | τρηχείας:** lit. 'jagged battle lines': the enjambed epithet evokes the enemies' bristling spears. The disciplined use of phalanx-type formation and tactics contributed to the Spartans' own military success. **σπουδῆι** 'by strenuous effort'. **κῦμα μάχης:** the metaphor draws on the epic comparison of armies to waves (cf. *Il.* 15.381–4, which compares the Trojans breaching the wall of the Achaean camp to waves battering a ship).

23–34 The man who dies nobly in battle wins rewards not only for himself, but also for his family and descendants.

23 ἐν προμάχοισι: cf. 16 above.

24 ἄστυ... εὐκλεΐσας: the glory is communal, not simply personal or familial (cf. ξυνὸν δ' ἐσθλὸν τοῦτο, 15).

25–6 ἀσπίδος ὀμφαλοέσσης: though not a feature of contemporary armour, the Homeric phrase 'bossed shield' is used for its heroic resonance. **πρόσθεν ἐληλαμένος,** 'pierced from the front', emphasizes the fact that the man faced his death and did not flee: cf. Tyrt. 11.19–20 αἰσχρὸς δ' ἐστὶ νέκυς κατακείμενος ἐν κονίηισι | νῶτον ὄπισθ' αἰχμῆι δουρὸς ἐληλαμένος.

27–8 For the brave warrior mourned by all, cf. Callin. 1.17–19*. **κέκηδε:** perf. used in present sense ('is distressed').

29–30 ἀρίσημοι 'pointed out': both the war hero (in his burial mound) and his family enjoy a new prominence. **παίδων... ἐξοπίσω:** cf. Sol. 13.32* (in a less reassuring context) ἢ παῖδες τούτων ἢ γένος ἐξοπίσω.

31–2 The promise of eternal fame crowns the list of rewards. **οὐδέ... ἀπόλλυται...|... ἀθάνατος:** the war hero's transcendent status is god-like; cf. Callin. 1.19* ζώων δ' ἄξιος ἡμιθέων.

33–4 ἀριστεύοντα... μαρνάμενον: epic vocabulary further elevates the fallen soldier. **γῆς πέρι καὶ παίδων:** the same phrase is used by Callinus

(1.6*); cf. Tyrt. 10.13–14 θυμῶι γῆς πέρι τῆσδε μαχώμεθα καὶ περὶ παίδων | θνήσκωμεν. **θοῦρος Ἄρης:** another Homeric phrase (e.g. *Il.* 24.498 τῶν μὲν πολλῶν θοῦρος Ἄρης ὑπὸ γούνατ' ἔλυσεν), echoing the warrior's own θοῦρις ἀλκή (9). **ὀλέσηι:** for the omission of ἄν, see on Sol. 13.9–10*.

35–42 The returning victor enjoys special privileges for the rest of his life.

35–6 κῆρα τανηλεγέος θανάτοιο 'the doom of death's long sorrow': cf. *Il.* 8.70 ἐν δ' ἐτίθει δύο κῆρε τανηλεγέος θανάτοιο. **νικήσας . . . ἕληι:** lit. 'and by his victory achieves his glorious spear-prayer'. **αἰχμῆς . . . εὖχος:** Homeric warriors often pray to the gods to direct their spear-casts (e.g. Diomedes' prayer to Athena, *Il.* 5.114–20, fulfilled at 5.290–1); the gen. αἰχμῆς denotes the prayer's topic. **ἀγλαόν:** cf. Callin. 1.6*.

37–42 These lines are adapted in the *Theognidea* (935–8) to describe the honour that comes to the rare man who has both virtue and good looks. Similarly, [Thgn.] 1003–6 reproduce lines 13–16 above except for the change of νέωι (14) to σοφῶι. On the *Theognidea*'s reuse of elegy (especially Tyrtaeus, Solon, and Mimnermus), see Noussia-Fantuzzi 2010: 55–65.

37 ὁμῶς νέοι ἠδὲ παλαιοί: the esteem of young and old is repeatedly stressed: cf. 27, 41–2.

38 πολλὰ . . . τερπνά: a few of these 'many joys' are spelled out in what follows (39–42).

39–40 γηράσκων 'as he grows old'. **μεταπρέπει:** the verb ('stand out among', with dat.) is frequently used of heroes in epic (e.g. *Il.* 2.579, describing Agamemnon, πᾶσιν δὲ μετέπρεπεν ἡρώεσσιν). **οὐδέ . . . | . . . ἐθέλει:** the potentially negative feelings of his fellow citizens are denied. **βλάπτειν:** with genitives of separation, 'deprive him of his due respect and rights'.

41–2 All give up their seats for the war hero, a traditional mark of respect. Contrast Xenophanes' complaint about the athletic victor, καί κε προεδρίην φανερὴν ἐν ἀγῶσιν ἄροιτο (2.7*).

43–4 Tyrtaeus concludes with a rousing exhortation. **ταύτης . . . ἀρετῆς:** emphatic, continuing the emphasis on *this* form of excellence (cf. ἥδ' ἀρετή, 13) and recapping the point of the priamel. **τις ἀνήρ** 'every man': cf. Callin. 1.5*. **πειράσθω:** 3rd sg. imperative of πειράομαι ('let every man now endeavour'). **θυμῶι** 'with all his heart': cf. Tyrt. 10.13–14 (quoted at 33–4 above). **μὴ μεθιεὶς πολέμου** 'not slacking in the fight': see on Callin. 1.3* μεθιέντες.

MIMNERMUS

Mimnermus of Smyrna was active in the second half of the seventh century. He is said to have mentioned an eclipse of the sun (dateable to 6 April 648: fr. 20), while various fragments look back to a battle of the

660s in which the Smyrnaeans repelled an attack by the Lydians under Gyges, and one (14*) may have been written in the final decade of the seventh century, as Smyrna was once again threatened by the Lydians, now led by Alyattes. In later tradition, Mimnermus was connected to the more prominent city of Colophon, whose foundation and alliance with Smyrna he celebrated (9.3, 10), but his work as a whole points to Smyrna as his homeland. By the Hellenistic period, Mimnermus' poetry circulated in two books, known as *Smyrneis* and *Nanno*. Callimachus remarked, 'Of the two the delicate ... showed that Mimnermus is sweet, but the big woman did not' (fr. 1.11–12 Harder), where the shorter poems of *Nanno* are preferred to the lengthy *Smyrneis*. (Callimachus also alludes here to the poems' names, since νᾶνος = 'dwarf', while Smyrna was an Amazon, a 'big woman', who gave her name to the city (Strabo 14.1.4).)

Smyrneis was an extended narrative elegy that commemorated the recent war against Gyges and the Lydians (cf. Simonides' Plataea Elegy*), complete with an epic-style proem invoking the Muses (13) and a vivid account of the close fighting (13a); it may also have described the city's foundation, as did (for example) Xenophanes' later poem on the foundation of Colophon. (Bowie 1986: 29–30 argues that Mimn. 9, dealing with the Smyrnaeans' migration from the Peloponnese to Asia Minor, also comes from the *Smyrneis* and that it was falsely ascribed to the *Nanno* by Strabo.)

Nanno took its name from an *aulos*-player (i.e. not a citizen woman) loved by Mimnermus, but she does not feature in any of the extant fragments. As a collection of shorter elegies, *Nanno* treated a variety of subjects suitable for sympotic performance, from reflective pieces on desire, pleasure, and the loss of youth (1*, 2*, 3–7) to mythological narratives (11–11a (Jason), 12* (the Sun), 19 (Niobe), 21 (Antigone and Ismene)). Mimnermus' later reputation as creator of the genre of love elegy (Prop. 1.9.11 *plus in amore ualet Mimnermi uersus Homero*; cf. Hunter 2013) makes the loss of his poems about Nanno all the more frustrating, but the fame of his love poetry should not be allowed to obscure the variety of his work.

Mimnermus 1

Source: Stobaeus 4.20.16.

The poem (which may be complete: cf. 1n.) falls into two halves, the first on the pleasures of love and youth, the second on the evils of old age. The speaker's celebration of erotic joy (life is not worth living without it, he declares) is as decisive and extreme as his condemnation of getting old. Mimnermus' portrayal of ageing is unusually negative: here, instead of the conventional transition from foolish youth through sober maturity to respected old age (cf. Sol. 27*), Mimnermus magnifies the contrast between youth and old age by introducing in the middle of line 5 a sudden shift from the first stage, which is delightful but brief, to the final one, which is no better than death (cf. Mimn. 2.10*). This 'anthem to youth' (Falkner 1995: 130) is presented from the perspective of a youthful speaker (note line 2 'may I die when these things no longer interest me'), contrasting with the wistful retrospective viewpoint of fr. 2*.

1 The rhetorical double question (intensified by the omission of ἐστί) immediately focuses our attention on the value of 'golden Aphrodite'. τίς δὲ βίος: inceptive δέ (*GP* 172), if indeed this is the beginning of the poem, gives the opening a conversational liveliness ('What's life, what's pleasure ...'). χρυσῆς Ἀφροδίτης: though gods are often associated with gold, Aphrodite is the only deity in early Greek poetry who is herself 'golden' (the epithet is later extended to Artemis by Bacchylides, 11.117); the metaphor expresses her power to dazzle and allure.

2 τεθναίην: an arresting wish, rejecting the joyless and sexless old age that lies ahead. ταῦτα: the vagueness is intriguing, making us wonder what exactly could be so important, and preparing for the answer in the following line. μέλοι: the subordinate temporal clause takes the optative by assimilation with τεθναίην (cf. Smyth §2186b, Goodwin §558).

3 The tricolon's pleonasm emphasizes the speaker's one-track mind. κρυπταδίη φιλότης: the phrase 'secret love-making' is used of adultery at *Il.* 6.161 (so too κρυπταδίης εὐνῆις at Hes. *WD* 329), but the speaker can hardly be celebrating such an offence, and here it refers to the clandestine love-affairs of the young. Nonetheless, the possibility of pre-marital sex for young women (γυναιξίν, 5) is shocking. μείλιχα δῶρα: the language of 'gifts' suggests the reciprocity of love-making.

4–5 οἷ' 'which are' (lit. 'such things as are', οἷα). ἥβης ... ἁρπαλέα 'the enticing blossoms of youth': flower imagery is frequently used in Greek poetry to express youth's fleeting and natural beauty (cf. Mimn. 2.3*). Here, by implication, the 'flowers' of sexual pleasure flourish briefly and are to be seized all the more eagerly. ἁρπαλέα (from ἁρπάζω, 'seize') implies 'rapturous', 'all-consuming' as well as 'to be snatched'; cf. ἁρπαλέως 'greedily'. ἀνδράσιν ἠδὲ γυναιξίν: the enjambment stresses the erotic pleasure of both sexes.

5–6 ὀδυνηρόν 'painful': for the inescapable physical degeneration of old age, compare Sappho's 'Tithonus poem' (fr. 58, restored by West): ἔμοι δ' ἄπαλον πρίν] ποτ' [ἔ]οντα χρόα γῆρας ἤδη | ἐπέλλαβε, λεῦκαι δ' ἐγ]ένοντο τρίχες ἐκ μελαίναν· | βάρυς δέ μ' ὁ [θ]ῦμος πεπόηται, γόνα δ' [ο]ὐ φέροισι, | τὰ δή ποτα λαίψηρ' ἔον ὄρχηϲθ' ἴϲα νεβρίοιϲι. ἐπέλθηι 'comes upon', personifying old age as a hostile force. γῆρας: the key word is enhanced by enjambment. ὅ ... τιθεῖ '[old age] which makes a man both ugly and worthless':

Mimnermus not only draws attention to the ugliness (and sexlessness: cf. line 9) of old age, but also links the old man's appearance to his moral and social standing. This reverses the aristocratic ideal of καλοκἀγαθία (the unity of beauty and virtue) and presents all people, including the rich and wellborn, as equally condemned to a loathsome and loveless old age. **αἰσχρόν:** for the loss of good looks, cf. Mimn. 5.5–6 τὸ δ' ἀργαλέον καὶ ἄμορφον | γῆρας ὑπὲρ κεφαλῆς αὐτίχ' ὑπερκρέμαται. **κακόν:** the conjecture makes a more pointed claim (see above) than the transmitted καλόν, '[old age] which makes even a handsome man ugly' (with Doederlein's ὅμως for ὁμῶς).

7 φρένας ἀμφί: for postpositive ἀμφί, and the φρένες ('heart') as the seat of cognition and emotion, cf. Hes. *Theog.* 554 χώσατο δὲ φρένας ἀμφί, *HHAp.* 273 σὺ δὲ φρένας ἀμφὶ γεγηθώς. **τείρουσι** 'wear away': cf. *Il.* 4.315 (Agamemnon wishes that Nestor's physical strength matched his spirit) ἀλλά σε γῆρας τείρει ὁμοίϊον.

8 αὐγὰς . . . ἠελίου: the old man's inability to enjoy such elemental beauty marks the misery of his condition; cf. Mimn. 2.2*, where youthful growth is nourished by the sun's rays.

9 ἐχθρός . . . γυναιξίν 'hated by boys and scorned by women': the balanced clauses present pederastic and heterosexual liaisons as complementary aspects of the sex life of the adult male (cf. Sol. 24.5–6 παιδός τ' ἠδὲ γυναικός, ἐπὴν καὶ ταῦτ' ἀφίκηται, | ὥρη, Introduction §4), but also as equally impossible for the ugly old man. **ἀτίμαστος:** the adjective (occurring only here) denotes the old man's loss of τιμή from women, compounding his sexual alienation. At Mimn. 5.7 old age itself is ἐχθρὸν ὁμῶς καὶ ἄτιμον.

10 οὕτως ἀργαλέον: old age is similarly 'painful' at Mimn. 2.6* and 5.2; this picks up on ὀδυνηρόν (line 5 above). **θεός:** Zeus, who gives Tithonus γῆρας, ὃ καὶ θανάτου ῥίγιον ἀργαλέου (Mimn. 4.2) and is responsible for mankind's hard existence: οὐδέ τίς ἐστιν | ἀνθρώπων ὧι Ζεὺς μὴ κακὰ πολλὰ διδοῖ (Mimn. 2.15–16*).

Mimnermus 2

Source: Stobaeus 4.34.12.

Like Mimn. 1*, this may be a complete poem (1n.) and falls into two halves, the first on the brevity of youth (1–8), the second on the miseries of old age (9–16). While youth is carefree (the young 'know nothing', 4–5), old age is full of suffering (poverty, childlessness, and illness are singled out). Once again (cf. Mimn. 1.5–10*), ageing leads to anxiety and isolation rather than serenity and esteem.

1–5 The 'men as leaves' theme is a traditional motif already in Homer, but whereas *Il.* 6.146–9 (often thought to have been adapted here by Mimn.: see Griffith 1975) and 21.462–7 emphasize the ephemerality of each mortal generation, Mimnermus' stress is on the brevity of youth. There is therefore no reason to see him engaging directly with the Homeric similes, but rather using a commonplace idea for his own ends (cf. Kelly 2015: 22–4).

1 ἡμεῖς δ': for inceptive δέ, see on Mimn. 1.1*. **οἷά τε φύλλα:** so-called epic τε, with relative, used in generalizing statements (cf. line 13 below ὧν τε, Mimn. 1.6*) or those describing habitual action (cf. line 8 below ὅσον τ'): *GP* 521–4. **φύλλα φύει:** alliteration (and *figura etymologica*, whether correct or not) marks the basic idea of fecundity; so too with αἶψ' αὐγῇς αὔξεται in the following line.

1–2 πολυάνθεμος ... | ἔαρος 'the flowery season of spring': the natural world mirrors the beauty and brevity of 'youth's bloom' (ἄνθεσιν ἥβης, 3; cf. ἥβης ἄνθεα, Mimn. 1.4*). **αὔξεται:** the subject (φύλλα, object of φύει) is understood from its opening thematic position, 'when they quickly grow in the sun's rays'. **ἠελίου:** the uncontracted epic–Ionic form, as always in Homer, except for Ἥλιος at *Od.* 8.271.

3 τοῖς (= τούτοις) ἴκελοι (lit. 'like them') maintains the focus on φύλλα. **πήχυιον ἐπὶ χρόνον** 'for a short time' (lit. 'for a cubit's length of time'). The cubit is the distance from elbow to tip of middle finger, and its use to measure time, first attested here, is parallel to such expressions as δάκτυλος ἀμέρα (Alcaeus fr. 346.1). **ἄνθεσιν:** instrumental dative (LSJ τέρπω II.2).

4–5 πρὸς ... | ... ἀγαθόν 'knowing neither the bad nor the good that come from the gods': in our youthful ignorance we are unaware of the inevitable changes of fortune that will end our happiness. As in the final lines (15–16), the emphasis is on the inescapability of suffering, dispensed by the gods.

5 Κῆρες are traditionally bringers of death, but Mimnermus' 'Dooms' bring old age as well, to suit his focus on the miseries of ageing. **μέλαιναι:** the epithet creates an effective contrast between our youth 'in the rays of the sun' (2) and the 'dark Dooms' that are always standing beside us (παρεστήκασι).

6 γήραος ἀργαλέου: see on Mimn. 1.10*.

7 θανάτοιο: i.e. an early death, before the misery of old age takes hold.

7–8 Once again the central idea of fleeting youth is expressed in imagery of natural growth (ἥβης καρπός ~ ἄνθεσιν ἥβης, 3) and the sun. **μίνυνθα:** adverbial, 'for a short time', modified by ὅσον. **ὅσον ... ἠέλιος** 'for as long as the sun's light is spread upon the earth', i.e. for a single day, and thus even briefer than the leaves' flourishing πήχυιον ἐπὶ χρόνον (3). **κίδναται:** κίδναμαι (passive of κίδνημι) is found only in poetry; σκεδάννυμαι (standard in prose) is similarly used of the sun's rays at Aesch. *Persae* 502–3 πρὶν σκεδασθῆναι θεοῦ | ἀκτῖνας.

9 αὐτὰρ ... ὥρης 'but when this, the fulfilment of youth, passes by'. **τέλος** suggests a state of perfection. **παραμείψεται:** short-vowel aorist

subjunctive. ὥρης: used earlier for a season of the year (1), the word reinforces the connection between natural and human flourishing.
10 αὐτίκα δή: emphatic, 'straightaway'. **τεθνάναι** 'to be dead': the first syllable is short (so-called Attic correption, before a mute–liquid combination). **βέλτιον** 'it is better' (with ellipse of ἐστί, as often in gnomic statements). **βίοτος**: epic equivalent of βίος. For the thought 'it's better to be dead than stay alive' in the context of old age, cf. Mimn. 4.2 γῆρας, ὃ καὶ θανάτου ῥίγιον ἀργαλέου.
11 πολλά ... κακά: three examples follow (ἄλλοτε ... ἄλλος ... ἄλλος): poverty, childlessness, and illness. **ἐν θυμῶι** locates the evils at the centre of our awareness. **ἄλλοτε οἶκος:** here the initial digamma originally in ϝοἶκος prevents hiatus; contrast δ' ἔργ' in the next line, where the original digamma is ignored. For ἄλλοτε in hiatus, see on Archil. 13.7*.
11–12 οἶκος | τρυχοῦται '(one man's) household is consumed': see on Sol. 4.21–2* (τρύχεται). **πενίης ... πέλει** 'and a painful life of poverty is his'. **πενίης ... ἔργ':** the struggles faced by the poor (lit. 'works of poverty'); see on Sol. 13.41–2*.

13–14 Since children were meant to support elderly parents, see to their funeral rites, keep alive their memory, and continue the family line, the lack of children would be felt with particular intensity as death approached. But ἱμείρων (14) also suggests an instinctive longing for children, and parental love free of self-interest. **ἐπιδεύεται** 'lacks' (+ gen.). **κατὰ γῆς ... εἰς Ἀΐδην:** emphatic tautology, as κατὰ γῆς itself already points to the underworld.

15–16 νοῦσον ... θυμοφθόρον 'a disease that wears down his heart' (rather than 'a life-destroying disease', since death has already been declared preferable to being old). **Ζεύς:** Achilles famously described the two jars of Zeus, one containing evil things, the other good; the best mortals can hope for is a mixture of the two, and no human life is free of suffering (*Il.* 24.527–33). **διδοῖ:** an epic–Ionic contracted form (= δίδωσι).

Mimnermus 12

Source: Athenaeus, *Scholars at Dinner* 11.469f–70b.

This fragment is quoted in a section of Athenaeus devoted to drinking cups: 'Mimnermus says in the *Nanno* that Helios crosses to the east as he sleeps in a golden bed made specifically for this purpose by Hephaestus, and he makes a riddling allusion to the hollow shape of the cup (αἰνισσόμενος τὸ κοῖλον τοῦ ποτηρίου). He puts it as follows: Ἠέλιος μὲν γὰρ κτλ.' The myth of Helios' night-time voyage around the waters of Ocean from west to east in a golden cup or bowl is used by many authors from Archaic epic onwards (Pisander's *Heraclea* fr. 5 Bernabé; e.g. Stes.

fr. 185 PMG, Aesch. fr. 69 R). West 1997: 507 claims that 'Mimnermus describes the eternal course of the Sun-god and his steeds, no doubt to contrast it with the numbered days of man' (cf. Fränkel 1975: 213), but the poet's emphasis is rather on the never-ending work undertaken by Helios and his horses (1–3), and so if any contrast with mortals is implied, it is more likely to be along those lines: cf. Gerber 1970: 111 'Mimnermus may have introduced this account of the Sun's daily toil as proof (note γάρ in v. 1) that not only men, but even gods, must endure hardships.'

1–4 The stress on continual work prepares for the depiction of the soundly sleeping god (5–8).

1 γάρ: the particle may support the idea that this is not the beginning of the poem (cf. Gerber, quoted above), but the presence of such particles as γάρ and ἀλλά at the start of elegiac pieces could aid their performance at *symposia*, where a poem might be used to pick up on, or contradict, the ideas expressed in the previous speaker's contribution. **ἔλαχεν:** the idea of a god's 'lot' (apportioned by Zeus) is a familiar one in early Greek thought (e.g. Hes. *Theog.* 73–4), but whereas the emphasis is usually on the welcome honours (τιμαί) given to each deity, here Helios' lot is πόνος, far from the ideal state of the gods 'who live at ease' (ῥεῖα ζώοντες, e.g. *Il.* 6.138). **ἤματα πάντα** 'day after day' (lit. 'all the days that are').

2 οὐδέ ... ἄμπαυσις ... οὐδεμία 'never any rest': similar admiration for the 'tireless' sun is expressed in the Homeric phrase Ἠέλιον ... ἀκάμαντα (*Il.* 18.239, 484).

3 ἵπποισίν τε καὶ αὐτῶι: Helios' horses and chariot are first mentioned in *HHDem.* 63, 88. The cyclic *Titanomachy* specified two male and two female horses (fr. 7 Bernabé). **ῥοδοδάκτυλος:** this formulaic epithet ('rosy-fingered Dawn') is usually taken to refer to rose-coloured rays of light spreading through the sky, creating a pattern like a spread hand, but it could refer to a single 'finger' of light at the horizon (cf. Alcaeus fr. 346.1 δάκτυλος ἀμέρα). If the epithet evokes the fragrance, beauty, and erotic associations of the flower, 'rosy-fingered Dawn' might also imply 'with beautiful hands displaying as a rose the essence of Aphrodite, or in a word, "sexy"' (Allen 1993: 101–2; cf. Irwin 1994).

4 Ὠκεανόν ... οὐρανόν: the sky was conceived as a dome covering the round flat earth, which was in turn surrounded by the river Ocean. The goddess Dawn precedes the sunrise, rising into the sky (εἰσαναβῆι) from the east. Mimn. fr. 11a depicts Helios' rays stored in a golden chamber at the eastern edge of the river Ocean. **εἰσαναβῆι:** aor. subjunctive of repeated action.

5–7 The detailed description of Helios' 'bed' or 'couch' (εὐνή, 5) is a 'riddling allusion' (see Athenaeus' comment in the introduction above) to the cup fashioned by Hephaestus.

5 πολυήρατος: the epithet is particularly apt for the exhausted god's intricately crafted 'bed', as it can mean both 'very lovely' and 'much longed for'.

6 κοΐλη 'hollow': an initial clue to the 'riddle' of the bed/cup. As the standard Homeric epithet for ships, κοῖλος is also well suited to a vehicle that carries Hephaestus around the waters of Ocean (see line 7 below for the cup's handles as ship's oars). **ἐληλαμένη** 'forged': perf. part. passive of ἐλαύνω ('to drive'), used of metal-working in the sense 'beat out'.

7 χρυσοῦ τιμήεντος: gen. of material, the appropriate metal for divine handiwork; cf. *Il.* 18.474–5 (Hephaestus prepares to forge arms for Achilles) χαλκὸν δ' ἐν πυρὶ βάλλεν ἀτειρέα κασσίτερόν τε | καὶ χρυσὸν τιμῆντα καὶ ἄργυρον. **ὑπόπτερος** 'winged' (of the cup's handles), enabling it to skim swiftly over the surface of the water (ἄκρον ἐφ' ὕδωρ). Some depictions of the cup in early Greek vase-painting show the handles as wings. The image evokes a comparison to the 'wings' which are a ship's oars.

8 εὕδονθ': agreeing with τόν (5), the participle takes us back to Helios, after the description of his 'bed'. **ἁρπαλέως** connotes intensity ('soundly') as well as pleasure ('gladly', cf. Mimn. 1.4*), an apt end to the day's labours.

8–9 Ἑσπερίδων... Αἰθιόπων: i.e. from the extreme west to the extreme east. Hesiod describes the Hesperides as daughters of Night, who tend the golden apples that grow beyond the western edge of Ocean (*Theog.* 215–16). The Ethiopians, at the edge of the known world, are generally depicted positively in Greek thought as being better than ordinary people and enjoying a special relationship with the gods. At *Od.* 1.23–4 they are divided into two groups, western and eastern, but their association with the east/sunrise is primary and more prevalent, and their king, Memnon, was the son of Eos/Dawn.

9–10 ἵνα... | ἑστᾶσ': Helios' horses and chariot await the new dawn. It is left unexplained how they themselves are transported overnight from west to east. One ancient author (Pherecydes 18a Fowler, quoted by Athenaeus, 11.470c) placed the horses in the same 'bed' as their master, but Mimnermus avoids such a crowded cup. **ἠριγένεια**: Dawn is born (the root γεν-) early (ἠρι-) each day.

11 ἔνθ'... υἱός 'and there Hyperion's son mounts his other vehicle'. **ἐπέβη**: gnomic, or timeless, aorist, expressing the sun's regular action. **ἑτέρων** 'other': i.e. his chariot, in contrast to his 'bed', described at length in the previous sentence. **ὀχέων**: the plural (ὄχεα) is regularly used by Homer of a single chariot. **Ὑπερίονος υἱός**: in Homer, Hyperion (popularly derived from ὑπὲρ ἰών, 'he that moves on high') is usually an epithet of the Sun, but most authors, including Mimnermus, follow the tradition used by Hesiod, where Hyperion is the father of the Sun (and also of the Moon and Dawn: *Theog.* 371–4). As it ends with a hexameter, the fragment is clearly incomplete. The poem may have concluded soon after by returning, in ring composition, to the god's daytime labours, but the narrative may equally well have taken a new turn.

Mimnermus 14

Source: Stobaeus 3.7.11.

Mimnermus recalls hearing of a warrior of the previous generation who excelled in battle against the Lydians, and contrasts his heroism with the qualities displayed by – most probably (see on τοῖον, line 2 below) – contemporary citizens of Smyrna. The piece may come from the *Smyrneis*, which commemorated the glorious victory over Gyges and the Lydians in the 660s, or it could be part of a separate exhortatory elegy that looked back to the same war (as Tyrt. 5–7* look back to the so-called First Messenian War). Smyrna was eventually destroyed by the Lydians under Alyattes *c*. 600, and it is tempting to link the poem to that disaster, but it may equally well refer to some earlier crisis calling for military action. In either case, the speaker is challenging his audience to match the fighting spirit of their elders. (Stobaeus quotes the fr. under the heading Περὶ ἀνδρείας (3.7.11).)

Mimnermus' portrayal of an exceptional warrior single-handedly routing the enemy reworks the pattern of a Homeric *aristeia* (cf. Swift 2015b: 100–1). His warrior is like Achilles, the best of all fighters (οὐ γάρ τις κείνου δηίων ἔτ᾿ ἀμεινότερος φώς, 9), and like Diomedes, who similarly decimated a foreign opponent with the support of Athena (τοῦ μὲν ἄρ᾿ οὔ ποτε πάμπαν ἐμέμψατο Παλλὰς Ἀθήνη | δριμὺ μένος κραδίης, 5–6). The passage also adapts a topos of Homeric battle exhortation, where warriors are spurred on by being compared to great fighters of the past. So Agamemnon, for example, seeks to motivate Diomedes by comparing him unfavourably with his father, Tydeus (*Il.* 4.370–400). In contrast to epic, however, which looks back to the distant world of mythological heroes, Mimnermus invokes the example of the previous generation, and he gains his knowledge of the past not only from the Muses (whom he invoked in the poem's proem: fr. 13), but also from the eyewitness reports of his fellow citizens (ἐμέο προτέρων πεύθομαι, οἵ μιν ἴδον, 2).

1 οὐ μὲν δὴ κείνου γε: the repeated negatives used to describe the warrior's achievements (cf. 5 τοῦ μὲν ἄρ᾿ οὔ ποτε πάμπαν, 9 οὐ γάρ τις κείνου) underline the contrast with the feeble fighters of today. **κείνου:** the identity of the famous warrior was presumably well known to the audience (or may have been made explicit in lines now missing). **μένος καὶ ἀγήνορα θυμόν** 'might and warlike spirit'. The phrase is used by Odysseus as he tries to placate Ajax in the underworld: δάμασον δὲ μένος καὶ ἀγήνορα θυμόν (*Od.* 11.562). In Homer, 'when a man yields to his θυμός ἀγήνωρ, his actions have negative effects for other men' (Graziosi and Haubold 2003:

66), but the phrase is wholly positive here. Fowler 1987: 46 observes '[the poem's] subject [i.e. martial exhortation] engenders a larger number of epicisms than is normal in this poet'; see below on πυκινὰς κλονέοντα φάλαγγας (3), φῶτα φερεμμελίην (4), δριμὺ μένος κραδίης (6), προμάχους (6), αἱματόεν<τος ἐν> ὑσμίνηι πολέμοιο (7), φυλόπιδος κρατερῆς | ἔργον (10–11).

2 τοῖον 'such (as yours)': given the tradition of battle exhortation, a contrast with the fighting spirit of the speaker's audience is the likeliest scenario, though others are imaginable: e.g. Bowie 1986: 29 'The narrative could have run: "Then x and his *hetairoi* were hard pressed: his *hetairoi* began to panic and retreat; not such ..."'. Moreover, as Swift 2015b: 101 notes, 'Since we lack the poem's wider context, we should be cautious of assuming that it was accusatory overall: if, for example, the lines were spoken by a character in the heat of battle, and were followed by a description of his companions' courageous rallying, our interpretation of the tone would be quite different.' **πεύθομαι** ('I learn'), with the information in the accusative (μένος ... | τοῖον) and its source in the genitive (ἐμέο προτέρων), as in πυνθάνεσθαί τινός τι. πεύθομαι is the preferred form in epic. **ἐμέο προτέρων:** lit. 'from those before me', i.e. 'from my elders'. The warrior's fame endures from one generation to the next, a key theme of military exhortation (cf. Irwin 2005: 19). The speaker is too young to have fought at the battle itself, which matches the traditional date of Mimnermus' birth, *c*. 670, and the defeat of Gyges in the 660s. West changed the transmitted ἐμεῦ to ἐμέο; cf. *Il.* 10.124 ἐμέο πρότερος, though that is the only instance of the intermediate form in Homer (ἐμεῖο > ἐμέο > ἐμεῦ). **οἵ μιν ἴδον:** as Swift 2015b: 101 observes, 'The description is vivid and exciting: we are encouraged to imagine the older men's story as a visual narrative, with the details of location, military equipment, and the hero's dynamic movement through the battleline.'

3–4 '[who saw him] routing the close-packed ranks of the Lydian cavalry on the plain of Hermus with his ash-spear'. **ἱππομάχων:** Herodotus describes the Lydians of Croesus' time (560–546 BC) as superb horsemen (1.27.3, 79.3). **πυκινὰς ... | ... πεδίον:** the deployment of epic phraseology underlines the warrior's prowess: e.g. *Il.* 5.93–4 (Diomedes' *aristeia*) ὡς ὑπὸ Τυδεΐδηι πυκιναὶ κλονέοντο φάλαγγες | Τρώων, 5.96 θύνοντ' ἂμ πεδίον πρὸ ἔθεν κλονέοντα φάλαγγας. **Ἕρμιον:** the river Hermus (now the Gediz), known to Homer (*Il.* 20.392) and Hesiod (*Theog.* 343), runs into the Aegean Sea north of Smyrna (cf. Hdt. 1.80.1). The possibility that Mimnermus' own name commemorates the battle (μίμν- + Ἕρμος, 'he who resists at the Hermus') is attractive, but names ending in -ερμος were common among Ionian Greeks of the time. (If the etymology is accepted, Mimnermus' birth would of course need to be dated after the battle *c*. 660.) **ἂμ:** apocope of ἀνά before a labial (ἂν before dentals, e.g. ἄν τοῦ τοίχου; ἄγ before gutturals, ἄγ γύαλα). **φῶτα:** the use of poetic φώς ('man') to add a description is characteristic of epic, e.g. *Il.* 7.136 τοῖσι δ' Ἐρευθαλίων πρόμος ἵστατο, ἰσόθεος φώς. **φερεμμελίην** 'carrying an ash-wood spear': the epithet, found only here, may have been preferred to Homeric ἐϋμμελίης in order to create alliteration and avoid hiatus.

5 Παλλὰς Ἀθήνη: the goddess had a large temple in the centre of Smyrna, and so she is fit to judge the local hero's courage.

6 δριμὺ . . . κραδίης 'his heart's fierce might'.

6–7 εὖθ' . . . | σεύαιθ' 'when he rushed': optative (3rd sg. aor. middle) of repeated action in the past (Goodwin §532). **αἱματόεν<τος . . . πολέμοιο** 'in the combat of bloody war': once again typically Homeric language (e.g. *Il.* 9.650 οὐ γὰρ πρὶν πολέμοιο μεδήσομαι αἱματόεντος) emphasizes the fighter's bravery.

8 βιαζόμενος 'defying [the enemy's sharp missiles]': the meaning 'overpower' is more common, but the sense here parallels βίαι + gen. 'in spite of'. **βέλεα:** javelins, spears, arrows.

9–10 οὐ . . . | ἔσκεν 'no man of the enemy remained his better'. **ἀμεινότερος:** a rare double comparative, formed from ἀμείνων. **ἔσκεν:** 3rd sg. epic imperfect of εἰμί, with durative aspect.

10–11 ἐποίχεσθαι . . . ἔργον: lit. 'at going about the task of harsh war', another expression with an epic colouring: e.g. *Il.* 6.491–2 καὶ ἀμφιπόλοισι κέλευε | ἔργον ἐποίχεσθαι, 16.208 φυλόπιδος μέγα ἔργον, 18.241–2 παύσαντο δὲ δῖοι Ἀχαιοὶ | φυλόπιδος κρατερῆς καὶ ὁμοιΐου πολέμοιο. **ὅτ' . . . ἠελίοιο:** West's supplement (= line 12) <εἴκελα χαλκείοις τεύχεσι λαμπόμενος> is the neatest suggestion so far: 'when he advanced, his bronze armour gleaming like the swift sun's light' (εἴκελα, n. pl. used adverbially). The interpretation favoured by some, 'so long as he moved in the rays of the swift sun' (i.e. as long as he was alive), is untenable, since the bare dative 'in the rays' (αὐγῆισιν) and 'he moved' or 'he lived/was carried through life' for φέρετο are impossible. φέρετο in the sense 'he rushed/advanced' is a standard epic term in a battle context, but the clause is incomplete. **ὠκέος ἠελίοιο:** for the sun's swift chariot and horses, see Mimn. 12.9*.

SOLON

Solon (c. 640–560 BC) is a central figure in the early history of Athens. Politician, legislator, and poet, he is the first Athenian (and the only one before Aeschylus in the 470s–450s) whose works have survived, and his poems were one of the main sources for later historians of the period. As archon in 594/3, he introduced reforms that affected almost every area of the Athenian state (see further below), and later tradition celebrated him as a wandering wise man, one of the Seven

Sages. Thus Solon's reputation for wisdom and moderation (the latter a recurring idea in his political poems: see esp. 4c, 5*, 6*, 7, 36*, 37) led Herodotus, for example, to depict his encounter in Sardis with Croesus, king of Lydia, who fatally ignores Solon's reflections on the dangers of excessive wealth and the uncertainty of human life (Hdt. 1.29–33). By the late fifth century Solon had become a quasi-legendary figure honoured in hero-cult (Kearns 1989: 198), hailed by some as the founding hero of Athenian democracy, by others as the guardian of a more conservative ancestral constitution (*patrios politeia*). Such attempts to co-opt Solon's authority have influenced his presentation in the ancient sources, but we can still be confident that there is more history than myth in the surviving accounts of his laws and reforms (cf. Rhodes 2006: 259).

Solon's main economic reforms came in response to growing tensions between rich Athenian overlords and poor farmers. Solon's solution, commonly known as the 'shaking-off of burdens' (or *seisachtheia*: see Sol. 36*), probably meant that the farmers were no longer obliged to render up a sixth of their produce to their overlords; it also liberated those Athenians who had been enslaved for debt, repatriated those who had been sold abroad, and made the future practice of enslavement for debt illegal (cf. Stanley 1999: 210–18, Harris 2002, Forsdyke 2006: 347).

Solon's political reforms were geared to extending decision-making power beyond a narrow aristocratic elite. He created a new council (βουλή) of 400 members to consider business for the assembly. He also divided the citizenry into four classes based on the size of their annual harvest; although only the three highest classes could hold political office, the poorest were allowed to attend the assembly and thus have a say in the running of the state. As with Solon's new legal code (cf. 36.18–20*), which gave all citizens access to the courts, the egalitarian thrust of his policies makes Solon a key figure in the development of democracy at Athens. By weakening the power of the wealthy elite and their inherited privileges, and by focusing on the cohesion and benefit of the community as a whole, Solon laid the foundations for the classical concept of the free Athenian citizen, who is expected to play a part in running the city (cf. Manville 1990: 124–56, Lewis 2006: 6).

Thus we cannot really separate 'Solon the poet' from 'Solon the politician', and the role of the poet as a public figure in Archaic and Classical Greece is nowhere clearer than with him. Moreover, we can see how Solon's skills as a poet, especially his striking use of language, simile, metaphor, and persona, enabled him to influence his audience, persuading them of the need for change and the wisdom of his policies. But it would be a mistake to see Solon as exclusively a political writer, since he also deals with homosexual desire (25), travel (28), food (38–40), gnomic reflections on human life and happiness (14, 16–18, 23, 26, 27*), and even the untrustworthiness of poets (20, 29). Indeed, excluding the Theognidea, we have more elegy from Solon than anyone else (*c*. 230 lines), including the longest surviving elegiac poem before the Hellenistic period (13*).

As regards the chronology of the poems, some political pieces are likely to predate Solon's archonship (e.g. 4*, 4a, 4c), while others are evidently later because they defend his reforms (5*, 34, 36*, 37) or boast of having resisted the chance to become a tyrant (32–3). Though most of Solon's works were composed for performance at *symposia*, whether among like-minded *hetairoi* or to persuade fellow aristocrats of the need for reform, we cannot rule out performance in more public settings (for example, at public meetings or city festivals: see 1–3*, 36*). In any case, as far as the political poems are concerned, it is striking how, unlike Alcaeus or Theognis, for example, who address an audience that shares their social and political views, Solon must balance the competing demands of different sections of Athenian society, and so uses all his rhetorical skill to persuade the listener to accept his political and ethical values.

With a historically significant figure like Solon it is particularly tempting to interpret the primary narrator in a simple biographical manner, but while Solon's poetry clearly draws on his own experiences as a politician and legislator, he too must fashion a convincing authorial persona (see Introduction §3). His self-presentation underlines his role as a moderate and impartial reformer, not a revolutionary, and by drawing on the language, ethics, and theology of Homer and Hesiod (especially in 4* and 13*), Solon imbues his commitment to justice and communal values with the authority of traditional wisdom.

Solon 1–3

Solon's poem (originally 100 lines long, according to Plutarch, *Sol.* 8.2) engages with Athens' war against Megara for control of the island of Salamis. Occupying a strategic position in the Saronic Gulf, Salamis was important to the trade routes of both cities, and its capture was a significant event in the early expansion of Athenian power (*c*. 600 BC). As in the martial elegies of Callinus and Tyrtaeus, the speaker of *Salamis* stages a dramatic call to arms. So skilful is Solon's evocation of crisis and public exhortation that later tradition presented him rushing into the agora to perform the poem (Plut. *Sol.* 8.1–2). Though it is not impossible that the work was composed for a public occasion rather than the *symposion*, the 'agora' is likely to be based on a misunderstanding of the poem's opening lines (see on 1.2*). Only eight lines survive, but they are enough to show Solon's skilled use of persona (as quasi-herald in 1*) and emotion (shame in 2* and 3*), building on the elegiac tradition of martial exhortation.

Solon 1

Source: Plutarch, Solon 8.1–2.

Plutarch quotes these lines as the beginning of the poem. αὐτός intensifies both the following words, stressing not only that the speaker himself has come from Salamis (and so has witnessed events there personally), but also that he is acting as his own herald. κῆρυξ: the image evokes the sacred inviolability and trust invested in the role of herald (cf. κήρυκες Διὸς ἄγγελοι ἠδὲ καὶ ἀνδρῶν, Il. 1.334; κήρυκες … Διΐ φίλοι, 8.517), encouraging the audience to see Solon as a credible messenger acting in the best interests of Athens. ἱμερτῆς: Salamis is 'lovely' or 'desirable', a common epithet for cities or islands, especially one's homeland (cf. Σπάρτης ἱμερόεσσα πόλις, Tyrt. 4.4*), but here also reminding Solon's (Athenian) audience that Salamis is worth going to war over. κόσμον . . . θέμενος 'adopting (lit. composing) song, an ordered form of words, instead of speech'. Solon plays on the incongruity of a singing herald, while also advertising his skill as a poet, whose message will be all the more memorable for being in verse. κόσμον ἐπέων: in apposition to ὠιδήν (cf. Sol. 13.21–2* θεῶν ἕδος αἰπὺν ἱκάνει | οὐρανόν). The phrase κόσμον ἐπέων is also used by Parmenides: δόξας δ' ἀπὸ τοῦδε βροτείας | μάνθανε κόσμον ἐμῶν ἐπέων ἀπατηλὸν ἀκούων (fr. 8.51–2 DK = D8.56–7 Laks–Most). The 'orderly array' of poetry is also claimed by Simonides: 11.23* τόνδ[ε μελ]ίφρονα κ[όσμον ἀο]ιδῆς. For praise of poetry sung κατὰ κόσμον, cf. Od. 8.489, HHHerm. 433. κόσμος denotes civic order and good government (e.g. πόλεων κόσμοι, Pl. Prt. 322c), and so bolsters Solon's claim to be offering sound political and military advice. ἀντ' ἀγορῆς: already in Homer ἀγορή can mean simply 'speech' as well as the 'assembly' where speeches are made (cf. Il. 2.788 οἱ δ' ἀγορὰς ἀγόρευον); its misconstrual here as 'before the assembly' may well be the origin of the idea that Solon performed Salamis in the agora of Athens. (A statue of Solon commemorating his intervention was set up in the agora of Salamis in the early fourth century BC: Aeschin. Against Timarchus 25, Dem. On the False Embassy 19.251.) Most scholars are sceptical, favouring the symposion (so too Bowie 1986: 19), but the possibility of performance before a broader audience cannot be definitively excluded (cf. Thomas 1995: 111–12); on public elegy, see Introduction §§1–2.

Solon 2

Source: Diogenes Laertius, *Lives of the Philosophers* 1.47.

Diogenes, who quotes these lines, describes them as having a particular appeal for the Athenians, presumably because of their ebullient patriotism.

1–2 εἴην . . . | . . . πατρίδ' ἀμειψάμενος: to exchange his homeland is a shocking wish for Solon to express before his fellow Athenians, underscoring the national disgrace of abandoning the struggle for Salamis. **τότ'** 'in that case', i.e. 'if we give up fighting for Salamis', emphasized by the preceding particle δή (cf. *GP* 228). **Φολεγάνδριος ἢ Σικινήτης:** the use of Pholegandros and Sicinos, minor islands in the southern Cyclades, exploits mainlanders' contempt for poorer, less developed islanders (cf. Iolaus at Eur. *Hcld.* 84–5, οὐ νησιώτην, ὦ ξένοι, τρίβω βίον, | ἀλλ' ἐκ Μυκηνῶν σὴν ἀφίγμεθα χθόνα). Moreover, the southern Cyclades had been colonized by Dorians from the Peloponnese, so Solon's wish is effectively to become Dorian instead of Ionian, a shaming declaration for his Athenian audience to hear.

3–4 Solon's quotation of anonymous, shaming criticism mirrors the use of τις-speeches in Homer (for Hector's particular concern with 'what people will say', cf. *Il.* 6.459–61, 22.106–10), a connection reinforced by the epic phrases αἶψα γάρ and μετ' ἀνθρώποισι. **Ἀττικός** (like Ἀθηναίου in line 2) implicates Solon's Athenian audience in the blame to come. **οὗτος ἀνήρ:** for the contemptuous use of οὗτος, cf. LSJ C 3. **τῶν Σαλαμιναφετέων** 'one of those Salamis-ceders'. Solon's sarcastic neologism (Σαλαμιναφέτης, from Σαλαμίς + ἀφίημι) gives the imaginary insult a punchy, humiliating ending. Moreover, the neologism itself hints at the widespread notoriety of losing Salamis ('Salamis-ceder' will become a familiar term), making the Athenians' shame all the more intense.

Solon 3

Source: Diogenes Laertius, *Lives of the Philosophers* 1.47.

Diogenes continues by quoting these lines. We do not know if 3* followed 2* in the original poem (the asyndeton makes it unlikely). In any case the transition from evoking shame (2*) to urging battle (3*) is typical of martial exhortation (cf. Callin. 1*, Tyrt. 10, 11, 12*). **ἴομεν:** 1st pl. epic short-vowel subjunctive, with lengthened iota. The move from critical 'I' (in 2*) to united 'we' rallies the Athenians behind the war. **μαχησόμενοι . . . ἀπωσόμενοι:** future participles expressing purpose (Goodwin §840, *CGCG* §52.41). **ἱμερτῆς:** marked by enjambment, and stressing again that Salamis is worth the fight: see on Sol. 1.1*. **χαλεπόν τ' αἶσχος:** strong language of disgrace; for Homeric *aischos* and its root meaning of 'ugliness', see Cairns 1993: 54–5. ἀπωσόμενοι: the middle form of ἀπωθέω is typically used in epic of driving back the enemy (e.g. *Il.* 8.206 Τρῶας ἀπώσασθαι) and so evokes the image of Solon and the Athenians physically repelling disgrace as they go to fight the Megarians for control of Salamis.

Solon 4

Source: Demosthenes 19.254–6.

Demosthenes quotes this poem to illustrate Solon's patriotism, which he contrasts with the treacherous behaviour of his opponent Aeschines (*On the False Embassy*, delivered in 343 BC). For Demosthenes and his audience, Solon embodied the ideal Athenian statesman, an enemy of greed and corruption, who enabled Athens to flourish. The poem's insistence on restraining the city's wealthy elite, whose conduct has led to the enslavement of poorer citizens (23–5), suggests composition before Solon's reforms. Though the transmitted text lacks some verses, the lacunae are unlikely to be large (see 11, 23–5nn.), and it is the second longest poem of Solon's to have survived (13* being by far the longest). Having stressed the gods' concern for Athens (1–4), Solon analyses the threat posed to the whole city by the selfish and unjust conduct of its citizens, especially its wealthy leaders (5–29). He ends with a personal warning to his fellow citizens to avoid lawlessness and embrace order, which is the solution to their troubles (30–9).

One of the most striking features of Sol. 4* is the way it applies the language of epic combat to civil war (*stasis*), and so suggests that the dichotomies of war versus peace, and enemy versus self, do not work in contemporary Athens (see on 3–4, 9–10, 12–13, 19–20). Solon draws on traditional conceptions of personified Justice (*Dikē*) and Lawfulness (*Eunomia*), and enlivens his analysis with striking imagery that makes abstract ideas concrete and easier to grasp: the foundations of Justice (14), the wounded city (17), slumbering war (19), evil leaping into the home (28), the flowers of ruin (35), and so on (for Solon's use of imagery in general, see Noussia-Fantuzzi 2010: 67–77; on this poem specifically, Henderson 2006).

Solon's insistence on humanity's personal responsibility for their suffering is a leitmotif of 13* as well, yet here there is even more emphasis on the repercussions of individual crime for the whole community. The poem's stress on social cohesion and the rule of law makes it an eloquent statement of Greek (and not solely Athenian) *polis* ideology.

1–8 The opening lines encapsulate the central argument of the poem: the gods will never destroy Athens (1–4), but its foolish citizens will

(5–8) – unless they take Solon's advice. By denying that the gods are to blame, Solon reinforces not only the Athenians' own culpability for their city's collapse but also their responsibility for finding a solution (cf. Sol. 11.1–4*).

1–4 Traditional epic language (the 'portion/dispensation' of Zeus, 'blessed, immortal gods', 'stout-hearted' Athena, 'of the mighty sire', etc.) evokes the enduring power and concern of the gods.

1 ἡμετέρη δὲ πόλις: though (as usual) we cannot be certain this is the opening of the poem, 'our state' grabs the audience's attention, while also implying that Solon has everyone's interests in mind. For the particle δέ used to begin a speech, see *GP* 172–3; it serves here to create a sense of spontaneous performance.

2 φρένας ('intentions') stresses the gods' active care for Athens.

3–4 offer the ultimate reassurance for an Athenian audience, the protection of their 'guardian' (ἐπίσκοπος) goddess. **ὀβριμοπάτρη:** the epithet ('daughter of a mighty father') is unique to Athena and triggers the audience's awareness of her role in epic as Zeus's favourite child and the enforcer of his will (e.g. *Il*. 5.747, *Od*. 3.135; cf. Allan 2006: 20–1), enhancing the status of both Athena and her favourite city. **χεῖρας ὕπερθεν ἔχει:** a familiar gesture of divine protection (e.g. *Il*. 24.374, where Priam thinks a god may be helping him, but ironically does not understand how). Athena, then, will assuredly oppose the city's enemies, which makes the threat from within Athens itself (5–8) all the more disturbing, for (it is implied) even divine protection cannot help if you are fighting your own people.

5–16 The causal (and moral) sequence 'greed, *hybris*, punishment' is typical of Archaic and Classical Greek thought; see on 9–10 below. Irwin 2005: 164 calls lines 5–8 'essentially a barrage of Hesiodic themes'.

5–6 αὐτοί ... | ἀστοί 'the citizens themselves'. Solon makes clear that all Athenians are susceptible to the temptations of greed and injustice, not just the rich. Enjambment emphasizes the key word (cf. ὕβριος in line 8). **ἀφραδίηισιν** 'by their foolish actions'. **χρήμασι πειθόμενοι** 'persuaded by wealth'. Solon is the earliest Greek thinker to analyse the dangers of an unlimited desire for wealth (cf. Sol. 13.71–3*, where the desire is described as insatiable). On Solon's stand against avarice and its importance to politics of the Classical period, see Balot 2001: 79.

7 δήμου θ' ἡγεμόνων ἄδικος νόος: a new subject added to the previous one (rather than a new sentence). Solon's focus now moves to 'the leaders of the people', the ruling class whose crimes are described in lines 9–14. Solon's view of leadership is traditional (and spelled out in detail in both Homer and Hesiod): the good leader protects his community and does not endanger it by the selfish pursuit of wealth and power. But although Solon is part of a wider Archaic tradition criticizing the selfishness and

COMMENTARY: SOLON 4   137

luxury of aristocrats (cf. Donlan 1973: 147–54), his insistence on treating the δῆμος fairly is unusually clear and tied to the contemporary crisis in Athens. οἷσιν ἑτοῖμον 'for whom [much pain] is ready and waiting', with ἐστί understood.

8 ὕβριος ἐκ μεγάλης: epic–Ionic gen. sg. of ὕβρις, 'as a result of their great insolence'; *hybris* embraces a wide range of insulting and/or outrageous actions, as the following lines make clear.

9–10 focus on typical benefits of peace ('the festivities of the banquet'), but make clear that the citizens are not capable of enjoying them. Solon is thus undermining the traditional dichotomy of war versus peace – one might think, for example, of the city at war and the city at peace depicted on Achilles' shield, where there are two modes: either you are at war, where there is bloodshed, but also divine support and opportunity to win glory; or you are at peace, where there is law and order, and the pleasures of stable life such as weddings and feasts (*Il.* 18.490–540). But Solon departs from this by suggesting that in his world, though the Athenians are formally at peace, they have civil strife, which disrupts the dichotomy of enemy versus self and is harder to manage. **κατέχειν κόρον** 'to restrain excess' (i.e. their insatiable desire for more). For the 'Archaic chain' of *koros* (satiety or greed) leading to *hybris* (arrogance) punished by *atē* (ruin, or the delusion leading to it), cf. e.g. Sol. 4.34–5*, 6.3–4*, 13.11–13*, 13.71–6*, Thgn. 44–52*, 153–4, 227–32. One of the blessings of *Eunomia* is therefore the halting of *koros* (see line 34). **εὐφροσύνας ... δαιτός:** the leaders cannot even feast properly, i.e. their excess extends to food and drink. The gluttonous suitors of the *Odyssey* begin a long Archaic tradition (especially prominent in poetry about the *symposion*: cf. Xenoph. 1*) which identifies excessive consumption with moral disorder. **κοσμεῖν** 'to arrange (in an orderly fashion)': for the word's connection with feasts, cf. Pind. *Nem.* 1.21–2 ἔνθα μοι ἁρμόδιον | δεῖπνον κεκόσμηται.

11 At least two hexameters are missing either side of the pentameter line 11, but the already substantial list of hybristic acts (9–14) suggests the gap was not much bigger (cf. Faraone 2008: 173). **πλουτέουσιν:** for the consequences of unjustly acquired wealth, cf. Sol. 13.7–13*, Hes. *WD* 320–6. **πειθόμενοι** 'relying on' + dat.

12–14 These lines describe the greediness of the Athenian elite, but do so using the language of a sacked city (note especially ἀφαρπαγῆι, 13), where the enemy run amok and plunder shrines (here the shrine of *Dikē* herself). This pillaging, however, is internal: there is no 'us' versus 'them' as in a real war, and the selfishness of the factions is condemned. Neither sacred nor public property is safe. The lust for unjust wealth leads to anarchy. **τι:** adverbial: 'in any way'. **φειδόμενοι** 'sparing', emphasized by enjambment between distichs (cf. 25). **ἀφαρπαγῆι,** 'by plunder', marks the forcefulness of the stealing; cf. 34.1 (on those Athenians who demanded a redistribution of land) οἱ δ' ἐφ' ἁρπαγῆισιν ἦλθον. ἄλλοθεν ἄλλος: an epic formula (e.g. *Il.* 9.311, also at line-ending). For epic formulas in elegy, see Introduction §5. σεμνὰ Δίκης θέμεθλα 'the venerable foundations of Justice', conjuring up the image of an altar, temple, or statue dedicated to the personified goddess – all imposing structures that inspire reverence. Kicking the altar of *Dikē* is a consequence of excessive wealth and greed at Aesch. *Ag.* 381–4 and *Eum.* 538–41.

15–16: For Justice overcoming *hybris* in the end, cf. Hes. *WD* 213–18, concluding παθὼν δέ τε νήπιος ἔγνω. Solon's thought is traditional (cf. Lloyd-Jones 1983: 44–5), but adapted to suit the political crisis in Athens. σιγῶσα: the goddess' silence is menacing. τῶι . . . χρόνωι: on justice 'slow but sure', see also Sol. 13.25–32*. πάντως ἦλθ': gnomic aorist, 'certainly comes'. ἀποτεισομένη: future participle expressing purpose (Goodwin §840, *CGCG* §52.41), 'to exact punishment'.

17 With 'this' (τοῦτ', 17) Solon refers back to the crisis outlined in 5–16, comprising both the outrageous behaviour of the citizens and the ensuing vengeance of *Dikē*. ἤδη ('already') stresses how urgent the crisis is. The combination of present (ἔρχεται) and gnomic aorist (18 ἤλυθε and 20 ὤλεσεν) gives Solon's analysis a general validity that bolsters its application to the social breakdown in contemporary Athens. πάσηι πόλει: all suffer, not just those carried away by greed. Solon's emphasis on the collective good was an important contribution to the development of Greek political thought: cf. Vlastos 1993: 38. ἕλκος ἄφυκτον 'as an inescapable wound', in apposition to τοῦτο. The metaphor figures the city as a social organism; for the 'body politic' in Greek thought, see Brock 2013: 69–82.

18 ἐς . . . δουλοσύνην 'and swiftly it [the city] falls into vile slavery', i.e. the subjugation of the many to the few, as the leading citizens pursue their own interests with no regard for the wider community; lines 23–5 further specify the enslavement of the poor.

19–20 Civic turmoil and death are presented as the inevitable result of gross inequality and exploitation; cf. Thgn. 39–52*. ἥ: the relative clause elaborates upon its antecedent, δουλοσύνην. στάσιν ἔμφυλον: lit. 'strife within the tribe', as rival aristocratic factions compete for money and power. στάσις in the sense 'civil war' is first attested here; cf. Thgn. 51* στάσιές τε καὶ ἔμφυλοι φόνοι ἀνδρῶν, Hdt. 8.3 στάσις γὰρ ἔμφυλος πολέμου ὁμοφρονέοντος τοσούτωι κάκιόν ἐστι ὅσωι πόλεμος εἰρήνης. πόλεμον θ' εὕδοντ' ἐπεγείρει: for war awakened from its 'sleep', cf. *Il.* 20.31 (of Zeus) πόλεμον δ' ἀλίαστον ἔγειρε; the common metaphor is made more sinister by being applied to internal conflict (rather than fighting external enemies). ἐρατὴν . . . ἡλικίην: Solon evokes (typically Homeric) pity for the loss of 'lovely youth', but the context of civil war makes their destruction peculiarly shocking.

21–2 ἐκ . . . δυσμενέων 'at the hands of its enemies'. As στάσιν (19) and φίλους (22) make clear, however, the city's enemies are its own citizens.

ταχέως: destruction comes quickly; cf. 18 ταχέως. πολυήρατον: Athens is 'much-loved', like 'beloved' Salamis (Sol. 1.1*, 3.2*). τρύχεται: lit. 'consumed', suggesting the careless waste of the city's resources. ἐν συνόδοις τοῖς ἀδικέουσι φίλους 'in gatherings of those who wrong their friends'. The damning word (φίλους, i.e. their fellow Athenians) is delayed for maximum effect.

23–5 Solon gives a specific example of how 'these evils' (ταῦτα . . . κακά) are undermining Athenian society, as some of its poorest citizens are sold into slavery abroad. In 36*, a defence of his political achievements, Solon boasts of liberating and repatriating these Athenians. στρέφεται 'roam at large'. πραθέντες . . . δεθέντες: aor. pass. participles, from πέρνημι ('I sell'; cf. 36.9*) and δέω ('I bind'). The indignity is underlined by the *figura etymologica* δεσμοῖσι . . . δεθέντες. At least one (pentameter) line is lost after 25, the sense of which may be preserved in garbled form in a single MS.: παίκακα (sc. πάγκακα) δουλοσύνης ζυγὰ φέρουσι βία.

26–9 As Will 1958: 309 remarks, 'The picture of the city haunted to its last nook by evil is one of the great visions of Greek poetry.' The verbs (ἔρχεται, ὑπέρθορεν, εὗρε) characterize the κακόν as an unstoppable creature, echoing the personified evils that 'roam at large' (στρέφεται, 23). δημόσιον . . . οἴκαδ' ἑκάστωι: the evil is 'public' but invades every household. αὔλειοι . . . θύραι 'the courtyard doors refuse to hold it back any longer'. ὑψηλὸν δ' ὑπὲρ . . . ὑπέρθορεν: repetition heightens our sense of the evil's 'leap'. πάντως 'assuredly' (cf. 16). φεύγων . . . ἧι: 3rd sg. pres. subj. of εἰμί, used in a periphrastic construction with the participle (cf. Rijksbaron 2006: 126–7, *CGCG* §52.51, Bentein 2016), 'even if he flees'. ἐν μυχῶι . . . θαλάμου: a Homeric phrase (like αὔλειοι . . . θύραι), 'to the innermost recess of his room'. The everyday details (yard, doors, wall, room) encourage the audience to picture their own homes under attack.

30–8 Having catalogued the city's troubles, Solon now offers a clear-cut solution.

30 ταῦτα refers back to the whole description of unjust behaviour and its consequences (5–29). **θυμὸς . . . με κελεύει** 'my heart bids me'. An epic phrase, lending authority to Solon's moral and political advice. After lengthy third-person analysis of the Athenians' folly, the declaration of Solon's first-person perspective is arresting. **διδάξαι . . . Ἀθηναίους:** all Greek poets were expected to teach as well as entertain (cf. Ar. *Frogs* 1053–6), but Solon adopts an explicitly didactic persona, reminiscent of Hesiod's condemnation of greedy kings who abuse justice (*WD* 248–64). Solon aims to teach 'the Athenians' in general, not a narrow aristocratic elite, since even if the poem were composed with the *symposion* in mind, it could also be reperformed and read in other contexts (see Introduction §2).

31–9 Δυσνομίη and Εὐνομίη are personified powers in Hesiod (*Theog.* 230, 902), where the former is daughter of Eris (Strife), and the latter is daughter of Zeus and Themis, and has Dike (Justice) and Eirene (Peace) among her sisters. Since Solon has already in effect enumerated the bad effects of Disorder (5-29), he recaps them here in a single line (31) as a foil to the extensive and artful description of Good Order and her benefits (32-9). As an encomiastic list of Eunomia's varied powers (note how she is the active subject of the many verbs), the passage has a hymnic quality (similar in manner and content to Hesiod's catalogue of Zeus's powers: WD 5-8), whose solemnity is enhanced by an elevated style, including chiasmus (34-5, 36-7), asyndeton and epigrammatic brevity (34), numerous metaphors (34-7), successive verbs in first position (35-8), and ring composition (ἄρτια πάντ', 32 ~ πάντα ... ἄρτια, 39).

32 εὔκοσμα καὶ ἄρτια 'well ordered and fitting'. Eunomia restores the *kosmos* ('order') which was the one of the hallmarks of peace (κοσμεῖν ... ἐν ἡσυχίηι, 10).

33 πέδας 'shackles'. Unlike the chains binding the poor and enslaved (25), these are merited.

34 The double chiasmus (object–verb, verb–object, object–verb) includes a meaningful juxtaposition of Solon's fundamental concepts (παύει κόρον, ὕβριν ἀμαυροῖ); see on line 9 above. **τραχέα λειαίνει** 'makes the rough smooth'; cf. Isa 40.4 (NRSV) 'the uneven ground shall become level, | and the rough places a plain'. **ἀμαυροῖ** 'weakens'.

35 αὐαίνει ... φυόμενα '[she] shrivels up the budding flowers of delusion'. A striking double metaphor. Already in Hesiod, Zeus ἀγήνορα κάρφει ('withers the proud', WD 7), and Solon's 'flowers of *atē*' are part of a wider pattern of imagery in Greek thought that associates human wickedness with (excessive) vegetal growth: see Michelini 1978, esp. 39-40 on botanical metaphors of *hybris* and *atē*. αὐαίνω is Attic, otherwise αὐαίνω. **ἄτης ἄνθεα:** normally emblematic of flourishing life, flowers here become a symbol of human delusion and suffering.

36-7 εὐθύνει ... δίκας σκολιάς 'straightens out crooked judgements'. A traditional metaphor for the restoration of distorted justice: cf. Hom. *Il.* 16.387 [Zeus grows angry at men] οἳ βίηι εἰν ἀγορῆι σκολιὰς κρίνωσι θέμιστας, | ἐκ δὲ δίκην ἐλάσωσι, Hes. *WD* 9 (addressed to Zeus) δίκηι δ' ἴθυνε θέμιστας. **ὑπερήφανα ... | πραΰνει** 'restrains (lit. soothes) arrogant behaviour'.

37-8 παύει ... | παύει: the repetition underlines Eunomia's power to end civil strife. **διχοστασίης:** the word (lit. 'standing apart') is first attested here, and similarly applied to civic discord at Thgn. 78.

39 πάντα ... ἄρτια: 31-9n. **ἄρτια καὶ πινυτά** 'fitting and rational'. Mirroring its reassuring opening (1-4), the surviving text concludes on an optimistic note (the ring composition suggests we have a complete poem, lacunae excepted): under Eunomia (ὑπ' αὐτῆς, 38) the Athenians can end the disorder and violence threatening their society.

COMMENTARY: SOLON 5

Solon 5

Source: [Aristotle], *Athenian Constitution* 11.2–12.1.

These lines are quoted to illustrate Solon's policy of putting the safety of Athens first, even at the risk of being hated by both the people (δῆμος) and the notables (γνώριμοι), who were equally disappointed by his reforms. The poem itself does not spell out the detail of Solon's policies (hence their divergent interpretation in the ancient sources: cf. 1n.), but its vagueness and generality are deliberate, since the goal is not to engage in a technical discussion of the Athenian constitution, but to assert Solon's impartiality in balancing the competing demands of both the δῆμος and the elite. (34, 36*, and 37 defend Solon's political achievements in similar terms, but in iambics.) The poem is carefully structured not only to reflect the idea of balance – each group is given equal attention: 1–2 on the δῆμος, 3–4 on the elite – but also to underline Solon's active authority and concern for all Athenians: he is the agent of the main verbs (ἔδωκα, ἐφρασάμην, ἔστην, εἴασ'), and the final couplet is devoted to his success in preventing 'an unjust victory' for either side. The poem is calculated to appeal to as wide a set of the Athenian audience as possible.

1–2 In epic it is the major heroes who are granted a γέρας as symbol of their τιμή, and these awards represent the appreciation of the wider community. Here, by contrast, it is the common people who are granted 'privilege', and this 'striking departure from heroic language' (Irwin 2005: 231) magnifies both the people's status and Solon's own, as he claims the authority to dispense privileges and determine honour. Ancient sources disagree over the precise 'privilege' referred to here, and its limits ('as much as is sufficient'): the author of the *Athenian Constitution* connects the poem to the cancellation of debts which annoyed the rich as well as to the people's disappointment that Solon did not carry out a complete redistribution of property (11.2), while Plutarch quotes it as evidence of Solon claiming credit for increasing the power of the popular courts (*Sol.* 18). But the poem's vagueness is productive, since as well as avoiding controversial detail, it allows Solon to appeal as much as possible to all sides. Above all, the language of *timē* and *geras* likens Solon to the ideal Homeric leader, who (unlike Agamemnon in the *Iliad*) knows how to apportion honour and privilege so as to create social harmony. τόσον . . . ἀπαρκεῖ 'as much privilege as is sufficient for them'. The limits of popular power are stressed, reassuring the wealthy that their own privileges will not be removed. Plutarch has κράτος ὅσσον ἐπαρκεῖ, but the *Athenian Constitution*'s papyrus text is superior, since it preserves the language of γέρας and τιμή, while ἀπαρκεῖ better expresses Solon's insistence on not giving too much. τιμῆς: partitive gen., with both participles, 'neither detracting from their honour nor giving more'. ἐπορεξάμενος: aor. middle part. of ἐπορέγω. Some interpret this to mean 'nor reaching out to take [honour] for myself', but the context (what constitutes 'sufficient' honour for the people) makes 'nor giving more' much likelier (cf. Mülke 2002: 187–8). Moreover, the implicit reaction to 'a new charge brought against Solon' (Noussia-Fantuzzi 2010: 288) would be rather sudden and distracting.

3–4 Power and wealth are explicitly connected. ἀγητοί 'admired for' (causal dative). ἀεικές appeals to the elite's heightened sense of their own status: 'suffer no indignity (lit. have nothing shameful)'.

5–6 A clever, paradoxical refashioning of traditional military imagery, stressing Solon's fairness and concern for all Athenians. The idea of protecting one's fellow citizens with the shield evokes the behaviour of the good hoplite, but Solon is able to cover *both* sides with his shield, whereas a real hoplite could cover only one comrade. Solon, then, is not only a good Homeric leader (cf. 1–2n.) but also a kind of super-hoplite, on whom everyone depends. By uniting all citizens under one shield, and by raising the possibility of civil strife (especially in the 'unjust victory' of one side over another), the image emphasizes Solon's success as reconciler and peacekeeper. ἔστην: emphatic first position, focusing our attention on Solon himself. ἀμφιβαλών ... ἀμφοτέροισι: the repetition of ἀμφί underlines the care shown to both sides. Rhodes 1981: 172–3 considers it 'likelier that Solon claimed to have held out his shield not in protection of both sides but in defence against both'. However, both the use of ἀμφιβάλλω ('I cast around', 'cover') and the previous lines' emphasis on Solon's concern for each side support the idea of protection rather than opposition. κρατερὸν σάκος: the epic-sounding phrase characterizes Solon as a resolute protector. ἀμφοτέροισι: dative of advantage. εἴασ': 1st sg. aor. of ἐάω, 'and did not allow', underlining Solon's refusal to favour one side over the other.

Solon 6

Source: [Aristotle], *Athenian Constitution* 11.2–12.1.

Having cited 5* as proof of Solon's opposition to the excessive demands of both the δῆμος and the wealthy elite, the author of the *Athenian Constitution* quotes these lines to demonstrate Solon's view of 'how the masses [πλῆθος] should be handled' (12.2). But although the people are expected to 'follow their leaders' (1), the poem is not limited to an elite view from above, for it expresses the importance of moderation for both groups.

1 δῆμος ... ἕποιτο: a patrician view of the people and their leaders, showing how far Solon's picture of a well-governed society differs from that of the Athenians of later centuries who tried to claim him as the originator of their democratic system.

2 μήτε... βιαζόμενος 'neither released nor restrained too much'. The image presupposes that the δῆμος needs to be controlled, with violence (βία) if necessary: cf. Sol. 36.16*. **ἀνεθείς:** aor. part. pass. of ἀνίημι, 'let loose'.

3–4 Solon deploys a piece of gnomic wisdom ('excess breeds *hybris*') to support (γάρ) his specific political advice on how best to treat the δῆμος. But like all *gnōmai*, Solon's observation is meant to apply generally, and is a warning to both the people and their leaders to be moderate (cf. Sol. 4.5–8*, where both groups are corrupted by wealth). For if the ruling elite repress or exploit the people too much, they risk violent insurrection, resulting even in tyranny. Theognis reworks Solon with a predictably aristocratic bias (τίκτει τοι κόρος ὕβριν, ὅταν κακῶι ὄλβος ἕπηται | ἀνθρώπωι καὶ ὅτωι μὴ νόος ἄρτιος ἦι, 153–4): in Solon excess is a danger for everyone (note the universalizing ἀνθρώποις ὁπόσοις), not just the low-born (Theognis' κακός). As Desmond 2006: 52–3 shows, this 'Archaic law of wealth' (i.e. excessive wealth as the cause of *hybris*) flourished in Greek literature and thought throughout antiquity, and (p. 53) 'contributed to the latent sense of the virtues of the non-hubristic poor'. **τίκτει:** similar genealogies of morals (particularly involving *hybris*, as parent or child) are found throughout Greek literature: e.g. Aesch. *Eum.* 533–4 δυσσεβίας μὲν ὕβρις τέκος ὡς ἐτύμως, Soph. *OT* 873 ὕβρις φυτεύει τύραννον. On breeding metaphors, see also on Sol. 4.35*. **κόρος ὕβριν:** the juxtaposition encourages the audience to think of the next link in the chain κόρος–ὕβρις–ἄτη, i.e. the ruin that awaits those made arrogant by their prosperity: cf. Sol. 4.9–10*, 13.11–13*. **νόος ἄρτιος** 'soundness of mind': compare the ἄδικος νόος of the wealthy elite at Sol. 4.7*; ἄρτιος also defines decent behaviour at Sol. 4.32* and 4.39*.

Solon 9

Source: Diodorus Siculus, *Universal History* 9.20.2; 19.1.4 (3–4); Diogenes Laertius, *Lives of the Philosophers* 1.50 (1–4); Plutarch, *Solon* 3.6 (1–2).

The authors who quote frr. 9–11 – Diodorus, Diogenes, and Plutarch – see Solon reacting to the tyranny of Peisistratus, whether warning the Athenians of its emergence (9–10) or blaming them for its establishment (11). The latter point is chronologically unlikely, however, since Solon was probably dead by the time of Peisistratus' second (successful) attempt to establish a tyranny *c.* 556. Moreover, Peisistratus is nowhere named, and 11.3 speaks vaguely of 'these men'. So it seems that the later biographical tradition could not resist connecting these two famous figures, the 'father' of democracy and the tyrant of Athens. Nonetheless, even if Solon does not have Peisistratus specifically in mind (and could even be reacting to much earlier troubles, *before* his archonship in 594/3), these texts confront the dangers of demagogues and their rhetoric, and are testimony to the political upheaval that made Peisistratus' rise to autocratic power possible. Solon's own claim in frr. 32–3 that he had the chance to become a tyrant but resisted it shows that the concept of one-man rule was in the air in Athens, a possibility reinforced by the spread of tyranny around the Greek world in this period (see Introduction §4).

1–4 These lines take the form of a priamel, a series of parallel statements throwing the last into relief: as sure as snow and hail come from clouds, and thunder follows lightning, so is a city destroyed by men who are given too much power. They are also a foil to lines 5–6, for the use of nature imagery underlines the inevitability of the city's ruin (one cannot halt natural processes), unless the Athenians heed Solon's concluding advice. As elsewhere (e.g. fr. 12, where the sea, calm or stormy, probably represents the state of a city), Solon's accessible imagery makes abstract political ideas easier to understand.

1 πέλεται: a poetic word, equivalent to γίγνεται. **μένος:** the force of nature foreshadows the violence of the tyrant.

3–4 πόλις ὄλλυται: cf. Sol. 4.1* ἡμετέρη δὲ πόλις . . . οὔποτ' ὀλεῖται. **μονάρχου:** dependent on δουλοσύνην ('enslavement to a monarch'). The word μόναρχος is first attested here (and soon after in Thgn. 52*), though μοναρχία was already rejected by Alc. 6.27. Some follow Diodorus in reading the metrically equivalent τυράννου (Diod. Sic. 19.1.4; he has μονάρχου at 9.20.2), but it is apt that Solon should use the rarer and more vivid word to underline the absoluteness of one-man rule, stressing, with δουλοσύνην, the citizens' loss of freedom (cf. Sol. 4.18*). **ἀϊδρίηι** 'through their own ignorance', i.e. about the consequences of autocratic rule (cf. Sol. 11.5–8*). The juxtaposition δῆμος ἀϊδρίηι calls attention to the people's own share of responsibility for their loss of power. **ἔπεσεν:** gnomic aorist (Goodwin §155).

5 λίην δ' ἐξάραντ' 'having raised [someone] too high', masc. acc. sg. aor. part. of ἐξαίρω, 'I raise in status, exalt', referring back to the δῆμος as subject, with τινα understood. As in Sol. 11.3* αὐτοὶ γὰρ τούτους ηὐξήσατε, it is the citizens themselves who are at fault. **κατασχεῖν** 'restrain'. Contrast Sol. 36.22* and 37.7, where it is the δῆμος itself that is to be kept in check.

6 ἀλλ' ἤδη 'so now is the time'. An urgent ending: there is still a chance to resist the rise of a tyrant. **<καλά>:** West's supplement gives more specific advice than the others so far proposed (<τινα>, <περί>, <τάδε>).

Solon 10

Source: Diogenes Laertius, *Lives of the Philosophers* 1.49.

Diogenes, our only source for these lines, claims that when Solon rushed into the assembly to warn the Athenians of Peisistratus' plans for a coup, the latter's supporters accused Solon of being mad, prompting this response. The story is suspiciously similar to Plutarch's account of events surrounding the *Salamis* poem, where Solon, feigning madness, is said to have rushed into the agora to deliver his advice (1–3*). In any case, these verses make no mention of tyranny, and could equally well be construed as a response to criticism of the numerous reforms made during Solon's archonship. Their mixture of sarcasm and self-confidence makes for a forceful persona. δείξει... | δείξει: anaphora underlines the speaker's certainty. δή: for the particle used ironically, giving 'the effect of inverted commas', see *GP* 234–5; hence 'my "madness"' or 'my so-called madness'. μανίην μὲν ἐμήν: alliteration and assonance draw attention to the (mistaken) accusation. Moreover, as Mülke 2002: 215 observes, since μανία could denote a prophetic state of divine inspiration, the word is doubly ironic: what his opponents call insanity is not only sound reasoning but also a true vision of the city's future. βαιὸς χρόνος 'a short time'. For time bringing the truth to light, cf. Sol. 36.3* ἐν δίκηι Χρόνου; its grandiloquence contrasts with the speaker's snappiness here. ἀληθείης... ἐρχομένης: genitive absolute. The verb suggests the truth's willingness to make itself public. ἐς μέσον 'into the open': later a byword for democratic transparency and equality; cf. Hdt. 3.142.3 (Maeandrius replacing the tyrant Polycrates of Samos) ἐγὼ δὲ ἐς μέσον τὴν ἀρχὴν τιθεὶς ἰσονομίην ὑμῖν προαγορεύω.

Solon 11

Source: Diodorus Siculus, *Universal History* 9.20.2; Diogenes Laertius, *Lives of the Philosophers* 1.51; Plutarch, *Solon* 30.8 (1–4, 5–7).

Solon emphasizes the Athenians' own responsibility for the rise of tyrannical leaders (so too 9.3–4*). Despite the views of the ancient sources, it is unlikely that these lines refer to Peisistratus: see on 9* above, and Rihll 1989: 279–80, who observes that fr. 11 does not fit with the other surviving evidence concerning Peisistratus' first coup (especially Hdt. 1.59.6 and Thuc. 6.54.5–6). The first two couplets expose the Athenians' complicity in their own 'slavery'; the second two explain how such foolishness was possible, namely, their failure to grasp the deceptiveness of political rhetoric.

1–4 For the thought – the gods are not to blame, you are – cf. Sol. 4.1–8*. κακότητα 'badness' is further defined in what follows as the addressees' culpable stupidity. ἐπαμφέρετε: 2nd pl. present imperative of ἐπαναφέρω ('ascribe'). τούτους: as with the unspecified ἄνδρες μεγάλοι of Sol. 9.3*, the speaker leaves it to the audience to work out who 'these men' are (unless their identity was made clear in an earlier, lost part of the poem). Such vagueness about who the powerful are is useful from a performative standpoint, not least because it makes the poem transferable to other Greek communities, giving Solon's poetry a wider audience. ηὐξήσατε: 2nd pl. aor. of αὐξάνω ('for you yourselves (emphatic αὐτοί) increased the power'). ῥύματα δόντες: lit. 'by giving them means of protection'. Many see an allusion to bodyguards (as employed by Peisistratus and other tyrants: e.g. Plut. *Sol.* 30.3), but ῥύματα ('defences') probably refers here to more intangible forms of political support. 'Bodyguards' narrows the focus too much, since the 'slavery' of line 4 is the citizens' loss of political autonomy in general. Diogenes' ῥύσια ('sureties', 'seized property') is defended by some (e.g. Rihll 1989, albeit as a reference to Draco's earlier laws), but makes for a rather confusing scenario. κακὴν . . . δουλοσύνην: cf. Sol. 4.18*, 9.4*.

5–6 Solon contrasts the individual citizen's fox-like cunning in pursuing his own interests (εἷς μὲν ἕκαστος) with the collective stupidity of the whole group (σύμπασιν δ'), which allows them to be outwitted by their powerful masters. ἀλώπεκος ἴχνεσι 'in the fox's tracks'. The cunning of the fox is proverbial: e.g. Archil. 185, where the fox tricks the boastful and pretentious monkey. σύμπασιν . . . νόος: a phenomenon of mass psychology, exploited by tyrants ancient and modern. χαῦνος 'empty': cf. 34.4 (on those who hoped for a redistribution of land) χαῦνα μὲν τότ' ἐφράσαντο.

7–8 The distinction between mere words (γλῶσσαν ... καὶ ... ἔπη) and actual deeds (ἔργον) is a staple of Greek thought, especially in the analysis of political rhetoric. ὁρᾶτε suggests the audience's mesmerized gaze as they experience the crafty orator in action. αἱμύλου: the adjective can mean both 'flattering' and 'wily', and is the *mot juste* for the manipulative orator who rises to power by telling his audience what they want to hear. εἰς ἔργον . . . γιγνόμενον 'at what is actually being done': cf. Sol. 4.15* τὰ γιγνόμενα πρό τ' ἐόντα. οὐδέν: adverbial, 'not at all'.

Solon 13

Source: Stobaeus 3.9.23.

At seventy-six lines (and probably a complete poem), Solon's so-called *Elegy to the Muses* is the longest extant elegy from the pre-Hellenistic period. Solon begins with a prayer to the Muses for justly acquired wealth, free from Zeus's punishment (1–32), goes on to survey the emptiness of men's hopes and the variety of their attempts to make a profit or ward off evil (33–62), then returns to the basic uncertainty of human life (63–70) – except for, as he concludes, the certainty that the excessive desire for wealth will

trigger god-sent ruin (71–6). The poem thus combines general reflection on human optimism and fallibility with more specific moralizing on the corrosive effects of greed and the inescapable reach of Zeus's punishment (which spans generations: 25–32n.). As is typical of Greek ethical thought, Solon's emphasis on mortal ignorance and vulnerability enhances the audience's awareness of their shared humanity, while the focus on greed and ruin underlines the threat posed by injustice to the individual, his descendants, and wider society. (The poem is quoted by Stobaeus (3.9.23) under the heading 'On Justice'.)
  Many scholars have found the poem 'rambling' (e.g. Gerber 1970: 124 'Solon seems to be writing as he is thinking, rather than thinking before he writes'), and many have sought to pin it down to a single, underlying idea (e.g. wealth, wisdom, *atē*, divine justice), but its paratactic style is typical of Archaic poetry, and the poem as a whole is conceptually both coherent and powerful. (For a detailed discussion and overview of previous scholarship, see Noussia-Fantuzzi 2010: 133–6, Gagné 2013: 226–49.) The poem's concern with the unjust pursuit of wealth means it has much in common with Solon's other political poems (especially 4*), not least because greed, *hybris*, and injustice form the ultimate political background to all Solon's work (whether in government, law, or poetry).

1–6 Solon's invocation features many of the standard features of ancient Greek prayer: direct address of the power(s) concerned (enriched with epithets: ἀγλαά, 1), their genealogy and location (1–2), the call to hearken to the speaker (κλῦτέ μοι εὐχομένωι, 2), followed finally by the request itself (ὄλβον … δότε …, 3–6): cf. e.g. *Il.* 1.37–42; Pulleyn 1997: 133–55. Petitioners often list their previous services too, but as a poet Solon can leave implicit his special relationship with the Muses and the honour paid to them by his works. Moreover, as this poem attests, the power of the Muses is not limited to poetry: in Hesiod, for example, the Muses help kings make 'straight judgements' (*Theog.* 85–6), and they possess a wide range of knowledge from Homer onwards (cf. Allen 1949: 64–5). The Muses' all-encompassing wisdom will not only ensure (so Solon hopes) prosperity and repute, but will also help humans cope with the uncertainty of life.
  1 Μνημοσύνης … τέκνα: Hesiod describes the union of Zeus and Memory, with nine nights of sex producing nine daughters (*Theog.* 53–62). An alternative genealogy made them the offspring of Earth and Ouranos (cf. Alcm. 5 fr. 2 *PMGF*, Mimn. 13), but Solon uses the more traditional version, not least because Zeus's punishment of wrongdoing will be a central theme of the poem (11–32, 71–6). In addition, the role of Memory enhances Solon's authority to impart his own views, building

on traditional wisdom and enabling his conception of wealth and success to become part of the Athenians' collective morality.

2 Πιερίδες: Pieria, the region north of Mt Olympus, was the Muses' birthplace; cf. Hes. *Theog.* 53, Simon. 11.16*.

3–4 The two gifts (prosperity and reputation, the first from gods, the latter from men) are arranged chiastically. ὄλβον embraces all aspects of a successful life (cf. Sol. 27* for some of its main components) and depends on more than material wealth, though Solon desires that too, if honestly gained (7–8). πρός... πρός: with genitive, 'from'. θεῶν μακάρων: all good things come from the gods; cf. *Theog.* 96–7 ὁ δ' ὄλβιος, ὅντινα Μοῦσαι | φίλωνται. πρὸς ἁπάντων | ἀνθρώπων: as the enjambment underlines, Solon is not merely concerned with how he is seen by a narrow aristocratic elite, but hopes to enjoy the esteem of all his fellow citizens. δόξαν ἔχειν: cf. Tyrt. 12.9*.

5–6 γλυκὺν ὧδε φίλοις, ἐχθροῖσι δὲ πικρόν: the chiasmus and juxtaposition ('friends, enemies') stresses the traditional distinction between helping friends and harming enemies, one of the cardinal principles of ancient Greek morality (e.g. Hippon. 115.14–16*; cf. Blundell 1989: 26–49). αἰδοῖον... δεινόν: a successful life is (among other things) to be respected by one's friends and feared by one's enemies.

7–15 Solon distinguishes between justly acquired wealth and its opposite (7–8), then elaborates on their respective benefits (9–10) and dangers (11–15).

7–8 Chiasmus and enjambment highlight the rejection of dishonest wealth. χρήματα 'wealth', not 'money', since coinage was introduced into Athens a generation after Solon in the mid-sixth century BC (cf. Seaford 2004: 130–1, 165). ἀδίκως: for the elite's unjust riches, similarly punished in the end by Δίκη, cf. Sol. 4.11–16*. πεπᾶσθαι: perf. inf. of πάομαι ('possess'). ὕστερον... δίκη: the profound implications of such delayed retribution are explored in due course (29–32). The asyndeton is explanatory ('... I do not want, for ...'): Smyth §2167b. ἦλθε: gnomic aor., expressing certainty.

9–10 δῶσι: for the omission of ἄν in relative clauses with the subjunctive, see Goodwin §540; cf. lines 11, 29, 30, 55, 76. παραγίγνεται... | ἔμπεδος '[god-given wealth] abides by a man, secure'. ἐκ... κορυφήν: πυθμήν can refer to the bottom of a jar or cup, so 'from the bottom of the storage jar to the top' or 'from the bottom of the cup to its lip'. Gagné 2013: 230–1 argues for the latter, seeing a reference to the poem's sympotic context, but the former better expresses the immediate idea of material prosperity.

11–32 After a single couplet on honest wealth, Solon details at length the consequences of its opposite: *hybris* and *atē* (11–15), unforeseen punishment from Zeus (16–25), which can afflict even future generations (25–32).

COMMENTARY: SOLON 13

11–13 for the connection between unjust (or excessive) wealth, *hybris*, and *atē*, see on Sol. 4.9–10* and 6.3–4*. **τιμῶσιν:** cf. Theognis' complaint on men who marry for money, χρήματα μὲν τιμῶσι (189*). **κατὰ κόσμον:** cf. Sol. 4.10*, 4.32*; also Thgn. 677 χρήματα δ' ἁρπάζουσι βίηι, κόσμος δ' ἀπόλωλεν. ἔρχεται ... πειθόμενος | ... ἕπεται: the bad kind of wealth is personified as disorderly (οὐ κατὰ κόσμον), undependable (οὐκ ἐθέλων), and depraved (ἀδίκοις ... πειθόμενος). ἀναμίσγεται ἄτηι 'is mixed with ruin'.

14–15 The first of two similes in quick succession (cf. 17–25). Nowhere else does Solon use them so densely; the only other similes in the surviving fragments are 36.26–7* (Solon himself like a wolf) and 37.9–10 (like a boundary-marker). **ἀρχῆς ... πυρός** 'which (i.e. ruin, defining ἄτηι, 13) from a small beginning grows like [that of] fire'. **φλαύρη ... ἀνιηρή** 'paltry ... lethal': the contrast expresses *atē*'s irresistible growth.

16 οὐ γὰρ δήν 'for not long-lasting [are mortals' violent deeds]'.

17 Πάντων ἐφορᾶι τέλος: a traditional expression of Zeus's supreme power: cf. e.g. Archil. 177* for Zeus as overseer of men's deeds (good and bad), and Semon. 1.1–2* for his control over the outcome (τέλος) of all things.

17–25 Solon's longest simile compares Zeus's punishment (Ζηνὸς ... τίσις, 25) to a sudden storm (ἐξαπίνης ... | ... ἄνεμος, 17–18) in spring (ἠρινός, 19). As often in Homer's extended similes of the natural world, Solon takes a topic familiar to his audience (the weather, and its unpredictable violence) and creates a picture of unexpected destruction (cf. *Il.* 16.384–92, where an angry Zeus sends a storm to punish human injustice). The indiscriminate violence of the storm, and its effect upon sky (18–19, 21–2), sea (19–20), and earth (20–1), prepare for the all-embracing τίσις of Zeus, which engulfs even the innocent (25–32). At the same time, however, the image ends with the storm's cleansing effect, which leaves the sun shining in a cloudless sky (22–4), suggesting also the positive impact of Zeus's justice.

18 διεσκέδασεν 'scatters': gnomic aor. (so too ἔθηκεν, 22), expressing the scene's timeless familiarity.

19–20 πολυκύμονος, 'swelling with many waves', is first attested here. **ἀτρυγέτοιο:** an obscure Homeric epithet, whose likeliest meaning is 'tireless' (see on Thgn. 247–8*). **πυθμένα:** the sea-floor is stirred up; cf. πυθμένος (10).

21 δηιώσας: aor. act. part. of δηϊόω, 'to ravage'. The violent wind flattens the crops (πυροφόρον) and undoes human industry (καλὰ ἔργα). **ἔργα** 'fields' (i.e. land that has been 'worked'): see on Tyrt. 5.7*. **καλά:** the epithet expresses the farmer's pride in the product of his labour (cf. πίονα γαῖαν, 23). **ἕδος αἰπύν** 'high seat'.

22 αἰθρίην, 'clear sky', is first attested here. The stress on sight and clarity (αἰθρίην ... ἰδεῖν, | λάμπει ... | καλόν, ... ἰδεῖν, 22–4) enhances the vividness of the image.

23 ἠελίοιο μένος: for the force of nature, cf. Sol. 9.1* χιόνος μένος ἠδὲ χαλάζης.

24 καλόν: adverbial, and emphasized by enjambment (as in 19 ἠρινός, 20 πυθμένα, 21 δηιώσας). ἀτάρ is 'progressive, with little or no idea of contrast' (*GP* 53). νεφέων ... ἕν 'not a single cloud'. Ring composition (cf. νεφέλας, 18) brings the scene to a close.

25 τίσις: i.e. the *atē* which follows *hybris*: cf. ὑφ' ὕβριος (11), ὕβριος ἔργα (16).

25–8 stress Zeus's admirable patience, as he avoids lashing out every time he is provoked by human wickedness. ἐφ' ἑκάστωι: neuter, 'at every thing', i.e. every transgression. ὀξύχολος, 'quick to anger', is first attested here. αἰεὶ ... διαμπερές: lit. 'for ever ... continually'; the temporal adverbs stress Zeus's permanent vigilance. οὐ ἑ λέληθε '[the man with a sinful heart] does not escape him': the gnomic perfect expresses a general truth (Goodwin §154), in this case the infallibility of Zeus. πάντως ... ἐξεφάνη 'for he is revealed, without fail, in the end', taking the sinful man as subject. Mülke 2002: 280 sees Zeus as the more probable subject, 'and he assuredly reveals himself in the end', but the former avoids the sudden change of focus and makes for better continuity with what follows (ἀλλ' ὁ μὲν ... ὁ δ' ...).

29–32 This famous passage spells out the consequences of Solon's fundamental idea, πάντως ὕστερον ἦλθε δίκη (8). Belief in delayed punishment, endured by later generations, is a traditional element of Greek moral and religious thinking: e.g. Thgn. 197–208; see Parker 1983: 201–2. (For 'the sins of the fathers' in Near Eastern thought, including the Old Testament, cf. West 1997: 511.) To lament Solon's use of a primitive 'dogma' (Vlastos 1993: 47) misses the point, for belief in the hereditary transmission of guilt remained a basic moral concept throughout antiquity. Leaving aside its ethical problems (also discussed in antiquity: e.g. [Thgn.] 731–52, challenging the notion that the innocent should pay for their ancestors' crimes), the idea proved so useful and enduring because it helped people make sense of the indisputable fact that evildoers are not always punished and the innocent suffer, while the threat of one's descendants being punished (and one's line potentially extinguished) constituted a powerful sanction. Herodotus' emphasis on Croesus' descent from the wicked Gyges illustrates the principle, while his inclusion of Solon shows their shared moral view: Hdt. 1.29–33. *Pace* Gagné 2013: 248, Solon is not developing a new notion of ancestral fault 'now extended to the entire collectivity of the *polis*', but deploying conventional wisdom, since the principle's universality, and the concept of inherited guilt, are already clear in Homer's account of the fall of Troy (cf. Allan 2006: 6).

29–30 φύγωσιν | ... κίχηι: subjunctives in general relative clause, with conditional force, 'and if some themselves escape ...'. **κίχηι:** the *mot juste* for being 'overtaken' by fate: cf. Hector's realization, νῦν αὖτέ με μοῖρα κιχάνει (Il. 22.303). ἐπιοῦσα, 'pursuing', personifies the gods' punishment as an inescapable attack.

31 ἤλυθε: gnomic aor. (cf. ἦλθε, 8). **πάντως** 'for certain': the hallmark of divine justice; cf. 8, 28. **αὖτις** 'at some other time' is menacingly unspecific. **ἀναίτιοι:** the suffering of the innocent proves the inevitability of divine punishment.

32 παῖδες... ἢ γένος ἐξοπίσω: cf. [Thgn.] 205–6 ἀλλ' ὁ μὲν αὐτὸς ἔτεισε κακὸν χρέος οὐδὲ φίλοισιν | ἄτην ἐξοπίσω παισὶν ἐπεκρέμασεν; also Tyrt. 12.30* (in a more positive context of enduring glory) καὶ παίδων παῖδες καὶ γένος ἐξοπίσω.

33–62 Having established that only Zeus has a comprehensive vision of human crime and punishment, and that only the gods can guarantee lasting prosperity, Solon turns to the emptiness of men's hopes, as they think all will turn out well (33–6), indulge comforting thoughts of escaping misfortune (37–42), and toil to ensure wealth and wellbeing with no certainty of success (43–62).

33–6 Human optimism is universal (ὁμῶς ἀγαθός τε κακός τε, 33) but misleading. **νοέομεν:** the change from the third-person analysis of Zeus's justice (9–32) to first-person plural ('we think') unites speaker and audience in the condition of human ignorance, making the poet's moral advice more palatable. **εὖ ῥεῖν:** the conjecture ('run well'; lit. 'flow'), in the context of δόξαν ('expectation'), is supported by [Thgn.] 639–40 πολλάκι πὰρ δόξαν τε καὶ ἐλπίδα γίνεται εὖ ῥεῖν | ἔργ' ἀνδρῶν, βουλαῖς δ' οὐκ ἐπέγεντο τέλος. **πρίν τι παθεῖν:** 'learning through suffering' is a traditional motif of Greek moralizing; cf. Hes. WD 218 παθὼν δέ τε νήπιος ἔγνω. **ἄχρι δὲ τούτου** 'until this point'. **χάσκοντες** 'with gaping mouths', i.e. in eager expectation. **κούφαις ἐλπίσι:** the deceptiveness of hope is proverbial: cf. Hes. WD 498–501, Semon. 1.6–10*, [Thgn.] 637–8. **τερπόμεθα:** the final word ('delight') underlines how deluded we humans are.

37–42 Three examples (one couplet each) illustrate the vanity of human optimism.

37–8 πιεσθῆι: 3rd sg. aor. subj. pass. of πιέζω ('oppress'). **κατεφράσατο** 'he thinks' (gnomic aor.): an imposing word (lit. 'he considers deep in his mind'), in final position, which underlines how ingrained the sick man's hope is.

39–40 These lines probably refer to one man (note the stress on ἄλλος) rather than two, who is in fact low-born (δειλός) and ugly (μορφὴν οὐ χαρίεσσαν ἔχων), but considers himself noble (ἀγαθός) and handsome (καλός). **καλός:** with δοκεῖ ἔμμεναι understood.

41–2 ἀχρήμων: first attested here. **πενίης... ἔργα:** lit. 'works of poverty', i.e. the struggles faced by the poor; the same periphrasis at Mimn.

2.12*, variants at line 16 above ὕβριος ἔργα, Sol. 4.37* ἔργα διχοστασίης. **βιᾶται** 'constrain', with neuter pl. subject.

42 κτήσασθαι: the aor. infinitive is common 'in prophecies ... and other expressions of confidence about the future' (West 1966: 339 on Hes. *Theog.* 628), and there is no need to adopt Sylburg's κτήσεσθαι (as do Campbell and Gerber).

43–62 A catalogue of professions: sea-merchant (43–6), farmer (47–8), craftsman (49–50), poet (51–2), seer (53–6), doctor (57–62). In the first three there is an emphasis on profit (κέρδος) and making a living (βίοτος) which continues the poem's reflections on wealth, while the last two focus on the human experts' limited knowledge and their inability to avert what is fated.

43–6 highlight the dangers of the sea. Hesiod's ideal was to be able to make a living without resorting to seafaring: *WD* 236–7, 618–94. **σπεύδει**: the first word stresses the eagerness with which each figure in the ensuing catalogue pursues his fortune. **ἄλλοθεν ἄλλος**: cf. Sol. 4.13*. **ἀλᾶται** 'roams', in search of profit, but also suggestive of the dangers of sea-travel. **ἰχθυόεντ'**: fish were thought to consume the bodies of the dead (e.g. *Il.* 21.122–7). The adjective is separated from πόντον by a whole verse: such a striking hyperbaton is rare outside lyric and, along with line-initial position and enjambment, emphasizes the threat posed to sailors. **φορεόμενος** 'tossed'. **φειδωλὴν ... θέμενος** 'with no regard for life and limb': τίθεσθαι/ θέσθαι + verbal noun is a poetic periphrasis for the verb itself (= ψυχῆς φειδόμενος), lit. 'with no sparing of life'.

47–8 τέμνων ... | λατρεύει: each word expresses the endless, exhausting effort of agriculture. **εἰς ἐνιαυτόν** 'the whole year round'. **καμπύλ' ἄροτρα** 'the curved plough': symbolic of the farmer's life in general. For how to build and operate a plough, see Hes. *WD* 427–47 (good luck).

49–50 As patron gods of handicrafts (cf. *Od.* 6.232–4), Athena and Hephaestus were often associated, but especially so in Athens, where (among other connections) Athena had a statue in the major temple of Hephaestus overlooking the agora (see Burkert 1985: 220). **πολυτέχνεω**: first attested here, stressing the god's versatility. **ἔργα δαείς**: aor. pass. part. of δάω, 'who has learned the skills'. **ξυλλέγεται**: lit. 'brings together'; middle voice, i.e. for his own use.

51–2 As is traditional in ancient accounts of poetic skill (σοφίη), these lines stress the combination of divine inspiration (Μουσέων πάρα δῶρα) and hard-earned human knowledge (ἐπιστάμενος): as the bard Phemius puts it, αὐτοδίδακτος δ' εἰμί, θεὸς δέ μοι ἐν φρεσὶν οἴμας | παντοίας ἐνέφυσεν (*Od.* 22.347–8). **Ὀλυμπιάδων**: cf. line 1 above. **πάρα**: where the preposition follows its noun, the accent is 'thrown back' (anastrophe: Smyth §175, *CGCG* §§24.37, 60.14). **ἱμερτῆς**: the poet's skill is 'longed for' (cf. Sol. 1.1*, 3.2*) by audiences. **σοφίης**: σοφίη can denote technical skill, whether in carpentry (*Il.* 15.412) or playing the lyre (*HHHerm.* 483). This is its earliest surviving use for poetry, though the idea of the poet's professional skills and knowledge is traditional. **μέτρον** 'measure', i.e. the rules of poetic composition. **ἐπιστάμενος:** the gift is divine, but the poet's expertise is his own: cf. Archil. 1.2* Μουσέων ἐρατὸν δῶρον ἐπιστάμενος.

53–6 A seer can discern the approach of evil (κακόν ... ἐρχόμενον), but not even his skill can avert what is fated (τά ... μόρσιμα). **ἄναξ ἑκάεργος Ἀπόλλων:** an epic line-ending (e.g. *Il.* 21.461). The etymology of ἑκάεργος is disputed, but it was construed in antiquity as ὁ ἕκαθεν ἐργαζόμενος ('he who works from afar') or ὁ ἕκαθεν εἴργων ('he who wards off from afar'). **ἔθηκεν ... | ἔγνω:** gnomic aorists, expressing certainty of action, with different subjects (Apollo and the seer). **ἀνδρί:** dative of disadvantage (Smyth §1481, *CGCG* §30.49). **ὧι ... θεοί** 'if the gods favour him', i.e. the seer. **συνομαρτήσωσι:** 3rd pl. aor. subj. of συνομαρτέω (first attested here), 'attend on'; cf. 9–10n. **οὔτε ... ἱερά** 'neither augury nor sacrifice', i.e. by studying the flight of birds or the entrails of sacrificed animals. **ῥύσεται** 'will ward off' (LSJ ἐρύω B 3).

57–62 Doctors too, despite their skills, cannot guarantee health. Since medicine was highly regarded – one might compare, for example, the first stasimon of *Antigone*, where medicine is listed as the crowning item in a catalogue of skills that characterize human progress (354–64) – Solon's insistence on its limitations is all the more striking. On the portrayal of medicine in Greek literary texts, see Allan 2014: 260–2. **Παιῶνος:** gen. sg. of the Ionic form Παιών. Paean (Παιάν) is a god in his own right in Homer, where he also operates as physician to the gods (e.g. *Il.* 5.401–2). By the Classical period Paean was identified with Apollo, but Solon can still speak of him as an individual power. **ἰητροί:** with εἰσί understood, 'others ... are doctors'. **καὶ ... τέλος:** καί is intensive, '*even* they can give no guarantees'. For τέλος in the sense 'power to decide or control the outcome', cf. Semon. 1.1–2*.

59–62 Two contrasting examples – one of failure, the other of unexpected success – illustrate the limits of human medicine. **ἐξ ὀλίγης ... μέγα:** the juxtaposition underlines pain's often baffling origins. **λύσαιτ'** 'can provide relief': 3rd sg. aor. middle opt. The middle voice suggests the doctor's own interest in the treatment. **ἤπια φάρμακα:** the epic phrase (e.g. *Il.* 11.830) highlights in this case the inefficacy of the doctor's traditional methods. **κυκώμενον:** present pass. part. of κυκάω (lit. 'to mix, stir'); the image expresses the disease's disturbing effects, both physical and mental. **νούσοισι ... ἀργαλέαις:** the repetition (cf. νούσοισιν ὑπ' ἀργαλέηισι, 37) connects the deluded optimism of the sick to the doctor's unpredictable success. **ἁψάμενος χειροῖν:** a mere touch of the hands and the patient is suddenly (αἶψα) cured.

63–70 Following on from the various examples of human struggle and ignorance (33–62), Solon returns to the gods' central role in directing human fortunes (cf. 16–32). The principle of alternation (63–4) – i.e. that no human life is free from misfortune and the best one can hope for is a mixture of good and bad – is fundamental to Greek thinking about mortal limitations. Its classic exposition is the meeting between Achilles and Priam (*Il.* 24, especially 525–33), where the inevitability of suffering underscores the importance of the characters' shared humanity. Solon uses the principle to emphasize the uncertainty of any action's outcome, since the gods can change everything (65–70).

63–4 τοι: the particle (equivalent to 'you know'), repeated at 65, is 'very frequent in gnomic writing' (*GP* 542–3) and reinforces Solon's use of traditional wisdom. **ἄφυκτα** 'inescapable': cf. 55–6 on τὰ μόρσιμα. ἄφυκτος is first attested in Solon (cf. 4.17*), but the idea (one cannot escape what the gods give) is a staple of Greek moralizing.

65–6 κίνδυνος 'risk'. **οὐδέ ... | ... ἀρχομένου** 'and no one knows, when a thing starts, how it will turn out'. Simple language for a central idea. **μέλλει:** the periphrastic future (μέλλω + inf.) emphasizes the unpredictable outcome. **σχήσειν:** fut. inf. of ἔχω used intransitively, 'how it is going to turn out': cf. Soph. *Ajax* 684 εὖ σχήσει.

67–70 As at 59–62, Solon gives two contrasting examples, one of failure, the other of unexpected – and in this case undeserved – success. One man tries to do well (ὁ μὲν εὖ ἔρδειν πειρώμενος), but ends up ruined; another is incompetent (τῶι δὲ κακῶς ἔρδοντι), but is granted success by the gods. **οὐ προνοήσας** 'without foreseeing it', with ἔπεσεν (gnomic aor., stressing the fact of the well-intentioned man's fall). **θεός:** no particular god or goddess is meant, since all can shape a man's 'fate': cf. Μοῖρα ... | ... θεῶν (63–44). **ἄτην:** only when 'disaster' strikes does he realize his error; cf. 33–6. For intentional *hybris* punished by *atē*, cf. 11–13, 75–6. **περὶ πάντα** 'in every respect'. **ἔκλυσιν ἀφροσύνης:** lit. 'an escape from folly' (in apposition to συντυχίην ἀγαθήν, 'a good outcome'), i.e. freedom from the negative consequences of his incompetence.

71–6 The text ends with ring composition (a popular closural technique, suggesting we have the complete poem) as Solon returns to the opening themes of right and wrong ways of pursuing wealth (cf. 7–8), the danger of *hybris* and *atē* (11–13), and the certainty of Zeus's punishment (29–32). The focus earlier had been on the means by which wealth is attained, here it is the related desire for too much of it: greed, like unjustly acquired wealth, leads eventually to ruin. For the 'Archaic law of wealth' and its vitality in later Greek thought, see on Sol. 4.9–10* and 6.3–4*.

71–3 τέρμα 'limit'. **πεφασμένον** 'revealed': perf. pass. part. of φαίνω. **γάρ:** proving the preceding claim about human nature (71). **νῦν ἡμέων,**

'us now', ties the general observation to Solon's Athens in particular. πλεῖστον: by focusing on those who already have the largest share of resources, Solon underscores how insatiable the human desire for wealth is. διπλάσιον σπεύδουσι 'strive for twice as much'. τίς ἂν κορέσειεν ἅπαντας; a rhetorical question, implying (as 74–6 make explicit) that only if humans show restraint can the chain of κόρος–ὕβρις–ἄτη be broken. For greed as a threat to social cohesion, cf. Sol. 4.9* οὐ γὰρ ἐπίστανται κατέχειν κόρον. Sol. 24 states the ideal: one should be content with just enough to get by, since (among other things) 'no one goes to Hades with all his countless possessions' (7–8).

74–6 The final antithesis between *kerdos* ('profit') and *atē* ('ruin') sums up the poem's reflections on the improper and corrupting pursuit of wealth. τοι: cf. 63–4n. ὤπασαν: 3rd pl. (gnomic) aor. of ὀπάζω ('grant'), regularly used of gifts from the gods. ἐξ αὐτῶν: i.e. as a result of their κέρδεα (whether excessive wealth or wealth unjustly gained). Since ἄτη can also mean 'loss' in a financial sense (cf. Hes. *WD* 352 μὴ κακὰ κερδαίνειν· κακὰ κέρδεα ἶσ' ἄτῃσι), Solon's connection of *kerdos* with *atē* is doubly apt. ἥν (= ἄτη) ... | ... ἄλλοτε ἄλλος ἔχει: the polyptoton ('now one man, now another') underlines the inevitability of Zeus's retribution (cf. 16–32). τεισομένην: future (middle) participle expressing purpose, 'to punish them'. ἄλλοτε ἄλλος: for hiatus in this phrase, see on Archil. 13.7*.

Solon 27

Source: Philo, *On the Creation of the World* 104; Clement of Alexandria, *Miscellanies* 6.144.3; Anatolius, *On the Decad* (p. 37 Heiberg).

Solon's 'Ten Ages of Man' is quoted by ancient authors dealing with both the division of human life (Philo, Clement) and the number seven (Anatolius) and is referred to by several authors in Latin, indicating its popularity throughout antiquity. Its division of the (male) human life cycle into ten seven-year phases is unique (most poetic treatments make do with four: childhood, youth, adulthood, old age), but Solon is probably drawing on popular beliefs about maturation that made use of seven-year periods, as found in later medical texts of the Classical period (losing baby teeth at seven, beginning puberty at fourteen) – indeed, the Hippocratic treatise *On the Hebdomads* speaks of seven such periods, which may remind us of Shakespeare's 'Seven Ages of Man' (*As You Like It*, II.7).

The structure is simple but effective, with a couplet devoted to each seven-year period (for the one deliberate exception, see 13–14n.). Six of the nine couplets are enjambed, and variety comes from the different types of development (physical, social, political, and intellectual) displayed at each stage. The poem is particularly valuable for what it reveals about standard Greek conceptions of manliness, good citizenship,

156   COMMENTARY: SOLON 27

and the successful human life. Solon speaks in general terms, avoiding explicit references to (for example) Athenian age-rituals or the required age for particular political offices, so that his broad categories – powerful soldier and athlete, husband and father, wise and eloquent citizen – have the widest possible appeal.

1–2 The ancient Greeks show comparatively little interest in child development, seeing children as pre-rational beings who take time to become interesting. They often retroject behaviour of the adult on the child (e.g. Heracles strangles snakes as an infant because he will be a strong hero), but there is little evidence of our idea of childhood as a crucial formative period that shapes one's ultimate character. A child's acquisition of language and reason were seen as gradual (and interconnected) processes, from 'a bestial state with bestial noises' (Thomas 2010: 197) to rationality and speech. ἄνηβος ἐὼν ἔτι νήπιος: ἄνηβος (lit. 'not fully grown') reinforces νήπιος ('child'), which denotes the immature, pre-rational state of the young; hence νήπιος in the sense 'foolish, without forethought' when applied to adults, as often in Homer: e.g. *Il.* 16.46 μέγα νήπιος (the narrator on the doomed Patroclus). ἕρκος ὀδόντων: the typically epic phrase (most frequent in the exclamation ποῖόν σε ἔπος φύγεν ἕρκος ὀδόντων;), normally used by and of fully grown heroes, is here amusingly applied to milk teeth. φύσας ἐκβάλλει: the juxtaposition underlines the rapidity of the child's development, as if the boy no sooner grows the teeth than he spits them out. πρῶτον, 'for the first time', reminds us that he will lose his teeth again as an old man.

3–4 τελέσηι θεός: the thought 'with god's help' is particularly appropriate in a culture where many children did not survive their early years. ἥβης . . . γεινομένης 'he shows the signs of puberty's onset'. The variety of bodily changes defies expression in a single line, hence the catch-all σήματα, which are elaborated in the following couplet.

5–6 γένειον . . . | λαχνοῦται 'his chin grows fuzzy'. The first sign of a beard is one of the most common markers of childhood's end, and of the transition to male maturity, in Greek literature and art (e.g. *Od.* 11.317–20, on the teenage giants Otus and Ephialtes, killed by Apollo). ἀεξομένων . . . | . . . ἀμειβομένης: genitive absolutes, varied by chiasmus (verb–noun, noun–verb). ἄνθος: the skin's changing 'bloom' marks the transition from the delicate beauty of youth (explicitly erotic in Sol. 25: ἔσθ' ἥβης ἐρατοῖσιν ἐπ' ἄνθεσι παιδοφιλήσηι, | μηρῶν ἱμείρων καὶ γλυκεροῦ στόματος) to the vigour and desirability of the adult male.

7–8 μέγ' ἄριστος | ἰσχύν: acc. of respect, 'is far best in strength'. The Homeric μέγ' ἄριστος is apt, defining the age when men are most heroic in their fighting strength and physical prowess. πείρατ': Stadtmüller's conjecture for the transmitted σήματα (perhaps copied from line 4) or μνήματα is convincing, since πεῖραρ ('decision', 'determination') well expresses the idea that acts of physical strength (e.g. warfare or athletics) are a test of ἀρετή (here 'manliness') or – as we might say – separate the men from the boys.

9–10 Although men had public roles denied to women, their domestic duties as husband and father could be as important to ancient Greek ideals of masculinity as the roles of wife and mother were to female status and identity. ὥριον 'it is time' (plus acc. and inf., with ἐστί understood). Similarly, Hesiod advises men to marry 'not far short of thirty or much beyond it' (adding γάμος δέ τοι ὥριος οὗτος), while the bride should be five years beyond puberty (*WD* 694–7). παίδων... γενεήν: the continuation of the οἶκος by the begetting of children (especially sons) was seen as a central element of a successful marriage; cf. Harrison 1968: 1.18. εἰσοπίσω 'to follow after him'.

11–12 As man ages, so the focus moves from physical to mental excellence. περὶ πάντα καταρτύεται 'is being trained in every way'. ἀπάλαμνα: the word denotes both 'reckless' and 'feckless' behaviour, and both senses reinforce the idea of 'discipline' present in καταρτύω. ἔθ' ὁμῶς... θέλει 'no longer equally disposed [to do stupid things]'.

13–14 The peak of a man's intellectual and rhetorical abilities covers two seven-year periods (43–9, 50–6), handled in a single couplet. *Pace* Faraone 2008: 66, there is no reason to think a couplet is missing or these lines are a later addition. These are the prime years of a man's engagement in public life, and both the interrupted pattern and the emphatic fourteen (ἀμφοτέρων τέσσαρα καὶ δέκ' ἔτη) draw attention to the extent of these valuable years. μέγ' ἄριστος: the repeated epic phrase (and acc. of respect, νοῦν καὶ γλῶσσαν: cf. 7 above) is appropriate, since the ideal Homeric man is 'both a speaker of words and a doer of deeds' (*Il.* 9.443).

15–16 A man's skill in speech and thought grow 'weaker' (μαλακώτερα), but as Anhalt 1993: 52 remarks, 'For Solon, the significant fact about the aging process is not the physical deterioration which may accompany it, but the opportunity it provides for intellectual development.' Cf. Sol. 18 γηράσκω δ' αἰεὶ πολλὰ διδασκόμενος; Falkner 1995: 153–68. πρὸς μεγάλην ἀρετήν: lit. 'with respect to great excellence', i.e. in speaking and thinking (which he achieved at his peak).

17–18 For seventy years as the natural measure of a human life, compare Solon's words to Croesus in Herodotus (probably influenced by this poem): ἐς γὰρ ἑβδομήκοντα ἔτεα οὖρον τῆς ζόης ἀνθρώπωι προτίθημι (1.32.2). Contrast Sol. 20, where Solon corrects Mimnermus' wish to live to sixty (Mimn. 6) to eighty. τὴν δεκάτην (sc. ἑβδομάδα)... τελέσας 'if he were to complete the tenth age'. κατὰ μέτρον ἵκοιτο: lit. 'and reach the measure'; μέτρον implies that seventy is the 'full measure' or 'limit' of a human life (cf. LSJ I.4). ἄωρος ἐών: ring composition with ἄνηβος ἐών (1), rounding off the life cycle. The litotes 'not before his time' and the receipt of his 'allotted share' (μοῖραν) reinforce the appropriateness of death at this age, thus avoiding a doleful conclusion.

Solon 36

Source: [Aristotle], Athenian Constitution 12.4.

This poem is one of the most fascinating surviving examples of the political use of iambus in the Archaic period. As in the elegiac fr. 5*, Solon defends his policies as being in the best interests of all Athenians, and boasts of his resistance to the extreme demands made by both the δῆμος and their wealthy opponents. By focusing on the liberation of the Athenian land (3–7) and its citzens (8–15), Solon foregrounds the damage to Athenian society caused by greed, debt, and enslavement, and presents his unbiased reforms as having prevented civil war (22–5).

The Aristotelian *Athenian Constitution* quotes the text in connection with Solon's cancellation of debts and liberation of enslaved debtors, a process it calls *seisachtheia* ('shaking-off of burdens'), while Plutarch (*Sol.* 15.5–6) applies the term, which he claims was invented by Solon, to the ending of debt slavery and the removal of ὅροι from mortgaged land (cf. 6n.). However, the term *seisachtheia* is nowhere attested in the surviving Solonian texts and may well be a later invention, while the lack of contemporary evidence means that the precise details of the policies celebrated in 36* are disputed (for a defence of the Aristotelian account, see de Ste. Croix 2004: 109–28).

Nonetheless, the broad themes of liberation, repatriation, impartiality, and incorruptibility are clear, as is Solon's skill in presenting his achievements in the best possible light. He begins by declaring that he fulfilled all the promises he made to the people (1–2), then justifies this claim in three long sentences (3–7, 8–15, 15–20) that cumulatively stress not only the range of his concerns (the land of Athens, enslaved citizens both at home and abroad, the creation of a fair legal system) but also his dynamism and authority, underlined by a plethora of first-person verbs (ξυνήγαγον 1, ἐπαυσάμην 2, ἀνεῖλον 6, ἀνήγαγον 9, ἔθηκα 15, ἔρεξα, διῆλθον, ὑπεσχόμην 17, ἔγραψα 20, ἤθελον 22, ἐστράφην 27) and a concluding simile that places him at the centre of events in a dramatically striking way (26–7).

1–2 The opening (rhetorical) question engages the audience immediately and marks the speaker's confidence. Its unusual phrasing (lit. 'the reasons why I called the people together, which of these had I not achieved when I stopped?') foregrounds Solon's initiative in calling a

COMMENTARY: SOLON 36

public meeting to resolve the crisis. ἐγώ: placed first, underlining Solon's authority (cf. 5, 20). πρὶν τυχεῖν: for Solon achieving all he said he would, cf. 17 below; also 34.6 ἃ μὲν γὰρ εἶπα, σὺν θεοῖσιν ἤνυσα.
3–7 Solon draws on the tradition of swearing oaths by Earth (cf. e.g. *Il.* 19.258–63, where Agamemnon swears by Zeus, Earth, Helios, and the Erinyes that he never slept with Briseis), invoking the 'greatest' (4) of deities as a powerful 'witness' (3) to the truth of his opening claim (ταῦτ', referring back to 1–2). Earth is doubly appropriate here, since her own 'liberation' is Solon's first achievement (5–7).
3 συμμαρτυροίη . . . ἄν: the verb is first attested here; the prefix συμ- emphasizes the goddess' close support. ἐν δίκηι Χρόνου 'in the court of Time'. A bold metaphor, personifying Chronos (along with Earth) as an arbiter of justice; one might compare Solon's contemporary, the philosopher Anaximander of Miletus, who claimed that existing things 'give justice and reparation to one another for their injustice in accordance with the ordinance of Time' (κατὰ τὴν τοῦ χρόνου τάξιν, DK 12 B1). More often, as at Sol. 4.16*, justice is said to come 'in time' (i.e. at last). δίκη ('judgement') here signifies the place where justice is determined (cf. LSJ IV.2).
4 μήτηρ . . . Ὀλυμπίων: for Earth as mother of all, including the Olympian gods, cf. Hes. *WD* 563, *Theog.* 45–6, 117–18.
5 ἄριστα: adverbial, modifying συμμαρτυροίη. Γῆ: the delayed name (like ἄριστα) adds to the impact of her intervention. μέλαινα: a standard poetic epithet for earth, emphasizing its fertility (cf. Sol. 38.4–5). The darkening of upturned earth after ploughing is miraculously represented in gold on the shield of Achilles: *Il.* 18.548–9. τῆς ἐγώ: as Mülke 2002: 374 observes, the positioning of ἐγώ after τῆς creates 'a direct and positive relationship' between the goddess and the speaker.
6 ὅρους . . . πεπηγότας 'whose mortgage stones, fixed far and wide, I removed'. Some have doubted the traditional interpretation of ὅροι as markers of mortgaged land and a sign of indebted 'sixth-parters' or *hektēmoroi*, but see de Ste. Croix 2004: 107–28. In any case, line 7 makes clear that the stones symbolize (in Solon's view) a damaging state of servitude between small farmers and their overlords. Contrast 37.8–9, where Solon himself is the boundary (ὅρος), in a positive sense, between the δῆμος and its enemies: ἐγὼ δὲ τούτων ὥσπερ ἐν μεταιχμίωι | ὅρος κατέστην. This striking image (a 'boundary-marker' set in 'the place between two armies') emphasizes that their conflict is best resolved not by civil war but by peaceful agreement (i.e. a lawful boundary-marker), a symbol of reconciliation embodied by Solon himself: see Allan 2018: 126–7. πεπηγότας: perf. part. of πήγνυμι.
7 The goddess was herself enslaved (δουλεύουσα), stressing the outrageous treatment of the poor who work the land.

160   COMMENTARY: SOLON 36

8–15 describe Solon's measures to end the suffering of his fellow Athenians, focusing on three separate groups (demarcated by πολλούς δ' ... | ... τούς δ' ... | ... τούς δ'): those sold into slavery abroad (8–10), those forced to flee by economic hardship (10–12), and those enduring slavery in Athens (13–15).

8 θεόκτιτον: the city's founding by Athena rather than human settlers was naturally a source of pride; cf. Sol. 4.3–4*.

9 πραθέντας 'sold' (as slaves); cf. Sol. 4.23–5*. Though not spelled out, the likeliest cause of their status is enslavement for debt, a practice ended by Solon's legislation.

9–10 ἄλλον ἐκδίκως, | ἄλλον δικαίως 'some illegally, others legally'. In other words, even if some were sold in line with the law then in force, the practice itself is abhorrent and has been ended by Solon. Those enslaved 'illegally' may have included victims of kidnapping.

10–11 ἀναγκαίης ... | χρειοῦς 'compelling need' (gen. sg. of χρειώ). Again, probably a reference to debt (and the threat of enslavement). Economic hardship was a common cause of migration: cf. e.g. Hesiod's father, who moved from Cyme on the coast of Asia Minor to Ascra in Boeotia 'fleeing evil poverty' (*WD* 635–8).

11–12 γλῶσσαν ... | ἱέντας: the loss of their native dialect is singled out as a particular privation for the Athenian refugees. Just as the Greek language marked identity vis-à-vis 'barbarians', so did its component dialects, in opposition to other regions of Greece. Since Attic and Ionic shared most features, the audience will think more of those areas of the Greek world where other Greek dialects (Doric, Aeolic, Arcado-Cypriot) were spoken. The dialects were mutually intelligible (cf. Morpurgo Davies 1987: 12–13), but it was possible to poke fun at other people's way of speaking Greek (as, for example, the Laconian dialect of the Spartans in Aristophanes' *Lysistrata*). ἵημι is regularly used of speaking a language (as well as uttering inarticulate cries): cf. Thuc. 3.112.4, where the Athenian general Demosthenes deploys Messenians in the front ranks, Δωρίδα τε γλῶσσαν ἱέντας, to outwit the enemy. **ὡς ... πλανωμένους** 'so far and wide their wanderings'. West's δή for ἄν removes the unwanted potentiality, since these people really are refugees. Their repatriation by Solon has restored them to their mother-tongue.

13 ἐνθάδ' αὐτοῦ: emphatic repetition, 'right here'. The first two groups suffered abroad, while the third endured the shame of slavery in their own city. **ἀεικέα**: cf. Sol. 4.25* δεσμοῖσί τ' ἀεικελίοισι.

14 ἤθη δεσποτέων τρομεομένους, 'trembling at their masters' whims', stresses the dehumanizing powerlessness of the slave. Note the synizesis of -έω- and -εο-, each scanned as one long syllable.

15 ἐλευθέρους ἔθηκα: a triumphant conclusion to Solon's catalogue of achievements.

15–17 Solon defends his actions (ταῦτα ... | ... | ἔρεξα) as the fitting together (ξυναρμόσας) of 'force' and 'justice'. The use of force (βίη), usually associated with tyranny (e.g. Sol. 32.2–3, 34.8), is here exercised in the interests of the community (cf. Irwin 2005: 221–30). **κράτει** 'in power' or 'by my power', but in either case during Solon's period of office. **ὁμοῦ ... ξυν(αρμόσας)**: the pleonasm underlines the surprising unity of two principles ('might' and 'right') that are typically opposed (e.g. Hes. *WD* 274–8). The need for βίη acknowledges the resistance of Solon's wealthy opponents, but its combination with δίκη asserts the rightness of Solon's reforms. The dichotomies of force and justice, power and wisdom, became central ideas in later discussions of the best statesman; for Solon the wise legislator as a precursor to the Platonic ideal of the philosopher-king, see Desmond 2011: 71–3. **διῆλθον** 'I completed'. **ὡς ὑπεσχόμην:** Solon reiterates his opening claim (1–2) that he fulfilled all his promises to the Athenians; cf. Sol. 34.6 ἃ μὲν γὰρ εἶπα, σὺν θεοῖσιν ἤνυσα.

18–20 Verbal and syntactic parallels with 15–17 (δίκην ξυναρμόσας ~ ἁρμόσας δίκην, ἔρεξα ~ ἔγραψα) present Solon's legal reforms as a further example of his pursuit of the public good. **θεσμούς:** only here in his surviving poetry does Solon refer to his achievements as a lawgiver (excluding the doubtful hexameter fr. 31). Athenians throughout the Classical period continued to refer to their legal system as 'the laws of Solon', despite the revisions made to them in the intervening centuries. For the extant fragments (ranging from criminal law to religious regulations), quoted by later authors, see Ruschenbusch 2010. **ὁμοίως ... κἀγαθῶι** 'for the lowly and the noble man equally'. The principle that all citizens are equal before the law (or ἰσονομία) became a central tenet of democratic ideology in the Classical period. **εὐθεῖαν ... δίκην:** lit. 'fitting straight justice for each man'. Solon's laws naturally embody Eunomia, which εὐθύνει ... δίκας σκολιάς (Sol. 4.36*). **ἔγραψα:** the word's marked position (last in sentence, first in line) underlines Solon's pride in a crucial feature of his legislative reforms, namely the laws' inscription on ἄξονες (revolving pillars) set up on the Acropolis (cf. Sickinger 1999: 29–31). Their publication fostered equal access to the laws (even the illiterate poor could ask for them to be read aloud) and made it harder for aristocratic Athenian officials to favour their own interests. Solon also made it possible for citizens to launch appeals against magistrates' decisions.

20–2 Solon imagines the conduct of an inferior man as a foil to his own good leadership. **κέντρον:** the 'goad' metaphor, applied to political control, typically describes the conduct of a tyrant (cf. Thgn. 847–50, Aesch. *Ag.* 1624). Solon draws on this idea to evoke the possibility that another man would have used his power tyrannically, whipping up the people for his own ends rather than using the goad (as Solon did: ὡς ἐγώ, 20) to keep them in line (οὐκ ἂν κατέσχε δῆμον, 22). Solon's use of the 'goad' exemplifies his prudent use of 'force' (βίη, 16) and figures the δῆμος as something that needs to be properly controlled (cf. Sol. 6.2*; also Sol. 37.6, repeating the phrase οὐκ ἂν κατέσχε δῆμον). The animal imagery continues in the simile of the wolf and the dogs in the final lines (26–7). κακοφραδής τε καὶ φιλοκτήμων 'unscrupulous and greedy'. For the dangers of greed, whether among the δῆμος itself or the ruling elite, cf. Sol. 4.5–14*, 33.5, 34.1–2.

22–5 The style is compact and punchy (see below); a full translation will help to clarify: 'If I had been willing to do what the people's opponents then desired, and in turn to do what the other party planned for them, this city would be mourning many men.' To demonstrate his own excellence as a leader, Solon imagines the bloody consequences if he had yielded to the demands of either side. In Sol. 37 he similarly rebukes both sides for complaining that they did not get what they wanted. ἃ . . . ἥνδανεν 'what pleased their (i.e. the δῆμος's) opponents'. τότε: i.e. during Solon's archonship. ἃ . . . φρασαίατο 'what the others (i.e. the δῆμος) would have contrived for them' (3rd pl. epic–Ionic aor. optative middle of φράζω). The vagueness of the phrase is sinister, but the threat of violence is made explicit in the following line. ἄν . . . ἐχηρώθη 'would have been bereft of' (3rd sg. aor. passive of χηρόω). For the catastrophe of civil war, cf. Sol. 4.19–22*, 4.37–8*, 5.5–6*. ἥδ' . . . πόλις: the emphatic final position of 'this city' underlines the key idea that Solon considered what was best for the community as a whole, unlike the rival factions of the previous lines.

26–7 Solon's wolf simile is highly ironic and stresses the ingratitude of the Athenians who attacked him because of his reforms. Although Solon worked for the whole community, their reaction has forced him into the role of the wolf (see below), while the two sides, the δῆμος and its opponents, have united (like a pack of dogs) to attack him, despite their incompatible interests. As with the shield simile of Sol. 5*, the animal simile here evokes Homeric epic, and adapts epic imagery to suit the new and disturbing context of civil war. In contrast to the shield simile, however, where Solon stands in the middle protecting both sides, here he is forced into the middle because he is under attack from all sides. τῶν οὕνεκ' 'for these reasons', i.e. because Solon refused to take sides (as explained in 22–5). The phrase echoes line 1 (τῶν . . . οὕνεκα), and the ring composition links Solon's opening claim (he achieved all his goals) with its consequence (he is attacked unfairly by all sides). ἀλκήν ('defence') continues the martial imagery of civil war in 22–5. πάντοθεν . . . | . . . ἐν κυσὶν πολλῇισιν: the scene ('on every side ... among many dogs') stresses Solon's heroic isolation as both groups turn on him and outnumber him. ὡς . . . λύκος: the simile only becomes clear with the final word, enhancing its impact. Since the wolf can have positive as well as negative associations in Greek thought, Solon's image works in different ways, but all to his advantage. As an animal known for its independence – cf. the fable (*Fab.* 346 Perry) of the 'free' wolf, who rejects the easy but 'slavish' life of the dog – it highlights Solon's courage in sticking to his principles and refusing to serve either side. On the other hand, the wolf's reputation as a selfish predator (even turning on its fellow wolves to get its prey: cf. *Il.* 4.471–2) emphasizes Solon's unfair treatment as an outsider, as he, the saviour of his community, is attacked by the group (the dogs) and cast in the role of the anti-social animal.

THEOGNIS

Theognis of Megara was probably active around the middle of the sixth century BC. It has been argued that references in his poetry point to an earlier date during the tyranny of Theagenes at Megara (*c.* 640–600; West 1974: 65–71), but the alleged historical allusions are unconvincing (cf. Lane Fox 2000: 37–40), and Theognis' warnings against the rise of tyranny would be equally valid in the mid-sixth century (see on 39–52* below). Chronographers dated his *floruit* to the Olympiads of 552–541. Theognis is the only poet in this volume whose work survives in a medieval manuscript tradition, yet most of the 1389 lines transmitted under his name are excerpts from other poets (including Tyrtaeus, Mimnermus, and Solon) or are composed by later imitators. Because the surviving verses were taken at different times from separate anthologies (each including the work of several poets), it is difficult to isolate the work of the original Theognis (cf. Bowie 1997). The main criterion used to identify genuine verses has been to single out those addressed to his young male lover, Cyrnus (also called Polypaïdes). This results in around 300 lines of 'authentic' Theognis, but caution is needed here, since later imitators could easily have mimicked the original poet's technique (for Cyrnus' name as potentially the 'seal' of Theognis, see on 19–20 below).

The poet's persona is that of an embittered aristocrat, a man who has lost his estates in a pro-democracy revolution and, perhaps forced into exile (cf. 1197–202*), now hopes for revenge (337–40*, 361–2). Theognis abhors the common people, who are ignorant and untrustworthy (69–72*). He laments the disappearance of class distinctions (53–68*) and complains that intermarriage has diluted aristocratic blood lines (183–92*). Theognidean poetry thus captures the anxiety of aristocratic communities throughout Greece in the Archaic period, as their rule was threatened by the emergence of democracies or by demagogues who rose to power on popular support and then set themselves up as tyrants (cf. 39–52*). His defence of established privilege and his detestation of the vulgar and the *nouveaux riches* made his elegies a popular choice at aristocratic *symposia* (cf. 237–54*), where their performance helped build group and class solidarity in the face of threatening change. In addition to elitist political ideology, the collection contains a wide range of standard sympotic themes, from gnomic moralizing on friendship, luck, and death to celebrations of drinking and love (both heterosexual and homosexual: cf. 1225–6*). As the largest corpus of early Greek elegy, the poems give us a good sample of the social and moral attitudes circulating at *symposia* in the Archaic period and beyond.

19–26

After a series of invocations (to Apollo, Artemis, and the Muses and Graces) comes a long sequence of poetry addressed to Cyrnus (19–254). The poet's emphasis on his own name, city, skill, and fame in 19–26 will have made them an attractive 'prologue' in the eyes of later compilers.

19–20 Κύρνε ... | ... ἔπεσιν 'Cyrnus, as I practise my poetic craft let a seal be set on these verses'. **Κύρνε:** the name occurs 76 times in the corpus, always in the vocative (so too with Polypaïdes, 9 times). Cyrnus, like Theognis, is as much a persona as a real person, and may well be invented for the poet's didactic purpose (cf. Hesiod's wastrel brother Perses in *Works and Days*). The name Cyrnus is very rare, and the patronymic Polypaïdes is not attested elsewhere (Selle 2008: 373). (Intriguingly, Hesychius says that Cyrnus means 'illegitimate child', so we may have 'bastard son of the man of many children' (Cyrnus, Polypaïdes), an addressee of precarious status within the social hierarchy defended by Theognis.) The range of Theognis' advice creates a portrait of a naïve and at times ungrateful young man in need of instruction in aristocratic values. **σοφιζομένωι:** the emphatic first word (following the vocative) immediately draws attention to Theognis' expertise (σοφία: see on Sol. 13.52*). **σφρηγίς:** the seal is a mark of authenticity. It is a mistake to limit its reference to one thing (the name of Cyrnus or Theognis being the most frequent suggestions: cf. Gerber 1997b: 124–7, Bakker 2017: 108–9), since the seal refers to the whole of Theognis' poetry, that is, both his distinctive (didactic) persona and the quality of his work, which will ensure that it cannot be interfered with (20–1). **ἔπεσιν:** the plural ἔπεα, which refers more commonly to hexameter epic, can also refer to poetry in general (cf. Alcm. fr. 39 ϝέπη τάδε καὶ μέλος).

20–1 λήσει ... κλεπτόμενα 'their theft will never go unnoticed'. Theognis anticipates the risk of plagiarism (someone intentionally 'stealing' his lines) and false attribution (verses 'stolen' and given to another), dangers that applied both to written texts of his work and to their performance at *symposia*. Ironically, our uncertainty over what counts as genuine

Theognis, and the presence of other poets in the corpus, belie the speaker's confidence in the effectiveness of his 'seal'. οὐδέ ... παρεόντος: lit. 'nor will anyone exchange something worse for the good that is there', i.e. no one will be able to get away with altering the text or attributing the work of inferior poets to Theognis.

22-3 By naming himself, Theognis seeks not only to guarantee the correct attribution of his poetry, but also to ensure his immortality. **πᾶς τις:** everyone will recognize Theognis' poetry, so distinctive is its 'seal'. **ὀνομαστός** 'famous' (with ἐστί understood): the praise is spoken by others, making it all the more genuine. In addition, the universal fame of Theognis' verses will make them harder to fake or interfere with.

24 ἀστοῖσιν ... δύναμαι: despite his fame beyond Megara (πάντας δὲ κατ' ἀνθρώπους, 23), the content of Theognis' poetry (i.e. its political and social reflections) means that he cannot please all his fellow citizens (ἀστοῖσιν δ', with δέ pointing the contrast, which is further enhanced by matching sounds: ὀνομαστός· | ἀστοῖσιν). Solon faced a similar problem: ἔργμασι (γὰρ) ἐν μεγάλοις πᾶσιν ἁδεῖν χαλεπόν (fr. 7).

25-6 Theognis reassures his friend (Πολυπαΐδη): if not even Zeus can please everybody (proverbial wisdom, so indisputable: cf. Thgn. 811–14), Cyrnus should not worry if Theognis' poetry arouses opposition. **οὖν:** the reading οὖν for ὁ (found on a late third-century BC ostracon (potsherd) from Egypt: *P. Berol.* 12319) is preferable, since the article with the god's name is foreign to hexameter, elegiac, and lyric poetry. **οὔθ' ὕων ... οὔτ' ἀνέχων** 'whether he sends rain or holds it back': the same example is used at Soph. fr. 524.3–4 R (spoken by Agamemnon) ἐπεὶ οὐδ' ὁ κρείσσων Ζεὺς ἐμοῦ τυραννίδι | οὔτ' ἐξεπομβρῶν οὔτ' ἐπαυχμήσας φίλος. **πάντεσσ' ἁνδάνει** echoes πᾶσιν ἁδεῖν (23) and reinforces the poet's comparison of himself to Zeus.

27–30

The first distich encapsulates the collection's central relationship (Theognis will pass on to Cyrnus the aristocratic values he himself learned as a boy, 27–8), the second some of its key markers of excellence (prestige, success, and wealth, 29–30).

27 σοί ... εὖ φρονέων 'with good will towards you': the older man's concern for the wellbeing of his young protégé (and lover) was a basic tenet of the aristocratic (and pederastic) system of education; cf. Dover 1978: 202, Introduction §4. **σοὶ δ' ἐγώ ... ὑποθήσομαι:** the juxtaposed pronouns (σοὶ δ' ἐγώ; cf. Hesiod *WD* 286 σοὶ δ' ἐγὼ ἐσθλὰ νοέων ἐρέω, μέγα νήπιε Πέρση) and the use of a standard term of moral instruction (ὑποτίθημι) underline the roles of educator and pupil.

28 ἀπὸ τῶν ἀγαθῶν: throughout the corpus Theognis deploys typical aristocratic terms of moral and social evaluation, allying himself with the ἀγαθοί/ἐσθλοί (well-born, morally good), in opposition to the κακοί/δειλοί (low-born, bad). **παῖς ἔτ' ἐών:** the importance of learning good conduct when young was a popular topic of gnomic literature; cf. Phocylides fr. 15 χρὴ παῖδ' ἔτ' ἐόντα | καλὰ διδάσκειν ἔργα. For the foolishness of youth, see on Sol. 27.1* παῖς μὲν ἄνηβος ἐὼν ἔτι νήπιος. **ἔμαθον:** with the final word Theognis emphasizes that he too had to go through the process of learning aristocratic values, justifying his current didactic purpose.

29–30 πέπνυσο 'be sensible'; imperative of πέπνυμαι (perf. passive of πνέω with present sense). **μηδ'... | ...μηδ':** the first μηδέ introduces the imperative ἕλκεο (2nd sg., ἕλκομαι, 'do not amass for yourself'), giving the specific advice heralded by πέπνυσο, the second μηδέ links the two adjectives ('from disgraceful or unjust deeds'), the third and fourth connect the three objects ('prestige, success, or wealth'). **τιμὰς ... ἀρετάς:** the plural refers to concrete examples of esteem and excellence, i.e. material honours and great achievements.

31–8

These lines are probably separate from 27–30 (as West 1974: 150 remarks, 'ταῦτα μὲν οὕτως ἴσθι (31) is surely the summation of a longer paragraph than 29–30'), but their central idea (associate with, and learn from, ἀγαθοί rather than κακοί) makes it easy to see why they have been placed after 27–30.

31–2 προσομίλει: for the familiar idea 'good/bad company leads to good/bad development', cf. Eur. *Andr.* 683–4 ἡ δ' ὁμιλία | πάντων βροτοῖσι γίγνεται διδάσκαλος. **ἔχεο** 'cling to': middle imperative + gen. (cf. LSJ ἔχω C 2 'lay hold on, take advantage of').

33–4 πῖνε καὶ ἔσθιε: Cyrnus will eat and drink with ἀγαθοί at the *symposion*, where aristocratic manners and ideology are inculcated, and where Theognis' poetry is performed (Introduction §2). For the kinds of food available at *symposia*, cf. Xenoph. 1.9–10*. **ἄνδανε ... δύναμις** 'and please those whose power is great': here it is still the ἀγαθοί who have money and influence, in contrast to other scenarios, where Theognis' cherished social hierarchy has been destroyed (53–68*, 183–92*).

35–6 ἐσθλῶν ... ἀπ' ἐσθλά: quoting these words, Aristotle argues that one can learn virtue from associating with good people (*NE* 1170a12, 1172a14). **μαθήσεαι:** for Cyrnus as pupil, see on ἔμαθον (line 28 above). **καὶ ... νόον** 'even the sense that you have'.

COMMENTARY: THEOGNIS 31-8, 39-52   167

37–8 μαθών . . . ὁμίλει: reiterating the message of μαθήσεαι (35) and προσομίλει (31, ring composition). **εὖ συμβουλεύειν:** for Theognis' concern to benefit Cyrnus, cf. εὖ φρονέων (27).

39–52

The poet fears that the corrupt behaviour of the city's leaders will lead to civil war and the rise of a tyrant. The dictator need not be Theagenes (c. 640–600), since Theognis can be expressing some fifty years later the fear of a new Megarian tyranny, exploiting his audience's awareness of the past. Though his political sympathies are very different from Solon's, Theognis here echoes the Athenian's diagnosis of civic degeneration, where the elite ruin their city for the sake of personal gain (46, e.g. Sol. 4.11*), sparking factional strife (51, Sol. 4.19*) and a descent into one-man rule (52, Sol. 9*).

39 Κύρνε, κύει: alliteration grabs Cyrnus' attention (and ours). **κύει:** the image of a 'pregnant' city is a striking extension of the metaphorical 'body politic': cf. Sol. 4.17*, where the city suffers an 'inescapable wound'. The unusual picture is intensified by the birth of a full-grown man, 'a corrector' (40). **πόλις ἥδε:** Megara (within the world of the poetic persona), but the non-specific phrasing guides the audience to think of similar tensions in other cities, including their own, and encourages reperformance of the poem in different communities (cf. Bakker 2017: 104).

40 εὐθυντῆρα . . . ἡμετέρης: lit. 'a straightener of our wicked insolence'. Greek narratives about the emergence of tyrants often emphasize their role as (harsh) restorers of justice, who come as a consequence of wicked behaviour (Irwin 2005: 227); compare Solon's combination of justice with force, ὁμοῦ βίην τε καὶ δίκην ξυναρμόσας (Sol. 36.16*), and his teaching of Eunomia (lawfulness), which 'straightens out crooked judgements' (εὐθύνει . . . δίκας σκολιάς, Sol. 4.36*). With 'our', it soon becomes clear, Theognis is insisting on the culpability of his own elite class, whose dishonesty and greed have brought the city to breaking point.

41–2 ἀστοὶ μέν . . . ἡγεμόνες δέ: the poet distinguishes between 'self-controlled' (σαόφρονες) citizens and their intemperate aristocratic leaders. (By contrast, Solon criticizes all Athenians for giving in to the temptations of greed and injustice: Sol. 4.5–8*.) **ἔθ'**, 'still', leaves open the possibility that the people could change, stressing the dangerous political situation. **τετράφαται:** 3rd pl. perf. middle, 'have begun to fall'; for τρέπεσθαι (middle) + infinitive = 'begin to', cf. Thuc. 2.65.10 ἐτράποντο καθ' ἡδονὰς τῶι δήμωι καὶ τὰ πράγματα ἐνδιδόναι.

168   COMMENTARY: THEOGNIS 39-52, 53-68

43–4 ἀγαθοί ... | ... κακοῖσιν: Theognis distinguishes between those who are truly good and a subset of the elite (the ἡγεμόνες, 41) who have proven to be bad. Thus his criticisms of the latter do not undermine his basic commitment to the system of aristocratic privilege.

45–6 specify particular examples of shocking behaviour (ὑβρίζειν, 44), and the leaders' crimes are marked by extensive alliteration. **δῆμόν τε φθείρωσι** 'and they destroy the people': corrupting them, so that they are no longer σαόφρονες (41). **δίκας τ' ἀδίκοισι διδῶσιν** 'and give judgements in favour of the unjust': the perversion of justice leads to popular disaffection and the emergence of an authoritarian ruler (see on line 40 above). **οἰκείων ... κράτεος** 'for private profit and power': the poet makes use here of the 'Archaic chain' linking greed (οἰκείων κερδέων, 46), arrogance (ὑβρίζειν, 44), and ruin (φθείρουσι, 45; δημοσίωι σὺν κακῶι, 50): see on Sol. 4.9–10*.

47 ἔλπεο ... ἀτρεμίεσθαι 'do not expect that city to remain unshaken for long' (ἀτρεμίεσθαι: future infinitive after a verb of expectation).

48 μηδ' εἰ 'even if'. **νῦν ... ἡσυχίηι:** i.e. the current calm is precarious.

49–50 reiterate the dangers expressed in 44–6. **κέρδεα ... ἐρχόμενα:** 'profit that comes with public ill'. **δημοσίωι σὺν κακῶι:** cf. Sol. 4.26* οὕτω δημόσιον κακὸν ἔρχεται οἴκαδ' ἑκάστωι.

51–2 Theognis rounds off his analysis of the city's perilous condition (cf. κύει, 39) by summing up a universal pattern of decline (the plurals are generalizing: στάσιες ... φόνοι ... | μούναρχοι). **στάσιες:** civil war, as factions fight for supremacy. **ἔμφυλοι φόνοι** 'slaughter within the clan': cf. στάσιν ἔμφυλον (Sol. 4.19*). **μούναρχοί τε:** enjambment caps the descent into tyranny. For the decadence of the elite resulting in one-man rule, cf. Sol. 9.3–4 ἀνδρῶν δ' ἐκ μεγάλων πόλις ὄλλυται, ἐς δὲ μονάρχου | δῆμος ἀϊδρίηι δουλοσύνην ἔπεσεν. **πόλει ... τῆιδε** returns to the poem's initial focus, the fate of Theognis' own city: πόλις ἥδε (39). Ring composition suggests a complete poem. **τῆιδε ἅδοι:** hiatus at word-juncture, though rare, is found in epic and elegy with words originally beginning with digamma (τῆιδε (ϝ)άδοι). Of the 50 instances of hiatus in Theognidea, 19 involve digamma (Seele 2008: 122). Nonetheless, digamma is more often neglected (cf. Thgn. 24* πᾶσιν ἀδεῖν) and does not prevent elision (cf. Thgn. 26* πάντεσσ' ἀνδάνει).

53–68

Theognis condemns the social change that has made the common herd superior to the aristocracy, and urges Cyrnus to fake friendliness towards these upstarts, while in fact recognizing their moral failings. The piece is characterized by strong antithesis – the town versus the country (53–6), low-born deceivers versus the righteous elite (59–60,

65–8) - and inversion (the κακοί/δειλοί are now the ἀγαθοί/ἐσθλοί and vice versa, 57–8).

53 Κύρνε . . . ἄλλοι 'Cyrnus, this city is a city still, but its people are very different': Theognis distinguishes between the city (πόλις μέν), with which he still identifies, and its inhabitants (λαοὶ δέ), not all of whom are to his liking. **δὲ δή**: strongly adversative (*GP* 259).

54 οὔτε δίκας . . . νόμους: ignorance of justice shows lack of civilization (as with the monstrous Cyclops: ἄγριον, οὔτε δίκας εὖ εἰδότα οὔτε θέμιστας, *Od.* 9.215).

55–6 Since the possession of justice distinguishes humans from animals (cf. Hesiod's fable of the hawk and the nightingale, *WD* 202–12), its lack encourages Theognis' presentation of the common people as beast-like and sub-human. **ἀμφὶ πλευραῖσι** 'around their sides'. **δορὰς αἰγῶν**: goatskins (and other animal skins) were typically worn by poorer rustics and slaves. **κατέτριβον**: lit. 'wore out (i.e. to tatters)', a contemptuous detail, sneering at the people's poverty. **ἔξω . . . τῆσδ' . . . πόλεος**: their rightful place, according to the speaker. **ἔλαφοι**: the timidity and cowardice of deer were proverbial: cf. Achilles' insulting address to Agamemnon, οἰνοβαρές, κυνὸς ὄμματ' ἔχων, κραδίην δ' ἐλάφοιο (*Il.* 1.225) and Agamemnon's attempt to rouse the Achaeans, τίφθ' οὕτως ἔστητε τεθηπότες ἠΰτε νεβροί; (*Il.* 4.243). Such associations enhance Theognis' indignation at the people's newly acquired authority. **ἐνέμοντο** 'lived': but since νέμομαι can also be used of animals (in the sense 'pasture/graze'), its deployment here strengthens the simile.

57–8 The two blunt, incredulous, statements, followed by an exasperated question, underline the speaker's outrage. **ἀγαθοί . . . ἐσθλοί | . . . δειλοί**: by using the traditional polarized terms of aristocratic superiority (ἀγαθοί/ἐσθλοί versus κακοί/δειλοί) Theognis makes the inversion of social class all the more shocking. **καὶ . . . ἀγαθοί** 'and now they are the gentry': the tone of ἀγαθοί is contemptuous, since these people are emphatically not 'well-born'; the complaint is effectively 'and now they are in charge', i.e. former 'goatskin wearers' now occupy the privileged position in the city once enjoyed exclusively by the aristocracy (the true ἀγαθοί). **Πολυπαΐδη**: the patronymic stresses Cyrnus' good birth (unless he is illegitimate: cf. on Thgn. 19–20*) and thus encourages his shared anger at the city's social revolution. **τίς . . . ἐσορῶν**; the question ('who can stand the sight of this?') presents Theognis' disgust as natural and correct.

59–60 The terms ἀγαθοί/ἐσθλοί/δειλοί (57–8) imply moral worth as well as social class, and Theognis now turns to the moral failings of the new elite. **ἀπατῶσιν . . . γελῶντες**: their cheating and mockery reveal their bad character, in implied contrast to the honesty of Theognis and his friends. The fact that they treat their own group in this way (emphasized by the repetition ἀλλήλους . . . ἐπ' ἀλλήλοισι) adds to the condemnation, since they lack the solidarity of Theognis' aristocratic *hetaireia*. Kurke 1989: 540 sees in the phrase 'a contemptuous aristocratic periphrasis for the practice of retail trade', but the allusion to lower-class trade, while well suited to Theognis' aristocratic persona, is hard to detect, and one would need more explicit reference to the agora or money to make this connection. **οὔτε . . . ἀγαθῶν:** lit. 'having knowledge neither of what is bad nor of what is good', i.e. with no moral sense. Some understand γνώμας as 'modes of thought' and the genitives as masculine rather than neuter, 'knowing the ways of thinking neither of the base nor the noble', but since the previous verse concerns dishonest conduct, a reference to awareness of moral principles (rather than men) seems more suitable.

61–2 Nothing can justify making any of these men a friend: cf. Thgn. 113–14 μήποτε τὸν κακὸν ἄνδρα φίλον ποιεῖσθαι ἑταῖρον, | ἀλλ' αἰεὶ φεύγειν ὥστε κακὸν λιμένα. **τῶνδε . . . ἀστῶν** reinforces the idea that these boors (55–6) now live in the town. **Πολυπαΐδη:** the patronymic again marks the difference between the noble Cyrnus and the arrivistes (see on 57 above). **ἐκ θυμοῦ:** lit. 'from the heart' (cf. Achilles on Briseis: ἐγὼ τὴν | ἐκ θυμοῦ φίλεον, δουρικτητήν περ ἐοῦσαν, *Il.* 9.342–3), so here 'your true friend'. **χρείης . . . μηδεμιῆς** 'for any reason' (cf. LSJ χρεία III.1 'use, advantage, service').

63–5 δόκει: 2nd sg. present imperative. **πᾶσιν:** i.e. all 'these townspeople' (61), the so-called ἀγαθοί (57), whose true nature (κακοί/δειλοί) is soon revealed (65–8). **ἀπὸ γλώσσης** 'in word alone', as opposed to ἐκ θυμοῦ (62); cf. Thgn. 979 μή μοι ἀνὴρ εἴη γλώσσηι φίλος, ἀλλὰ καὶ ἔργωι. **χρῆμα . . . | σπουδαῖον** 'but share with none of them any serious matter whatsoever'. **συμμείξηις:** 2nd sg. aor. subjunctive of συμμείγνυμι. **σπουδαῖον:** emphatic enjambment.

65–8 reiterate their cheating, faithlessness, and lack of moral principle (cf. 59–60). **γάρ** 'for (if you do befriend them)'. **ὀιζυρῶν** 'miserable', in a condemnatory rather than sympathetic sense. **ὥς . . . οὐδεμία:** lit. 'since there is no trustworthiness in their actions'. **ἔπ'** = ἔπεστι. **δόλους . . . πολυπλοκίας** 'treachery, deceit, and cunning': a barrage of synonyms, hammering the point home. πολυπλοκία is found only here, but cf. Thgn. 215–16 πουλύπου ὀργὴν ἴσχε πολυπλόκου, ὃς ποτὶ πέτρηι, | τῆι προσομιλήσηι, τοῖος ἰδεῖν ἐφάνη. **ἐφίλησαν:** ingressive aorist, 'have grown to love'. **οὕτως ὡς** 'just like': more forceful than simple ὡς. **μηκέτι σωιζόμενοι** 'past all salvation': the new elite may be beyond hope, but Theognis leaves open the possibility of the city's eventual deliverance (echoing the opening idea: πόλις μὲν ἔθ' ἥδε πόλις, 53), if Cyrnus and his kind can reassert their dominance.

119-28

Theognis laments that it is easier to detect adulterated gold and silver than it is to tell a person's true character. To wish for a clear outward sign of a person's inner (and real) self became a popular motif (e.g. Eur. *Hipp.* 925-7), as did the analogy between false metals or coinage and deceptive human character: cf. Eur. *Med.* 516-19, where, as here, the ease of detecting counterfeit gold is contrasted with the difficulty of identifying bad people.

119 χρυσοῦ . . . ἄτη 'the damage caused by counterfeit gold and silver can be endured'. **κιβδήλοιο:** the trick involved putting a precious-metal exterior around a base-metal core. For the comparison of good/noble people to unalloyed coins (of silver and gold) and bad/low-born people to inferior coinage (bronze plated with silver), see Ar. *Frogs* 718-37. **ἀνσχετός** (epic variant of ἀνασχετός) sets up a contrast with the 'unendurable' harm of a false friend (121-4).

120 ἐξευρεῖν: various methods for detecting adulterated metals were available, including weighing, melting, and the use of touchstones (for the latter, cf. Thgn. 415-18, 447-52, 1105-6). **ἀνδρὶ σοφῶι** 'an expert'.

121-2 φίλου . . . ἀνδρός: the deceiver's identity as a friend is foregrounded. **ἐνὶ στήθεσσι . . . | . . . ἐν φρεσὶν ἦτορ:** an Attic drinking-song features the wish that one could open up a man's breast to examine his mind and check his honesty (889 *PMG*). **ψυδρός** 'lying' (a rare alternative to ψευδής). **δόλιον . . . ἦτορ:** contrast Thgn. 77-8, where a trustworthy man is said to be worth his weight in gold and silver.

123-4 κιβδηλότατον 'the most fraudulent thing': the rare fourth-foot caesura stresses the word (see Introduction §5). **γνῶναι . . . ἀνιηρότατον** 'to discover it involves the greatest pain of all'. **τοῦτ':** i.e. that a friend is not who he seems.

125-8 For the difficulty (and importance) of recognizing a 'counterfeit man', cf. Thgn. 117-18 κιβδήλου δ' ἀνδρὸς γνῶναι χαλεπώτερον οὐδέν, | Κύρν', οὐδ' εὐλαβίης ἐστὶ περὶ πλέονος.

125 οὐδὲ γὰρ εἰδείης: Aristotle cites these lines, beginning οὐ γὰρ ἄν (*Eth. Eud.* 1237b13), but potential optative without ἄν is not unusual.

126 πρὶν . . . ὑποζυγίου 'until you have tested it like a beast of burden' (i.e. to see whether it can carry a load). **πειρηθείης:** 2nd sg. aor. pass. opt. of πειράω (with gen.), 'to test, make trial of'; the subordinate temporal clause takes the optative by assimilation with εἰδείης (cf. Smyth §2186b, Goodwin §558).

127 οὐδέ . . . ἐλθών 'nor can you judge it (i.e. a man's or a woman's character) as if inspecting (lit. coming to) something in season': the image here comes from agriculture (following on from the pack-animal of the previous line), namely, checking the quality of a product that has reached maturity. Camerarius suggested ἐς ὤνιον ('as if inspecting something for sale'), but the transmitted reading ὥσπερ ποτ' ἐς ὥριον ἐλθών makes good sense, and the breach of Hermann's Bridge (stating that the fourth biceps is normally undivided) is attested elsewhere in Theognis (e.g. 1171 γνώμην, Κύρνε, θεοὶ θνητοῖσι διδοῦσιν ἀρίστην).

128 ἰδέαι 'appearances': the final word sums up the central problem of the whole piece. The word ἰδέα is first attested here.

183–92

Theognis complains that although his fellow Megarians breed their animals from the best possible stock, they themselves are now marrying for money, leading to intermarriage between ἀγαθοί and κακοί, which has spoiled human bloodlines (γένος; cf. 190–1). For the erosion of class distinctions, see also Thgn. 53–68*, and for humans compared to animals, Thgn. 126*. As a staunch aristocrat, Theognis considers eugenics (ἀγαθοί breeding with ἀγαθοί) essential for maintaining human excellence and social order. The discrete sequence of thought suggests a complete poem.

183–5 Animal husbandry was an essential part of life in most Greek settlements, and Theognis' opening appeal to the importance of successful breeding creates a commonly accepted premise for his argument. The poet has chosen three different animals to make his point, including the lowly donkey, the implication being that if people want the best breeding partner even for a beast of burden, they should be all the more discriminating in the selection of their husbands and wives. **κριοὺς . . . | εὐγενέας** 'with rams, donkeys, and horses, Cyrnus, we seek out the purebred': the key idea (good birth) is emphasized by enjambment. **κριούς:** sheep could be bred for high-quality wool and cheese, a valuable source of income. Later Classical sources point to Megara as an important exporter of woollen clothing (Ar. *Ach.* 519, *Peace* 1002, Xen. *Mem.* 2.7.6). **ὄνους:** famously hardy and versatile animals, integral to the ancient economy and daily life; cf. Griffith 2006: 205–28. **ἵππους:** as symbols of nobility, wealth, and social prestige, horses are the obvious choice to illustrate good breeding. For the extensive technical literature on horse-keeping in antiquity, see Anderson 1961. **καί . . . | βήσεσθαι** 'and everyone wants them to breed (lit. 'to mount', future inf. of βαίνω) from good stock'. The future infinitive after verbs of wishing makes the reference to the future particularly prominent (Goodwin §113), underlining here the hope that one will find the best breeding partner for one's animals.

185–8 detail the pervasive greed of the ἀγαθοί/ἐσθλοί, as both men (185–6) and women (187–8) willingly debase themselves. **κακὴν κακοῦ** 'a worthless daughter of a worthless father'. **γῆμαι . . . οὐ μελεδαίνει** 'does not mind marrying'. ἤν... διδῶι 'if he (the father) gives him (the ἐσθλὸς ἀνήρ) a lot of money'. The bride's dowry (χρήματα may refer to property as well as money) outweighs the noble man's scruples about class. οὐδὲ ... ἀναίνεται 'nor does a woman refuse': as with οὐ μελεδαίνει (185), the negative underlines the bad choice being made. πλουσίου: the key condition is emphasized by pause and position, 'provided that he is wealthy'. ἀφνεὸν ... ἀντ' ἀγαθοῦ 'a rich man rather than a man of worth'.

189–90 restate the complaints of 185–8, but with a male subject in each scenario (noble or low-born groom). **μέν:** the solitary particle emphasizes χρήματα, 'It's money they value'. **ἔγημε | ... ἔμειξε:** gnomic aorists, underlining the general truth embodied in the complaint. **πλοῦτος ... γένος** 'wealth corrupts blood': asyndeton highlights the speaker's trenchant conclusion. **ἔμειξε:** lit. 'mixes up': cf. μίσγεται (192). Since μείγνυμι can also mean 'have sex with', it is a particularly apt word to express Theognis' hostile view of such 'mixed' marriages and their consequences. The idea of 'mixing' is prevalent in Archaic Greek thought, especially in the Presocratics, with theories ranging from Parmenides' 'oneness of being' to the atomists' belief in the random mixture of atoms forming our universe. For an attempt to link various thinkers' 'fear of diversity' to the development of political thought in ancient Greece, see Saxonhouse 1992.

191–2 οὕτω ... | μαυροῦσθαι 'so don't be surprised, Polypaïdes, that the citizens' stock is fading'. **ἀστῶν:** not the entire citizen body, but the elite, who are the only people Theognis cares for.

237–54

Theognis describes in great detail the unique gift of immortality through poetry that he has bestowed upon Cyrnus (237–52) and complains of his ingratitude (253–4). The poem also celebrates the sympotic setting that is the context for Theognis' work: the poet looks forward to future performances (239–43), which will spread Cyrnus' fame (and his own) throughout the Greek world (247–8). This is one of the longer pieces in the Theognidea; it may well be complete. West 1974: 42 suggested that 'the disproportion between 237–52 and 253–4 may have been less in the complete original', but the abruptness and punchiness of the final complaint are effective. The grander style deployed here – marked by metaphor (the wings of song in 237–9, 247–50), simile (ὥσπερ μικρὸν παῖδα, 254), and numerous epic formulae and epithets (e.g. ἐπ' ἀπείρονα πόντον, 237, ὑπὸ κεύθεσι γαίης | ... εἰς Ἀΐδαο δόμους, 243–4, ἰχθυόεντα ... πόντον ἐπ' ἀτρύγετον, 248) – is well suited not only to the central idea of the power of poetry, but also to the speaker's emotional state, as he condemns his protégé's disrespect and deception.

237–9 The speaker evidently describes a wondrous gift (for with it one can fly 'over the boundless sea and all the earth with ease'), but does so allusively, engaging the audience's curiosity. σοὶ μὲν ἐγώ: Cyrnus' debt to Theognis is immediately stressed, preparing for the breakdown in reciprocity revealed at the end, αὐτὰρ ἐγών . . . παρὰ σεῦ (254). πτέρ': a popular metaphor for poetry, first attested here. σύν: with instrumental dative. ἀειρόμενος 'soaring' (lit. 'lifted up'). ῥηϊδίως: emphatic enjambment.

239–43 reveal how Cyrnus' fame will manage to spread so widely. Composing for performance primarily at *symposia* (see Introduction §2), Theognis looks to similar convivial settings where pipes are played and elegiac poems are sung. θοίνηις . . . | . . . πάσαις 'you will be present at every dinner and feast': pleonasm (θοίνηις . . . καὶ εἰλαπίνηισι) and enjambment (ἐν πάσαις) heighten the honour conferred upon Cyrnus by his (virtual) presence at these gatherings, not just in Megara but throughout Greece. πολλῶν . . . στόμασιν explain Cyrnus' miraculous omnipresence: though physically absent, he will be present as the subject of song. Given the nature of the relationship between speaker and addressee, the phrase (lit. 'lying on the lips of many') also has erotic connotations, enhanced by the 'lovely young men' (νέοι ἄνδρες | . . . ἐρατοί, 241–2) who will sing about Cyrnus. Although Theognis here foregrounds the role of oral transmission in circulating his poetry, his worries about plagiarism, false attribution, and alteration (see on Thgn. 20–1*) envisage written texts too and assume that his audience is not restricted to those attending *symposia* or similar occasions (see Introduction §6). σύν 'accompanied by'. αὐλίσκοισι: as the diminutive of αὐλός, αὐλίσκος suggests shorter and therefore higher-pitched pipes. Aristoxenus (fr. 101 Wehrli), writing in the fourth century BC, speaks of five kinds of aulos, the highest pitched being the 'girl-type' (*parthenioi*), followed by the 'boy-type' (*paidikoi*), the latter perhaps envisaged here, though we cannot be certain these categories applied in Theognis' day. λιγυφθόγγοις: lit. 'clear-voiced', a compliment to the skill of the aulos-player, but also creating a pleasing harmony with the λιγέα (242) singing voices of the young men. εὐκόσμως, 'orderly', further characterizes their singing, but may also suggest the decency and good conduct of the young men themselves. καλά . . . λιγέα 'with beautiful, clear voices' (adverbial accusatives).

243–52 Having described the remarkable expanse of Cyrnus' fame (ἐπ' ἀπείρονα πόντον | . . . καὶ γῆν πᾶσαν, 237–8, ἐν πάσαις, πολλῶν, 240), Theognis now turns to its endurance through time; for in addition to transmitting aristocratic values to his protégé, Theognis has bestowed upon him an undying name (ἄφθιτον ὄνομα, 246), which makes Cyrnus' failure to reciprocate (253–4) all the more unjust.

COMMENTARY: THEOGNIS 237-54 175

243-4 The sudden focus on Cyrnus' death and his containment below the earth creates a deliberate contrast with his movement throughout Greece (237-9) and his association with active youth (241-3). Only Theognis' poetry, it is strongly implied, can save Cyrnus' memory from extinction. For the links between death, Hades, memory, and poetry used in a less friendly fashion, cf. Sapph. fr. 55 (said to be addressed to an uncultured woman) κατθάνοισα δὲ κείσηι οὐδέ ποτα μναμοσύνα σέθεν | ἔσσετ' οὐδὲ †ποκ'† ὕστερον· οὐ γὰρ πεδέχηις βρόδων | τῶν ἐκ Πιερίας, ἀλλ' ἀφάνης κἀν Ἀΐδα δόμωι | φοιτάσηις πεδ' ἀμαύρων νεκύων ἐκπεποταμένα. **ὑπὸ κεύθεσι ... | ... δόμους**: cf. *Il.* 22.482-3 (Andromache to Hector) νῦν δὲ σὺ μὲν Ἀΐδαο δόμους ὑπὸ κεύθεσι γαίης | ἔρχεαι. **δνοφερῆς ... γαίης** 'down in the dark depths of the earth' (a transferred epithet, or hypallage). **πολυκωκύτους** 'full of wailing', attested only here, may be a new coinage by Theognis to stress the bleakness of Hades.

245-6 Homeric language of fame and immortality underlines not only Cyrnus' quasi-heroic privilege but also Theognis' status as a poet whose work is capable of such enduring influence. **μελήσεις | ... ἀνθρώποις** 'you will be in men's thoughts'. **ἄφθιτον ... ὄνομα**: cf. Thgn. 23* ὀνομαστός (the poet on his own fame). Appropriately, ὄνομα is followed here by the only use of Cyrnus' name in the entire poem (247).

247-8 The naming of multiple geographical features (mainland, islands, mountains, rivers, harbours, etc.) is a technique often used to stress wide expanse, especially when describing divine power: cf. *HHAp.* 20-1 πάντηι γάρ τοι, Φοῖβε, νομὸς βεβλήαται ὠιδῆς, | ἠμὲν ἀν' ἤπειρον πορτιτρόφον ἠδ' ἀνὰ νήσους. The pairing here of 'mainland and islands' emphasizes Cyrnus' universal repute (and, again, the extent of the poet's popularity). **στρωφώμενος**, 'roaming', implies free, unhindered movement. **ἰχθυόεντα ... ἀτρύγετον** 'crossing the fish-filled, untiring sea': the Homeric epithets suggest the effort and dangers of sea travel (see on Sol. 13.43-6*), which Theognis' verses effortlessly overcome. **ἀτρύγετον**: a notoriously obscure word, probably formed from ἀ-privative + τρύχω, 'unwearied, indefatigable'. The alternative meaning 'barren' (from ἀ-privative + τρυγάω, 'harvest') is less likely if the sea is full of fish; cf. Hippon. 128.4*.

249-50 οὐχ ... ἐφήμενος 'not riding on the backs of horses', as a young aristocrat like Cyrnus would often do. **πέμψει** 'will escort': a sense often used (as here) of helpful deities (e.g. *Od.* 11.626 Ἑρμείας δέ μ' ἔπεμπεν ἰδὲ γλαυκῶπις Ἀθήνη). **ἀγλαὰ ... ἰοστεφάνων** 'the splendid gifts of the violet-garlanded Muses': i.e. 'my poems', but elevated by ornate and honorific description. **δῶρα ἰοστεφάνων**: for hiatus before digamma ((ϝ)ῖον, cf. Lat. *viola*), see on Thgn. 51-2*.

251-2 πᾶσι ... | ... ὁμῶς 'for all who care about them and for future generations alike you will be a subject of song': **μέμηλε**: the subject is Μουσάων δῶρα. **καὶ ἐσσομένοισιν ἀοιδή**: a quintessentially epic expression for poetry's role in preserving fame: cf. *Od*. 8.579–80 (Alcinous on the fall of Troy) τὸν δὲ θεοὶ μὲν τεῦξαν, ἐπεκλώσαντο δ' ὄλεθρον | ἀνθρώποισ', ἵνα ἦισι καὶ ἐσσομένοισιν ἀοιδή, *Il*. 6.357–8 (Helen on Hector and herself) οἷσιν ἐπὶ Ζεὺς θῆκε κακὸν μόρον, ὡς καὶ ὀπίσσω | ἀνθρώποισι πελώμεθ' ἀοίδιμοι ἐσσομένοισι. **ὄφρ'... ἠέλιος** 'as long as earth and sun exist': the verb (ἦι) is understood.

253–4 Theognis' lengthy promise of immortal fame gives his final terse complaint particular force. **ὀλίγης ... αἰδοῦς** 'even a little respect': this is more than just the deference due to the older generation, for as part of the custom of aristocratic pederasty, their relationship is not only social and political, but also sexual (see Introduction §4), and αἰδώς here refers to the sexual favours owed by Cyrnus in return for Theognis' many kindnesses (the focus has been on the gift of poetic immortality, but the audience would also be aware of Cyrnus' moral and political education). The formal language of 'respect' avoids explicitness, but the amatory relationship explains what kind of betrayal Theognis is alluding to. For earlier erotic allusions, see 240–2 above. **ὥσπερ μικρὸν παῖδα:** the language again hints at the breakdown of their age-based relationship, as Theognis, the elder mentor who deserves respect, is treated like a child. The power of boys over older lovers is a frequent theme of sympotic poetry: e.g. Anacr. 360 *PMG* ὦ παῖ παρθένιον βλέπων | δίζημαί σε, σὺ δ' οὐ κλύεις, | οὐκ εἰδὼς ὅτι τῆς ἐμῆς | ψυχῆς ἡνιοχεύεις.

337–40

Theognis prays to Zeus. The desire to 'help friends and harm enemies', cardinal principles of ancient Greek ethics (first combined at *Od*. 6.182–5), is often expressed as a prayer: cf. Sol. 13.5–6* (to the Muses), Sapph. 5.6–7 (to Aphrodite and the Nereids); Thgn. 869–72 present a negative variation ('may the sky fall upon me if I don't help, etc.'), and Thgn. 1107–8 lament having brought 'joy to my enemies and trouble to my friends'. Some link Theognis' various comments on the sweetness of revenge (e.g. 361–2, 363–4) to his hatred of the Megarian tyrant Theagenes (see the introduction above), but the poet nowhere names the tyrant or his enemies (contrast Alcaeus, who names both), and the poems' generality make them well suited to reperformance in a variety of contexts.

337–8 τίσιν: Theognis wants to 'repay' both groups equally (τῶν τε φίλων ... | τῶν τ' ἐχθρῶν). Cognates and compounds of τίνω ('I pay') are commonly used in expressions of reciprocal justice and repayment in kind (cf. ἀποτεισάμενον, 340). **οἵ με φιλεῦσιν:** an idea already implicit in φίλων, but spelling it out underlines their kindness to the speaker and his debt to them. **μεῖζον ... δυνησόμενον** 'by overpowering them': μεῖζον is adverbial accusative (neuter); the future participle looks forward to the fulfilment of his prayer. The acc. δυνησόμενον after μοι (subject of the participle) is a common anacoluthon.

339–40 χοὔτως = καὶ οὕτως (crasis): i.e. if my prayer is granted. **μετ'... θεός** 'a god among men': the exalted comparison emphasizes the speaker's great pleasure in both friendship and revenge. **ἀποτεισάμενον** 'having paid back both groups'. **μοῖρα... θανάτου**: for this familiar epic expression, cf. Sol. 20.4 ὀγδωκονταέτη μοῖρα κίχοι θανάτου, correcting Mimn. 6 αἲ γὰρ ἄτερ νούσων τε καὶ ἀργαλέων μελεδωνέων | ἑξηκονταέτη μοῖρα κίχοι θανάτου.

805–10

Theognis explains to Cyrnus that envoys to Delphi must report the god's response exactly. Like many other Greek cities, Megara consulted Delphi on significant political matters, and it was important to prevent oracular responses from being falsified or invented. (Theognis need not be implying that Cyrnus or someone else in their circle had been appointed as an envoy.) The piece is neatly constructed, with the first and third couplets focusing on the honesty of the delegate (θεωρός) himself, the second on the role of the priestess as the god's messenger.

805–6 τόρνου... | ... φυλασσόμενον 'An envoy, Cyrnus, must take care to be straighter than a pair of compasses, a plumb line or a set square'. **τόρνου... γνώμονος**: tools used to create circles, straight lines, and right angles. **θεωρόν**: this standard term for an envoy sent to consult an oracle on a state's behalf is first attested here (Rutherford 2013: 97–8). **εὐθύτερον**: the tools rely on straight lines, but the moral connotations of εὐθύς are equally apt.

807–8 present the envoy entering the innermost sanctuary (adyton) and communicating directly with the priestess. **ᾧτινι** 'the one to whom'. **Πυθῶνι** 'at Pytho', i.e. Delphi, so named when the serpent killed by Apollo rotted away (πύθω = 'I rot'); cf. *HHAp*. 371–4. Hudson-Williams' κ' ἐν for κεν is unnecessary, since the locative dative Πυθῶνι is well attested. **θεοῦ... ἱέρεια** 'the god's priestess' (the Pythia of Apollo). **χρήσασ'** 'in her response': aor. part. of χράω ('I proclaim'), frequently used of oracular pronouncements. **ὀμφὴν σημήνηι** 'communicates the oracle': lit. 'reveals the voice' (of Apollo, understood from the previous line). For the oracle's enigmatic 'signs', cf. Heraclitus' description οὔτε λέγει οὔτε κρύπτει ἀλλὰ σημαίνει ('he neither declares nor conceals, but gives a sign', fr. 93 DK). **πίονος ἐξ ἀδύτου** 'from the rich temple': cf. *Il.* 5.512 πίονος ἐξ ἀδύτοιο (of Apollo's temple at Troy). As a major influence in Greek politics since the eighth century, the sanctuary at Delphi amassed considerable wealth.

809–10 Oracles might be given orally or in writing, but in either case envoys were trusted to preserve their original formulation (presumably by writing down oral communications correctly as soon as possible). Cases of deliberate manipulation by envoys are attested (cf. Rutherford 2013: 106). Hexameter oracles, issued occasionally at Delphi, would be harder to tamper with. οὔτε τι γὰρ προσθεὶς ... | οὐδ' ἀφελών: cf. Deut 4.2 (NRSV) 'You must neither add anything to what I command you nor take away anything from it, but keep the commandments of the LORD your God with which I am charging you.' φάρμακον 'a cure', i.e. for the problem which motivated the consultation in the first place. πρὸς θεῶν ἀμπλακίην 'sacrilege in the eyes of the gods' (rather than 'harm from the gods', as in Rutherford 2013: 93): to be a θεωρός was a sacred office (cf. Soph. *OT* 114, where Laius' status as an envoy returning from Delphi makes his killing by Oedipus even more shocking), and tampering with oracles was an offence against the gods as well as one's community.

1197–202

Theognis laments the loss of his land, which is now farmed by others. The speaker's distress is poignantly triggered by a bird's cry, which reminds him of the season for ploughing. Some take the poem as evidence that Theognis had been driven into exile as well as dispossessed (cf. 1202*). The piece skilfully reworks a passage of Hesiod (see below, and Hunter 2014: 128–31) to emphasize the injustice done to Theognis.

1197–9 Hesiod points to the crane's southward migration across Greece (in late October or early November) as a sign of the ploughing season: φράζεσθαι δ', εὖτ' ἂν γεράνου φωνὴν ἐπακούσῃς | ὑψόθεν ἐκ νεφέων ἐνιαύσια κεκληγυίης, | ἥ τ' ἀρότοιό τε σῆμα φέρει καὶ χείματος ὥρην | δεικνύει ὀμβρηροῦ (*WD* 448–51). There are several echoes here: ὄρνιθος φωνήν ~ γεράνου φωνήν, ὀξὺ βοώσης ~ κεκληγυίης, ἤκουσ' ~ ἐπακούσῃς, ἥ τε βροτοῖς ἄγγελος ἦλθ' ἀρότου ~ ἥ τ' ἀρότοιό τε σῆμα φέρει. **ὀξὺ βοώσης:** for the strident cries of migrating cranes, cf. *Il.* 3.2–6 (a simile for the advancing Trojans). **ἀρότου | ὡραίου** 'ploughing in good season': cf. Hes. *WD* 616–17 τότ' ἔπειτ' ἀρότου μεμνημένος εἶναι | ὡραίου.

1199 Compare Hes. *WD* 451 (continuation of the quotation above) κραδίην δ' ἔδακ' ἀνδρὸς ἀβούτεω, 'and it [the crane's cry] stings the heart of the man without oxen'. Theognis' κραδίη is similarly affected, but for a very different reason: not because he lacks oxen, but because his land and animals have been stolen from him. **μέλαιναν** is proleptic, 'it struck my heart and made it black'. Blackening of the κραδίη (and related organs such as φρένες and σπλάγχνα) is a sign of emotion, usually fear, anxiety, or anger (for the last, cf. *Il.* 1.103–4 on Agamemnon: μένεος δὲ μέγα φρένες ἀμφὶ μέλαιναι | πίμπλαντ'). Here a mixture of anger and melancholy is present.

1200–1 give the reasons for Theognis' 'black heart'. The repetition of μοι marks his personal turmoil. ὅττι: causal particle ('because'), as often after expressions of emotion. εὐανθεῖς . . . ἀγρούς 'others possess my flower-covered fields': the speaker's focus on the beauty of his lost land is touching. ἡμίονοι 'mules' (offspring of male donkey and mare) were essential to ancient agriculture and transportation (cf. Thgn. 183*). κυφόν 'curved': the syllable -όν is lengthened by caesura.

1202 A perplexing line ('because of †the other memorable† sea-voyage'). ναυτιλίη could refer to the cause of Theognis' dispossession (for example, a sea-voyage into exile) or its consequence (he must resort to seafaring to make a living). On balance some reference to a journey away from Theognis' lost home seems likeliest, even if we cannot reconstruct its exact form (μάλα μισητῆς (Hertzberg, Crusius), 'greatly hated', is worth considering). For the miseries of exile, cf. e.g. Thgn. 209–10 οὐδείς τοι φεύγοντι φίλος καὶ πιστὸς ἑταῖρος· | τῆς δὲ φυγῆς ἐστιν τοῦτ᾽ ἀνιηρότερον. Alternatively, Gerber (Loeb) thinks it likely that 'Theognis has lost his land because of a disastrous sea voyage', but he offers no suggestion for the first half of the line. By contrast, building on Young's νήστεις ('fasting' or 'on an empty stomach', hence 'working non-stop', referring to the mules) for μνηστῆς, West 1974: 165 argued, 'If the mules are particularly pressed for time, it is because they have started late, and if it is because of the trading voyage, the latter has been extended; of the possible reasons for that, the one that suits the context is commercial success.' His *IEG²* apparatus offers *exempli gratia* τῆς Σαμίης νήστεις. Such a memory of former success would certainly move the poem's nostalgia, but the thought process is laboured, and a complaint about exile is much more likely.

1225–6

ἀγαθῆς: the proverbial statement 'there is nothing better than a good wife' is often followed by the qualification 'and nothing worse than a bad one': cf. Hes. *WD* 702–3 οὐ μὲν γάρ τι γυναικὸς ἀνὴρ ληΐζετ᾽ ἄμεινον | τῆς ἀγαθῆς, τῆς δ᾽ αὖτε κακῆς οὐ ῥίγιον ἄλλο, echoed by Semon. 6 γυναικὸς οὐδὲν χρῆμ᾽ ἀνὴρ ληΐζεται | ἐσθλῆς ἄμεινον οὐδὲ ῥίγιον κακῆς. Theognis stresses here the more optimistic view. For the ideal of harmony (ὁμοφροσύνη, 'like-mindedness') between husband and wife, see *Od.* 6.180–5. γλυκερώτερον: the comparative form γλυκίων is more common in Theognis (as elsewhere). γυναικός: the topic of the speaker's extravagant praise is revealed only with the final word. μάρτυς ἐγώ 'I can testify to that': boasting of his wife's virtues enhances Theognis' own standing. σὺ . . . ἀληθοσύνης: a compressed expression, lit. 'and you make yourself [a μάρτυς of] my truthfulness', i.e. by marrying a good woman yourself. Once his period as Theognis' protégé and lover is over, Cyrnus is expected (like all men) to take on the adult responsibilities of marriage and fatherhood. ἀληθοσύνη is a *hapax*, one of 30 in 1431 verses (Selle 2008: 129), a strikingly high number, whose significance is complicated by the composite nature of the collection (see the introduction above).

XENOPHANES

Fr. 8 tells us that Xenophanes began his career as a wandering poet and thinker aged twenty-five, and that he has been on the road 'throughout the land of Greece' for the past sixty-seven years. Assuming that he left Colophon when it was captured by the Persians *c.* 545, fr. 8 suggests that he was born around 570 and was still active at the age of 92 around 478. His long life is matched by a wide range of interests, from theology and epistemology to sympotic etiquette (1*) and the civic benefits of intellectual thought (2*). Despite the criticisms of Heraclitus ('much learning does not teach sense', fr. B 40 DK = D20 Laks–Most) and Aristotle ('he said nothing that was clear … [and was] rather too unsophisticated', *Metaph.* A5 986b18–27), Xenophanes is an important figure in the development of early Greek philosophy and rationalism (cf. Lesher 1992: 3–7, Heitsch 1994, Bryan 2012: 6–57). His tone is often opinionated and polemical, and turned against a variety of targets: traditional stories of divine warfare (1.21–4*), the standard anthropomorphic view of divinity (B 14*), the mindless worship of athletes (2*), the damaging effects of luxury (3*), the bizarre theories of rival philosophers (7–7a*), and many others.

Rather than adopt the new medium of literary prose to communicate his ideas (as, for example, Anaximander of Miletus had done), Xenophanes chose to use the most commonly performed types of verse (dactylic hexameters and elegiacs), and did so in order to reach the widest possible non-specialized audience (cf. Granger 2007; for the use of iambic metre, see 14*). Thus, for all his pride in his own σοφίη (2.12*), Xenophanes addressed a popular audience rather than an intellectual elite, seeking to correct widespread misconceptions, whether about the gods, the natural world, or the value of clever people like himself.

Xenophanes 1

Source: Athenaeus, *Scholars at Dinner* 11.462c.

Poetry composed for the *symposion* often reflects on the context of its own performance and may even (as here) take the *symposion* as its central theme (cf. Hobden 2013: 22–65 on 'metasympotics', Clay 2016: 207–10, Introduction §2). This (probably) complete poem, quoted by Athenaeus to illustrate a '*symposion* full of every delight', is one of the best surviving examples of such metasympotic literature, outlining not only the ideal physical preparations for the *symposion* (1-12) but also various rules for the conduct of party-goers (13-24). Strikingly, as regards proper behaviour, Xenophanes links together the refinement of social conduct and the positive moral effects of certain kinds of poetry: songs that celebrate 'noble deeds' (19) spur the audience on to pursue virtue and are therefore to be commended, while those that describe violent conflict among gods and heroes are 'useless' (23) and should be avoided, since they offer false and pernicious paradigms of moral education (cf. Ford 2002: 46-66).

1-12 *Symposia* took place in the ἀνδρών, with drinking groups as large as thirty, reclining one or two per couch around the room. All symposiasts were male, but slaves, performers, and prostitutes of both sexes were on hand to serve them. Xenophanes makes no mention of professional acrobats, dancers, and musicians, focusing instead on the guests' own performance and the selection of appropriate subjects for their songs.

1-2 Explanatory γάρ (emphasized by δή) indicates that something is missing from the start, but it need be no more than a couplet or two (to the effect 'Our party can begin ... For now the floor is clean, etc.'). ζάπεδον is a secondary formation from δάπεδον ('floor'): see Richardson 1974: 254 (on *HHDem.* 283), West 1974: 188-9. Floors of cement or mosaic were easier to sweep and swab down. For the images on ἀνδρών mosaic floors (mythological scenes, exotic flora, the god Dionysus, and much else), see Franks 2018. **καθαρόν** (with ἐστί understood) modifies the two nouns that follow as well, stressing the cleanliness and ritual purity of the room, the drinking group, and the vessels. The same adjective is later applied to the water (8) and the men's words about the gods (14), creating a further link between physical cleanliness and the 'purity' of the group's piety and morality. **κύλικες**: wine-cups came in a variety of shapes, as did mixing-bowls (κρητήρ, 4) and wine-jars (κεράμοις, 6); they were often decorated with self-reflexive images related to the actions of the symposiasts (cf. Lissarrague 1991, Lynch 2012).

2-3 ἀμφιτιθεῖ: Ionic equivalent of ἀμφιτίθησι. The subject (ἄλλος μέν, followed by ἄλλος δ') is left unexpressed (cf. *GP* 166), but is easily understood from the context ('one servant puts woven garlands on us, another offers ...'). **εὐῶδες μύρον**, 'fragrant perfume', combines with the smell of wine (6), frankincense (7), and flowers (11) to create a pleasing convivial atmosphere. Since perfumes were often associated with sex and sensuality (e.g. Ar. *Lys.* 938-45), this may also hint at the sexual gratification on offer (see on 1-12 above).

4 μεστὸς ἐϋφροσύνης 'full of good cheer': contrast Sol. 4.9-10*, where it is characteristic of Athens' dysfunctional leaders that their εὐφροσύναι ('festivities') are marked by excess and disorder.

5–6 ἄλλος... ἑτοῖμος: ἐστί again understood. ὅς... προδώσειν 'which promises never to run out'; for the verb used idiomatically of the 'failure' or running dry of liquids, cf. Hdt. 7.187.1 προδοῦναι τὰ ῥέεθρα τῶν ποταμῶν. **μείλιχος,** 'gentle', reinforces the personification of the wine. **ἄνθεος ὀζόμενος** 'with a flowery bouquet'.

7–8 ἁγνήν 'sacred': frankincense (λιβανωτός) became widely used in religious worship and was burned at weddings (Sapph. 44.30) as well as *symposia*. **ἵησιν** 'sends up' (in the rising smoke). **ψυχρὸν... καθαρόν:** the description 'cold, fresh, and pure' emphasizes the water's suitability for drinking, whether on its own or combined with wine in the mixing-bowl (κρητήρ, 4), to a strength set by the symposiarch; for ancient discussion of the proper ratio of water to wine, see West 1978: 308 on Hes. *WD* 596, which recommends three parts water to one of wine. Xenoph. 5 insists on putting the water in the mixing-bowl before the wine. The drinking of unmixed wine was a sign of barbarism (cf. Anac. 356b). 'Civilized' symposiasts got drunk slowly, though the rowdy procession (κῶμος) afterwards might result in no less mayhem.

9–10 παρκέαται 'lie to hand': Ionic 3rd pl. form with apocope (= παράκεινται). **ξανθοί:** the loaves are golden-brown, and the appetizing nature of the spread is further emphasized in the next line, where the table is 'laden with cheese and rich honey'. **γεραρή,** 'splendid' or 'lordly', stresses the host's generosity and the honour (γέρας) shown to the guests. Understandably, the speaker's focus is on the big buffet table, not the low tables set before each drinker. **τυροῦ... ἀχθομένη:** the genitive is modelled on expressions of fullness (cf. μεστὸς ἐϋφροσύνης, 4).

11–12 βωμὸς... ἂν (= ἀνά) **τὸ μέσον:** a (small) central altar, where the frankincense was burned (cf. ἐν δὲ μέσοις, 7). **πάντηι πεπύκασται** 'is covered on every side': alliteration encourages the reader to dwell on (and so visualize) the colourful scene. **μολπή... θαλίη** 'song and festivity pervade the house'. **ἀμφὶς ἔχει:** lit. 'encompasses', 'enfolds' (ἀμφίς is a poetic form of ἀμφί).

13–24 Having established the ideal sympotic setting, Xenophanes now specifies the kind of poetry to be performed by the guests (whether they sing their own compositions or those of others). It is first and foremost poetry with a 'reverent' and 'pure' vision of the gods (εὐφήμοις μύθοις καὶ καθαροῖσι λόγοις, 14), since this will encourage in its listeners the pursuit of moral excellence (μνημοσύνη καὶ τόνος ἀμφ' ἀρετῆς, 20). Xenophanes' rejection of traditional stories of divine and heroic conflict (οὔ τι μάχας διέπειν... | ... ἢ στάσιας σφεδανάς, 21–3) was taken up most enthusiastically by Plato, who notoriously banned the prestigious and popular genres of epic and tragedy from his ideal state, and (like Xenophanes) envisioned an alternative sanitized tradition of song, with a positive and morally improving portrayal of divine and human conduct (e.g. *Republic* Books 2–3, *Laws* 2.655–6, 7.817a–d, 9.858c–e).

COMMENTARY: XENOPHANES 1   183

13–14 χρή governs a succession of infinitives (ύμνεῖν, 13; πίνειν, 17; αἰνεῖν, 19; διέπειν, 21; ἔχειν, 24), giving a series of moralizing precepts. **πρῶτον:** as soon as the performances begin. **θεόν** refers to divinity in general rather than a specific deity (for Xenophanes' rationalized pantheon, see on B 14* DK below). **εὔφρονας:** like the wine-jar itself (μεστὸς ἐϋφροσύνης, 4), the men are 'of good cheer' (i.e. have had a drink or two) and so all the more in need of being reminded to censor their songs. **εὐφήμοις . . . λόγοις** 'with reverent stories and pure words': the content matches the 'purity' of the setting (see on καθαρόν, line 1 above).

15–17 εὐξαμένους . . . | πρήσσειν 'praying for the ability to do what is right': the strikingly moralistic prayer (far from the usual request that the gods bring success or prosperity) chimes with Xenophanes' unusually rigorous piety. The goal of moral excellence (ἀρετή) is restated in line 20. The postponement of caesura to the fourth foot in line 15 is very rare (see Introduction §5); its effect is to stress the importance of their prayer (εὐξαμένους). **ταῦτα . . . | ὕβρεις:** lit. 'for indeed (ὧν = οὖν) these things (i.e. just acts), not acts of *hybris*, lie closer to hand'; προχειρότερον here cannot mean 'easier', since the road to virtue is proverbially harder (cf. Hes. *WD* 287–92), but means either 'more obvious' in the sense 'more obviously correct' (a nuance readily supplied by the context) or 'more straightforward' ('good acts are more straightforward than crimes', i.e. do not have unpleasant consequences).

17–18 πίνειν δ': the infinitive (still dependent on χρή, 13) introduces a new instruction, namely not to drink so much that one cannot get home on one's own. Warnings against excessive drinking are a staple of sympotic poetry (e.g. Thgn. 211–12, 467–96). Plato's model of self-control, Socrates, is able to outdrink his fellow symposiasts, tucking the last ones up as day breaks, before going about his usual daily routine and heading home unaided (*Symp.* 223c–d). **ὁπόσον κεν ἔχων:** a breach of Hermann's Bridge (stating that the fourth biceps is normally undivided), hence 'vix κ' ἐνέχων' in West's apparatus, but this also occurs in line 19 (and elsewhere in Xenophanes). **ἀφίκοιο:** the second-person singular addresses the call for moderation directly to each listener (or reader). **ἄνευ προπόλου** 'without an attendant'. **μὴ πάνυ γηραλέος** acknowledges that some will need help nonetheless ('unless you're very old').

19–20 ὃς ἐσθλὰ . . . ἀναφαίνει: lit. 'who brings noble things to light', i.e. the poetry he performs focuses on morally edifying material. **ὡς . . . ἀρετῆς** 'so that there may be recollection of and striving for excellence'. ἦι (Ahrens) is preferable to οἱ (Koraes) since it puts the focus on the poetry's effect on the symposiasts rather than the performer himself. **τόνος ἀμφ' ἀρετῆς:** Koraes' suggestion is closest to the manuscripts' τὸν ὅς and makes good sense: cf. ξυναῖσι δ' ἀμφ' ἀρεταῖς τέταμαι ('I strive for achievements that benefit the community', Pind. *Pyth.* 11.54).

21-4 Having praised morally improving poetry, Xenophanes now rejects its opposite, focusing on traditional stories of divine and heroic conflict, since they are central to epic, the most popular and influential genre of Archaic poetry, and offer bad moral paradigms that legitimize violence and discord. Anacreon delivers a comparable rejection of strife and warfare, but from the very different perspective of a love poet: οὐ φιλέω, ὃς κρητῆρι παρὰ πλέωι οἰνοποτάζων | νείκεα καὶ πόλεμον δακρυόεντα λέγει, | ἀλλ' ὅστις Μουσέων τε καὶ ἀγλαὰ δῶρ' Ἀφροδίτης | συμμίσγων ἐρατῆς μνήσκεται εὐφροσύνης (fr. 2 W). **οὔ τι:** for οὐ (as an alternative to μή) after χρή (13), see Smyth §2714. **διέπειν** 'relate, handle', but its Homeric use in the sense 'marshal' (cf. ὣς ὅ γε κοιρανέων δίεπε στρατόν, *Il.* 2.207) makes it particularly apt for this context. **Τιτήνων:** the older generation of gods defeated by Zeus and the Olympians and imprisoned in Tartarus (cf. *Il.* 8.478–81, Hes. *Theog.* 617–719, *HHAp.* 335–6). Hesiod (*Theog.* 133–8) names six male and six female Titans, offspring of Earth (Gaia) and Sky (Ouranos). The quelling of the Titans, like that of the Giants (see below), was often used in poetry and art to symbolize the triumph of civilized order over primal chaos, but for Xenophanes these battles represent distasteful examples of divine misconduct. **Γιγάντων:** superhuman but mortal beings, created when blood from the castrated Ouranos fertilized Gaia (Hes. *Theog.* 185). The Olympians overcame an attack from them with the help of Heracles. Along with [Hes.] fr. 43a.65 MW ἐν Φλέγρηι δ]ὲ Γίγαντας ὑπερφιάλους κατέπεφ[νε, from the *Catalogue of Women*, composed *c.* 580–520 BC, this is the earliest explicit literary reference to the Gigantomachy, though it is already present in art in the late seventh century. **Κενταύρων:** wild creatures (human above, horse below) whose lust, violence, and craving for wine sparked conflict with a range of heroes (including Heracles, Peleus, and Theseus). For the battle between the Lapiths (a Thessalian clan) and Centaurs, caused by the latter's drunken attack on the new bride of the Lapith king Pirithous, cf. *Il.* 1.262–8, 2.742–4, *Od.* 21.295–304. **πλάσματα** 'fabrications': the negative connotations of πλάσμα (lit. 'anything formed or moulded'), first attested here, imply that such stories of divine and heroic conflict are misleading images of reality. Moreover, as Ford 2002: 58 observes, 'The metaphor suggestively connects singers' false tales with the false, anthropomorphic images of divinity that are sculpted and painted by men.' **τῶν προτέρων,** 'of men of old', evokes above all Homer and Hesiod, underlining Xenophanes' break with epic tradition and foregrounding his new and 'pure' sympotic entertainments. Since it was normal to honour one's poetic predecessors, the caustic phrasing marks Xenophanes' radical approach. **στάσιας σφεδανάς** 'violent factions': songs that depict the partisan politics of civil strife (e.g. Thgn. 53–68*, Alc. fr. 129) are similarly to be avoided, since they too have 'nothing useful' to offer the sympotic group or the wider community (contrast Sol. 4.19*, where poetry is intended to resolve στάσις). οὐδὲν χρηστόν, 'nothing useful', completes Xenophanes' argument: stories of violent conflict (whether among gods or mortals) contribute nothing to individual morality or the cohesion of the community; indeed, they actively undermine both. On Xenophanes' concern for 'law and order' and the communal benefits of his own wisdom, cf. 2.11–12*, 2.19*. For χρηστός as 'useful to the city', see Dover 1974: 296–9. θεῶν ... ἀγαθήν 'and one should (cf. χρή, 13) always have due consideration for the gods'. Xenophanes' pious religious poetry is echoed by Plato, who admits into his ideal city only ὕμνους θεοῖς καὶ ἐγκώμια τοῖς ἀγαθοῖς (*Rep.* 607a).

Xenophanes 2

Source: Athenaeus, *Scholars at Dinner* 10.413c–14c.

This may well be a complete poem. It has two roughly equal sections: the first claims that athletic prowess is not worth as much as Xenophanes' wisdom (1–12); the second explains why this is so, focusing on the security and prosperity brought to the entire community by the intellectual's skills (13–22). As we know from epinician poetry, victors in the major Panhellenic games could excite considerable envy (e.g. Pind. *Pyth.* 11.29–30, Bacchyl. 13.199–209) and had to balance self-glorification with an insistence that they were bringing honour to the whole community (cf. Lys. 19.63). Despite these tensions, however, successful athletes were widely admired, and Xenophanes' criticism of the honours granted to them (including meals at public expense and cash rewards) is deliberately provocative (akin to his denigration of iconic poets like Homer and Hesiod: 1.21–2*). He further sharpens the challenge to conventional opinion by claiming that it is his own intellectual achievements which truly deserve such public recognition and reward.

Tyrtaeus had used skill in running and wrestling as a foil for the superior value of the brave soldier (Tyrt. 12.1–2*), but Xenophanes' denial of the public benefit brought by successful athletes goes much further. Euripides' satyr play *Autolycus* echoed both Tyrtaeus and Xenophanes in its attack on selfish and socially useless athletes: 'What successful wrestler, runner, discus thrower or boxer has defended his ancestral city by winning a wreath?' (fr. 282.16–18 K); wreaths should be given to men who are 'wise and brave', who can lead their city 'with moderation and justice', and whose words 'end wars and factional strife' (23–8). With a similar emphasis on what is socially productive, Xenophanes' σοφίη leads to 'good government' (εὐνομίη, 19) and a prosperous community (πιαίνει ... μυχοὺς πόλεως, 22). One can easily imagine this celebration of brains over brawn going down well at a *symposion* of like-minded intellectuals; but even a group of sporty aristocrats could enjoy it, though they might treat it in a more humorous manner, as a kind of utopian revenge of the nerds.

1–12 A lengthy priamel of sporting events (1–5) and civic benefits (6–9) builds to a surprising conclusion: that it is brain power, not athletic prowess, which deserves the city's highest honours.

1–5 ταχυτῆτι ποδῶν covers all the running events: *stadion* (a length of the stadium, almost 200m at Olympia), *diaulos* (there and back), *dolichos* (twelve laps at Olympia), and race in armour; cf. Pind. *Ol.* 1.95 (on Olympia) ἵνα ταχυτὰς ποδῶν ἐρίζεται. **τις:** all four Panhellenic games featured separate events for men and boys, but mention of the *pankration* (see below) and the civic benefits listed by Xenophanes make it clear he is thinking of adult male competitors. **ἄροιτο:** 3rd sg. aor. optative, ἄρνυμαι, 'win'. **πενταθλεύων** (participle) 'competing in the pentathlon', a combination of long-jump, *stadion*, discus, javelin, and wrestling. **ἔνθα . . . Ὀλυμπίηι** 'where the precinct of Zeus <lies> by Pisa's stream at Olympia'. As the oldest and most prestigious athletic competition (cf. Pind. *Ol.* 1.1–7), the Olympic Games stand here for all the major contests and the opportunities for victory they offered. **Πίσαο:** epic genitive of Πίσης, -ου (LSJ give only the feminine Πίσα). Pisa was the district around Olympia; 'Pisa's stream' is a periphrasis for the river Alpheus (cf. 21 Πίσαο παρ' ὄχθας). **ῥοῆις:** dative pl. **παλαίων:** since there were no weight classes in wrestling (or in boxing and the *pankration*, the other two fighting events), bigger men had the advantage. The winner was the first to throw his opponent to the ground three times. **πυκτοσύνην ἀλγινόεσσαν** 'the painful art of boxing': fist-fights were brutal and continued uninterrupted until one of the competitors was unable to fight or gave up. Bare leather straps covered the hands; padded gloves and head protection were used only in training. **πυκτοσύνην . . . ἔχων:** the periphrasis (ἔχων also governs ἄεθλον) is more ornate than the simple participle πυκτεύων (πυκτοσύνη is found only here) and makes it possible to use the epithet (cf. *Il.* 23.653 αὐτὰρ ὃ πυγμαχίης ἀλεγεινῆς θῆκεν ἄεθλα). **εἴτε . . . καλέουσιν** 'or that terrifying contest they call *pankration*': the increasingly grand style satirizes the absurdly high regard enjoyed by these men. Like a modern cage-fighter, the pankratist (who fought with bare hands) could do almost anything to dominate his opponent (only biting, scratching, and eye-gouging were prohibited), hence the name *pankration* ('complete test of strength'). This event was confined to adult men at Olympia in the Archaic and Classical periods. On Greek combat sports, see Poliakoff 1987.

6–9 Tyrtaeus' war hero is honoured by all and given privileged seating (12.37–42*), but Xenophanes' victorious athlete gets this and more, underlining the gap between public benefit and reward. For criticism of

COMMENTARY: XENOPHANES 2   187

athletes and their rewards as a way of boosting the status of rival professionals, including poets and philosophers, see Stewart 2017b: 169–73. ἀστοῖσίν ... προσορᾶν 'he would appear more glorious in the eyes of the citizens'. προεδρίην ... ἐν ἀγῶσιν: the iota in προεδρίη (first attested here) is scanned long. Front-row seating at games and other spectacles such as the theatre was a widespread way of honouring public benefactors or distinguished visitors. ἄροιτο: the repetition (line 1) marks the irrational and unjust coupling of athletic skills (1–5) and civic rewards (6–9). καί ... | ... πόλεως 'and he would have (lit. there would be) meals from the public store by grant of the city': a valuable lifelong perk granted to victorious Olympic athletes by many *poleis*. Xenophanes' emphasis on communal goods and decision-making (δημοσίων κτεάνων | ἐκ πόλεως) highlights the issue of the athletes' social utility (cf. Sol. 4.12* κτεάνων ... δημοσίων). The privilege of food at public expense is used to similarly shocking effect by Plato, when the condemned Socrates argues that as a poor man who has benefited the state, he is more deserving of this honour than any Olympic victor (*Apol.* 36d–e). καὶ δῶρον ... κειμήλιον εἴη 'and a gift that would be a valued possession for him': the epic phrasing (cf. *Od.* 1.311–12 δῶρον ... | ... ὅ τοι κειμήλιον ἔσται) enhances the honour granted to the athlete. While wreaths were the official prize at the major games, sizeable gifts (including money) could be granted by the victor's city. Xenophanes' wording suggests a precious object (cf. LSJ κειμήλιον '(κεῖμαι) *anything stored up as valuable, treasure*'), for example a decorated bowl, tripod, weapon, or piece of raw metal (such prizes are awarded by Achilles at Patroclus' funeral games (*Il.* 23.262–897)). Solon is said to have set the reward for victory in the Isthmian Games at 100 drachmas and in the Olympic Games at 500 drachmas (Plut. *Sol.* 23).

10 εἴτε καὶ ἵπποισιν, lit. 'or also with horses', is to be understood with νίκην τις ἄροιτο (1), 'or if he won with horses', returning to the imagined sporting programme (cf. εἴτε παλαίων | ... εἴτε τὸ δεινὸν ἄεθλον, 3–5). Equestrian events (races of four-horse chariots and single horses) were particularly expensive, and while envy or resentment of such extravagance was always possible, particularly in democratic communities (cf. Thuc. 6.16.1–3 for Alcibiades' awareness of this), admiration for equestrian victories was widespread even in more egalitarian circles, since they were felt to bring honour to the entire community.

10–11 πάντα is emphatic, 'he would get *all* that', envisaging an athlete who receives (undeservedly) every conceivable honour. οὐκ ... ἐγώ 'without being worthy of it as I am': the core of Xenophanes' complaint; ἐγώ contrasts forcefully with the general τις ('someone') at the beginning and end (1, 21).

11–12 ῥώμης ... | ... σοφίη: the brain/brawn antithesis is a staple of Greek literature (e.g. *Il.* 23.315 μήτι τοι δρυτόμος μέγ' ἀμείνων ἠὲ βίηφι), though the foremost heroic figures (Achilles, Odysseus) have both.

ἡμετέρη σοφίη is delayed for maximum impact. The plural ἡμετέρη (following ἐγώ) is not unusual (e.g. Thgn. 504–5 ἀτὰρ γνώμης οὐκέτ' ἐγὼ ταμίης | ἡμετέρης), but usefully encourages future performers to identify with the speaker's proud intellectualism. σοφίη is to be understood here in the broadest sense, covering all Xenophanes' brainy achievements, from his skill as a poet (cf. Sol. 13.52*) to his expertise in government (the focus of 19–22). For the idea 'brain does more to save a city than brawn', see the introduction above, and compare the debate between Zethus and Amphion in Eur. *Antiope* frr. 183–9, 193–202 K.

13–14 νομίζεται points to the habitual practice (νόμος) of athletic honours. μάλα strengthens εἰκῆι ('haphazard, random'), 'but this custom is completely irrational'. οὐδὲ ... | ... σοφίης 'nor is it right to value strength above good expertise'.

15–18 Four of the six events mentioned in 1–10 are redeployed, with running placed first in the opening priamel (1) and last here because it is 'the most admired of all physical feats in which men compete' (τόπερ ἐστὶ πρότιμον, | ῥώμης ὅσσ' ἀνδρῶν ἔργ' ἐν ἀγῶνι πέλει, 17–18). ἀγαθός describes the good boxer, pentathlete, wrestler, and runner, varying the construction each time (nominative πύκτης, infinitive πενταθλεῖν, accusative παλαισμοσύνην, and dative ταχυτῆτι ποδῶν). Its use encourages (a critical) comparison with τῆς ἀγαθῆς σοφίης at the end of the previous line (14). λαοῖσι μετείη, 'were among the people', situates the victorious athlete back home, preparing for the claim that he contributes little of importance to his community (19–22). οὐδὲ μέν 'nor again'. τόπερ ... πέλει: Xenophanes includes the strongest counter-case to his argument: i.e. not even in the case of the most honoured athlete (the runner) can one speak of benefit to the community as a whole.

19 The four conditional clauses ('For not even if, etc.', 15–17) build to a forceful conclusion, which makes clear the civic basis of Xenophanes' argument: what makes his σοφίη superior to the achievements of the best athletes is its contribution to the public good. τοὔνεκεν ... εἴη 'would the city for that reason be better governed'. ἐν εὐνομίηι: cf. Solon's extensive praise of Εὐνομίη (4.32–9*) and Tyrt. 4*. Plato echoes these sentiments when he claims that the guardians of his ideal state will live more happily than any Olympic victor: νίκην τε γὰρ νικῶσι συμπάσης τῆς πόλεως σωτηρίαν ('for the victory they have won is the preservation of the whole community', *Rep.* 465d7–8).

20–2 Xenophanes rounds off his argument with a final appeal to the public good, framed this time in economic terms. σμικρὸν ... χάρμα: 'little joy' is tendentious, since there is ample evidence from literature, archaeology, and art that athletic victories were greatly enjoyed by all levels of society (cf. Miller 2004). Thus, Xenophanes' attempt to link 'joy' here solely with economic prosperity makes for a misleadingly narrow view of the pleasure derived from the victor's success. **νικῶι:** 3rd sg. present optative (νικώιη in Attic). **Πίσαο παρ' ὄχθας** takes us back to the opening scene (πάρ Πίσαο ῥοῆις, 3). **οὐ ... πόλεως** 'for that does not enrich the city's treasury'. By focusing on economic gain, Xenophanes also suggests the cost to the city of granting additional prizes to athletes (cf. 9 above). How exactly his own σοφίη will improve the city's finances is not spelled out, though it is implied that the 'good government' he creates will be the catalyst. **πιαίνει**, lit. 'fatten', is well chosen, since it evokes the notorious gluttony of athletes; cf. Eur. *Autolycus* fr. 282 K, which Athenaeus quotes originally in connection with gluttony (though, as was noted in the introduction above, its focus is much more political) before citing this poem of Xenophanes as Euripides' inspiration (*Scholars at Dinner* 10.413c–14c). **μυχούς:** lit. 'innermost parts' (of a building), where valuables were stored, hence 'storehouses'.

Xenophanes 3

Source: Athenaeus, *Scholars at Dinner* 12.526a.

Athenaeus quotes this fragment as evidence of the corrupting influence of Lydian luxury: 'According to Phylarchus (*FGrH* 81 F 66), the Colophonians were originally austere in their habits, but after they ran aground on the reef of luxury and became friends and allies of the Lydians, they went out with their hair elaborately decorated with gold jewellery, as Xenophanes says: [fr. 3]'. The Colophonians' 'addiction to luxury' (as Athenaeus calls it elsewhere: 12.524b) became proverbial, but here Xenophanes, a native of Colophon, pointedly blames their degeneration on the Lydians, and focuses on the wealthy elite as the worst offenders. Criticisms of moral degeneration such as this embody the socially productive effect of poetry insisted upon in Xenoph. 1* and 2*. If this comes from a sympotic elegy, it is interesting to see it reject the kind of aristocratic luxury celebrated in other such poems (see on ἁβροσύνας, line 1 below; cf. Sol. 4.9–10*). However, since Xenophanes is said to have written a poem on the foundation of Colophon (Diog. Laert. 9.20), it may well come from a historical elegy written for performance at public festivals (cf. Bowie 1986: 31–2).

1 **ἁβροσύνας**, 'luxury', is seen here as a symptom of decadence and decline; contrast the positive ἁβροσύνη ('luxuriance, delicacy, refinement') of hair, cosmetics, and adornment in, for example, Sappho and Anacreon (e.g. Sapph. fr. 58.25 ἔγω δὲ φίλημμ' ἁβροσύναν). **μαθόντες:** by contrast, the poem's audience are to learn from the mistakes made by the poet's fellow citizens. **ἀνωφελέας**, 'unprofitable, useless', defines the citizens' expense as going beyond respectable needs. By contrast, Xenophanes' own expertise is useful (1.23*) and profitable (2.22*) for

the whole community. παρὰ Λυδῶν: Colophon was an Ionian Greek city, but located in Lydia (cf. Hdt. 1.142). Lydia itself enjoyed great natural wealth (not least from mining) and expanded its power considerably under the Mermnad dynasty (c. 700–546). Already in Archilochus, the first Mermnad king, Gyges, and all his gold are dismissed (Archil. 19*; cf. Hdt. 1.14), and in Xenophanes' time the mainland Greek cities of Asia Minor (including Colophon) came under the rule of the last Mermnad, Croesus (560–546), who forced them to pay tribute (Hdt. 1.6). Writing from free Lesbos and Sparta, Sappho and Alcman can see fancy Lydian dress as glamorous and desirable (Sapph. frr. 39, 98; Alcm. 1.67–9), but the experience of Xenophanes and his fellow citizens (the latter at least now living under Persian rule: see below on τυραννίης, 2) creates a more hostile attitude. For the Lydians 'living luxuriously' and their subsequent defeat by the Persians, cf. Aesch. *Persians* 41–3 ἀβροδιαίτων δ' ἕπεται Λυδῶν | ὄχλος, οἵτ' ἐπίπαν ἠπειρογενὲς | κατέχουσιν ἔθνος, and line 2 below.

2 ὄφρα ... στυγερῆς, 'while they were free from hateful tyranny', refers to the period before the Persian king Cyrus' conquest of Croesus' kingdom in 547–546 (rather than Colophon's earlier destruction by the Lydians in the reign of Alyattes c. 600–590, *pace* Lane Fox 2000: 40); the Ionian Greeks' ensuing revolt from Cyrus was repressed by his general Harpagus c. 545 (Hdt. 1.169–70). Although Herodotus (1.169) refers to this as the 'second enslavement' of the Ionians (treating their domination by Lydians and then Persians as comparable blows to Greek freedom), this fragment focuses on the latter as the major rupture, since the Persians were more obviously non-Greek than the cosmopolitan Lydians, their subjects were more clearly subordinate members of a vast empire, and it was quite possibly this event which led to Xenophanes leaving his homeland (see the introduction above on fr. 8). The speaker also implies that this 'tyranny' was a result of the Colophonians' luxurious and soft lifestyle, an idea prevalent in subsequent Greek thinking about the Persian Wars, especially in Herodotus, where the once hardy Persians are themselves enervated by the opulence of their empire (indeed, Hdt. 1.71 identifies the Persians' conquest of Lydia as the first step in their decadence) and come to grief when opposed by tough-living Greeks: cf. Hdt. 9.82, and especially 9.122, the final paragraph of the work, where Cyrus himself forewarns the Persians of the dangers of conquest and luxury. So Xenophanes is partially blaming his fellow citizens for their own suffering. Theognis, who was active in the mid-sixth century and so may also be thinking of Colophon's recent conquest by the Persians, is more explicit: ὕβρις καὶ Μάγνητας ἀπώλεσε καὶ Κολοφῶνα | καὶ Σμύρνην· πάντως, Κύρνε, καὶ ὕμμ' ἀπολεῖ (1103–4). **τυραννίης:** τυραννίη (here with iota scanned long) is a rarely found equivalent of τυραννίς (cf. Archil. 19.3*, rejecting the power of Gyges the Lydian: μεγάλης δ' ούκ ερέω τυραννίδος).

3–4 ἤιεσαν: 3rd pl. imperfect of εἶμι ('they would go'). **εἰς ἀγορήν**: the central civic space, where citizen assemblies were held. The word's political tenor underlines the frivolity of the Colophonians, who spend their time showing off rather than governing their city. **παναλουργέα** (παν + ἅλς + ἔργον) ... **ἔχοντες** 'wearing robes all of purple': purple dye was very costly (it took c. 12,000 sea-snails to produce just 1.5 grams of dye), and so the adjective (attested only here) stresses the citizens' ostentatious luxury. Colophon ceased to be a rich city after its subjugation by the Persians, and fifth-century Athenian tribute lists show it making only a modest contribution to the 'Delian League' (or Athenian empire). **οὐ ... χείλιοι** 'no less than (ὥσπερ = ἤ: cf. LSJ ὥσπερ IV) a thousand': the large number suggests that nearly every member of the wealthy elite has succumbed to self-satisfied preening. **ὡς ἐπίπαν**, 'usually', points to regular displays.

5–6 The language (especially αὐχαλέοι 'boastful', ἀγαλλόμενοι 'glorying', and δευόμενοι 'drenched') presents an unattractive scene. **αὐχαλέοι**: attested only here. **χαίτηισιν ... εὐπρεπέεσσιν** 'glorying in their finely coiffured hair'. Xenophanes' contemporary Asius of Samos refers to elaborately combed and decorated hair when he condemns the luxury of his fellow Samians (fr. 13 Bernabé). Fancy hair is presented positively elsewhere, especially in maiden-songs (e.g. Alcm. 1.70). **ἀγαλλόμενοι**: the synecphonesis (-οι εὐ- scanned as one long syllable) is rare but possible (cf. *Il.* 2.651 Ἐνυαλίωι ἀνδρειφόντηι, *Od.* 1.226 εἰλαπίνη ἦε, Sapph. 1.11 ὠράνω αἴθερος), and there is no need for Wilamowitz's ἀγαλμένοι. Some editors feel there should be a reference to the gold ornaments mentioned by Phylarchus (in the Athenaeus passage quoted above) and see ἄγαλμα in the transmitted ἀγάλλομεν; hence such conjectures as χαίτης ἐν ἀγάλμασιν (Hermann), χαίτηισιν ἀγάλμασί τ' (Bergk). **ἀσκητοῖς ... δευόμενοι** 'drenched in the scent of elaborately prepared unguents': strictly speaking, ὀδμήν is acc. of respect after ἀσκητοῖς ('elaborately prepared in respect of their scent'). Each word hammers home the vanity and profligacy of the Colophonian elite.

Xenophanes 7–7a

Source: Diogenes Laertius, *Lives of the Philosophers* 8.36.

In a section devoted to satirists who poked fun at Pythagoras, Diogenes cites these lines as evidence for the doctrine of metempsychosis: 'As regards Pythagoras having become different people at different times, Xenophanes attests to this in an elegy which begins with the line: [fr. 7]. What he says about him goes like this: [fr. 7a].' Though Xenophanes' philosophical writings are mainly in hexameters, here he uses elegy to parody a notorious theory of a controversial contemporary (Pythagoras was born, like Xenophanes, *c.* 570); these verses are the earliest surviving response to Pythagoras' belief in the transmigration of the soul. Whereas Empedocles (*c.* 490–430) marvelled at Pythagoras' claim to have knowledge extending back 'ten or twenty human generations' (fr. B 129 DK = D38 Laks–Most), Xenophanes is far less generous, mocking the theory by presenting Pythagoras as able to recognize the soul of a friend in the yelping of a puppy. No less pointedly, Heraclitus (active *c.* 500) accused Pythagoras of selecting from the writings of others in order to 'manufacture a wisdom for himself – a thing of much learning and wicked artifice' (fr. B 129 DK = D26 Laks–Most). Despite these criticisms, Pythagoras achieved superhuman status among his followers, and was a major influence on Plato (among others), especially through his ideas on the immortality and transmigration of the soul (cf. Burkert 1972: 120–3).

1 νῦν ... λόγον 'now I shall move on to another story': the transitional phrase (cf. the hymnic closing formula σεῦ δ' ἐγὼ ἀρξάμενος μεταβήσομαι ἄλλον ἐς ὕμνον, e.g. *HHAphr.* 293) presents a narrator capable of telling a variety of separate tales, and perhaps more than one about Pythagoras; cf. Hesiod's didactic λόγοι addressed ostensibly to his brother Perses (e.g. *WD* 106 εἰ δ' ἐθέλεις, ἕτερόν τοι ἐγὼ λόγον ἐκκορυφώσω). **δείξω ... κέλευθον** 'and will show the way': Xenophanes parodies the philosophical metaphor of the path (κέλευθος/ὁδός) of intellectual reflection: cf. Parmenides fr. B 2.1–4 DK (= D6 Laks–Most) εἰ δ' ἄγ' ἐγὼν ἐρέω, κόμισαι δὲ σὺ μῦθον ἀκούσας | αἵπερ ὁδοὶ μοῦναι διζήσιός εἰσι νοῆσαι· | ἡ μὲν ὅπως ἔστιν τε καὶ ὡς οὐκ ἔστι μὴ εἶναι, | Πειθοῦς ἐστι κέλευθος (Ἀληθείηι γὰρ ὀπηδεῖ). The use of κέλευθος to describe a path of song or poetry (e.g. Pind. *Isthm.* 4.1 ἔστι μοι θεῶν ἕκατι μυρία παντᾶι κέλευθος) also creates a cheeky *double entrendre*: the poet's path/song will show Pythagoras pursuing a ludicrous line of reasoning. Diogenes' citation of these fragments suggests that some lines are lost between them, which, given the satirical opening, are likely to have contained further parody of Pythagorean thought.

2–3 καί ποτέ ... φασίν, 'and they say that once', often introduces anecdotes or exemplary scenes, here giving the event, talked about by others, an air of credibility. **στυφελιζομένου σκύλακος** 'as a puppy was being thrashed': genitive absolute; the rare fourth-foot caesura (see Introduction §5) underlines the animal's distress. **ἐποικτῖραι:** Pythagoras' admirable concern for the mistreated animal sets up the humour of the following lines, where his pity's absurd cause is revealed. Xenophanes' joke assumes his audience will be familiar with the Pythagorean belief that the immortal human soul could pass into other living beings. (This resulted in certain restrictions, said by some ancient sources to be a total

COMMENTARY: XENOPHANES 7-7A, B 14 DK

ban, on the consumption of meat: Burkert 1972: 180–5.) **τόδε φάσθαι ἔπος:** the anecdote's credibility is enhanced by the quotation of the philosopher's actual words. Xenophanes may also be poking fun at the Pythagoreans' fervent belief in the words of their master, summed up in the mantra αὐτὸς ἔφα (cf. Diogenes Laertius 8.46 ἐφ' οὗ καὶ τὸ Αὐτὸς ἔφα παροιμιακὸν εἰς τὸν βίον ἦλθεν).

4–5 παῦσαι, μηδὲ ῥάπιζ᾿ 'stop, don't beat him': the double imperatives mark Pythagoras' alarm and urgent intervention. **ἐπεί ... | ψυχή** 'for in fact it's the soul of a friend': ἀνέρος (epic gen.) and the enjambment of ψυχή emphasize the unexpected recognition (man as dog). **τὴν ... ἀΐων** 'which I recognized when I heard its voice': Pythagoras' reasoning ridicules not only the theory of transmigration, but also the notion that one could detect the presence of a dead friend in a dog's yelp. As in Empedocles (cf. fr. B 117 DK = D13 Laks–Most 'For I have already been a boy and a girl and a bush and a bird and a scaly fish in the sea'), the Pythagorean soul retains its identity and remembers previous incarnations (an idea rejected by Plato). **φθεγξαμένης:** genitive following a verb of perception (ἀΐων): Smyth §1361, *CGCG* §30.21.

Xenophanes B 14 DK (= D12 Laks–Most)

Source: Clement of Alexandria, *Miscellanies* 5.109.1–2.

Clement quotes this fragment as evidence of Xenophanes' belief that 'god is one and incorporeal'. Xenophanes was highly critical of traditional religious beliefs, and this piece mocks one of his favourite targets, anthropomorphism, which he rejects elsewhere as being both culturally specific ('The Ethiopians make their gods black and snub-nosed, the Thracians red-haired and blue-eyed', fr. B 16 DK = D13 Laks–Most) and part of a self-centred pattern of thought that is hard to escape (fr. B 15 DK = D14 Laks–Most: if cows or horses or lions could draw, they would represent their gods in their own image). So, to clarify Clement's formulation, Xenophanes' gods are 'incorporeal' in the sense that they are non-anthropomorphic, and his 'one god' is the main figure in a refined (i.e. rationalized and moralized) divine pantheon: 'men should sing of god with reverent stories and pure words ... and one should always have due consideration for the gods' (1.13–4*, 1.24*). Thus Xenophanes' break with the traditional gods of heroic myth and popular belief is radical: 'Homer and Hesiod attributed to the gods all the things which among men are matters of reproach and blame: stealing, adultery, and deceiving one another' (fr. B 11 DK = D8 Laks–Most). In their place he offers a supreme rational being, ruling within a conflict-free polytheism, a vision that influenced many later thinkers, especially Plato.

COMMENTARY: XENOPHANES B 14 DK

While Xenophanes' other critiques of conventional religion are in hexameters (or, in fr. 1*, elegiacs), this piece is composed in an epodic metre consisting of an iambic trimeter followed by a hexameter (see Introduction §5). The combination of hexameters and iambics was used in the contemporary (i.e. sixth-century) mock epic *Margites*, and Xenophanes draws here on the parodic associations of the mixture (already present in the humorous inscription on 'Nestor's cup', *c*. 750–700, *CEG* 454) to sharpen his satirical attack on anthropomorphic conceptions of divinity. Later tradition referred to these theological fragments as σίλλοι ('lampoons'). This was the title of a third-century work by the sceptic philosopher Timon, which included Xenophanes taking on the role of Timon's guide through the underworld, in a parody of epic scenes of *katabasis* (especially the 'Nekyia' of *Od.* 11).

1 ἀλλ'... θεούς 'but mortals suppose that the gods are born': the birth of the gods was a popular subject of Greek poetry and myth, and central to works like Hesiod's *Theogony* and the major Homeric Hymns. Its rejection here marks Xenophanes' highly untraditional theology. According to Aristotle, 'Xenophanes said: "Those who say the gods are born are as impious as those who say they die; for either way the result is that there was a time when they did not exist"' (*Rh.* 1399b18). ἀλλ' suggests a previous statement by Xenophanes on the true nature of the divine. As it happens, Clement quotes this fragment just after fr. B 23 DK (= D16 Laks–Most) 'There is one god, greatest among gods and men, not at all like mortals in body or in thought' (εἷς θεὸς ἔν τε θεοῖσι καὶ ἀνθρώποισι μέγιστος, | οὔ τι δέμας θνητοῖσιν ὁμοίιος οὐδὲ νόημα). **δοκέουσι:** criticism of popular opinion (δόξα) is a staple of pre-Socratic philosophy: e.g. Parm. fr. B 1.28–30 DK (= D4 Laks–Most) χρεὼ δέ σε πάντα πυθέσθαι | ἠμὲν Ἀληθείης εὐκυκλέος ἀτρεμὲς ἦτορ | ἠδὲ βροτῶν δόξας, ταῖς οὐκ ἔνι πίστις ἀληθής.

2 τὴν σφετέρην... τε 'and have clothes, a voice, and a body just like theirs': specific and familiar features of anthropomorphism are scrutinized sarcastically. Some translate 'and have clothes, a voice, and a body of their own', but Xenophanes' focus is on the *human-centred* image of the gods which mortals mistakenly 'suppose' (δοκέουσι) to be true. On the unbridgeable divide between gods and humans in Xenophanes' thinking, see Warren 2013. **δέμας:** cf. fr. B 23 DK (quoted above on line 1). According to Xenophanes, god's physicality is totally different from that of humans: he perceives with his whole being (fr. B 24 DK = D17 Laks–Most), does not change or move (fr. B 26 DK = D19 Laks–Most), and controls everything with his mind (fr. B 25 DK = D18 Laks–Most); cf. Finkelberg 1990: 109–13.

HIPPONAX

Hipponax of Ephesus was active probably around the mid-sixth century BC. The Parian Marble gives his *floruit* as 541/540, and this is supported by Pliny the Elder's statement (*HN* 36.11) that he was alive in the 60th Olympiad (540–537). These dates chime with the only chronological hint in the poetry itself, when Hipponax refers to the tomb of Attales (whose brother Alyattes, the father of Croesus, died in 561) as a familiar landmark for those travelling from Lydia to the coast of Asia Minor (fr. 42). A later dating to the reign of the Persian king Darius (521–486), attested by Proclus (*Chrest.* 7 ap. Phot. *Bibl.* 239), is possible (cf. Degani 1984: 19–20) but seems on the whole less likely. The Suda (s.v. Ἱππῶναξ) reports that Hipponax was banished from Ephesus by the (otherwise unknown) tyrants Athenagoras and Comas, and moved to Clazomenae, another Ionian city. Although there is little sign of political engagement in the surviving poetry, exile is a regular theme in ancient poetic biographies, and Hipponax's low-life persona is a likely candidate for expulsion. In any case, fr. 1, 'O Clazomenians, Bupalus has killed', suggests that his quarrel with the sculptors Bupalus and Athenis (discussed below) was located in Clazomenae.

Ancient commentators refer to two books of Hipponactean iambics (frr. 118a, 142; cf. 92.14–15*). Much of what survives is quoted by ancient lexicographers and metricians particularly interested in obscure words and the poet's choliambic metre (see below), but we can still appreciate the variety of Hipponax's work, which ranges from sophisticated parody of prayer (3–3a*, 32*, 34*) and epic (128*) to scurrilous abuse (e.g. 12* on the 'mother-fucker' Bupalus). The papyrus fragments, which offer a less filtered picture, confirm the power and range of Hipponax's poetry, not least his talent for invective and obscene comedy (cf. 92*, 115*, 117*), and help us appreciate why he was ranked alongside Archilochus and Semonides in the canon of iambic poets.

Distinctive of Hipponax is an ironic contrast between the poet's aristocratic name ('lord of horses'), often used by the narrator (32.4*, 36.2*, 37, 79.9, 117.4*), and the frequently low-class nature of his persona and actions: as a thief (3a*), for example, or a pauper begging Hermes for wealth (32*, 34*, 36*). Like Archilochus, who seduces a free-born woman (the sister of his former fiancée) and so destroys the family reputation of his enemy Lycambes (Archil. 196a*), Hipponax has illicit sex with the mistress of his enemy Bupalus (16–17*, 84). Yet Hipponax goes further than his iambic predecessors in depicting himself in unsavoury situations, as when he undergoes a degrading cure for impotence (92*). But although Hipponax often situates himself on the margins of respectable society, this does not mean that he simply rejects or ignores conventional values; on the contrary, as with Archilochus' condemnation of Lycambes for oath-breaking (Archil. 172–81*), Hipponax attacks a former friend for the same crime (115*) and criticizes others for stupidity (28), gluttony (26–26a, 118, 128*), theft (79, 117), and sexual perversion (12*, 70). To achieve its goal, blame poetry needs the audience to go along with the narrator's criticism of his targets, and Hipponax exploits his audience's received values in order to condemn his opponents (cf. Carey 2018: 12–13).

Hipponax's language reflects the often obscene and farcical situations he depicts (e.g. '[my arse was] spattering me with shit', 92.9*), and there is comic juxtaposition of high and low registers (as later in Aristophanes): dung-beetles, for example, advance like Homeric warriors (cf. 92.10–15*), and the narrator's prayers to Hermes veer between formal hymnic style ('Hermes, dear Hermes, son of Maia, Cyllenian', 32.1*) and the amusingly colloquial ('I'm bloody freezing', 32.2*). His unusually frequent use of Lydian and other foreign words mimics the everyday speech of eastern Greek cities such as Ephesus (cf. Hawkins 2013). For his wider Greek audience such local linguistic detail evokes a mixed culture on the edge of the civilized world and creates a variety of comic effects, as in the Lydian woman's spell (92*) or the use of πάλμυς, Lydian for 'king', to describe (among others) both Hermes and Zeus (3*, 38.1). No less distinctive of Hipponax's style (and first attested in his poetry) is the use of the so-called 'choliambic' or 'scazon' metre, which ends with a spondee (see Introduction §5). The three long syllables at the end have a dragging and intentionally clumsy effect, accentuating the humour of the poetry and (according to Demetrius, *On Style* 301) creating a broken metre that suits the vigorous abuse of the poet's enemies (cf. Boedeker 2016).

Hipponax's best known enemies were the brothers Bupalus and Athenis, who hailed from a famous Chian family of sculptors. According to later tradition (Plin. *HN* 36.12, Suda s.v. Ἱππῶναξ), Hipponax was strikingly ugly, and the brothers made a grotesque statue of him and exhibited it in public. Hipponax retaliated with such savage verses that the brothers hanged themselves. However, since Archaic sculpture did not present realistic likenesses of specific individuals (but rather idealizing images of naked youths (*kouroi*) and draped girls (*korai*)), this part of the story is likely to be a post-Hellenistic fiction intended to explain why Hipponax was at odds with a pair of sculptors. Bupalus and Athenis may have been real people (various external sources refer to works by them and their family: e.g. *CEG* 425, Paus. 4.30.6, 9.35.6), but Hipponax has made them part of his fictional world, using the iambic story-pattern of quarrel, abuse, and suicide, as seen in Archilochus' treatment of Lycambes and his daughters (cf. Archil. 172–81*, 196a*). Although the surviving fragments lack these narrative details, they do preserve other episodes in the

Bupalus song cycle (Athenis is mentioned only once: fr. 70.11 ῶθηνι): fr. 1 accuses Bupalus of killing someone, and 12–17* present a variety of unsavoury scenes, including Hipponax having sex with Bupalus' mistress Arete (so too probably fr. 84), while frr. 120–1 imagine a direct confrontation: 'Take my cloak, I'll punch Bupalus in the eye. I've got two right hands and my punches don't miss' (a brawl later recalled by Ar. *Lys.* 360–1). Hipponax's poetry is well suited to a range of performance contexts. Iambic poetry of the Archaic period, like most elegy, was written primarily for the *symposion*, but it could be performed at more inclusive public festivals (Introduction §2). Drawn from all social classes, a festival audience could enjoy Hipponax's scurrilous escapades or the next instalment in his revenge against Bupalus and Athenis, while the more elite setting of the *symposion* will have created an entertaining distance between the upper-class audience and the lower levels of society presented so graphically and comically by the narrator. The elite's fascination with the boorish behaviour of the lower classes is an important feature of Hipponax's later influence on the choliambic *mimiamboi* of the Hellenistic poet Hero(n)das (cf. Degani 1984: 50–6). By contrast, and illustrating the range of Hipponax's poetry, Callimachus adopts the persona of Hipponax returned from Hades at the start of his *Iambi* in order to criticize the quarrelling of contemporary scholars (cf. Kerkhecker 1999: 4–5, 11–48, Acosta-Hughes 2002: 21–59).

Hipponax 3–3a

These fragments are sometimes joined together, with fr. 3* introducing the invocation of Hermes in 3a*. This creates a plausible sequence, but Hermes is often addressed in Hipponax (e.g. 32*, 34*), and 3a* could well be performed in persona rather than being reported speech. Yet even taken separately, the fragments share features characteristic of Hipponax: an irreverent attitude to the gods and the conventions of prayer; a close relationship to Hermes, appealed to as god of thieves; and the use of unusual and foreign words.

Hipponax 3

Source: Tzetzes on Lycophron, *Alexandra* 219.

ἔβωσε: 3rd sg. Ionic aor. (restored in favour of the transmitted ἐβόησε), 'he called upon', with acc. of the person invoked. **Μαίης παῖδα:** the description is honorific (Hermes' mother was daughter of Atlas and one of the Pleiades), but also echoes the invocation itself, since reference to a god's lineage is a typical element of prayers (cf. Hippon. 32.1* Ἑρμῆ, φίλ' Ἑρμῆ, Μαιαδεῦ, Κυλλήνιε). Μαίη (for Μαῖα) is an Ionism. **Κυλλήνης πάλμυν** 'sultan of Cyllene': the description marks the speaker's culturally mixed milieu, but by comparing Hermes to a foreign potentate, it comically undercuts the speaker's appeal to the god's absolute power, and the effect is enhanced if what he is asking for is help with a burglary (see 3a*); cf. Hippon. fr. 38 'Zeus, father Zeus, sultan of the Olympian gods, why have you not given me lots of money?' **Κυλλήνης**: for Hermes' conception and birth on Mt Cyllene in Arcadia, see *HHHerm*. 1–19. The long syllable at the start of the third metron (-λή-) enhances the 'limping' effect of the choliambic metre (such lines, known as ischiorrogic, 'broken-hipped', are found 21 times in Hipponax, or roughly 14% of his iambics). **πάλμυν**: Hipponax uses πάλμυς (from the Lydian *qalmlus*, 'king': cf. Hawkins 2013: 188–90) of Hermes, Zeus, and the Thracian king Rhesus, 'sultan of the Aeneans' (72.7), and refers to a landmark in Lydia as 'the memorial of Tos, sultan at Mytalis' (42.4). Unlike τύραννος, derived from another Anatolian word for 'king', πάλμυς remained a local dialect word. Other Lydian borrowings include καύης ('priest', 4.1) and βάκκαρις ('perfume', 104.21).

Hipponax 3a

Source: Tzetzes on *Chiliades* 1.147.

Hipponax adapts the familiar form of a kletic hymn – that is, the use of multiple cult titles and epithets (κυνάγχα, Κανδαῦλα, φωρῶν ἑταῖρε) to summon a particular deity into the speaker's presence (δεῦρό μοι) – and gives it a comic twist, with the petitioner revealed as a burglar and Hermes as patron of thieves.

1 κυνάγχα 'dog-throttler': the pseudo-cult title (κυνάγχης is attested only here) looks forward to the god's assistance in neutralizing any guard dogs that threaten the speaker's plans (cf. Hippon. 79.9–10). The scene envisaged by Hipponax is a clever variation on Hermes' more familiar role as 'slayer of Argus' (Ἀργειφόντης), the all-seeing monster that Hera set to guard Io. **Μηιονιστὶ Κανδαῦλα** '"Candaules" in Maeonian': the speaker ingratiatingly displays his awareness of the god's titles and widespread power. The Lydian god Candaules (whose worship at Sardis included the sacrifice of puppies: Robertson 1982: 135) has become identified with 'Hermes dog-throttler'. Such syncretism, whereby foreign deities are equated with Greek ones, is a widespread feature of Greek ethnography, as when Herodotus equates Dionysus with Osiris, Apollo with Horus, and so on (Hdt. 2.144.2); cf. Allan 2004: 116–20. Candaules is also the name of an early Lydian king (*c*. 735–716; cf. Hdt. 1.7–12), though since 'the Greeks call him Myrsilus' (Hdt. 1.7), a recognized Anatolian name, Candaules was probably the royal name that he took when he came to power. Thus Candaules did not mean 'dog-throttler' in Lydian, but the

Lydian god's association with dogs underlies the syncretism with Hermes.
Μηιονιστί: a *hapax*. According to Herodotus (1.7), the Lydians were known as Maeonians until they came to be ruled by the family of Lydus, who is said to have predated the Heraclid dynasty which began *c.* 1221 BC. The terms Maeonia and Maeonian are used in poetry from Homer onwards (e.g. *Il.* 2.864–6).
2 φωρῶν ἑταῖρε 'comrade of thieves': Hermes is the great trickster god who helps intruders escape detection (cf. *Il.* 24.333–8). Apollo calls him 'leader of thieves': ἀρχὸς φηλητέων κεκλήσεαι ἤματα πάντα (*HHHerm.* 292). He helps burglars at Hippon. 79.9–10 and 32.6* (see ad loc.). **δεῦρο** requests the god's presence and active assistance, and the omission of the verb suggests not only the speaker's urgency but also his familiarity with the addressee (cf. Sapph. fr. 127 δεῦρο δηὖτε Μοῖσαι χρύσιον λίποισαι). **σκαπαρδεῦσαι:** aor. inf. σκαπερδεύω; a disputed *hapax*, though the likely reference here is to the activities of a burglar. A σκαπέρδα was a rope used in a tug-of-war game at the Dionysia (see LSJ), and so the sense is probably 'come and help me with this rope', as the speaker prepares to scale a high wall. (A connection with σκάπτειν, 'come here and chop for me [through this wall]', defended by Robertson 1982: 133, is less plausible linguistically.)

Hipponax 12–17

These fragments offer a selection of lurid episodes in the evolving drama of Hipponax's feud with Bupalus (for the origins of the Bupalus song cycle, see the introduction above). They are unlikely to come from a single poem, though 13–14 go together well, as do 16–17. Rather they present snapshots of the relationship between Hipponax, Bupalus, and a woman called Arete. For the original audience, familiar with the wider cycle of Bupalus poems, these scenes are instalments in a titillating story of infidelity and revenge, as Hipponax demeans his enemy Bupalus by having sex with his mistress (for Arete's relationship to both men, see on fr. 15*). As with Archilochus' Lycambes cycle (cf. Archil. 172–81*, 196a*), Hipponax's audience are able to place the individual episodes within a broader narrative. Bupalus and Arete are comically humiliated (as is the family of Lycambes), but the narrator's actions are disreputable too (as in Archil. 5* and 196a*).

Hipponax 12

Source: Tzetzes on *Posthomerica* 687, 'θήπεον'.

The only fragment to name both Bupalus and Arete presents them as engaged in deception (θηπέων) and graphic sex (ὑφέλξων τὸν δυσώνυμον δαρτόν).

1 τούτοισι refers back to the act of deception, e.g. 'with these words' or 'by these means'. θηπέων: a rare word, glossed by Hesychius as 'deceiving, flattering, marvelling at' (ἐξαπατῶν, κολακεύων, θαυμάζων); the first meaning best suits the context here, though the second is also possible (either way Bupalus and Arete are getting the better of the Erythraeans). τοὺς Ἐρυθραίων παῖδας: the epic-style periphrasis 'sons of the Erythraeans' (cf. Homeric υἷες Ἀχαιῶν, Aesch. *Pers.* 402 ὦ παῖδες Ἑλλήνων) strengthens the condemnation of Bupalus and Arete by enhancing the prestige of their victims. Erythrae was an Ionian community on the mainland opposite Chios (Bupalus' native island). According to Herodotus (1.142.3), the Chians and Erythraeans spoke the same dialect (a different one from Ionians in Lydia such as Hipponax's Ephesians), and the closeness of the two communities underlines Bupalus' wickedness in deceiving them.

2 μητροκοίτης 'mother-fucker' (a *hapax*), probably used here (as in English) as a general term of abuse, though a literal charge of incest would add to Bupalus' sexual depravity. Hippon. fr. 70.7–8 abuses an (unnamed) man, 'this godforsaken villain, who used to poke his sleeping mother's sea-urchin'. Βούπαλος ... Ἀρήτηι: a pun on Bupalus' name, comically etymologized as βου- ('bull-like') and -παλος (= φαλλός), i.e. 'Bull-Dick' or 'Big-Dick', would suit Hipponax's attack on his enemy's shameful lust (as argued by Rosen 1988: 32–7). (By contrast, Rosen's interpretation of 'Erythraeans' as 'Red Men' (from ἐρυθρός, 'red'), with reference to the red glans of the penis, '"deceiving the Red Men" in that he is able to outdo them with his own erection' (pp. 36–7), involves a rather forced translation of θηπέων.) In addition, Arete's Homeric name ('prayed for (from the gods)'), borne by the queen of the Phaeacians, seems deliberately chosen to play up the clash with the woman's sordid adventures here. Moreover, ἀρητός can mean 'accursed', and so her name also chimes with her disreputable behaviour.

3 καὶ <μήν>: one manuscript omits καί, so that the missing start of the line may have contained, for example, a finite verb before the participle (<x–> ὑφέλξων τὸν δυσώνυμον δαρτόν). ὑφέλξων ... δαρτόν: Masson's conjecture for the unmetrical ἄρτον ('bread') creates a suitably graphic scene, with Bupalus 'preparing to draw back his accursed foreskin'. ὑφέλξων: future participle (ὑφέλκω), expressing Bupalus' intention (Smyth §2044, *CGCG* §52.41). δυσώνυμον, a typically epic and tragic word, apt for curses, creates an amusing clash of registers and vocabulary when combined with δαρτόν. δαρτόν: usually used of the flayed skin of sacrifical animals, δαρτός has the anatomical sense 'foreskin'; compare the use of δέρμα (~ δέρω, 'flay') at Ar. *Knights* 29 ὁτιὴ τὸ δέρμα δεφομένων ἀπέρχεται ('because masturbators get their skins peeled off').

Hipponax 13-14

These fragments, which probably come from the same poem, are cited (in this order) in Athenaeus' discussion of πέλλα/πελλίς, a broad-based vessel used as a milk-pail. Arete is hosting a drinking-party, but she has no proper drinking-cups, and so her guests take turns in drinking from a bucket. The scene parodies the conventions of the *symposion*, presenting Arete and her friends as low-life characters whose attempts to ape the parties of the elite end in farce and slapstick (a slave falls on a drinking-cup and smashes it). Yet if Hipponax is present at the party himself, which seems implicit in the narrator's focus on Bupalus and Arete (e.g. 14.2–3* ἄλλοτ' αὐτός, ἄλλοτ' Ἀρήτῃ | προὔπινεν), we have a further sign of his own unsavoury lifestyle.

Hipponax 13

Source: Athenaeus, *Scholars at Dinner* 11.495c–d.

1 ἐκ πελλίδος 'from a pail': the partygoers' readiness to use such a large and unsuitable vessel suggests excessive drinking and lack of self-control, a breach of one of the basic rules of a well-run *symposion* (see on Xenoph. 1.17–18*). πίνοντες: the use of the third person in fr. 14* (ἔπινον, προὔπινεν) suggests the same perspective here ('they were drinking'). But even if Hipponax is describing the disgraceful behaviour of others, he is still present and part of their set.

1–2 οὐ . . . | κύλιξ 'she didn't have a cup' (the double γάρ explains why the pail was needed): the amusing revelation that Arete had only a single cup to start with (now broken by a slave) underlines the absurdity of her attempt to hold a drinking-party. The κύλιξ was the most common type of drinking-cup, with a broad, shallow bowl and two opposing handles. αὐτῆι: she (Arete) is the host, a risqué usurpation of a traditionally male role. ὁ . . . κατήραξε 'as the slave had fallen on it and smashed it': a vivid, comic detail which encourages us to imagine a raucous and dissolute scene as the party gets out of hand. κατήραξε recreates the sound of the shattered cup.

Hipponax 14

Source: Athenaeus, *Scholars at Dinner* 11.495d.

2 ἔπινον 'they were drinking (from the pail)' (3rd pl. imperf.) rather than 'I was drinking' (1st sg.), given the disgrace involved and because the narrator is describing the drinking of Arete and another man (αὐτός . . . Ἀρήτῃ), most probably Bupalus.

2-3 ἄλλοτ'... ἄλλοτ'... | προὔπινεν 'now he, and now Arete would drink a toast' (lit. 'would drink first'): the partygoers mimic the formal etiquette of a *symposion*, where a drinking-cup is passed around, but the use of a bucket renders the scene ludicrous. The focus on Bupalus' and Arete's drinking emphasizes their excess, an effect intensified by the imperfect tenses (ἔπινον, προὔπινεν) expressing repeated action at the start of successive lines.

Hipponax 15

Source: Choeroboscus, *On the Canons of Theodosius* i.268.32.

The speaker's incredulous question, 'Why have you made your home with that rogue Bupalus?', is addressed to a woman, probably Arete, and suggests a triangular relationship in which Hipponax not only has sex with Arete (cf. 16–17*) but also criticizes her for her poor choice of lover or husband (see below on συνοίκησας).

τάλαντι: the adjective, usually compassionate in tone ('suffering', 'wretched', etc.), can also be abusive (e.g. τάλαν, 'you wretch!').
συνοίκησας: 2nd sg. unaugmented aor. The woman has moved in with Bupalus, and the speaker's tone suggests his jealous disapproval of her perceived infidelity. But if Hipponax has been sleeping with Arete behind Bupalus' back, his criticism both of her choice and of Bupalus is hypocritical. συνοικέω can mean 'live in wedlock' as well as 'cohabit' and so opens up the possibilty that Arete has become Bupalus' wife and is not merely a cohabiting mistress. If so, Bupalus will incur mockery by taking such a promiscuous woman as his wife, and if Hipponax continues to sleep with Arete after this meeting (an exact timeline of the relationship is not to be expected), the disgrace done to Bupalus by their adultery will be all the greater – as will the shame of Arete and the fault of Hipponax himself.

Hipponax 16–17

These fragments may come from a single poem in which Hipponax describes arriving at Arete's house (16*) for a night of sex (17*). The audience's awareness of Hipponax's feud with Bupalus would enable them to interpret this as an act of revenge as well as lust. Another fragment depicts the narrator having sex on the floor with an unnamed woman (probably Arete): their affair is secret ('keeping a look-out through the doors ... in case ... should catch us naked', Hippon. 84.12–14), and the narrator rejoices in the harm he is doing to his enemy ('and I was fucking ... saying "to hell with Bupalus"', 84.16–18).

Hipponax 16

Source: Herodian, *On Anomalous Words* ii.924.14.

δεξιῶι ... | ... 'ρωιδιῶι 'with a heron on the right', a lucky sign. The name ἐρωιδιός was applied to several species of heron (cf. Thompson 1895: 58–9, Arnott 2007 s.v. Erôdios). They were birds of good omen (e.g. Plut. *Mor.* 405d; cf. Mynott 2018: 255). As a bird sacred to Aphrodite (*Etym. Magn.* ῥῳδιός), the heron signals Hipponax's intentions with Arete.
'ρωιδιῶι: aphaeresis is otherwise limited to prepositions in Hipponax: e.g. 84.20 δὴ 'πί. (These lines are quoted by Herodian for the trisyllabic form of ἐρωιδιός.) **παρ' Ἀρήτην** 'to Arete's place': presumably the same house which she used for her low-class *symposion* (13–14*) and which she shares with Bupalus (15*). **κνεφαῖος ἐλθών**, 'arriving in the dark', suits a surreptitious night of sex. **κατηυλίσθην** 'I set up camp': καταυλίζομαι has strong military overtones (e.g. [Eur.] *Rhesus* 518 νῦν μὲν καταυλίσθητι). Thus the final word casts Hipponax's sexual conquest as a military campaign, a familiar Greek metaphor for male sexual domination (cf. Archil. 23.17–21, where the male speaker teasingly presents himself as a city sacked by his female addressee). Hipponax parodies epic elsewhere (see 128*); here he uses military language ('making camp for a night') to suggest both vigilance (this is a secret affair) and victory over his enemy. Some go further and see parody of a specific moment in the *Iliad*, where Athena sends a heron on the right as a good omen for Odysseus' and Diomedes' night-time raid on the Trojan camp (10.274–6): cf. Degani and Burzacchini 2005: 46–7. Whether an audience would detect such a specific reference is uncertain, but the narrator's deployment of the sex-as-war analogy would be clear.

Hipponax 17

Source: *Etymologicum Genuinum* λ 156.

It is tempting to view this scene as the climax of Hipponax's night-time 'sexpedition' to Arete's house (fr. 16*).

κύψασα ... μοι 'bending over for me': κύπτω is often used in sexual or obscene contexts, describing sexual penetration from behind (vaginal and anal) or fellatio (Archil. 42* combines both). Hippon. 129 parodies the *Odyssey* by changing Καλυψοῦν to Κυψοῦν: 'How did he come to Bendova's isle?' (West's translation). **πρὸς τὸ λύχνον** 'towards the lamp': lamps often feature in erotic scenes (cf. Ar. *Eccl.* 7–9, where Praxagora invokes a lamp as co-conspirator: 'We reveal our plot to you alone, and rightly, for in our bedrooms too you stand close by as we attempt Aphrodite's manoeuvres'). If 16–17* come from the same poem, Hipponax's arrival at Arete's in the dark (16.2* κνεφαῖος) contrasts with their encounter in the lamplight here.

Hipponax 32 and 34

These fragments probably belong together and may have formed a complete poem (though part of line 3 is now missing). Like several other fragments (cf. Hippon. 3a*, 35, 36*, 38, 39), they parody the conventions of prayer, adopting an amusingly irreverent attitude to the gods and mixing the high-flown language of invocation with gross and bathetic materialism, e.g. 'Zeus, father Zeus, sultan of the Olympian gods, why have you not given me lots of money?' (fr. 38). Here an impoverished and freezing Hipponax asks Hermes for a variety of gifts, culminating in a shameless request for a huge amount of money (32*). He then justifies his demands in a ludicrously self-pitying tone (34*).

Hipponax 32

Source: Heliodorus in Priscian, *On the Metres of Terence* iii.428.24 (1–2); Tzetzes on Lycophron, *Alexandra* 855 (1, 4–6); Plutarch, *The Stoics Talk More Paradoxically than the Poets* 6.1058d, *On Love of Wealth*, 2.523e, *Against the Stoics on Common Conceptions* 20.1068b (2–4).

1 Ἑρμῆ . . . Ἑρμῆ 'Hermes, dear Hermes': by addressing Hermes as a φίλος the speaker seeks to create (or implies that he already enjoys) a close and affectionate relationship with the god, and the ingratiating tone is strengthened by the honorific epithets ('Maia's son', 'born on Cyllene'). **Μαιαδεῦ, Κυλλήνιε:** Hippon. 35 deploys a similarly flattering invocation: ἐρέω γὰρ οὕτω· "Κυλλήνιε Μαιάδος Ἑρμῆ". **Μαιαδεῦ:** the metronymic form Μαιαδεύς is found only here. It may be a coinage by the poet to mark the speaker's particularly flattering and manipulative tone. **Κυλλήνιε:** a pure iambic line, followed by scazons. Maia conceived and gave birth to Hermes on Mt Cyllene in Arcadia; cf. Hippon. 3* ἔβωσε Μαίης παῖδα, Κυλλήνης πάλμυν.

2–3 ἐπεύχομαί τοι, 'I pray to you' (τοι = σοι), completes the speaker's formal appeal. The solemn prayer style (complete with lineage and birthplace) clashes humorously with the linguistic register and content of what follows. **κάρτα . . . | . . . βαμβαλύζω** 'for I'm t-t-terribly cold and my teeth are chattering': alliteration (κάρτα . . . κακῶς, lit. 'very much and terribly') ingeniously suggests the speaker's shivering, which is confirmed by the onomatopoeic βαμβαλύζω (attested only here). The second part of the line probably continued to emphasize the speaker's physical distress (e.g. 'and my chilblains are bursting', if 34.4* echoes the language of this fragment, as do 34.1–3*: ῥιγῶ ~ ῥίγεος; δὸς χλαῖναν ~ ἔδωκας οὔτέ κω χλαῖναν; κἀσκερίσκα ~ ἀσκέρηισι).

4–6 A cheeky catalogue of requests which goes well beyond what is needed. The diminutive forms for tunic, sandals, and shoes (κυπασσίσκον | καὶ σαμβαλίσκα κἀσκερίσκα) initially downplay the size of Hipponax's demands, but the effect is comically overturned by his final request for a massive amount of gold.

4 χλαῖναν 'a cloak': a warm outer garment seems at first a reasonable request, given the narrator's condition, but his demands quickly escalate: cloak *and* tunic, sandals *and* winter shoes, plus an entire fortune. **Ἱππώνακτι:** the introduction of poets' names is not uncommon in early Greek poetry (e.g. Hes. *Theog.* 22 αἵ νύ ποθ' Ἡσίοδον καλὴν ἐδίδαξαν ἀοιδήν, where Hesiod refers to himself in the third person, or Sapph. 1.19–20 τίς σ', ὦ | Ψάπφ', ἀδικήει;, where Aphrodite addresses Sappho), and its frequency is part of the author's construction of the character 'Hipponax' (or 'Hesiod' or 'Sappho') as a figure within the text, whose identity is (re)animated in (re)performance. The name Hipponax is used to highlight the character's greediness (here and 36.2*), his disreputable conduct (fr. 37 'said they should pelt and stone Hipponax'), and his triumph over an enemy (117.4*).

4–5 All three diminutive forms are attested only here. They derive from Anatolian (probably Lydian) loanwords (κύπασσις, σάμβαλον, ἀσκέρα). **κυπασσίσκον** 'a nice little tunic': a κύπασσις (like the more common χιτών) was a simple everyday garment reaching to the mid-thigh, usually worn with a belt. **σαμβαλίσκα:** σάμβαλον, Ionic–Aeolic equivalent of σάνδαλον, 'sandal', separate adaptations of a foreign word. **κἀσκερίσκα** (= καὶ ἀσκερίσκα): ἀσκέρα, a fur-lined winter shoe.

5–6 χρυσοῦ | ... ἑξήκοντα: the contemporary (mid-sixth century) coin of the Lydian king Croesus (Κροίσειος στατήρ), for example, was made of pure gold (*c.* 11g each); sixty gold staters represented a stupendous amount of wealth. The diminutives ('a nice little tunic, etc.') neatly cue the punchline ('... and sixty million pounds'). **τούτέρου τοίχου:** lit. 'of/from the other wall', a disputed phrase. The likeliest explanation is that Hipponax is revealed to be invoking Hermes as god of thieves (as in fr. 3a*), i.e. '[money] from the other side of the wall' (for the sense 'the other side of *x*', cf. LSJ ἕτερος IV 2). Hipponax's entire request is thus doubly outrageous: he wants not merely a phenomenal amount of money and clothing, but goods stolen from someone else's house (cf. Ar. *Clouds* 1327 ὦ μιαρὲ καὶ πατραλοῖα καὶ τοιχωρύχε for 'housebreaker' as a term of abuse). In fr. 79, by contrast, Hermes helps someone burgle Hipponax's house, but the thief is later confronted at his place of work (a shop selling cheap wine).

Hipponax 34

Source: Tzetzes on Lycophron, *Alexandra* 855.

A connection with fr. 32* seems highly likely, as Hipponax attempts to justify his shameless catalogue of requests by complaining of the god's stinginess in the past. The speaker's self-pitying tone is enhanced by the repetition of his demands (for a cloak and shoes), which also underscores his greed. The final low detail of his 'bursting chilblains' caps the parody of formal prayer.

1 γάρ further justifies Hipponax's appeal to Hermes (cf. 32.2* κάρτα γὰρ κακῶς ῥιγῶ) and introduces his complaint of neglect. **οὐκ ... κω** (Ionic for πω), 'not yet', cheekily implies there is some obligation on the god to meet demands of this kind.

2–3 δασεῖαν ... | ... δασείηισι: the new and repeated detail ('thick', i.e. luxurious) emphasizes the speaker's excessive request. There is humour too in his focus on the quality of the cloak and shoes, overlooking the fact that they actually belong to someone else (see 32.6*). **φάρμακον ῥίγεος** 'a remedy against the cold': quasi-medical language, hinting at a serious threat to his health if his prayer is not answered. **οὔτ' ... | ... ἔκρυψας** 'nor have you wrapped my feet in thick fur shoes': κρύπτω ('cover') has connotations of protection (LSJ I 1), implying (as with οὐ ... κω above) the god's duty of care towards him. **χίμετλα** 'chilblains': the word (cognate with χεῖμα, 'cold, frost' and used by medical writers: Hippoc. *Epid.* 5.1.57) points to the exposed sores on Hipponax's feet and ends his self-justification on a comically vulgar and grotesque note. **ῥήγνυται** 'burst' (3rd sg. after neuter plural subject): a strong word, evoking a graphic image of exploding ulcers.

Hipponax 36

Source: Tzetzes on Aristophanes, *Wealth* 87.

Tzetzes quotes this fragment to show that Aristophanes took the idea of Wealth's blindness from Hipponax (see on τυφλός below). The speaker's complaint of divine neglect, his self-pitying tone, and his demand for a large amount of money all echo frr. 32* and 34* (as well as frr. 38–9). Hipponax's repeated use of this shameless persona attests to its popularity with contemporary audiences.

1 ἐμοὶ δὲ Πλοῦτος: the poem's main characters are immediately introduced and opposed. ἐμοί, placed first, emphasizes the speaker's self-interest; his identity is revealed by the equally marked Ἱππῶναξ (end of line 2 and first word of the god's imagined speech). Πλοῦτος: the son of Demeter and Iasion (Hes. *Theog.* 969–74) and the personification of wealth, especially (as is natural in a predominantly agricultural economy) that of the harvest (cf. *HHDem.* 488–9). Ploutos had no extensive mythology or formal cult, but as Hipponax and Aristophanes show, his embodiment of good fortune had comic potential. ἔστι ... τυφλός: the parenthesis imitates conversational style (perhaps constructing the listener as a sympathetic friend) and draws attention to a crucial detail. Although this is the earliest reference to Wealth's blindness, it is unlikely to have been a novel idea, given the unfair distribution of resources in Archaic Greece. In Aristophanes' play the god's blindness means he cannot distinguish between the good and the bad, the deserving and the undeserving (Ar. *Wealth* 87–97). Similarly, Hipponax's insistence that the god is 'utterly blind' (λίην τυφλός) and 'dim-witted' (δείλαιος ... τὰς φρένας, 4) implies that he himself, a deserving recipient of Wealth's blessings, has been unfairly passed over.

2 ἐς ... οὐδάμ' 'has never come to my house' (τὠικί' = τὰ οἰκία): Hipponax treats the god with unusual familiarity (so too Hermes in 3a*, 32*, 34*, Zeus in 38). His lack of reverence makes his bewilderment at Wealth's neglect of him all the more amusing. Ἱππῶναξ: the speaker's expectation that the god would address him by name emphasizes still further his disrespectful over-familiarity (on the use of Hipponax's name, cf. 32.4*).

3 μνέας ... τριήκοντα 'three thousand silver drachmas': lit. 'thirty minas of silver'. The value of the mina varied (*c.* 70–150 drachmas), but a notional 1 mina = 100 drachmas gives the sum above. In any case, thirty minas represented *c.* 13–20 kg of silver, a huge amount of wealth, like the sixty gold staters of fr. 32*. The god's imagined generosity is rendered even more fantastic by the addition of 'and lots of other stuff too' (καὶ πόλλ' ἔτ' ἄλλα).

4 δείλαιος ... τὰς φρένας 'No, he's an idiot' (lit. 'For he [is] feeble-minded', acc. of respect). Hipponax's response to the god's alleged neglect is shockingly, and comically, insolent. (The alternative translation, 'No, he's too hard-hearted', lacks the same impact.) The audience can enjoy his persona's effrontery, knowing that retribution is likely (fr. 37, 'said they should pelt and stone Hipponax', could come from such a scene). The choliambic fragment ends with an iambic trimeter (cf. 32.1* for the reverse).

Hipponax 68

Source: Stobaeus 4.22.35.

These lines neatly embody, and may even be taken to parody, the hegemonic tradition of Greek misogyny. They play cleverly with perspective (for whom exactly are these two days 'sweetest'?), and the final caustic twist, celebrating the woman's death, encourages us to reassess the speaker's viewpoint. For just as an Archaic audience can see beyond the grumpy persona of Hesiod, Semonides, or Theognis, including their negative attitude to women (Hes. *Theog.* 570–612, *WD* 59–99, Semon. 7*; contrast Thgn. 1225–6*), so here they are led to question the speaker's rejection of the benefits women bring, especially the bearing of children, which is strikingly elided (see below). We do not know who speaks these comically grouchy lines, but they suit the often outrageous and risible 'Hipponax' persona (e.g. 32*, 34*, 36*).

1 δύ' . . . ἥδισται 'two days in a woman's life bring most pleasure': the exact number encourages the audience to guess what the two days are and prepares for the witty surprise in the next line.

2 ὅταν . . . τις 'when a man marries her': the woman's sense of happiness at her marriage is called to mind, but crucially τις focuses on the man's perspective, preparing for the punchline. **κἀκφέρηι τεθνηκυῖαν** 'and when he carries her out dead for burial': since Greek gender ideology maintained that the *telos* of a woman's life was marriage and motherhood, we expect something like 'when he marries her and she bears a son'. But the sudden move from wedding to funeral reshapes their relationship: just as Pandora, the archetypal woman, is a 'beautiful evil' (Hes. *Theog.* 585), so the bride here appears wonderful on her wedding day (when she is still largely unknown to her new husband), but later turns out to be a curse that he is glad to be rid of (cf. Semon. 7.112–14*, where the narrator points out that all men tend to believe that their own wife is one of the good 'bee-women'). In other words, the wedding day may be 'most sweet' for husband and wife, but the punchline makes us realize that the statement as a whole is to be understood from the perspective of a hostile male speaker. His bias, which leads him to move straight from wedding to funeral and to omit the main purpose and pleasure of marriage (the bearing of children), is ludicrously extreme. The leap from wedding to funeral also represents a darkly comic variation on the familiar 'married to death' motif (e.g. Soph. *Ant.* 801–82; cf. the inscription on the Phrasicleia *kore* contemporary with Hipponax: 'Memorial of Phrasicleia: I shall always be called "maiden", having received this name from the gods instead of marriage'). This is normally applied to tragic young women who die too soon, i.e. before they have a chance to marry and bear children, but here the woman cannot die soon enough. Finally, there is sexual innuendo at the woman's expense, since a man may perceive the day of a woman's marriage as 'most pleasurable' because it is the first time he can have sex with her. The lines are often echoed by later comic poets and writers of epigram, one of whom makes the sexual jibe explicit: *Anth. Pal.* 11.381 (Palladas) πᾶσα γυνὴ χόλος ἐστίν· ἔχει δ' ἀγαθὰς δύο ὥρας, | τὴν μίαν ἐν θαλάμωι, τὴν μίαν ἐν θανάτωι.

Hipponax 92

Source: PSI 1089 (second-century AD papyrus from Oxyrhynchus); *P. Oxy.* 2174 fr. 24 (5–9); Tzetzes on *Il.* 1.273 (10–11).

The narrator recalls a magical rite performed by a Lydian woman. Another fragment of Hipponax describes (in the third person) how a man overcame impotence by making offerings to the Cabiri and smearing his penis with mulberry juice (fr. 78). Similarly, the rite here is most likely intended as a cure for impotence (cf. line 4 below), but is far more painful and degrading and is inflicted on the male narrator by an anonymous foreign woman. The scene is obscene and farcical: the narrator's testicles are thrashed with a fig branch, something is inserted into his anus, and he ends up spattered with his own excrement, which attracts an invasion of dung-beetles. Assuming the lines are spoken *in propria persona*, 'Hipponax' is recounting a particularly sordid escapade which marks him out as an unmanly and ludicrous figure on the margins of respectable society.

1 ηὔδα ... Λυδίζουσα 'she spoke in Lydian': the poetic αὐδάω makes for a solemn opening, but this is comically undercut by the lewdness that soon ensues. The woman is uttering a spell. Hipponax's Greek audience may have known very little about Lydian religion or magical practices, but the woman's methods confirm the dangerous potential of 'magic' or 'witchcraft', which is often associated in Greek thought with women or goddesses (e.g. Circe), especially foreigners (most notoriously Medea). The scene also plays with the elite and luxurious connotations of Lydian culture (cf. e.g. Sapph. frr. 39, 98 on fancy Lydian clothing), as the woman's cure descends into vulgar slapstick. **βασκι ... κρολεα:** this is probably intended as the Lydian equivalent of 'abracadabra' and may be a magical nonsense word borrowed into Hipponax's local Greek (Ephesian) vernacular. Later sources speak of Ἐφέσια γράμματα ('Ephesian letters [of the alphabet]'), strings of incomprehensible words uttered as protective spells (Suda s.v. Ἐφ. γρ.). Alternatively, a series of glosses by Hesychius ('βασκεπικρολεα: "hurry up over here" in Lydian', 'βαστιζα κρολεα: "come quickly" in Lydian', 'κρολίαζε: "come here quickly"') has been used to reconstruct the line, with the woman urging the narrator to approach and begin his cure, but it is unlikely that Hipponax's audience knew enough Lydian to decipher this, and Hesychius may well be guessing based on his vision of the scene. If, as Hawkins 2013: 166 suggests, the Lydian phrase here is translated into 'Arsish' (πυγιστί) in the following line (cf. Hippon. 3a.1* Ἑρμῆ κυνάγχα, Μηιονιστὶ Κανδαῦλα, where the Lydian equivalent of the Greek is given), Hipponax may have used real Lydian for τὸν πυγεῶνα παρ[(2), but again it seems unlikely that his audience will have known enough Lydian to realize this.

2 πυγιστί 'in Arsish': a comic neologism from πυγή (cf. Archil. fr. 187 τοιήνδε δ', ὢ πίθηκε, τὴν πυγὴν ἔχων), based on such forms as Λυδιστί/ Μηιονιστί, used of language. **τὸν πυγεῶνα παρ[:** like πυγιστί, πυγεών occurs only here and is another new coinage for 'arse'; the ludicrous effect is enhanced by alliteration, πυγιστί· "τὸν πυγεῶνα παρ[". For possible restorations (e.g. τὸν πυγεῶνα πάρ[εχέ μοι θᾶττον or πάρ[εχέ μῶκιστα), see Gärtner 2008. As subsequent events suggest, the Lydian woman inserts something into the narrator's anus to act as a stimulant, but her treatment backfires all too literally (9–10).

3 καί ... φαλ[: Hesychius' gloss, φάλα· ἡ μικρὰ κάρα, suggests Hipponax is punning here on the 'little head' of the narrator's penis, and the genitive probably depends on a verb of touching or grabbing, e.g. καί μοι τὸν ὄρχιν τῆς φαλῆς παρ-/προσέλκουσα, 'dragging me by my little cock she thrashed my ball(s), etc.' West's supplement καί μοι τὸν ὄρχιν τῆς φαλάκρης ἔλκουσα ('pulling my testicle by the bald patch') gives less good sense, especially as using the penis as a 'handle' or 'rope' is later a well-attested joke (e.g. Ar. *Wasps* 1341–4). **τὸν ὄρχιν:** this is probably singular for the unmetrical plural (ὄρχεις, Ion. ὄρχιες, 'testicles'), though it may be a reference to the narrator having only one testicle (or an undescended testicle), compounding his impotence.

4 κ]ράδηι συνηλοίησεν 'she thrashed [my ball(s)] with a fig branch': συναλοάω ('smash, crush') is a strong word, expressing the speaker's agony. **ὥσπ[ερ φαρμακῶι** 'like a scapegoat': Coppola's supplement is plausible, since Hipponax mentions elsewhere the practice of beating a scapegoat with fig branches (frr. 5, 6, 9) and lashing his penis (fr. 10). Since the *pharmakos* ritual could be used to counteract agricultural infertility caused by plague, famine, or drought, its application to the impotent narrator is appropriate. However, since the ritual ended in exile or death for the unfortunate victim, alluding to it here suggests that the Lydian woman's unconventional cure is truly a form of torture. Ancient Greek gender ideology emphasized the active, penetrating male and the passive, penetrated female, so that impotence was felt to be deeply shameful and unmanly. Standard treatments included various vegetables and plants (especially penis-shaped ones), which were ground down and drunk as a potion or rubbed on the body, as well as the use of erotic images: see McLaren 2007: 15–19.

5 .].τοις διοζίοισιν probably refers to branches 'with two knots or eyes' (LSJ δίοζος) or to something with two branches (όζος = branch). West 1974: 145 suggested 'forked appliances pinning his legs to the ground', translating 'fast[ened in] the stocks' (cf. διοζόομαι, 'branch out'). This is unlikely, since the narrator is probably to be imagined as standing rather than sitting or lying down (cf. 7–8, 12–13 below).

6 καὶ δὴ δυοῖσιν ἐν πόνοισ[ι 'and indeed [I was caught] in two torments', i.e. simultaneously being thrashed (7–8) and shitting himself (8–9). For 'I was caught', cf. πόνοισ[ιν εἰχόμην: Bossi, πόνοισ[ιν ἠγρεύμην: Knox.

7–8 ἤ . . . | . . . ἐμπίπτουσα 'from one side the fig branch ... me, descending from above': Coppola's ἔκνιζεν ('was pounding') and Knox's ἤλγυνεν ('was causing me pain') are plausible supplements, though the first is better, being more specific and vivid. **ἐμπίπτουσα** refers to the branch, which the Lydian woman, having grabbed the man's penis (see 3 above), is now bringing down on his testicle(s). Rather than picturing the man sitting or lying on the ground with the woman bent over him, we are probably to imagine both the man and the woman standing, with the man doubled over in pain (see on κατέβαλον below).

8–9 κ[. . . | παραψιδάζων βολβίτωι[: Latte's κ[ἄνθεν ὁ πρωκτός gives good sense, 'a[nd from the other side my arse], spattering me with shit'. **παραψιδάζων**, a *hapax* (cf. ψίδες, 'droplets', 'drizzle'), creates a striking and repulsive scene, as the anal stimulant backfires. **βολβίτωι:** the word usually refers to cattle dung: its use here (the only time it is applied to human excrement) intensifies the narrator's degrading condition.

10 ὦζεν . . . λαύρη 'the alleyway stank': λαύρα (Ion. λαύρη), a small lane or side street, enhances the sense of a furtive and shameful ritual as well as a stinking enclosed space.

10–15 The dung-beetles' attack, with its military language (ἐμπίπτοντε[ς | κατέβαλον, ἐμπεσόντες τὰς θύρα[ς) and large number of fighters (πλέονες ἢ πεντήκοντα) split into separate formations (οἱ μὲν . . . οἱ δὲ . . . οἱ δ'), recalls the type of epic simile where soldiers are compared to swarming wasps or bees (e.g. *Il.* 12.167–70, 16.259–65). The dung-beetles are themselves comically cast as mini-warriors, and whereas the Homeric insects fight in defence of their young (ἀμύνονται περὶ τέκνων, 12.170; ἀμύνει οἷσι τέκεσσι, 16.265), the beetles' aim is far from glorious.

10–11 κάνθαροι: κολεόπτερος is the general term for beetle, while κάνθαρος is used of the various species of dung-beetle (Beavis 1988: 157). **ῥοιζέοντες**, 'buzzing', 'whirring', is onomatopoeic. **κατ' ὀδμήν:** though obvious, the detail (coming after ὦζεν δὲ λαύρη) reinforces our awareness of the appalling smell.

12–13 τῶν ... κατέβαλον 'some of them attacked and knocked [me] down': humorous slapstick, as the puny insects overwhelm the speaker. The object of κατέβαλον is lost, but is more likely to be the shit-spattered narrator than the Lydian woman. κατέβαλον further confirms the idea that the man is being treated standing up. **οἱ δὲ τοὺς ὀδ. .[:** Knox's ὀδό[ντας ὤξυνον ('others whet their teeth') creates a suitably macabre image as a second division of dung-beetles prepares to attack. **14–15 οἱ ... | ... Πυγέλησι[:** the phrase combines two puns (unless they belong to separate clauses), the first on 'door' (θύρα) as 'anus' (as in the 'back-door' jokes of later comedy; cf. Henderson 1991: 199), the second on Pygela, a town near Ephesus, which was founded when some of Agamemnon's men were forced to stay there because of πυγαλγία ('buttock pain'; cf. Strabo 14.1.20), and whose name (derived from πυγή: see line 2 above) is here comically construed as 'Arseville', 'Buttocktown' or the like (cf. West's 'and others fell upon the Arsenal doors'). A marginal note on the papyrus at line 14 indicates it is line 800 of the roll, perhaps line 800 of Hipponax's first or second book.

Hipponax 115 and 117

The authorship of frr. 115–17, commonly known as the Strasbourg Epodes (after the city where the papyrus is now held), is a matter of much scholarly debate. (Fr. 116, omitted here, consists of three badly preserved lines in which no complete word is legible.) Fr. 117* probably contains the name Hipponax (117.4*), and its style and content are akin to what we know of his poetry, so it is very likely to be by him. Fr. 115*, however, has been thought to be much more typical of Archilochus in both language and theme. Thus some attribute both poems to Archilochus, some both to Hipponax, and others argue for separate authorship (115* by Archilochus, 117* by Hipponax), with the papyrus containing an anthology of different poets.

It is certainly true that 115* resembles Archilochus, both in its attack upon a friend who turns out to be an oath-breaker (cf. Archilochus' epodes against Lycambes: 172–81*) and its use of epic language and elevated rhetoric. However, Hipponax too is a master of invective aimed at punishing those who transgress social norms (e.g. 26–26a, 118, 128* on gluttony; 79 and 117* on theft; 12* and 70 on sexual perversion), and his appeals to Hermes and Wealth, for example, exploit the ideas of friendship and betrayal (32*, 34*, 36*). Moreover, we have only a small amount of Hipponax's work, and it is unwise to prescribe a single Hipponactean style based on a particular persona. Thus, although he often uses grand language to parodic effect (e.g. 128*), there is no reason to believe he could not deploy a high-flown tone seriously (as in 115*). Finally, if we

COMMENTARY: HIPPONAX 115

accept that Hipponax wrote 117*, we know that he composed epodes with the same metrical scheme as 115* (iambic trimeter followed by hemiepes, also used by Archilochus). In conclusion, although it is possible that the papyrus contained an anthology of different poets, it is no less probable that Hipponax composed two invectives in the same metre and was capable of varying his style to suit his goals. I therefore agree with the most recent editors of Hipponax (West 1989, Degani 1991, Nicolosi 2007) in ascribing both poems to him.

Hipponax 115

Source: P. Argent. 3 fr. 1.1–16 (second century AD).

The narrator revels in imagining his enemy shipwrecked, enslaved, and mistreated in a foreign land (4–13) before revealing the reason for his curse: his friend has broken his oaths and betrayed him (14–16). In praying for shipwreck rather than a safe voyage, the poem is a kind of inverted *propempticon* (cf. Hor. *Epode* 10, probably modelled on this poem). It is carefully constructed, with the reason for the speaker's curse held back, and the sudden revelation of his motives makes us more receptive to his complaint (cf. Thgn. 237–54*, where Theognis ends by declaring that Cyrnus disrespects and deceives him 'like a small child'). The abrupt shift from third-person invective (i.e. 'may he suffer ...', 4–13) to first-person anguish ('because I have suffered', 14–16) helps to guide our sympathy away from the enslaved figure towards the betrayed narrator himself. The former friend may have been named in the lost opening (1–3; the thief's name in 117* is also lacking); in any case, he is unlikely to be Bupalus, who appears elsewhere as a pure enemy and rival and not as a former friend (cf. 12–17*).

1–3 may have described the man setting out on his voyage, since he is already adrift by line 4.

4 κύμ[ατι] πλα[ζόμ]ενος 'driven on by the swell': cf. *Od.* 5.388–9 (of Odysseus) ἔνθα δύω νύκτας δύο τ' ἤματα κύματι πηγῷ | πλάζετο, which supports the singular κύμ[ατι] over κύμ[ασι].

5–13 The speaker imagines his enemy's reception by a barbarous people (5–9), dwells (in a parenthetic clause) on his future sufferings as a slave (7–8), then returns to the moment he is washed up on the foreign shore (9–13).

5–9 κἄν ... | ... αὐτόν 'at Salmydessus may top-knotted Thracians welcome him most kindly, naked ... and frozen stiff'. κἄν = καὶ ἐν (crasis). Σαλμυδ[ησσ]ῶι: a Thracian settlement on the south-west coast of the Black Sea, whose dangerous shallow waters and harbourless coast led to frequent shipwrecks: cf. [Aesch.] *Prometheus Bound* 726–7 τραχεῖα πόντου Σαλμυδησσία γνάθος | ἐχθρόξενος ναύτῃσι, μητρυιά νεῶν. According to Xenophon, the locals killed each other over the right to plunder ships that were wrecked there (*An.* 7.5.12–13). If the speaker's enemy is shipwrecked near Salmydessus, he is likely to be on a trading voyage to the Black Sea, compounding the reversal of his fortunes (from profit and success to slavery and suffering). The fertile Black Sea region, supplying grain, cattle, timber, metals, and much else, attracted Greek colonies and traders from the mid-eighth century onwards (Hdt. 4.85–6 emphasizes the region's huge scale): cf. Moreno 2007: 145–208. **γυμνόν** stresses the man's shameful and vulnerable condition. **εὔφρονε.[**: the most plausible supplement, εὐφρονέσ[τατα (cf. Gärtner 2008 for εὐφρονέ[στατοι), well expresses the speaker's sarcasm and *Schadenfreude*. **Θρήϊκες ἀκρό[κ]ομοι**: Homer uses the same phrase in a passage that emphasizes the fighting prowess of the Thracians, allies of the Trojans (*Il.* 4.533); here the distinctive epithet connotes their threatening exoticism, enhancing the isolation and vulnerability of the shipwrecked sailor. **λάβοιεν**, modified by εὐφρονέσ[τατα or the like, means 'receive hospitably' (LSJ λαμβάνω II 1 b), though the negative sense 'seize' is what the speaker really has in mind. **ῥίγει πεπηγότ'**: the physical detail (lit. 'stiff with cold') draws our attention to the man's extreme suffering and is all the more notable for being delayed.

7–8 The parenthetical clause captures the speaker's excitement as he anticipates his enemy's future as an abused slave. **ἀναπλήσει**: the future ('there he will endure many woes') is preferable to West's aorist optative ἀναπλῆσαι ('may he endure') as it is closer to the papyrus' ενθαναπλησει and better expresses the speaker's experience as he suddenly switches from merely wishing to vividly imagining and enjoying the scene. **πόλλ' ... κακά**: another Homeric phrase (cf. *Il.* 15.132 ἀναπλήσας κακὰ πολλά). The speaker's repeated use of traditional elevated language underlines his moral authority: he is right to resent his friend's treachery and to wish him destroyed. **δούλιον ἄρτον**, 'slaves' bread', recalls the Homeric δούλιον ἦμαρ (*Il.* 6.463, etc.), but focuses attention on the physical degradation caused by slavery, a shameful condition for a formerly free and healthy man. Hipponax speaks elsewhere of 'cheap figs and coarse barley bread' as δούλιον χόρτον, 'slaves' fodder' (26.5–6); it seems likely that such phrases were already proverbial for the miserable life of a slave: cf. e.g. Aesch. *Ag.* 1041 δουλίας μάζης.

9–13 These lines return to the moment when the speaker's enemy is washed up on the foreign shore, emphasizing his exhaustion and suffering. **ἐκ ... χνόου** '[as he emerges] from the brine': cf. *Od.* 6.226 ἐκ κεφαλῆς δ' ἔσμηχεν ἁλὸς χνόον ἀτρυγέτοιο, where χνόος refers to the salty crust coating the shipwrecked Odysseus. **φυκία ... ἐπιχ⟨έ⟩οι** 'may he vomit [lit. "pour forth"] much seaweed': ἐπιχ(έ)οι is preferable to ἐπέχοι ('may he have on him much seaweed', accepted by West) since it is closer to the papyrus' επιχοι and creates a more graphic and memorable image of physical distress (there is no need for another verb, *pace* Gärtner 2008 φυκία πόλλ' ἔτ' ἐμέοι). **κροτέοι . . . ὀδόντας** reinforces onomatopoetically how frozen the man will be (cf. ῥίγει πεπηγότ', 9); for the humiliation of chattering teeth, see Hippon. 32.3*. **ὡς . . . | . . . ἀκρασίηι** 'lying like a dog face down and powerless': the comparison to a dog (an animal often used in insults: e.g. *Il.* 22.345 μή με, κύον, γούνων γουνάζεο μὴ δὲ τοκήων) is made even more shameful by the additional details: the prostrate animal represents the man's abasement, and its lack of strength his helpless vulnerability. Moreover, the dog's reputation for deceit, used elsewhere by Hipponax (fr. 66 'and doesn't bite afterwards, like a sneaky dog'), helps prepare for the revelation of the man's treachery (15–16). **ἄκρον παρὰ ῥηγμῖνα** 'at the very [lit. outermost] edge': cf. ἄκρον ἐπὶ ῥηγμῖνα ἁλὸς πολιοῖο θέεσκον (*Il.* 20.229). ῥηγμίν, the place where the waves break (ῥήγνυται) on the shore, takes us back to the opening scene of the poem (κύμ[ατι] πλα[ζόμ]ενος, 4). **κυμα. . . .δου:** some reference to the breaking waves is likely, e.g. κυμάτων ὁμοῦ Diels (in Reitzenstein 1899: 859), κύματος λάβρου (Gärtner 2008).

14–16 The poem changes tone from acrimony to moral indignation and sadness as the speaker reveals the reason for his curse. There is a stylistic contrast between the more intricate syntax used to elaborate the curse and the short, punchy clauses used here to justify the grievance. The ending of the poem is indicated by a marginal mark in the papyrus. **ταῦτ' . . . ἰδεῖν** 'that is what I would like to see': ἰδεῖν marks the hoped-for switch from vividly imagining the scene (4–13) to actually seeing and enjoying it as fact. Wishes for revenge often focus on *seeing* the punishment enacted: e.g. *Il.* 6.284–5 (Hector on Paris) εἰ κεῖνόν γε ἴδοιμι κατελθόντ' Ἄϊδος εἴσω, | φαίην κε φρέν' ἀτέρπου ὀϊζύος ἐκλελαθέσθαι. **ἐθέλοιμ':** the move from third to first person focuses our attention on the narrator and encourages us to adopt his perspective, whereby he, and not the victim of his curse, is truly the wronged party. **ὅς . . . ἠδίκησε** 'for the man who wronged me': strictly speaking, ὅς lacks an antecedent, and the slight dislocation in syntax suggests the speaker's emotion. **λ[ὰ]ξ . . . ἔβη:** the already forceful imagery of 'trampling on oaths' (cf. Agamemnon on the truce-breaking Trojans, κατὰ δ' ὅρκια πιστὰ πάτησαν, *Il.* 4.157) is intensified by λάξ (lit. 'with the foot', here 'underfoot'), which is used elsewhere of violent movements (e.g. *Il.* 6.65 λὰξ ἐν στήθεσι βὰς ἐξέσπασε μείλινον ἔγχος, Hippon. 104.13 ἐν τῆι γαστρὶ λὰξ ἐνώρουσα). The language expresses the man's utter violation of his oaths. **τὸ . . . [ἐ]ὼν:** the revelation in the very last words of the poem that the man was once a friend is arresting and leads us to sympathize with the speaker as the victim of a personal betrayal. ἑταῖρος calls to mind the loyalty and mutual support of the aristocratic *hetaireia*, underlining the former friend's treachery.

Hipponax 117

Source: P. Argent. 3 fr. 2 (second century AD).

The third Strasbourg Epode is aimed at a thief whose victims have included Hipponax himself. Not only is the thief exposed, but it is revealed that he has been robbed in turn. For Hipponax's own shady involvement in theft, see 3a*, 32*.

2 χλαῖν[α: given Hipponax's own attempt to acquire a cloak by stealing (cf. 32.4*, 34.1*), this one is probably the target of, or may already have been stolen by, the thief addressed in the poem.

3 κυρτον: much depends on whether this is accented κύρτον ('fishing-basket') or κυρτόν ('bent, hunchbacked'). The former may suggest a scene in which the cloak has been stolen from a fisherman, 'who took it off so as not to get it wet when he was sinking his creel (κύρτος): the thief was waiting his chance nearby' (so West 1974: 146–7); this fits neatly with what follows (φιλεῖς | ἀγχοῦ καθῆσθαι, 'you like to sit nearby'), but takes us far from the *mise-en-scène*. More likely, therefore, is that the narrator is describing the 'hunchbacked' thief himself and linking his physical deformity to his moral depravity (for the link between looks and character, cf. Semon. 7.73–7*).

4–6 ταῦτα ... | ... κἀρίφαντος 'Hipponax ... knows this better than anyone, and Ariphantus knows too': what they know, probably from direct experience of his crimes, is that the addressee is a thief. There is a sharp irony in Hipponax the cloak-stealer (32.4*) suffering the same fate himself. The repetition ο]ἶδεν ... | ... οἶ]δεν emphasizes that the thief's shameful secret has been brought to light. Alternative scenarios seem on the whole less likely: Hipponax and Ariphantus 'know' simply because they witnessed the theft, but this is less effective as a source of hostility towards the thief; or they were themselves involved in the theft, but the phrase 'better than anyone' supports their being victims (unless it is read ironically). **Ἱππῶνα[ξ:** the narrator is probably referring to himself, since his own experience of the thief motivates his subsequent attack on him (6–11). For use of the poet's name, see 32.4*. **κἀρίφαντος:** Ariphantus, an attested Greek name, is used here as a witty *nom parlant*, 'very visible' (ἀρι- + φαίνομαι), highlighting the thief's exposure.

6–8 These lines comically juxtapose the high-flown style of a *makarismos* ('blessed is he who ...') with the low abuse of 'stinking thief' (πνέοντα φῶρα). **μηδαμά ... εἶδε** 'has never yet seen you': since his victims, Hipponax and Ariphantus, and his nemesis, Aeschylides, are all named, the identity of the thief may have been revealed in a lost part of the poem. **.]ρ[. .]ου** has attracted a variety of supplements, e.g. τ]ρ[άγ]ου Diehl ('with the stink of a goat'), a popular insult (for τράγου πνεῖν or ὄζειν, see LSJ τράγος). **φῶρα:** here a source of shame, though embraced by Hipponax elsewhere: cf. 3a.2* φωρῶν ἑταῖρε (invoking Hermes), 32.6*.

8–9 τῶι... | ... πολέμει 'quarrel now with the potter Aeschylides': the narrator addresses the thief directly (πολέμει: 2nd sg. present imperative).

10–11 These lines explain why the thief will be at odds with the potter. Unlike the sculptor Bupalus (frr. 12–17*), his fellow artisan Aeschylides has incurred Hipponax's admiration. **ἐκεῖνος ... ἀπαρτί]ης**, 'he has deprived [you of your household goods]', combines the motifs of 'the biter bit' (cf. Soph. *OC* 1025–7 γνῶθι δ' ὡς ἔχων ἔχηι | καί σ' εἷλε θηρῶνθ' ἡ τύχη· τὰ γὰρ δόλωι | τῶι μὴ δικαίωι κτήματ' οὐχὶ σώιζεται) and 'it takes a thief to catch a thief' (cf. Arist. *EE* 1235a9 ἔγνω δὲ φώρ τε φῶρα, καὶ λύκος λύκον). **ἠμερσέ[ν:** 3rd sg. aor. of ἀμέρδω, a poetic word expressing the narrator's tone of moral superiority. **πᾶς ... δό[λος** 'and all your dishonesty has been revealed': the items taken from his house included stolen goods. Alliteration (π–δ–π–δ) underlines the speaker's satisfaction.

Hipponax 128

Source: Athenaeus, *Scholars at Dinner* 15.698b.

These four lines are almost all that survive of Hipponax's hexameter poetry (the other two fragments, 129 and 129a, are only four words each). They are included here as an iambic poet's take on the epic style (for other examples, serious and comic, see Hippon. 115* and 92.10–15*). The lines are preserved by Athenaeus in a long quotation from Polemon of Ilium, who claimed that Hipponax was the 'inventor of the genre' of parody (εὑρετὴς τοῦ γένους). That is not quite true, since Archilochus often pokes fun at epic (e.g. the Telephus Elegy = 17a*) and even parodies the kind of epic invocation used here by Hipponax (cf. Archil. 117 τὸν κεροπλάστην ἄειδε Γλαῦκον), but whereas Archilochus engaged with epic in iambic and elegiac metre, Hipponax composes actual hexameters, making his satirical intentions much more obvious; hence the title 'inventor' of parody. (The mock-heroic *Margites*, contemporary with Hipponax, mixes hexameter with iambic lines.) On Hipponax's place in the tradition of epic parody, see Degani 1984: 187–205, Olson and Sens 1999: 5–12, Alexandrou 2016: 211–19.

The poem treats typical iambic themes – gluttony, lapses of etiquette, the abuse and destruction of an enemy – in grand epic language, creating a comic clash of register between high style and low content. Though it uses the form of an epic proem (see below), it may well be a complete poem in itself, taking us from the Muse's initial narration of the man's crimes to his eventual death, a compact tale suitable for memorization and recitation at *symposia* or festivals (cf. Introduction §2).

1–3 Μοῦσά μοι ... | ... ἔννεφ': Hipponax's mock-heroic hexameters offer a highly compressed parody of numerous features of Archaic epic proems, most obviously the invocation of the Muse, the request to sing through the narrator (μοι) of a particular person or theme, and the use of traditional formulae (2 οὐ κατὰ κόσμον, 3 κακὸν οἶτον ὀλεῖται, 4 παρὰ θῖν' ἁλὸς ἀτρυγέτοιο). Though it is often claimed that Hipponax is targeting the proems of the *Iliad* and *Odyssey*, his structure ('Muse, to me sing') is closer to that of the *Homeric Hymn to Aphrodite* (Μοῦσά μοι ἔννεπε ἔργα πολυχρύσου Ἀφροδίτης, 1) and the cyclic epic *Little Iliad* (Μοῦσά μοι ἔννεπε ἔργα, τὰ μήτ' ἐγένοντο πάροιθε, fr. 1.1 Bernabé), and it is clear that Hipponax has the epic tradition as a whole in mind (cf. Kelly forthcoming). For similar parody of prayer forms, see 3*, 3a*, 32*. **Εὐρυμεδοντιάδεα** 'the son of Eurymedon': patronymics are a regular feature of epic (e.g. *Il.* 1.1 Πηληϊάδεω Ἀχιλῆος), not least because of its interest in heroic descent and the pressure to outdo one's ancestors: cf. *Il.* 6.479 (Hector on Astyanax) καί ποτέ τις εἴποι "πατρός γ' ὅδε πολλὸν ἀμείνων". Eurymedon is named as the king of the arrogant Giants at *Od.* 7.56–66, but there is no reference to him elsewhere, and it seems unlikely that Hipponax could expect his audience to make the specific connection. (The same name is given to a charioteer of Agamemnon and a servant of Nestor: *Il.* 4.228, 8.114.) The Eurymedon was, however, a major river of Pamphylia in southern Asia Minor, and the description 'son of Eurymedon' could make the man sound both pompous and foreign; an allusion to a watery-sounding father would also complement the following image of the glutton as ποντοχάρυβδιν. **ποντοχάρυβδιν**, 'sea-swallower' (lit. 'sea-Charybdis', a *hapax*), pictures the man as someone who could drink the sea dry. Ironically the man who could drain the sea will die beside it (see line 4). The notorious whirlpool Charybdis was a feature of Argonautic myth predating the *Odyssey*. **τὴν ἐν γαστρὶ μάχαιραν**, 'the knife-in-the-guts', creates the grotesque image of a man whose greed prevents him from cutting up or even chewing his food: he swallows it whole and slices it internally. Vulgarities of the body are at home in iambus, not epic: cf. Hippon. 26–26a on a man who ate up his inheritance; 118 attacking a glutton called Sannus with 'a ravening beak like a heron's'; 114c on a man who defecates between courses so he can fit more in. **ὃς ... κόσμον**, 'who eats in no orderly fashion', with its charge of poor table manners after the extreme descriptions that precede it, is nicely timed comic bathos.

3–4 These lines predict the glutton's shameful and lonely death as his fellow citizens vote for his execution on the seashore. The gap between the man's crime (a big appetite) and his punishment is intentionally ludicrous. ψηφῖδι ... | βουλῆι δημοσίηι, 'with a vote ... by public decision', emphasizes the entire community's condemnation of his conduct. The language evokes the ritual rejection and killing of the *pharmakos* or scapegoat, whose ashes were scattered into the sea (cf. Hippon. frr. 5–10). Scapegoats were often selected in response to famine, so that there is an added joke in the implication that the man's greediness has led to such a disaster. κακὸν ... ὀλεῖται 'he will die a miserable death': Musurus' ψηφῖδι <κακῆι> would create an effective polyptoton (so too <κακός> Cobet, <κακῶς> Kalinka). παρὰ ... ἀτρυγέτοιο 'along the shore of the barren sea': the obscure epithet ἀτρύγετος ('unharvested' or 'unwearied': cf. Thgn. 247–8*) is here given a uniquely ironic charge by its context, the death of a glutton, who in life was fixated on what could be harvested and consumed. For the seashore as a place of suffering and death, cf. Hippon. 115*, 118E.

SIMONIDES

Simonides (*c.* 556–468) was born in Iulis on Ceos (the closest of the Cycladic islands to Attica, 19 km south-east of Cape Sounion) and was buried at Acragas in Sicily. For his chronology, see Molyneux 1992: 307–37; for his tomb, Callim. *Aetia* fr. 64. His long life and career are matched by an unusually wide variety of poetic genres, ranging from epigram to choral lyric (epinicia, dithyrambs, laments, encomia, maiden-songs): indeed, he is the first poet we know of to compose both lyric and elegy (see Introduction §1). A poet of international standing, Simonides worked all over the Greek world, and his clients included tyrants (Anaxilas of Rhegium, Hieron of Syracuse, perhaps Hipparchus of Athens) and royal families (e.g. the Scopadae of Thessaly) as well as individual athletes and cities. His professionalism and popularity encouraged versatility but also aroused envy: he is said to have been the first poet to compose for a fee, and he is presented in the biographical tradition as a money-grubber and miser (cf. Lefkowitz 2012: 55, Hunter 1996: 97–109).

Though our focus is Simonides' elegy on the battle of Plataea (479 BC, frr. 10–18 W), he commemorated the other famous battles of the Persian Wars in a range of styles: Marathon (490) in epigrams and perhaps elegy, Artemisium (480) in lyric and elegy, Thermopylae (480) and Salamis (480) in lyric, Plataea in epigrams and elegy (cf. frr. 531–6 *PMG*, frr. 1–4, 86 W, epigrams 5, 8–9, 15, 20(a) and (b) Page). His fellow Ceans fought in the naval battles of Artemisium and Salamis (Hdt. 8.1.2, 46.3). It seems likely (*pace* Kowerski 2005: 109–46) that Simonides composed both personal poems for the *symposion* and narrative elegy based on historical events, written for performance at public festivals: cf. Bowie 1986: 33–4, Introduction §2, and see further below.

Simonides' historical/military elegies on Artemisium and Plataea have antecedents in Tyrtaeus' poetry on the Messenian Wars (4–7*) and in Mimnermus' *Smyrneis* (14*), and one might also compare Semonides' *Archaeology of the Samians* (*Suda* iv.360.7 Adler) and Xenophanes' elegy on the foundation of Colophon (Xenoph. 3*); cf. Bowie 2001a, Lulli 2011: 51–86. But whereas Tyrtaeus and Mimnermus each looked back to a previous generation's victories over Messenians and Lydians, Simonides lived through the decisive Greek triumphs he commemorates. So as well as being a key example of a particular kind of elegy, the Plataea poem is important historically, since it represents a contemporary witness to the Persian Wars at least one generation before Herodotus, who himself considered Plataea, rather than Marathon or Salamis, the greatest victory of all (Hdt. 9.64.1).

The papyrus manuscripts (*P. Oxy.* 3965 and 2327) which supply most of what survives of the elegy have been edited and ingeniously reconstructed by Peter Parsons and Martin West (Parsons 1992, West 1993; Lobel 1954 first suggested Simonidean authorship of 2327). Photographs of the papyri are published in Parsons 1992, Boedeker and Sider 2001, and on the Oxyrhynchus papyri website: www.papyrology.ox.ac.uk/Poxy/. The papyri appear to come from different copies of a book containing all the elegiac poems of Simonides, or at least a substantial selection of his elegies on military (Artemisium, Plataea) and sympotic topics. Though none of the fragments gives a single complete line, enough is recoverable to give us some picture of the poem's structure and contents. It must have been at least 120 lines long and may well have been much longer. The standard text (West's *IEG*^{2}) contains numerous supplements, some more speculative than others, but I follow it in the main, not least because an unsupplemented text would be far less helpful in this context (frr. 12, 17, and 18 are too meagre to include). For many suggestions (not all discussed here) as to how the text may have read, see the apparatus criticus to *IEG*^{2}.

The poem as we have it begins with a hymn to Achilles, telling of his death and burial with Patroclus and the subsequent fall of Troy (10*, 11.1–14*), and saluting Homer's skill in giving glory to the warriors who fought there (11.15–18*). Bidding Achilles farewell, the speaker invokes the Muse to assist him in celebrating those who saved Greece at Plataea (11.19–28*). The narrative of the battle starts with the Spartans' march northwards to the Isthmus and the mustering of the Greek allies at Eleusis (11.29–45*). The remaining fragments present the opposing sides as they take up position on the plain (13*), report a prophecy concerning the outcome of the battle (14*), and describe the glorious role played by the Corinthians (15–16*).

A combination of hymn and battle narrative, the Plataea poem is a kind of mini-epic, or epyllion, in elegiacs. Mimnermus' *Smyrneis* is once again a precedent, with its invocation of the Muses (13), its account of the battle with Gyges and the Lydians (13a), and its celebration of Greek victory over a powerful and much larger barbarian aggressor (14*). Simonides equates the glorious fighters of the Persian Wars with the Greek heroes of the Trojan War, and this creates a parallel between Homer and himself (see on 10.5*, 11.15–18*). The language is elevated, and epic epithets and phrases are adapted to magnify contemporary history (e.g. 11.25* δούλιον ἦμ]αρ, 11.27* κλέος ... ἀθάνατο⟨ν⟩, 11.35* ἐπικλέα ἔργα Κορίν[θ]ου): cf. Poltera 1997: 541. In Simonides, as in Homer and Herodotus, the enemy are presented respectfully; nonetheless, their punishment is supported by the gods (cf. Simon. 11.12*, 14.7*). Trojan myth had long been used to reflect on contemporary wars (cf. Archilochus' Telephus Elegy = 17a*) or to underline the narrator's distinctive point of view (cf. Sapph. fr. 16 on love versus war), and Simonides is among the first to use heroic models to memorialize the Persian Wars, a technique mirrored in Aeschylus' *Persians*, produced in Athens in 472, where barbarian hybris and autocracy lead to defeat and disgrace (e.g. *Pers.* 353–432, 739–842). Moreover, the poetic immortality fashioned for the war dead by Simonides had a concrete parallel in the annual commemorative games held at Plataea, where cultic honours indistinguishable from those granted to heroes such as Achilles were offered to those who had died in defence of their homeland. (As Parker 1996: 135–7 observes, the term 'hero', in the sense 'recipient of hero-cult', is never applied to the war dead in the Classical period, but their honours are identical, and fifth-century Greeks (p. 137) 'heroized their benefactors as best they could'; cf. Bremmer 2006).

The Plataea elegy was probably performed at a Panhellenic event within a few years of the battle (cf. Rawles 2018: 78–83). Plataea itself is perhaps the likeliest venue, and it is possible the poem was written for the inaugural Eleutheria festival there, where the battle was commemorated every four years (cf. Parsons 1992: 6, Boedeker 1995: 222–3). Given the scale, Panhellenic vision, and heroizing intent of the work, it seems much likelier that it was designed for first performance at a grand public event rather than at a *symposion* (*pace* West 1993: 5), though subsequent reperformance at *symposia* would of course be perfectly possible, and highly desirable for the poet. If it was first performed at the Eleutheria festival, the poem was probably commissioned rather than performed in a competition (cf. Bowie 2001a: 60–1). Though some think it was commissioned by the Spartans or by Pausanias himself (cf.

11.33–4*), performance at Plataea and reference to other Greek states make it more plausible that it was commissioned by a group of leading states (Sparta, Athens, and Corinth supplied the most troops: cf. Hdt. 9.28–30) or by the Plataeans themselves. The poem is sometimes seen as biased in favour of the Spartans (e.g. Aloni 2001: 102–4), but Herodotus too is explicit about their key role at Plataea, where they 'outshone everyone else' and 'took on the toughest opponents and won' (9.71.1–2), while Aeschylus has the ghost of Darius attribute the Persian disaster at Plataea to 'the Dorian spear' (*Persians* 817), so Simonides is more likely to be reflecting the *communis opinio* in this respect, and he extends credit to other states (including Corinth, unlike Herodotus: cf. Simon. 15–16*, Hdt. 9.52, 69).

Simonides 10

Source: *P. Oxy.* 3965 fr. 22.

If we accept the text in line 5 suggested by West, this fragment appears to come from an invocation of Achilles. However, we cannot be certain that such an address belongs before fr. 11 (the poet could have returned to Achilles at the end) or that, even if it does, this is how the poem began. Simonides could have started, for example, by hymning Achilles' exploits before the Trojan War or those of his ancestors or descendants: 'father and forefather' (2) may refer to Peleus and Aeacus, or (more likely, if Achilles is the focus) to Neoptolemus and his offspring.

4 μελε]τῶν ὑπὲρ ἡμ[ετέρων 'for my composition': the poet requests Achilles' help in, and blessing upon, his 'cares' or 'efforts', a parallel to his later invocation of the Muse (11.20–2*).

5 κούρης εἰν]αλίης ἀγλαόφη[με πάϊ 'O son of the sea-nymph, glorious in your fame': the elaborate periphrasis is honorific (cf. 11.19–20*). **ἀγλαόφη[με:** a rare adjective, perhaps coined by Simonides (Poltera 1997: 374–5), who uses it again in the elegy for Artemisium (3.13), where it may refer to the Old Man of the Sea (cf. West 1993: 3–4). Allusion to Achilles' renown reminds us of Simonides' own role in conferring fame, as he equates the heroic κλέος of Achilles and the Danaans (11.15*) with that achieved by the victors of Plataea (11.28*).

Simonides 11

Source: *P. Oxy.* 2327 frr. 5 + 6 + 27 col. I + 3965 frr. 1 + 2.

This fragment, an amalgam of pieces from *P. Oxy.* 2327 (fr. 5 = lines 1–4, fr. 6 = lines 5–14, fr. 27 = right ends of lines 13–29) and 3965 (fr. 1 = lines 9–23, fr. 2 = lines 22–45), is the longest surviving passage of Simonides.

Its reconstruction gives us sizeable chunks of 45 verses that probably came towards the beginning of the poem (see on fr. 10*). A hymn to Achilles leads into an invocation of the Muse, followed by a detailed narrative of the battle, starting with the departure of the Spartan army under Pausanias. Epic structure – narrative preceded by a proemic hymn – is recreated here in elegy, and the transition too is handled in familiar epic style (see 11.19–20*). Recollection of the Trojan War creates an implicit analogy between the victorious Danaans, immortalized by Homer (11.15–18*), and the Greek forces at Plataea, celebrated by Simonides (11.23–8*).

1–18 describe Achilles' heroic death and funeral, the fall of Troy, and the Danaans' eternal glory, created by Homer, who was inspired by the Muses. How much of the hymn has been lost before these lines is unknown (cf. fr. 10*).

1–3 an epic-style simile compares the dying hero to 'a pine tree in the glades' which 'woodcutters fell'. παι[.] σ [: West's παῖ[σέ] σ [, 'struck you', is plausible. ἢ πίτυν, 'or a pine tree', suggests more than one point of comparison: e.g. *Il.* 16.482–4 (Sarpedon killed by Patroclus) 'He fell as an oak falls, or a poplar, or a tall pine which carpenters cut down in the mountains with whetted axes to make a ship's timber.' ὑλοτόμοι: cf. Soph. *El.* 97–9 μήτηρ δ' ἡμὴ χὠ κοινολεχὴς | Αἴγισθος ὅπως δρῦν ὑλοτόμοι | σχίζουσι κάρα φονίωι πελέκει.

4 ἤρωσ[: ἡρώησ[ε, aor. of ἐρωέω, 'gush' (of blood), is a possibility: cf. *Il.* 1.303 (Achilles to Agamemnon) αἶψά τοι αἷμα κελαινὸν ἐρωήσει περὶ δουρί.

5–6 Reference to the army (λαός) and possibly to Patroclus led to West's suggestion, 'great grief seized the army; they honoured you mightily, and with Patroclus' ashes mingled yours'. For the funeral and tomb of Achilles, cf. *Od.* 24.36–97. It has been argued that the elegy was commissioned by Pausanias for performance at the supposed grave of Achilles (near Sigeum at the mouth of the Hellespont), and that he did so to impress local Greeks with the power of Sparta (Schachter 1998), but a more Panhellenic location and purpose seem much likelier (see the introduction above).

7–8 Both Patroclus and Achilles were killed with Apollo's help (cf. *Il.* 16.849–50, 19. 416–17, 22.358–60), but the wider context (a hymn to Achilles) favours allusion here to the greater hero's death (cf. 11.18* ὠκύμορον).

9–12 The killing of Achilles is balanced by the destruction of Troy, as Paris' sin is punished by the gods. West's reconstruction of 9–10, 'Athena was at hand, and destroyed the famous town with Hera: they were angry with the sons of Priam', restores the deities most hostile to Troy. εἴνεκ' ... | ... δίκ[ης: the narrative is compressed, as Simonides takes us from the cause of the war (Paris' departure with Helen) to the final reckoning in just two lines. εἵνεκ'... κακόφρ[ονο]ς 'because of evil-minded Alexander': κακόφρων is not attested in epic (Paris' epithets in the *Iliad* are the honorific δῖος and θεοειδής), and its use here underlines the poet's explicit moralizing. θείης... δίκ[ης 'the chariot of divine justice destroyed': the likeliest object of the verb is Paris. The 'chariot of justice' is an image attested only here in Greek (Dike, the goddess of justice, usually sits enthroned); various deities use chariots (e.g. Hera, Athena, Iris, Aphrodite, Poseidon, and Zeus in the *Iliad*; Hades in the *HHDem*.), and one may also compare epic scenes where a deity acts as a hero's charioteer (cf. *Il*. 5.835–40, where Athena ousts Diomedes' charioteer Sthenelos and the axle creaks under her weight). Watkins 1995: 16 compares the 'chariot of Truth' in Indo-European poetics. The chariot is well suited here both to the immediate Trojan War setting and to the wider military context.

13–18 foreground Homeric poetry's role in immortalizing the Greek heroes of the Trojan War. A compressed account of the end of the war (13–14) leads into a more expansive reflection on the importance of poetic commemoration (15–18).

13–14 ἀοίδιμον, 'famous in song', looks forward to the praise of Homer in the following lines, but it is also a self-referential reminder of Simonides' own powers. ἀοίδιμος occurs only once in Homer, when Helen tells Hector that Zeus set an evil destiny upon Paris and herself, to make them ἀοίδιμοι for men to come (*Il*. 6.357–8); but whereas Helen fears notoriety, the poet here celebrates the Greeks' achievement in 'having sacked the song-famed city'. [οἴκαδ' ἵ]κοντο 'they made their homecoming': emphasis on those who survived and returned home is a positive counterweight to those who did not: Achilles and Patroclus (11.1–8*), and by extension the Greeks who died at Plataea. The heroes' various returns home from Troy (*nostoi*) were a popular topic in Archaic epic (most prominently in the *Odyssey* and *Nostoi*): cf. Danek 2015. ἀγέμαχοι Δαναοί 'the Danaan battle leaders': ἀγέμαχος is attested only here. The presence in elegy of Doric ἀγέμαχοι instead of Ionic ἡγέμαχοι is unusual but not impossible. Tyrtaeus, for example, uses some Doric forms in elegy, though it is true that he is a Spartan writing primarily for Doric speakers (cf. on Tyrt. 7.1*). Nonetheless, there is no absolute rule that bans all Doric forms from elegy, and we need not emend here to ἡγέμαχοι, or go even further and suggest other words (Rawles 2008, for example, proposes ἀγχέμαχοι, 'close-fighting'). It might be argued that the Doric ἀγέμαχοι is preparation for the later focus on the Spartan forces at Plataea (cf. 11.29–34*) or even a sign that the poem was commissioned by the Spartans or by Pausanias himself, but (as discussed in the introduction above) other Greek states played a role, and a Panhellenic commission and venue are more plausible. Moreover, the Doric form is applied to the Danaans, i.e.

all the Greeks who fought at Troy, and so rather than seeing ἀγέμαχοι as a response to Spartan patronage, it is best interpreted as part of the poem's Panhellenism. The restorations φέρτατοι ἥρ]ώων (Parsons) or ἔξοχοι ἥρ] ώων (Capra–Curti) give good sense, 'outstanding among heroes'.

15–18 celebrate the role of Homeric poetry in creating and preserving heroic fame. Homer's importance to the warriors of the Trojan War implicitly boosts Simonides' status as the poet who will immortalize their successors at Plataea.

15 οἷσιν . . . ἕκητι 'upon whom immortal glory has been poured thanks to a man': the contrast between ἀθά]νατον and ἀν[δρός] underlines the fact that a mortal man, a poet, can produce immortal fame. **ἀθά]νατον . . . κλέος:** a central idea of heroic poetry (cf. κλέος ἄφθιτον ἔσται (*Il.* 9.413) and the formula κλέος οὔποτ᾽ ὀλεῖται) which Simonides' elegy will extend to the heroized dead of his own time (11.28*): cf. Tyrt. 12.31–2* οὐδέ ποτε κλέος ἐσθλὸν ἀπόλλυται οὐδ᾽ ὄνομ᾽ αὐτοῦ, | ἀλλ᾽ ὑπὸ γῆς περ ἐὼν γίνεται ἀθάνατος. **κέχυται:** the image of 'pouring' fame likens it to a libation offered to the great heroes of the past. For the similar offerings made to heroes and the fifth-century war dead, see the introduction above.

16–17 ὅς: Homer, whose identity as the foremost chronicler of the Trojan War and the greatest epic poet is now so well established that he need not even be named: cf. Simon. 19.1–2 ἓν δὲ τὸ κάλλιστον Χῖος ἔειπεν ἀνήρ· | "οἵη περ φύλλων γενεή, τοίη δὲ καὶ ἀνδρῶν". **ἰοπ]λοκάμων . . . Πιερίδ[ων** 'the violet-haired Muses of Pieria': cf. Simon. fr. 555 *PMG* (on Maia, mother of Hermes) ἔτικτε δ᾽ Ἄτλας ἑπτὰ ἰοπλοκάμων φιλᾶν θυγατρῶν | τάνδ᾽ ἔξοχον εἶδος, ⟨ὅσ⟩αι καλέονται | Πελειάδες οὐράνιαι. 'Violet' refers to the hair's vibrant colour (though the word is sometimes mistranslated 'violet-wreathed'). The epithet ἰοπλόκαμος is confined to the Muses (cf. Pind. *Pyth.* 1.1), whose hair, like that of many other women and goddesses, is often praised in Greek poetry: e.g. *Il.* 18.407 Θέτι καλλιπλοκάμωι, Ibyc. fr. 303.1–2 *PMG* γλαυκώπιδα Κασσάνδραν | ἐρασιπλόκαμον Πριάμοιο κόραν. **Πιερίδ[ων:** for Pieria (the region north of Mt Olympus) as the birthplace and home of the Muses, cf. Hes. *Theog.* 53, *WD* 1, Sapph. frr. 55.3, 103.5, Sol. 13.2*. **δέξατο . . . | πᾶσαν ἀλη]θείην** 'received the whole truth': the idea that the poet acts as a conduit for the 'true' account of the heroic past granted to him by the Muses is central to Homeric poetry (e.g. *Il.* 2.485–6 ὑμεῖς γὰρ θεαί ἐστε πάρεστέ τε ἴστέ τε πάντα, | ἡμεῖς δὲ κλέος οἶον ἀκούομεν οὐδέ τι ἴδμεν). Hesiod's lying Muses showcase his distinctively different persona: ἴδμεν ψεύδεα πολλὰ λέγειν ἐτύμοισιν ὁμοῖα, | ἴδμεν δ᾽ εὖτ᾽ ἐθέλωμεν ἀληθέα γηρύσασθαι (*Theog.* 27–8); see Kelly 2008: 195–9.

17–18 καὶ . . . | . . . γενεή[ν, 'and made the short-lived race of demigods famous to later generations', foregrounds the poet's key role in connecting the audience to the earlier and different world of the heroes.

ἐπώνυμον: the sense 'famous' is an extension of the adjective's usual meaning, 'giving one's name to' or 'named after'; for Simonides' verbal creativity here, cf. Suárez de la Torre 1998. ὁπ[λοτέρ]οισιν: lit. 'younger men'. The passage is recalled by Theocritus, who clearly also understands Simonides' ἐπώνυμον as 'famous': εἰ μὴ θεῖος ἀοιδός ὁ Κήιος αἰόλα φωνέων | βάρβιτον ἐς πολύχορδον ἐν ἀνδράσι θῆκ' ὀνομαστούς | ὁπλοτέροις (16.44–6). ἡμ]ιθέων ... γενεή[ν: for the ἡμίθεοι, or men of the Heroic Age, cf. Il. 12.23 ἡμιθέων γένος ἀνδρῶν (where those who fell at Troy are viewed from the poet's own day), Hes. WD 159–60 ἀνδρῶν ἡρώων θεῖον γένος, οἳ καλέονται | ἡμίθεοι, προτέρη γενεὴ κατ' ἀπείρονα γαῖαν (those killed at Thebes and Troy); see on Callin. 1.19*. ὠκύμορον: the epithet (in the sense 'doomed to perish soon') is used only of Achilles in the *Iliad* (and always by Thetis: 1.417, 505, 18.95, 458), but here it is extended to all the heroes who fought at Troy. That even the race of heroes is 'short-lived' and must rely on poets like Homer to preserve their fame makes Simonides' efforts to immortalize contemporary human achievement all the more impressive.

19–20 The poet bids Achilles farewell as he moves to a new beginning: an invocation of the Muse, followed by the main narrative. ἀλλὰ σὺ μὲ]ν νῦν χαῖρε ... | ... αὐτὰρ ἐγώ: the transition replicates in elegy a pattern familiar from epic, especially in the Homeric Hymns, where the singer turns from his hymn to another song: e.g. *HHAp*. 545–6 καὶ σὺ μὲν οὕτω χαῖρε Διὸς καὶ Λητοῦς υἱέ· | αὐτὰρ ἐγώ καὶ σεῖο καὶ ἄλλης μνήσομ' ἀοιδῆς. The Homeric Hymns' farewells are of course addressed to divinities, but although Achilles was widely worshipped as a god (Hommel 1980), Simonides' poem treats him as one of the heroic and heroized dead, an ennobling parallel to the fallen at Plataea. θεᾶς ... | ... Νηρέος 'O son of the glorious goddess, daughter of Nereus of the sea': for both the honorific periphrasis and the connection with the sea, cf. Simon. 10.5* κούρης εἰν]αλίης ἀγλαόφη[με πάϊ. θεᾶς ἐρικυ[δέος υἱέ: cf. e.g. *HHHerm*. 550 Μαίης ἐρικυδέος υἱέ. υἱέ | κούρης ... Νηρέος: for Achilles as 'the son of Nereus' daughter', cf. Eur. *IT* 216–17 (Iphigeneia on her fate) νύμφαν, οἴμοι, δύσνυμφον | τῶι τᾶς Νηρέως κούρας, αἰαῖ.

20–2 'But I invoke you as my ally, illustrious Muse, if you have any care for men who pray.' ἐπίκουρον: the military metaphor suits the battle narrative to come, while the Muse's role as 'ally' implies the poet's equal status in their partnership, thus going well beyond the Homeric poet's persona as a mere channel for the Muses' superior knowledge (see on lines 16–17* above). Timotheus summons Apollo in his *Persians*, ἐμοῖς ἔλθ' ἐπίκουρος ὕμνοις (791.204–5 *PMG*). π[ολυώνυμε: for the sense 'much renowned, famous, celebrated' (rather than the more usual 'worshipped under many names'), cf. e.g. Hes. *Theog*. 785 πολυώνυμον ὕδωρ (referring to the water of Styx).

COMMENTARY: SIMONIDES 11

23–8 After the elaborate proem the song's central subject is finally revealed: the men who saved Greece from slavery, and their undying glory.

23–4 ἔντυνο]ν... | ἡμετ]έρης 'make ready too this pleasing song-array of mine'. **ἔντυνο]ν... μελ]ίφρονα κ[όσμον:** each word evokes a poem's proper arrangement: cf. *Hom. Hymn* 6.20 ἐμὴν δ' ἔντυνον ἀοιδήν; Pind. fr. 122.14 μελίφρονος... σκολίου; *Hom. Hymn* 7.59 γλυκερὴν κοσμῆσαι ἀοιδήν. In relation to poetry κόσμος denotes truthfulness and clarity as well as good order; see on Sol. 1.2* κόσμον ἐπέων ὠιδήν. **ἵνα... [μνή]σεται** 'so that someone may remember [the men who, etc.]': for the importance of remembrance, compare Simonides' eulogy on those who died at Thermopylae: εὐκλεὴς μὲν ἁ τύχα, καλὸς δ' ὁ πότμος, | βωμὸς δ' ὁ τάφος, πρὸ γόων δὲ μνᾶστις, ὁ δ' οἶκτος ἔπαινος (531.2–3 *PMG*). Herodotus has a similar memorializing purpose in his account of Greek success, but his distance from the Persian Wars allows him to be more generous to the other side, as his preface makes clear: ὡς μήτε τὰ γενόμενα ἐξ ἀνθρώπων τῶι χρόνωι ἐξίτηλα γένηται, μήτε ἔργα μεγάλα τε καὶ θωμαστά, τὰ μὲν Ἕλλησι, τὰ δὲ βαρβάροισι ἀποδεχθέντα, ἀκλεᾶ γένηται (Book 1 init.). **[μνή]σεται:** short vowel aor. middle subjunctive (-ηται).

25–6 West's reconstruction is based on two Simonidean epigrams (16.1, 20(a).3–4 Page): 'who held the line for Sparta and for Greece, that none should see the day of slavery'. The terror and poignancy of δούλιον ἦμαρ are a pervasive epic concern, typified by Hector's fears for his family (e.g. *Il.* 6.463).

27–8 οὐδ' ἀρε]τῆς ἐλάθ[οντο 'nor did they forget their valour': another epic theme; compare the Homeric antithesis μνήσασθε/λάθοντο δὲ θούριδος ἀλκῆς (e.g. *Il.* 16.356–7). **οὐρανομ[ήκ]ης:** a word for fame is likely to be missing (cf. Ar. *Clouds* 460–1, where the Clouds promise Strepsiades κλέος οὐρανόμηκες), supplied e.g. by φάτις δ' ἔχε]ν ('and their fame rose heaven-high'). **κλέος... ἀθάνατο⟨ν⟩** creates a parallel with the Danaans, who enjoy the ἀθά]νατον κλέος bestowed by Homer (line 15 above). Cf. Simon. *epigr.* 20(a).1 Page (probably referring to the battle of Salamis) ἀνδρῶν τῶνδ' ἀρετῆ[ς ἔσται κλέ]ος ἄφθι[τον] αἰεί.

29–34 The narrative of the battle begins with the Spartan army setting out, led by Pausanias. In contrast to Herodotus' account, where the Spartan ephors delay responding to the ambassadors from Athens, Plataea, and Megara for ten days (9.8.1–2) and the army sets out covertly at night (9.10), Simonides presents a resolute and well-ordered departure from Sparta. According to Herodotus (9.10.1, 11.3), Pausanias was put in command of 5,000 Spartiates, 35,000 helots (acting as light-armed troops), and 5,000 perioeci (free-born inhabitants of Laconia).

29–30 οἳ... | ὥρμησαν 'leaving the Eurotas and the city of Sparta, they set out': the subject of the verb is ἡγεμόνες (32). The 82 km-long Εὐρώτας ('abundantly-flowing') was the main river of Laconia, and it often represents the region (e.g. Eur. *Andr.* 437 ἢ ταῦτ' ἐν ὑμῖν τοῖς παρ' Εὐρώται σοφά;). **30–1 Ζηνὸς ... | ... Μενελάω[ι** 'accompanied by the horse-taming sons of Zeus, the Tyndarid heroes, and mighty Menelaus'. As Spartan heroes, cult figures (i.e. carved images) of Castor, Polydeuces, and Menelaus accompany the army to lend it support. According to Herodotus (5.75), the Spartans passed a law *c.* 506, following a disagreement between Cleomenes and Demaratus, stating that the two kings were not to campaign together, and that one of the Tyndaridae had to be left behind in Sparta with the remaining king. Assuming Herodotus is right, Simonides is either unaware of the law (which is quite possible, since he is not a Spartan) or chooses to ignore it in favour of a more impressive scene. Their role as fighters in Sparta is seen, for example, in the tradition that they invented war dances and that Spartan soldiers sang a hymn to Castor (τὸ Καστόρειον μέλος) as they lined up for battle (cf. Plut. *Lyc.* 22.2). **ἱπποδάμοις:** the epithet ἱππόδαμος is applied to Castor in epic (e.g. *Il.* 3.237, *Od.* 11.300), and both brothers are expert horsemen, constantly associated with horses in both literature and art: e.g. *Hom. Hymn* 17.5, 33.18 ταχέων ἐπιβήτορες ἵππων, Pind. *Ol.* 3.39 εὔιπποι; cf. *LIMC* 3.1, 567–93 s.v. Dioskouroi. Their horses are white, and they appear in myth as the λευκόπωλοι, riders of white horses, who abduct the two sisters, Phoebe and Hilaeira, known as the Leukippides. **Τυνδαρίδα]ις:** if the restoration is right, Castor and Polydeuces are presented as simultaneously 'sons of Zeus' and 'sons of Tyndareus', acknowledging their double nature. Some authors choose to emphasize their identity as sons of Tyndareus and Leda (e.g. *Od.* 11.298–304), others specify that only Polydeuces is the son of Zeus (e.g. Pind. *Nem.* 10.80–2), and yet others (like Simonides) describe them as sons of Zeus and as Tyndaridae in successive lines: cf. *Hom. Hymn* 33.1–2. As in the Homeric Hymn (which praises them as gods who rescue sailors from danger at sea), their connection with Zeus is given precedence by Simonides; this enhances both their status and the Spartan army's. For the tradition that the Dioscuri saved Simonides' life, see 510 *PMG.* **ἥρωσι:** although Laconia was the pre-eminent centre of their cult, the Dioscuri were worshipped throughout Greece. **Μενελάω[ι:** the hero shared a major shrine with Helen at Therapne (overlooking the Eurotas, *c.* 2.5 km south-east of Sparta), and a fragmentary commentary on Alcman (7 *PMG*), preserved on a first-century AD papyrus, says 'he is honoured in Therapne with the Dioscuri'. Though not the best fighter at Troy (cf. *Il.* 7.94–122, where his offer to face Hector in a duel is frankly rejected by Agamemnon), Menelaus is no slouch (as his defeat of Paris shows: *Il.* 3.340–82), and his heroic status at Sparta will have bolstered his position as a symbol of the state's military strength.

32 πατ]ρώιης ... π[ό]λεος, 'leaders of their ancestral city', refers to the (unnamed) Spartan officers commanded by Pausanias.

33–4 τοὺς ... | ... Παυσανίης 'whom the son of godlike Cleombrotus led out, the best man, ... Pausanias': an honorific introduction, with the commander's name in emphatic final position. Herodotus explains why the regent Pausanias was given the command: 'The right of leadership actually belonged to Pleistarchus, the son of [king] Leonidas, but he was still a child, and Pausanias was his guardian, as well as being his cousin' (9.10.2). Pausanias' career after Plataea was marred by allegations of tyrannical behaviour and medism (cf. Thuc. 1.94–5, 128–34). By contrast, Herodotus' portrait of him, especially in the Plataea narrative, is strikingly positive: he is not only strategically adept (as when he changes wings with the Athenians: Hdt. 9.46–8), but also pious (waiting for favourable omens before attacking: 9.62) and compassionate (refusing to mutilate the corpse of the Persian commander Mardonius: 9.78–9). Herodotus sums up his achievement at Plataea by saying 'he won the most glorious victory of all those we know' (9.64.2).

35–41 describe the army's progress via Corinth, Megara, and Eleusis, where the Athenian troops join them. Herodotus' fuller account of the advance (9.19) is useful for suggesting possible textual restorations.

35–6 καὶ ... Κορίν[θ]ου 'and the famous land of Corinth'. Some translate 'famous deeds' (e.g. Sider 2001), but the journey through different territories in these lines favours the sense 'tilled lands, fields' for ἔργα (see on Tyrt. 5.7*). The 'deeds' of Corinth are, however, extensively praised later (15*, 16*). For the first half of the line, West suggests αἶψα δ' ἵκοντ' Ἰσθμόν ('they quickly reached the Isthmus'). According to Herodotus, the Peloponnesian allies joined the Spartans at the Isthmus before they proceeded together to Eleusis (9.19.1–2). Ταντα**λ**ίδεω Πέλοπος, 'of Tantalid Pelops', suggests reference to the Peloponnese; hence West's νῆσου τ' ἐσχατιήν ('furthest boundary of Tantalid Pelops' island'), describing Corinth; and Parsons' νῆσον δ' ἐξέλιπον ('and left the island of Tantalid Pelops'). For Pelops giving his name to the entire Peloponnese, see on Tyrt. 12.7* οὐδ' εἰ Ταντα**λ**ίδεω Πέλοπος βασιλεύτερος εἴη.

37–8 Ν]ίσου πόλιν: Nisus, king of Megara, was son of Pandion (cf. 11.41* Παν]δίονος) and brother of Aegeus; the port of Megara was called Nisaea. The Simonidean epigram for the Megarian war dead was inscribed in the agora ὀμφαλῶι ἀμφίς | Νισαίων ('around the navel of the Nisaeans', 16.9–10 Page). ἔνθά περ ὤ[λλοι | ... φῦλα περικτιόνων 'where indeed the others [crasis of οἱ ἄλλοι] ... tribes of neighbouring men': if the restoration of Nisus/Megara is correct, and the Peloponnesian allies have already joined (lines 35–6), these lines probably refer to the mustering of the Megarians, 3,000 of whom fought at Plataea (Hdt. 9.28.6).

39–40 The combined (Peloponnesian and Megarian) forces reach the plain of Eleusis. θεῶν . . . | . . . πεδίον 'trusting in the omens of the gods, and they reached Eleusis' lovely plain': the supplements are guided by Herodotus' account (9.19.2): 'Once they had obtained favourable omens, the combined troops made their way from the Isthmus to Eleusis, where they once again offered up sacrifices.' Cf. σύν[οπλοι Parsons ('under arms together, allied', referring to the whole army), σὺν [αὐτοῖς West (the Peloponnesian and Megarian forces coming together). The Thriasian plain of Eleusis had been the scene of a miraculous portent the year before, when a vision of the great procession of the Eleusinian mysteries was seen there, marking the gods' protection of Attica (Hdt. 8.65).

41 Παν]δίονος ἐξε[λάσα]ντες, lit. 'of Pandion having marched out', probably refers to the Athenian troops joining the army at Eleusis (e.g. γῆς Παν]δίονος, 'marching out from the land of Pandion'). By contrast, West takes ἐξε[λάσα]ντες transitively as 'having driven out' and supplements Μηδείους γαίης ('driving the Persians from Pandion's land'). There is, however, no sign of such a rout in our historical sources, and in Herodotus the Persians withdraw voluntarily to fight near Thebes (9.12–15.3). Some mention of the Athenians is expected, given their notable role in the battle: e.g. killing the 300 best and bravest Persians (9.67) and breaching the Persian palisade (9.70). There is no reason to believe Simonides was writing from a particularly pro-Spartan (or anti-Athenian) perspective, which might lead him to suppress the Athenians' role: see the introduction above. Eight thousand Athenians fought at Plataea under the command of Aristides (Hdt. 9.28.6).

42 Κέκρ]οπος ἀντιθέου, 'of godlike Cecrops', describes the Athenians, emphasizing once again (after Pandion) their illustrious ancestry. Cecrops was widely considered the first king of Athens (as on the Parian Marble, *FGrH* 239 A), and his namesake Cecrops II, son of Erechtheus, was Pandion's father: Paus. 1.5.3, Apollod. 3.196, 204. Luppe 2008 suggests e.g. εἵποντ', ἐκγενέται Κέκρ]οπος ἀντιθέου. West reads μάν]τιος ἀντιθέου ('of the godlike diviner') and takes this as a reference to Teisamenus, the army's official seer (who, in return for his services, cannily obtained Spartan citizenship for himself and his brother: Hdt. 9.33–5), but the traces on the papyrus confirm Parsons' reading] τος. (The high horizontal stroke to the left of π/τι cannot be a nu, so West's reading is palaeographically impossible.) Nonetheless, Teisamenus does (probably) make an appearance later in the narrative: see 14*.

43 δαμάσαντ['having overcome': West (*IEG*² app. crit.) sees a possible reference to the engagement in which the Athenians killed the Persian cavalry commander Masistius (Hdt. 9.22–5); Parsons 1992: 38 suggests a look back to Artemisium or Salamis. All we can say with confidence is that, given the pace of the narrative so far and the content of frr. 13–14*, it is very unlikely to refer to the main battle.

44 εἴδομεν[, 'we saw', might come from a variation on the idea 'it was the biggest force (Persians) / greatest victory (Greeks) we have ever seen' popular with both poets and historians (see e.g. Thucydides, outdoing even Homer, on his war as greater than all those that preceded: 1.10.3, 21.2).

45 Fowler's εὐώ]νυμον ('favourable', used of omens) would fit well with Herodotus' emphasis: 'The omens [at Eleusis] were favourable, and so they continued on their way, accompanied now by the Athenian troops' (9.19.2); for more omens, see on lines 39–40* above. The word has another relevant military use in phrases like τὸ εὐώνυμον κέρας ('the left wing', e.g. Hdt. 6.111) or simply τὸ εὐώνυμον (without κέρας, Thuc. 4.96).

Simonides 13

Source: P. Oxy. 2327 fr. 27 col. ii.

Located in the column following 11.13–27* in P. Oxy. 2327, this fragment must have come shortly after fr. 11* (perhaps only ten or so lines on from 11.45*). It describes an encounter between Persians and Dorians on a plain, and may well refer to the Greek army's advance from the foothills of Mt Cithaeron near Erythrae to their second position on the Asopus river (see on line 11 below).

1–7 offer only the occasional glimpse of a word. At line 6 Gentili–Prato's μενε]πτόλε[μ-, 'steadfast in battle', would suit the narrator's view of the Greeks.

8–10 balance and contrast the Medes and Persians on one side with the sons of Dorus and Heracles on the other. **ὄφρ'... |... Περσῶν**: lit. 'so that from the Medes and Persians'. λαὸν ἅπαντ' ἐλάσαι, 'in order to drive away the whole army of the Medes and Persians', gives good sense. Herodotus presents a detailed account of the rise of the Medes until their conquest by Cyrus the Persian c. 550 (1.95–107). Nonetheless, Greek sources, including Herodotus himself, continue to use 'Mede' or 'Median' to refer to the Persians (e.g. τὰ Μηδικά for 'the Persian Wars': see Graf 1984: 18–19). The expanded phrase 'Medes and Persians' is used here to emphasize the extent and power of the Persian empire (cf. Xen. Cyr. 1.5.3 διαβάλλων τούς Μήδους καὶ Πέρσας, λέγων ὡς μεγάλα τ' εἴη ταῦτα ἔθνη καὶ ἰσχυρά). Though not enough of the poem survives to be certain, one can imagine Simonides (like Herodotus: see 9.62–3) acknowledging the strength and courage of the Persians, not least as a way of magnifying the achievement of the Greeks. **Δώρου...|... Ἡρακλέος**, '[to/for?] the sons of Dorus and Heracles', draws attention to the Peloponnesian forces, especially the Spartans (see on 11.29–34*), in preparation for their key role at Plataea (cf. Hdt.

232   COMMENTARY: SIMONIDES 13-14

9.71.1-2 and Aesch. *Persians* 817, quoted in the introduction above). The phrase 'sons of Dorus and Heracles' combines the two traditions concerning the origins of the Dorians in the Peloponnese: on one hand, Dorus, the mythical ancestor (two of the three Dorian tribes claimed descent from him via his grandsons Pamphylos and Dymas; the third from Hyllus, Heracles' son: cf. Tyrt. 19.8, Pind. *Ol.* 1.60-5); on the other, the Heraclidae, whose 'return' to the Peloponnese served as a charter myth (cf. Malkin 1994: 15-45) for the territorial claims of different Dorian states (Argos, Sparta, and Messenia): cf. e.g. Tyrt. 2.11-15, 'For Zeus himself, son of Cronus and husband of fair-crowned Hera, gave this state [Sparta] to the sons of Heracles, under whose lead we left windswept Erineos [in Doris in central Greece] and came to the broad sea-circled land of Pelops.'

11 οἳ] ... πεδίον, 'and when they into the plain', captures a movement by the Greek army, and the likeliest point in the campaign is when they moved from their first position on the slopes of Mt Cithaeron to the Asopus plain where the Persians were encamped (cf. Hdt. 9.25.2-3). The missing verb of motion is supplied e.g. by Βοιώτιον εὐρὺ κατῆλθον ('when they came down into the broad Boeotian plain'). Only with the description of the battle line in frr. 15-16* do we reach the army's third and final position at Plataea itself (cf. Hdt. 9.52). **εἰ]σωποὶ δ' ἔφ[α]νεν[**, 'and came into view', probably refers to the arrival of the Persians, seen from the Greek perspective; cf. Hdt. 9.31.1 (who makes clear the opposition of Persians and Spartans), 'So much for the arrangement of the Greek forces on the Asopus. The Persians ... came to Plataea, where they had heard that the Greeks were, and they moved up to the part of the Asopus which flows through that region. There Mardonius disposed his troops as follows. He placed the Persians opposite the Lacedaemonians.'

Simonides 14

Source: P. Oxy. 3965 fr. 21.

Lines 3-6, with their first-person speaker (λ]έγω) and references to a river (ποταμοῦ), disaster (κακ[όν), and the future (ἤματα πάντ[α), strongly suggest that Simonides has presented a prophecy by Teisamenus, the army's official seer, whose divination (according to Herodotus) led him to recommend a defensive strategy: 'The entrails gave favourable omens for the Greeks if they remained on the defensive, but not if they crossed the Asopus and took the fight to the enemy' (9.36). Herodotus' succinct report contrasts with the poem's more dramatic and personal declaration. For the possibility that Simonides has extended the seer's prediction beyond the immediate battle, see on lines 7-11 below.

COMMENTARY: SIMONIDES 14   233

2]αδον βαλλομε[ν: ὄμ]αδον βαλλομέ[νων σακέων, 'clash of blows on shields', illustrates one possibility, though βαλλομε[ν could equally refer to some kind of missile, most probably arrows; if so, it is noteworthy that, to judge from Herodotus, only the Athenians on the Greek side had archers at Plataea (cf. Hdt. 9.22.1, 60.3).

3–6 West's supplements (see app. crit.) produce an attractive version of Teisamenus' prophecy: 'I declare that, should the army force its way across the river first, a terrible and irresistible disaster will be theirs; but if they wait, a victory whose memory will last for ever.'

3 λ]έγω: even if we do not restore the verb, ἐγώ indicates direct speech. It has been argued that 'a divine speaker (like Nereus in [Simon.] 3.12 W²) would seem more appropriate in a poem' (Rutherford 2001: 48), but since Simonides has already named and celebrated the general Pausanias (11.33–4*), a prominent role for his seer would be more appropriate than a divine epiphany (of which there is no sign in Herodotus). **ποταμοῦ:** the river appears to be unnamed, which suggests that Teisamenus' strategic advice concerning the Asopus was already a well-known part of the Plataea story; cf. Aesch. *Persians* 805–6, produced in 472, 'They [the Persian army] remain where the Asopus waters the plain with its streams, bringing welcome enrichment to the Boeotians' land.'

5–6 ἀμαι]μάκετον, 'irresistible', suggests the Persians' huge military advantage: Herodotus records 350,000 (including 50,000 Greeks) fighting on the Persian side at Plataea versus 110,000 Greeks (38,700 hoplites, the rest light-armed troops: 9.30, 32). The Persian numbers are often thought to have been exaggerated in order to enhance the Greeks' miraculous victory (cf. Flower and Marincola 2002: 163 'estimates range from 120,000 to 30,000'). **μνή]μην:** for the Plataea elegy's role in preserving the memory of Greek heroism, see on 11.24–5* above. **ἤματα πάντ[α:** a common epic phrase (used 30 times in Homer, 26 of them at line-end); for another example in elegy, cf. Mimn. 12.1*.

7–11 The restoration by West 1993: 8 is worth pondering (Μήδους δ' ἐξ Ἀ]σί[η]ς ἐλάσει, νεύσαντο[ς Ἀθήνηι | ὀψὲ Διός, καὶ]νὴν συμμα[χ]ίην τελέω[ν | Ἄρης· εὐδά]φνωι γὰρ [ὑ]π[ὸ κ]ρηπῖδα τ[ανύσσει | νήσωι, ἄδην] ἐπά[γων εὐπ] ορίην β[ιότου, | παρβασιῶ]ν δὲ [δίκην λήψ]ει ποτὲ Φ[οῖβος Ἀπόλλων), though lines 9–10, where Ares extends a foundation under Delos (a reference to the Delian League formed in 478/477), are particularly speculative. Nonetheless, Simonides could certainly have presented a more elaborate version of the prophecy than we find in Herodotus (compare, for example, the ghost of Darius' detailed interpretation of the prophecies concerning Persia at Aesch. *Persians* 739–842).

7 ἐξ Ἀ]σί[η]ς ἐλάσει 'will drive out of Asia': if this is correct, 'Asia' here probably stands for 'Ionia', which had been under foreign control since its conquest by Croesus, beginning in 555 (cf. Hdt. 1.26), rather than referring to the entire continent of Asia, though to have the Persians driven that far is not an inconceivable prediction for a Greek victory song.

νεύσαντο[ς: if a god is nodding, it will be Zeus, since only he is portrayed as powerful enough to guarantee his decisions in this way (cf. *Il.* 1.524–30, 17.209). For the gods punishing the invaders, cf. e.g. Aesch. *Persians* 345–7 (on δαίμων τις at Salamis), 532–4 ('O Zeus the king! Now you have destroyed the army of the proud and populous Persians').

8]νὴν συμμα[χ]ίην φιλέω[ν, 'favouring a new alliance' (with και]νήν, or perhaps κοι]νήν, 'common alliance', cf. e.g. Isoc. *Plataean Oration* 14.21 ὑπὲρ τοῦ κοινοῦ τῶν συμμάχων), could be a reference to the Delian League, indicating that the poem was composed after its foundation in 478/477 but before it became widely resented by other Greek states as a tool of Athenian imperialism. Alternatively, assuming that the seer Teisamenus would be unlikely to make specific political predictions, the phrase συμμα[χ]ίην φιλέω[ν could refer to (e.g.) Zeus's admiration for the body of Greek allies who defeated the Persians at Plataea.

9 κ]ρηπῖδα: the likeliest 'foundation' is that of freedom, as in Pind. fr. 77 Maehler (on the sea battle of Artemisium in 479) ὅθι παῖδες Ἀθαναίων ἐβάλοντο φαενναν | κρηπῖδ' ἐλευθερίας; cf. Pind. *Pyth.* 4.138 βάλλετο κρηπῖδα σοφῶν ἐπέων ('he [Jason] laid the foundation of wise words'), 7.3 κρηπῖδ' ἀοιδᾶν (Athens as 'a foundation for songs'). The foundation metaphor is used by Darius' ghost as he introduces the Persian defeat at Plataea: κοὐδέπω κακῶν | κρηπὶς ὕπεστιν, ἀλλ' ἔτ' ἐκπιδύεται ('no solid floor yet lies beneath their woes, they well up still', though for the textual difficulties here see Garvie 2009: 312–13).

11]ει ποτεφ[could be εἴ ποτε, introducing a wish or prayer.

Simonides 15

Source: Plutarch, *On the Malice of Herodotus* 42 872d.

Frr. 15–16* are quoted by Plutarch as evidence against Herodotus' claim that only the Spartans, Tegeans, and Athenians engaged in direct combat with the Persians during the pitched battle at Plataea. Rejecting Herodotus' account of Corinthian cowardice (9.69), Plutarch argues as follows: 'Now so far as the Corinthians are concerned, the position they held while fighting the barbarians and the honour that resulted for them from the battle of Plataea may be seen from the following lines of Simonides [frr. 15–16*]. Simonides did not write these lines for a choral performance in Corinth or as an ode in honour of the city, but in an elegiac poem that simply records those events.' In contrast to Simonides, Herodotus' treatment of the Corinthians is indeed strikingly negative: they disobey Pausanias' orders (9.52), miss the main battle (9.69), and are not assigned a war grave at the site (9.85). The discrepancy between the two accounts, it has been suggested, may be due to the anti-Corinthian bias of Herodotus' Athenian sources (cf. Flower and Marincola 2002: 19). In any case, Simonides' extravagant praise of the Corinthians' bravery in the centre of the battle line suggests either that he had personal reasons for favouring them or (more likely) that the poem was commissioned by a group of leading states (Sparta, Athens, and Corinth supplied the most troops: cf. Hdt. 9.28–30) and that the terms of Simonides' appointment were explicitly Panhellenic (see the introduction above). Though frr. 15* and 16* come from the same poem, they were not consecutive (see on 16*).

1–3 almost certainly come from a larger catalogue of the Greek forces, detailing their origins and places in the battle line; this was a standard feature of both epic (e.g. *Il.* 2.494–779, 816–77 on Greeks and Trojans) and historical writing (cf. Hdt. 9.28.2–32.2 on Greeks and Persians at Plataea).

1 μέσσοις . . . ναιετάοντες 'and in the centre stood the men who dwell in Ephyra with its many springs'. Plutarch's comment that the poem shows 'the position they held while fighting the barbarians and the honour that resulted for them from the battle' (see above) is evidence that Simonides presented the Corinthians actually fighting in the centre against the Persians rather than simply being stationed there prior to the battle. **μέσσοις:** Herodotus has the 5,000-strong contingent of Corinthians placed on the outermost (right) edge of the centre (between the Tegeans and Potidaeans, 9.28.3), but Simonides' simple μέσσοις emphasizes their strategically essential role in holding the centre of the battle line between the Spartans on the right wing and the Athenians on the left. **Ἐφύρην:** Ephyra was an old name for Corinth: cf. *Il.* 6.152–3; according to Eumelus' cyclic epic *Corinthiaca*, Ephyra was the daughter of Oceanus and Tethys and wife of Epimetheus (fr. 1 Bernabé). By calling Corinth Ephyra as well as Glaucus' city (line 3), Simonides stresses the Corinthians' long and venerable history. **πολυπίδακα:** the epithet is used only of Mt Ida in Homer, and this is the first time it is used of another location (unless *Hom. Hymn* 19.30 ἐς Ἀρκαδίην πολυπίδακα is earlier than Simonides). Corinth had several sacred springs; for Peirene, the most famous, cf. e.g. Pind. *Ol.* 13.61 ἐν ἄστεϊ Πειράνας. **ναιετάοντες:** a poetic word, frequent in epic, often with acc. of place (e.g. *Od.* 9.21 ναιετάω δ' Ἰθάκην εὐδείελον).

2 παντοίης . . . πολέμωι, lit. 'skilled in every kind of excellence in war', stresses the Corinthians' contribution to the battle (unlike their inglorious role in Herodotus).

3 πόλιν . . . ἄστυ 'the Corinthian town, Glaucus' city': the epic-style amplification further dignifies the Corinthians. Glaucus, son of Sisyphus and Merope, was an early king of Corinth (cf. *Il.* 6.154–5, where his great-grandson Glaucus the Lycian boasts of descent from him). νέμοντες, 'inhabit', is a variation on ναιετάοντες (1), which it echoes. The manuscripts have νέμονται, but the active can have the same sense as the middle (LSJ νέμω III.1).

Simonides 16

Source: Plutarch, *On the Malice of Herodotus* 42 872d–e; *P. Oxy.* 3965 fr. 5.

Plutarch quotes 15* and 16* as separate pieces, so despite attempts to connect the two (e.g. οἳ καί (Ursinus), οἷον (Hermann), οἵπερ (Hiller), οἷοι (Diehl)), the initial dactyl or spondee of 16* is unknown, as is the length of the lacuna between the two fragments.

1 κάλλιστον . . . πόνων 'had the finest witness to their struggles': bearing witness to the victor's achievements is a leitmotif of praise poetry (cf. Pind. *Ol.* 4.3 for the poet himself as ὑψηλοτάτων μάρτυρ᾽ ἀέθλων). **ἔθεντο**: lit. 'they established for themselves' (aor. middle). **πόνων** stresses the Corinthians' actual fighting (see on 15.1* above).

2 χρυσοῦ . . . αἰθέρι '[a witness] of precious gold in the sky' (gen. of material): the kenning is easily deciphered, since the sun is proverbially all-seeing and thus often called upon to act as a witness (e.g. *Il.* 3.277 Ἠέλιός θ᾽, ὃς πάντ᾽ ἐφορᾷς καὶ πάντ᾽ ἐπακούεις, [Aesch.] *Prometheus Bound* 91 καὶ τὸν πανόπτην κύκλον ἡλίου καλῶ). Simonides used it again in at least one other elegy (fr. 87): ξεινοδόκων †δ᾽ ἄριστος ὁ χρυσὸς ἐν αἰθέρι λάμπων ('and best of witnesses, the gold that shines in the sky'). **χρυσοῦ τιμήεντος**: χρυσοῦ evokes the sun's colour and brightness, but also stresses (as does τιμήεντος) its value to human life; cf. Soph. *Ant.* 103–4 for the sun's rays heralding an army's victory, ὦ χρυσέας | ἁμέρας βλέφαρον. Helios' bed is of χρυσοῦ τιμήεντος at Mimn. 12.7*.

2–3 καί . . . | . . . πατέρων, 'which magnifies their fathers' far-famed glory and their own', emphasizes not only the Corinthians' illustrious past (cf. 15.1*), but also their success in living up to the expectations of their fathers, a fundamental feature of masculinity in patriarchal Greek society (both heroic and contemporary: cf. e.g. Soph. *Ajax* 462–72, 545–57, 1008–18). **σφιν**: dative of advantage (lit. 'for them'). **ἀέξει**: from ἀέξω, poetic form of αὔξω (αὐξάνω); cf. Pind. *Isthm.* 7.29 ἀστῶν γενεᾷ μέγιστον κλέος αὔξων. The sun 'increases' their glory by illuminating the achievements it has witnessed. **εὐρεῖαν κληδόνα**: the phrase (found only here) implicitly aligns the Corinthians who fought at Plataea with the heroes of epic, whose ultimate goal is εὐρὺ κλέος (cf. *Od.* 3.203–4 καί οἱ Ἀχαιοὶ | οἴσουσι κλέος εὐρὺ καὶ ἐσσομένοισιν ἀοιδήν).

WORKS CITED

Acosta-Hughes, B. 2002. *Polyeideia: the Iambi of Callimachus and the Archaic iambic tradition*, Berkeley
Adkins, A. W. H. 1985. *Poetic craft in the early Greek elegists*, Chicago
Alexandrou, M. 2016. 'Mythological narratives in Hipponax', in Swift and Carey 2016: 210–28
Allan, W. 2004. 'Religious syncretism: the new gods of Greek tragedy', *Harvard Studies in Classical Philology* 102: 113–55
Allan, W. 2006. 'Divine justice and cosmic order in early Greek epic', *Journal of Hellenic Studies* 126: 1–35
Allan, W. 2008. *Euripides: Helen*, Cambridge
Allan, W. 2014. 'The body in mind: medical imagery in Sophocles', *Hermes* 142: 259–78
Allan, W. 2018. 'Solon and the rhetoric of *stasis*', in Allan and Swift 2018: 113–29
Allan, W. and L. Swift, eds. 2018. *Moralizing strategies in early Greek poetry* (*Mouseion* LIX 15.1), Toronto
Allen, A. 1993. *The fragments of Mimnermus: text and commentary*, Stuttgart
Allen, A. W. 1949. 'Solon's prayer to the Muses', *Transactions of the American Philological Association* 80: 50–65
Aloni, A. 2001. 'The proem of Simonides' Plataea elegy and the circumstances of its performance', in Boedeker and Sider 2001: 86–105
Aloni, A. and A. Iannucci, eds. 2007. *L'elegia greca e l'epigramma dalle origini al V secolo. Con un'appendice sulla 'nuova' elegia di Archiloco*, Florence
Anderson, J. K. 1961. *Ancient Greek horsemanship*, Berkeley
Anderson, J. K. 1991. 'Hoplite weapons and offensive arms', in V. D. Hanson, ed. *Hoplites: the Classical Greek battle experience* (London) 15–37
Anhalt, E. K. 1993. *Solon the singer: politics and poetics*, Lanham, MD
Arnott, W. G. 1996. *Alexis: the fragments*, Cambridge
Arnott, W. G. 2007. *Birds in the ancient world from A to Z*, London
Bakker, E. J. 2017. 'Trust and fame: the seal of Theognis', in E. J. Bakker, ed. *Authorship and Greek song: authority, authenticity, and performance* (Leiden) 99–121
Balot, R. K. 2001. *Greed and injustice in Classical Athens*, Princeton
Barnes, H. R. 1995. 'The structure of the elegiac hexameter: a comparison of the structure of elegiac and stichic hexameter verse', in M. Fantuzzi and R. Pretagostini, eds. *Struttura e storia dell'esametro Greco* (Rome) 135–62
Bartol, K. 1993. *Greek elegy and iambus: studies in ancient literary sources*, Poznan

Beavis, I. C. 1988. *Insects and other invertebrates in Classical antiquity*, Liverpool
Bentein, K. 2016. *Verbal periphrasis in ancient Greek: have- and be- constructions*, Oxford
Blok, J. H. and A. P. M. H. Lardinois, eds. 2006. *Solon of Athens: new historical and philological approaches*, Leiden
Bloomer, W. M. 2013. 'The ancient child in school', in J. E. Grubbs and T. Parkin, eds. *Oxford handbook of childhood and education in the Classical world* (Oxford) 444–64
Blundell, M. W. 1989. *Helping friends and harming enemies: a study in Sophocles and Greek ethics*, Cambridge
Boardman, J. 1999. *The Greeks overseas: their early colonies and trade*, 4th ed., London
Boedeker, D. 1995. 'Simonides on Plataea: narrative elegy, mythodic history', *Zeitschrift für Papyrologie und Epigraphik* 107: 217–29
Boedeker, D. 2016. 'Coarse poetics: listening to Hipponax', in Swift and Carey 2016: 56–73
Boedeker, D. and D. Sider, eds. 2001. *The new Simonides: contexts of praise and desire*, Oxford
Bowie, E. L. 1986. 'Early Greek elegy, symposium and public festival', *Journal of Hellenic Studies* 106: 13–35
Bowie, E. L. 1990. '*Miles ludens*? The problem of martial exhortation in early Greek elegy', in Murray 1990: 221–9
Bowie, E. L. 1997. 'The Theognidea: a step towards a collection of fragments?', in G. W. Most, ed. *Collecting fragments – Fragmente sammeln* (Göttingen) 53–66
Bowie, E. L. 2000. 'Athenaeus' knowledge of early Greek elegiac and iambic poetry', in D. Braund and J. Wilkins, eds. *Athenaeus and his world* (Exeter) 124–35
Bowie, E. L. 2001a. 'Ancestors of historiography in early Greek elegiac and iambic poetry?', in N. Luraghi, ed. *The historian's craft in the age of Herodotus* (Oxford) 45–66
Bowie, E. L. 2001b. 'Early Greek iambic poetry: the importance of narrative', in Cavarzere *et al.* 2001: 1–27
Bowie, E. L. 2002. 'Ionian *iambos* and Attic *komoidia*: father and daughter, or just cousins?', in A. Willi, ed. *The language of Greek comedy* (Oxford) 33–50
Bowie, E. L. 2010. 'Stobaeus and early Greek lyric, elegiac and iambic poetry', in M. Horster and C. Reitz, eds. *Condensing Texts – Condensed Texts* (Stuttgart) 587–617
Bowie, E. L. 2016a. 'Quo usque tandem . . . ? How long were sympotic songs?', in Cazzato *et al.* 2016: 28–41

Bowie, E. L. 2016b. 'Cultic contexts for elegiac performance', in Swift and Carey 2016: 15–32
Bremmer, J. N. 2006. 'The rise of the hero cult and the new Simonides', *Zeitschrift für Papyrologie und Epigraphik* 158: 15–26
Brock, R. 2013. *Greek political imagery from Homer to Aristotle*, London
Brown, C. G. 1997. 'Iambos', in Gerber 1997a: 13–88
Brown C. G. 2018. 'Picturing a truth: beast fable, early *iambos*, and Semonides on the creation of women', in Allan and Swift 2018: 29–47
Bryan, J. 2012. *Likeness and likelihood in the Presocratics and Plato*, Cambridge
Budelmann, F. 2018. *Greek lyric: a selection*, Cambridge
Budelmann, F. and T. Power 2013. 'The inbetweenness of sympotic elegy', *Journal of Hellenic Studies* 133: 1–19
Burkert, W. 1972. *Lore and science in ancient Pythagoreanism*, trans. E. L. Minar Jr., Cambridge, MA
Burkert, W. 1985. *Greek religion*, trans. J. Raffan, Cambridge, MA
Burkert, W. 1992. *The orientalizing revolution: Near Eastern influence on Greek culture in the early Archaic age*, trans. M. E. Pinder and W. Burkert, Cambridge, MA
Cairns, D. L. 1993. *Aidōs: the psychology and ethics of honour and shame in ancient Greek literature*, Oxford
Calame, C. 1999. *The poetics of Eros in ancient Greece*, trans. J. Lloyd, Princeton
Cameron, A. 1995. *Callimachus and his critics*, Princeton
Campbell, D. A. 1976. 'The language of the new Archilochus', *Arethusa* 9: 151–7
Campbell, D. A. 1982. *Greek lyric: a selection of early Greek lyric, elegiac and iambic poetry*, 2nd ed., Bristol
Campbell, D. A. 1984. 'Stobaeus and early Greek poetry', in D. E. Gerber, ed. *Greek poetry and philosophy: studies in honor of Leonard Woodbury* (Chico, CA) 51–7
Carey, C. 1986. 'Archilochus and Lycambes', *Classical Quarterly* 36: 60–7
Carey, C. 2009. 'Iambos', in F. Budelmann, ed. *The Cambridge companion to Greek lyric* (Cambridge) 149–67
Carey, C. 2016. 'Mapping *iambos*: mining the minor talents', in Swift and Carey 2016: 122–39
Carey, C. 2018. 'Narrative, authority, and blame', in Allan and Swift 2018: 7–27
Carson, A. 1984. 'How bad a poem is Semonides fragment 1?', in D. E. Gerber, ed. *Greek poetry and philosophy: studies in honor of Leonard Woodbury* (Chico, CA) 59–71

Carson, A. 1990. 'Putting her in her place: woman, dirt, and desire', in D. M. Halperin, J. J. Winkler, and F. I. Zeitlin, eds. *Before sexuality: the construction of erotic experience in the ancient Greek world* (Princeton) 135–69
Catoni, M. L. 2010. *Bere vino puro*, Milan
Cavarzere, A., et al. eds. 2001. *Iambic ideas: essays on a poetic tradition from Archaic Greece to the late Roman empire*, Lanham, MD
Cazzato, V., et al. eds. 2016. *The cup of song: studies on poetry and the symposion*, Oxford
Clay, D. 2004. *Archilochus heros: the cult of poets in the Greek polis*, Cambridge, MA
Clay, J. S. 2016. 'How to construct a sympotic space with words', in V. Cazzato and A. Lardinois, eds. *The look of lyric: Greek song and the visual* (Leiden) 204–16
Cohen, E. E. 2015. *Athenian prostitution: the business of sex*, New York
Cooley, M. G. L. ed. 2017. *Sparta*, London
Corrêa, P. da Cunha 2007. 'A human fable and the justice of beasts in Archilochus', in P. J. Finglass, C. Collard, and N. J. Richardson, eds. *Hesperos. Studies in ancient Greek poetry presented to M. L. West on his seventieth birthday* (Oxford) 101–17
Dale, A. M. 1963. 'Stichos and stanza', *Classical Quarterly* 56: 46–60
D'Alessio, G. B. 2009. 'Defining local identities in Greek lyric poetry', in R. Hunter and I. Rutherford, eds. *Wandering poets in ancient Greek culture: travel, locality, and pan-Hellenism* (Cambridge) 137–67
Danek, G. 2015. '*Nostoi*', in M. Fantuzzi and C. Tsagalis, eds. *The epic cycle and its ancient reception* (Cambridge) 355–79
Davidson, J. 2007. *The Greeks and Greek love: a radical reappraisal of homosexuality in ancient Greece*, London
Dean-Jones, L. A. 1994. *Women's bodies in Classical Greek science*, Oxford
Degani, E. 1984. *Studi su Ipponatte*, Bari
Degani, E. 1991. *Hipponactis testimonia et fragmenta*, 2nd ed., Leipzig
Degani, E. and G. Burzacchini, eds. 2005. *Lirici greci: antologia*, 2nd ed., Bologna
Desmond, W. D. 2006. *The Greek praise of poverty: origins of ancient Cynicism*, South Bend, IN
Desmond, W. D. 2011. *Philosopher-kings of antiquity*, London
de Ste. Croix, G. E. M. 2004. *Athenian democratic origins*, Oxford
Dickey, E. 2007. *Ancient Greek scholarship*, Oxford
Dillon, M. 2002. *Girls and women in Classical Greek religion*, London
Donlan, W. 1973. 'The tradition of anti-aristocratic thought in early Greek poetry', *Historia* 22: 145–54
Dougherty, C. 1993. *The poetics of colonization: from city to text in Archaic Greece*, Oxford

Dougherty, C. 1994. 'Archaic Greek foundation poetry: questions of genre and occasion', *Journal of Hellenic Studies* 114: 35–46

Dover, K. J. 1974. *Greek popular morality*, Oxford

Dover, K. J. 1978. *Greek homosexuality*, London

Duplouy, A. and R. Brock, eds. 2018. *Defining citizenship in Archaic Greece*, Oxford

Eckerman, C. C. 2011. 'Teasing and pleasing in Archilochus' first Cologne Epode', *Zeitschrift für Papyrologie und Epigraphik* 179: 11–19

Falkner, T. M. 1995. *The poetics of old age in Greek epic, lyric, and tragedy*, Norman, OK

Faraone, C. 2008. *The stanzaic architecture of early Greek elegy*, Oxford

Faulkner, A. 2008. *The Homeric hymn to Aphrodite*, Oxford

Fenno, J. B. 2005. 'Semonides 7.43: a hard/stubborn ass', *Mnemosyne* 58: 408–11

Finkelberg, A. 1990. 'Studies in Xenophanes', *Harvard Studies in Classical Philology* 93: 104–67

Flower, M. A. and J. Marincola 2002. *Herodotus: Histories, Book IX*, Cambridge

Ford, A. 2002. *The origins of criticism: literary culture and poetic theory in Classical Greece*, Princeton

Ford, A. 2003. 'From letters to literature: reading the "song culture" of Classical Greece', in H. Yunis, ed. *Written texts and the rise of literate culture in ancient Greece* (Cambridge) 15–37

Forsdyke, S. 2006. 'Land, labor and economy in Solonian Athens: breaking the impasse between archaeology and history', in Blok and Lardinois 2006: 334–50

Forsyth, N. 1979. 'The allurement scene: a typical pattern in Greek oral epic', *Classical Antiquity* 12: 107–20

Fowler, R. L. 1987. *The nature of early Greek lyric: three preliminary studies*, Toronto

Fowler, R. L. 2000. *Early Greek mythography. Vol. 1: text and introduction*, Oxford

Fowler, R. L. 2013. *Early Greek mythography. Vol. 2: commentary*, Oxford

Foxhall, L., and J. Salmon, eds. 1998. *Thinking men: masculinity and its self-representation in the Classical tradition*, Abingdon

Fränkel, H. 1975. *Early Greek poetry and philosophy*, trans. M. Hadas and J. Willis, Oxford

Franks, H. M. 2018. *The world underfoot: mosaics and metaphor in the Greek symposium*, Oxford

Gagné, R. 2009. 'A wolf at the table: sympotic perjury in Archilochus', *Transactions of the American Philological Association* 139: 251–74

Gagné, R. 2013. *Ancestral fault in ancient Greece*, Cambridge

242   WORKS CITED

Garner, R. S. 2011. *Traditional elegy: the interplay of meter, tradition, and context in early Greek poetry*, Oxford
Gärtner, T. 2008. 'Kritische Bemerkungen zu den Fragmenten des Hipponax', *Wiener Studien* 121: 53–66
Garvie, A. F. 2009. *Aeschylus: Persae*, Oxford
Gentili, B. and C. Prato 1988–2002. *Poetarum elegiacorum testimonia et fragmenta*, 2nd ed., Leipzig
Gerber, D. E. 1970. *Euterpe: an anthology of early Greek lyric, elegiac and iambic poetry*, Amsterdam
Gerber, D. E. 1984. 'Semonides, fr. 1 West. A commentary', in D. E. Gerber, ed. *Greek poetry and philosophy: studies in honor of Leonard Woodbury* (Chico, CA) 125–35
Gerber, D. E., ed. 1997a. *A companion to the Greek lyric poets*, Leiden
Gerber, D. E. 1997b. 'Elegy', in Gerber 1997a: 91–132
Goldman, M. L. 2015. 'Associating the *aulêtris*: flute girls and prostitutes in the Classical Greek symposium', *Helios* 42: 29–60
Graf, D. F. 1984. 'Medism: the origin and significance of the term', *Journal of Hellenic Studies* 104: 15–30
Graham, A. J. 1983. *Colony and mother city in ancient Greece*, 2nd ed., Manchester
Granger, H. 2007. 'Poetry and prose: Xenophanes of Colophon', *Transactions of the American Philological Association* 137: 403–33
Graziosi, B. and J. Haubold 2003. 'Homeric masculinity: ΗΝΟΡΕΗ and ΑΓΗΝΟΡΙΗ', *Journal of Hellenic Studies* 123: 60–76
Gregory, J. W. 2007. 'Donkeys and the equine hierarchy in Archaic Greek literature', *Classical Journal* 102: 193–212
Griffith, M. 1975. 'Man and the leaves: a study of Mimnermos fr. 2', *California Studies in Classical Antiquity* 8: 73–88
Griffith, M. 2006. 'Horsepower and donkeywork: equids and the ancient Greek imagination (part one)', *Classical Philology* 101: 185–246
Griffiths, A. 1995. 'Non-aristocratic elements in Archaic poetry', in A. Powell, ed. *The Greek World* (London) 85–103
Halperin, D. M. 1990. *One hundred years of homosexuality and other essays on Greek love*, New York
Handley, E. 2007. 'Night thoughts (Archilochus 23 and 196a West)', in P. J. Finglass, C. Collard, and N. J. Richardson, eds. *Hesperos. Studies in ancient Greek poetry presented to M. L. West on his seventieth birthday* (Oxford) 95–100
Harris, E. M. 2002. 'Did Solon abolish debt-bondage?', *Classical Quarterly* 52: 415–430
Harris, E. M. 2006. 'Solon and the spirit of the laws in Archaic and Classical Greece', in Blok and Lardinois 2006: 290–318
Harrison, A. R. W. 1968. *The law of Athens*, 2 vols, Oxford

Harvey, A. E. 1955. 'The classification of Greek lyric poetry', *Classical Quarterly* 5: 157–75
Hawkins, S. 2013. *Studies in the language of Hipponax*, Bremen
Hedreen, G. 2006 '"I let go my force just touching her hair": male sexuality in Athenian vase-paintings of Silens and iambic poetry', *Classical Antiquity* 25: 277–325
Heirman, J. 2012. *Space in Archaic Greek lyric: city, countryside and sea*, Amsterdam
Heitsch, E. 1994. *Xenophanes und die Anfänge kritischen Denkens*, Mainz
Henderson, J. 1976. 'The Cologne Epode and the conventions of early Greek erotic poetry', *Arethusa* 9: 159–79
Henderson, J. 1991. *The maculate Muse: obscene language in Attic comedy*, Oxford
Henderson, W. 2006. 'The imagery of Solon, Fr. 4 West (3 Gentili–Prato)', *Acta Classica* 49: 129–36
Herington, J. 1985. *Poetry into drama: early tragedy and the Greek poetic tradition*, Berkeley
Hobden, F. 2013. *The symposium in ancient Greek society and thought*, Cambridge
Hommel, H. 1980. *Der Gott Achilleus*, Heidelberg
Hordern, J. H. 2002. 'Semonides, fr. 7.41–2', *Classical Quarterly* 52: 581–2
Horrocks, G. 2010. *Greek: a history of the language and its speakers*, Oxford
Hunter, R. 1996. *Theocritus and the archaeology of Greek poetry*, Cambridge
Hunter, R. 2013. 'One verse of Mimnermus? Latin elegy and Archaic Greek elegy', in T. D. Papanghelis, S. J. Harrison, and S. Frangoulidis, eds. *Generic interfaces in Latin literature: encounters, interactions and transformations* (Berlin) 337–50
Hunter, R. 2014. *Hesiodic voices: studies in the ancient reception of Hesiod's Works and Days*, Cambridge
Hussey, E. 1972. *The Presocratics*, London
Hutchinson, G. O. 2001. *Greek lyric poetry: a commentary on selected larger pieces*, Oxford
Irigoin, J. 2003. *La Tradition des textes grecs: pour une histoire critique*, Paris
Irwin, E. 1994. 'Roses and the bodies of beautiful women in early Greek poetry', *Echos du Monde Classique* 13: 1–13
Irwin, E. 2005. *Solon and early Greek poetry: the politics of exhortation*, Cambridge
Itsumi, K. 2007. 'What's in a line? Papyrus formats and Hephaestionic formulae', in P. J. Finglass, C. Collard, and N. J. Richardson, eds. *Hesperos. Studies in ancient Greek poetry presented to M. L. West on his seventieth birthday* (Oxford) 306–25
Kantzios, I. 2005. *The trajectory of Archaic Greek trimeters*, Leiden
Kearns, E. 1989. *The heroes of Attica*, London

Kelly, A. 2008. 'Performance and rivalry: Homer, Odysseus, and Hesiod', in M. Revermann and P. Wilson, eds. *Performance, iconography, reception: studies in honour of Oliver Taplin* (Oxford) 177–203
Kelly, A. 2015. 'Stesichorus' Homer', in P. J. Finglass and A. Kelly, eds. *Stesichorus in context* (Cambridge) 21–44
Kelly, A. (forthcoming) 'Homer and Hipponax'
Kerkhecker, A. 1999. *Callimachus' book of Iambi*, Oxford
Kilmer, M. F. 1993. *Greek erotica*, London
Kilmer, M. F. 1997. 'Painters and pederasts: ancient art, sexuality and social history', in M. Golden and P. Toohey, eds. *Inventing ancient culture: historicism, periodization and the ancient world* (New York) 36–49
King, H. 1998. *Hippocrates' woman: reading the female body in ancient Greece*, London
Kowerski, L. M. 2005, *Simonides on the Persian Wars: a study of the elegiac verses of the 'New Simonides'*, New York
Kurke, L. 1989. 'ΚΑΠΗΛΕΙΑ and deceit: Theognis 59–60', *American Journal of Philology* 110: 535–44
Kurke, L. 2000. 'The strangeness of "song culture": Archaic Greek poetry', in O. Taplin, ed. *Literature in the Greek world* (Oxford) 40–69
Lane Fox, R. 2000. 'Theognis: an alternative to democracy', in R. Brock and S. Hodkinson, eds. *Alternatives to Athens: varieties of political organization and community in ancient Greece* (Oxford) 35–51
Latacz, J. 1992. '"Freuden der Göttin gibt's ja für junge Männer mehrere ...": zur Kölner Epode des Archilochos (Fr. 196a W.)', *Museum Helveticum* 49: 3–12
Lear, A., and E. Cantarella 2008. *Images of ancient Greek pederasty: boys were their gods*, New York
Lefkowitz, M. R. 2012. *The lives of the Greek poets*, 2nd ed., Baltimore
Lennartz, K. 2000. 'Zum "erweiterten" Iambusbegriff', *Rheinisches Museum* 143: 225–50
Lennartz, K. 2010. *Iambos: philologische Untersuchungen zur Geschichte einer Gattung in der Antike*, Wiesbaden
Lesher, J. 1992. *Xenophanes of Colophon: fragments*, Toronto
Lewis, J. 2006. *Solon the thinker: political thought in Archaic Athens*, London
Lightfoot, J. L. 2009. *Hellenistic collection*, Loeb, Cambridge, MA
Lissarrague, F. 1991. *The aesthetics of the Greek banquet: images of wine and ritual*, trans. A. Szegedy-Maszak, Princeton
Lloyd-Jones, H. 1975. *Females of the species: Semonides on women*, London
Lloyd-Jones, H. 1983. *The justice of Zeus*, 2nd ed., Berkeley
Lobel, E. 1954. '2327: early elegiacs', *The Oxyrhynchus Papyri* 22: 67–76
Loraux, N. 1993. *The children of Athena: Athenian ideas about citizenship and the division between the sexes*, trans. C. Levine, Princeton

Luginbill, R. D. 2002. 'Tyrtaeus 12 West: come join the Spartan army', *Classical Quarterly* 52: 405–14
Lulli, L. 2011. *Narrare in distici: l'elegia greca arcaica e classica di argomento storico-mitico*, Rome
Luppe, W. 2008. 'Die Athener vor der Schlacht bei Plataiai (zu Simonides fr. 11 W²)', *Zeitschrift für Papyrologie und Epigraphik* 167: 4
Lynch, K. M. 2012. 'Drinking and dining', in T. J. Smith and D. Plantzos, eds. *A companion to Greek art* (Malden, MA) 525–42
MacLachlan, B. 1993. *The age of grace: charis in early Greek poetry*, Princeton
Malkin, I. 1994. *Myth and territory in the Spartan Mediterranean*, Cambridge
Manville, P. B. 1990. *The origins of citizenship in ancient Athens*, Princeton
Marrou, H. I. 1958. *A history of education in antiquity*, trans. G. Lamb, Madison
McClure, L. 1999. *Spoken like a woman: speech and gender in Athenian drama*, Princeton
McLaren, A. 2007. *Impotence: a cultural history*, Chicago
Merkelbach, R. and M. L. West 1974. 'Ein Archilochos-Papyrus', *Zeitschrift für Papyrologie und Epigraphik* 14: 97–113
Michelini, A. 1978. '"ΥΒΡΙΣ and plants', *Harvard Studies in Classical Philology* 82: 35–44
Miller, S. G. 2004. *Ancient Greek athletics*, New Haven
Molyneux, J. H. 1992. *Simonides: a historical study*, Wauconda, IL
Montana, F. 2015. 'Hellenistic scholarship', in F. Montanari, S. Matthaios, and A. Rengakos, eds. *Brill's companion to ancient Greek scholarship*. 2 vols. Vol. 1 (Leiden) 60–183
Moreno, A. 2007. *Feeding the democracy: the Athenian grain supply in the fifth and fourth centuries BC*, Oxford
Morgan, K., ed. 2003. *Popular tyranny: sovereignty and its discontents in ancient Greece*, Austin
Morgan, T. 1998. *Literate education in the Hellenistic and Roman worlds*, Cambridge
Morgan, T. 2005. 'The wisdom of Semonides fr. 7', *Cambridge Classical Journal* 51: 72–83
Morpurgo Davies, A. 1987. 'The Greek notion of dialect', *Verbum* 10: 7–28
Morrison, A. D. 2007. *The narrator in Archaic Greek and Hellenistic poetry*, Cambridge
Mülke, C. 2002. *Solons politische Elegien und Iamben (Fr. 1–13; 32–37 West): Einleitung, Text, Übersetzung, Kommentar*, Munich
Murray, O., ed. 1990. *Sympotica: a symposium on the symposion*, Oxford
Murray, O. 2018. *The symposion: dining Greek style. Essays on Greek pleasure 1983–2017*, ed. V. Cazzato, Oxford
Mynott, J. 2018. *Birds in the ancient world*, Oxford

Nelson, R. S. 2010. 'Byzantium', in A. Grafton, G. Most, and S. Settis, eds. *The Classical tradition* (Cambridge, MA) 152–8

Nesselrath, H.-G. 2007. 'Lucian and Archilochus, or: how to make use of the ancient iambographers in the context of the Second Sophistic', in P. J. Finglass, C. Collard, and N. J. Richardson, eds. *Hesperos. Studies in ancient Greek poetry presented to M. L. West on his seventieth birthday* (Oxford) 132–42

Nicolosi, A. 2007. *Ipponatte, Epodi di Strasburgo. Archiloco, Epodi di Colonia (con un'appendice su P. Oxy. LXIX 4708)*, Bologna

Nicolosi, A. 2013. *Archiloco: elegie*, Bologna

Nicolosi, A. 2016. 'Archilochus' elegiac fragments: textual and exegetical notes', in Swift and Carey 2016: 174–89

Nobili, C. 2011. 'Threnodic elegy in Sparta', *Greek, Roman, and Byzantine Studies* 51: 26–48

Noussia-Fantuzzi, M. 2010. *Solon the Athenian: the poetic fragments*, Leiden

Obbink, D. 2005. '4708. Archilochus, elegies (more of VI 854 and XXX 2507)', *The Oxyrhynchus Papyri* 69: 18–42

Obbink D. 2006. 'A new Archilochus poem', *Zeitschrift für Papyrologie und Epigraphik* 156: 1–9

Olson, S. D. and A. Sens 1999. *Matro of Pitane and the tradition of epic parody in the fourth century BCE*, Atlanta

Osborne, R. 2001. 'The use of abuse: Semonides 7', *Proceedings of the Cambridge Philological Society* 47: 47–64

Owen, S. 2003. 'Of dogs and men: Archilochus, archaeology and the Greek settlement of Thasos', *Proceedings of the Cambridge Philological Society* 49: 1–18

Page, D. L. 1936. 'The elegiacs in Euripides' *Andromache*', in C. Bailey, ed. *Greek poetry and life: essays presented to Gilbert Murray on his seventieth birthday* (Oxford) 206–30

Palmer, L. R. 1980. *The Greek language*, London

Parker, R. 1983. *Miasma: pollution and purification in early Greek religion*, Oxford

Parker, R. 1996. *Athenian religion: a history*, Oxford

Parker, R. 2000. 'Greek states and Greek oracles', in R. Buxton, ed. *Oxford readings in Greek religion* (Oxford) 76–108

Parker, R. 2011. *On Greek religion*, Ithaca

Parsons, P. J. 1992. '3965: Simonides, Elegies', *The Oxyrhynchus Papyri* 59: 4–50

Parsons, P. J. 2007. *City of the sharp-nosed fish: Greek lives in Roman Egypt*, London

Pellizer, E. and G. Tedeschi 1990. *Semonide: introduzione, testimonianze, testo critico, traduzione e commento*, Rome

Pfeiffer, R. 1968. *History of Classical scholarship from the beginnings to the end of the Hellenistic age*, Oxford
Poliakoff, M. B. 1987. *Combat sports in the ancient world: competition, violence, and culture*, New Haven
Poltera, O. 1997. *Le Langage de Simonide. Étude sur la tradition poétique et son renouvellement*, Bern
Pulleyn, S. 1997. *Prayer in Greek religion*, Oxford
Race, W. H. 1982. *The Classical priamel from Homer to Boethius*, Leiden
Rawles, R. 2008. 'Simonides fr. 11.14 W: "Close-fighting Danaans"', *Mnemosyne* 61: 459–66
Rawles, R. 2018. *Simonides the poet*, Cambridge
Reitzenstein, R. 1899. 'Zwei neue Fragmente der Epoden des Archilochos', *Sitzungsberichte der Königlich Preussischen Akademie der Wissenschaften zu Berlin* 45: 857–64
Renehan, R. 1983. 'The early Greek poets: some interpretations', *Harvard Studies in Classical Philology* 87: 1–29
Reynolds, L. D. and N. G. Wilson 2013. *Scribes and scholars: a guide to the transmission of Greek and Latin literature*, 4th ed., Oxford
Rhodes, P. J. 1981. *A commentary on the Aristotelian Athenaion politeia*, Oxford
Rhodes, P. J. 2006. 'The reforms and laws of Solon: an optimistic view', in Blok and Lardinois 2006: 248–60
Richardson, N. J. 1974. *The Homeric hymn to Demeter*, Oxford
Rihll, T. E. 1989. 'Lawgivers and tyrants (Solon, frr. 9–11 West)', *Classical Quarterly* 39: 277–86
Rijksbaron, A. 2006. *The syntax and semantics of the verb in Classical Greek: an introduction*, Chicago
Robertson, N. 1982. 'Hittite ritual at Sardis', *Classical Antiquity* 1: 122–40
Rosen, R. M. 1988. 'Hipponax, Boupalos, and the conventions of the *psogos*', *Transactions of the American Philological Association* 118: 29–41
Rosen, R. M. 2007a. *Making mockery: the poetics of ancient satire*, Oxford
Rosen, R. M. 2007b. 'The Hellenistic epigrams on Archilochus and Hipponax', in P. Bing and J. S. Bruss, eds. *Brill's companion to Hellenistic epigram* (Leiden) 459–76
Rösler, W. 1976. 'Die Dichtung des Archilochos und die neue Kölner Epode', *Rheinisches Museum* 129: 289–310
Rotstein, A. 2010. *The idea of iambos*, Oxford
Ruschenbusch, E. 2010. *Solon: Das Gesetzeswerk – Fragmente. Übersetzung und Kommentar*, Stuttgart
Rutherford, I. 2001. 'The new Simonides: toward a commentary', in Boedeker and Sider 2001: 33–54
Rutherford, I. 2013. *State pilgrims and sacred observers in ancient Greece: a study of theōriā and theōroi*, Cambridge

Saxonhouse, A. W. 1992. *Fear of diversity: the birth of political science in ancient Greek thought*, Chicago

Schachter, A. 1998. 'Simonides' elegy on Plataia: the occasion of its performance', *Zeitschrift für Papyrologie und Epigraphik* 123: 25–30

Schear L. 1984. 'Semonides Fr. 7. Wives and their husbands', *Echos du Monde Classique* 28: 39–49

Schmitt Pantel, P. 1992. *La Cité au banquet: histoire des repas publics dans les cités grecques*, Rome

Schwinge, E.-R. 1997. 'Tyrtaios über seine Dichtung (Fr. 9 G.–P. = 12 W.)', *Hermes* 125: 387–95

Seaford, R. 2004. *Money and the early Greek mind: Homer, philosophy, tragedy*, Cambridge

Selle, H. 2008. *Theognis und die Theognidea*, Berlin

Sickinger, J. P. 1999. *Public records and archives in Classical Athens*, Chapel Hill

Sider, D. 2001. 'Fragments 1–22 W^2: text, apparatus criticus, and translation', in Boedeker and Sider 2001: 13–29

Silk, M. S. 1974. *Interaction in poetic imagery with special reference to early Greek poetry*, Cambridge

Slings, S. R. 1976. 'Archilochus, the hasty mind and the hasty bitch', *Zeitschrift für Papyrologie und Epigraphik* 21: 283–8

Slings, S. R. 1987. 'First Cologne Epode', in J. M. Bremer, A. Maria van Erp Taalman Kip, and S. R. Slings, eds. *Some recently found Greek poems: text and commentary* (Leiden) 24–61

Slings, S. R. 1990. 'The "I" in personal Archaic lyric: an introduction', in S. R. Slings, ed. *The poet's I in Archaic Greek lyric* (Amsterdam) 1–30

Slings, S. R. 2000. 'Symposium: speech and ideology. Two hermeneutical issues in early Greek lyric, with special reference to Mimnermus', *Mededelingen der Koninklijke Nederlandse Akademie van Wetenschappen* 63: 5–33

Stanley, P. V. 1999. *The economic reforms of Solon*, St Katharinen

Stehle, E. 1997. *Performance and gender in ancient Greece: nondramatic poetry in its setting*, Princeton

Steinrück, M. 2000. *Iambos: Studien zum Publikum einer Gattung in der frühgriechischen Literatur*, Hildesheim

Steinrück, M. 2009. *Der neue Iambos: Studien zu den Formwegen eines griechischen Diskurses im Hellenismus und Kaiserzeit*, Hildesheim

Stewart, E. 2017a. *Greek tragedy on the move: the birth of a Panhellenic art form c. 500–300 BC*, Oxford

Stewart, E. 2017b. '"There's nothing worse than athletes": criticism of athletics and professionalism in the Archaic and Classical periods', *Nikephoros* 27: 155–76

Suárez de la Torre, E. 1998. 'El adjetivo ἐπώνυμος en la elegía por la batalla de Platea de Simónides (Fr. 11.17 West²)', *Lexis* 16: 29–32
Swift, L. 2010. *The hidden chorus: echoes of genre in tragic lyric*, Oxford
Swift, L. 2012. 'Archilochus the "anti-hero"? Heroism, flight and values in Homer and the new Archilochus fragment (P. Oxy. LXIX 4708)', *Journal of Hellenic Studies* 132: 139–55
Swift, L. 2014. 'Telephus on Paros: genealogy and myth in the "new Archilochus" poem (P. Oxy. 4708)', *Classical Quarterly* 64: 433–47
Swift, L. 2015a. 'Negotiating seduction: Archilochus' Cologne Epode and the transformation of epic', *Philologus* 159: 2–28
Swift, L. 2015b. 'Lyric visions of epic combat: the spectacle of war in Archaic personal song', in A. Bakogianni and V. Hope, eds. *War as spectacle: ancient and modern perspectives on the display of armed conflict* (London) 93–109
Swift, L. 2019. *Archilochus: the poems*, Oxford
Swift, L. and C. Carey eds. 2016. *Iambus and elegy: new approaches*, Oxford
Tarrant, R. 2016. *Texts, editors, and readers: methods and problems in Latin textual criticism*, Cambridge
Thomas, O. 2010. 'Ancient Greek awareness of child language acquisition', *Glotta* 86: 185–223
Thomas, R. 1992. *Literacy and orality in ancient Greece*, Cambridge
Thomas, R. 1995. 'The place of the poet in Archaic society', in A. Powell, ed. *The Greek world* (London) 104–29
Thompson, D'A. W. 1895. *A glossary of Greek birds*, Oxford
Tiverios, M. 2008. 'Greek colonisation of the northern Aegean', in G. R. Tsetskhladze, ed. *Greek colonisation: an account of Greek colonies and other settlements overseas*. Vol. 2 (Leiden) 1–154
Todd, S. C. 2007. *A commentary on Lysias, speeches 1–11*, Oxford
Tribulato, O. 2010. 'Literary dialects', in E. J. Bakker, ed. *A companion to the ancient Greek language* (Oxford) 388–400
Turner, E. G. 1980. *Greek papyri: an introduction*, Oxford
van Raalte, M. 1988. 'Greek elegiac verse rhythm', *Glotta* 66: 145–78
van Wees, H. 1999. 'Tyrtaeus' *Eunomia*: nothing to do with the Great Rhetra', in S. Hodkinson and A. Powell, eds. *Sparta: new perspectives* (London) 1–41
Verdenius W. J. 1977. 'Epilegomena zu Semonides, Fr. 7', *Mnemosyne* 30: 1–12
Vlastos, G. 1993. 'Solonian justice', in D. W. Graham, ed. *Studies in Greek philosophy, vol. I: the Presocratics* (Princeton) 32–56
Warren, J. 2013. 'Gods and men in Xenophanes', in V. Harte and M. Lane, eds. *Politeia in Greek and Roman philosophy* (Cambridge) 294–312
Watkins, C. 1995. *How to kill a dragon: aspects of Indo-European poetics*, Oxford

Węcowski, M. 2014. *The rise of the Greek aristocratic banquet*, Oxford
West, M. L. 1966. *Hesiod: Theogony*, Oxford
West, M. L. 1971. *Early Greek philosophy and the Orient*, Oxford
West, M. L. 1973. *Textual criticism and editorial technique*, Stuttgart
West, M. L. 1974. *Studies in Greek elegy and iambus*, Berlin
West, M. L. 1978. *Hesiod: Works and Days*, Oxford
West, M. L. 1982. *Greek metre*, Oxford
West, M. L. 1989–92. *Iambi et elegi Graeci ante Alexandrum cantati*, 2 vols, 2nd ed., Oxford
West, M. L. 1992. *Ancient Greek music*, Oxford
West, M. L. 1993. 'Simonides Redivivus', *Zeitschrift für Papyrologie und Epigraphik* 98: 1–14
West, M. L. 1997. *The east face of Helicon: west Asiatic elements in early Greek poetry and myth*, Oxford
West, M. L. 2006. 'Archilochus and Telephos', *Zeitschrift für Papyrologie und Epigraphik* 156: 11–17
Will, F. 1958. 'Solon's consciousness of himself', *Transactions of the American Philological Association* 89: 301–11
Wright, M. ed. (forthcoming) *Classical literature and quotation culture*
Yoffee, N. 2005. *Myths of the archaic state: evolution of the earliest cities, states, and civilizations*, Cambridge
Zanker, G. 2009. *Herodas: Mimiambs*, Oxford
Zetzel, J. E. G. 2018. *Critics, compilers, and commentators: an introduction to Roman philology, 200 BCE–800 CE*, Oxford

INDEX

Aesop 72, 76, 78, 84, 93, 98, 101
  See also fable
aetiology 3, 111
alliteration 15, 59, 95, 124, 130, 145, 167, 168, 182, 204, 210, 217
anacoluthon 177
anastrophe 100, 108, 152
anthropomorphism 75, 78
  rejection of 12, 180, 193–4
anus 13, 82, 203, 209, 210, 211, 212
Aphrodite 80, 82, 98, 122, 126, 176, 203, 205, 218, 224
apocope 129, 182
Apollo 63, 111, 153, 156, 164, 175, 177, 198, 199, 223, 226
Ares 58, 88, 98, 233
aristocracy 7, 10, 12, 71, 123, 131, 132, 137, 138, 139, 143, 148, 161, 163–76, 216
  See also hetaireia
Artemis 102, 103, 106, 122, 164
assonance 15, 59, 74, 145
asyndeton 60, 101, 109, 134, 140, 148, 173
Athena 60, 72, 120, 128, 130, 136, 152, 160, 203, 223, 224
athletes 118, 120, 156, 186–7, 219
  rejection of 180, 185–9
aulos 3, 5, 70, 110, 121, 174

beard 71, 72, 156
beer 69–70

caesura 16–17, 106, 171, 179, 183, 192
chiasmus 15, 58, 59, 100, 140, 148, 156
children
  development of 155, 156
  importance of 14, 91, 102, 103, 123, 125, 157, 208–9
  as means of revenge 73, 75, 78, 82, 84
choral song 1, 14, 18, 110, 114, 219, 234
civil war (*stasis*) 7, 12, 13, 135, 137, 138, 140, 142, 158, 159, 162, 167, 168, 184
closure 16, 105, 154
coinage 148, 171, 205, 207
  See also wealth

colloquialism 14, 15, 61, 70, 83, 97, 99, 196
colonization 11, 57, 59, 61, 65, 85, 111, 134, 214
consolation 3, 62, 65, 88
correption 125
crasis 75, 88, 97, 102, 177, 213, 229
cult, ritual 5, 57, 64, 131, 156, 181, 198, 207, 210, 211, 219, 221, 228

Demeter 4, 5, 102, 207
democracy 12, 13, 131, 143, 145, 161, 163, 187
dialect 14, 110, 160, 198, 200
  Attic 14, 75, 87, 90, 98, 125, 140, 160, 189
  Doric 1, 14, 110, 112, 115, 160, 224
  Ionic 1, 14, 74, 77, 87, 90, 94, 97, 98, 100, 104, 105, 107, 108, 109, 110, 111, 115, 117, 124, 125, 153, 160, 162, 181, 182, 197, 205, 206, 224
didactic poetry 3, 10, 20, 58, 86, 87, 91, 104, 139, 164, 166, 192
  parody of 5, 80, 86
digamma 105, 125, 168, 175
diminutive 174, 205
Dionysus 5, 181, 198, 199
domestic violence 94, 97
Dorian 111, 134, 222, 231, 232
double motivation 59, 66

eclipse 57, 120
ejaculation 15, 69, 70, 71, 85
elegy
  ancient terminology 2
  language of 14–15
  metre of 3, 16–17
  and lamentation 2, 62
  (re)performance of 2–3, 6, 7, 8, 65, 87, 133, 146, 189, 197, 221–2
  variety of 1–3, 57, 121
  and warfare 72, 106–7, 110, 116, 128, 219
elision 106, 168
enjambment 15, 74, 89, 100, 103, 108, 109, 119, 122, 134, 136, 137, 148, 150, 152, 155, 168, 170, 172, 174, 193

INDEX

epic
 contrast with 9, 13, 70, 107, 116, 128
 engagement with 58, 71, 80, 141, 162, 182, 184, 211, 221, 223, 235
 linguistic engagement with 3, 14–18, 60, 61, 62, 65, 66, 67, 74, 85, 86, 106, 129, 136, 173
 parody of 5, 61, 85, 89, 93, 94, 104, 194, 195, 203, 211, 217–18
epigram 3, 140, 209, 219, 227, 229
epinician 18, 20, 185, 219
etymology 129, 153, 200
 See also figura etymologica
euphemism 70, 82, 109

fable 4, 5, 58, 72–3, 75–6, 84, 91, 93, 98, 100, 101, 163, 169
fellatio 69, 85, 203
festivals 10, 79, 92, 221
 as venues for poetry 2, 5, 6, 7, 8, 79, 92, 110, 132, 189, 197, 218, 220, 221
figura etymologica 59, 102, 124, 139
food 19, 59, 93, 98, 113, 132, 137, 166, 187, 218
 See also gluttony

gender ideology 7, 10, 13–14, 64, 83, 92, 208, 210
 See also masculinity, misogyny, patriarchy, women
genitalia 69, 85
 female 69, 82, 203
 male 69, 70, 200, 209, 210, 211
genre 1, 2, 3, 4, 5, 9, 11, 14, 19, 91, 121, 182, 184, 217, 219
gluttony 91, 95, 97, 137, 189, 196, 212, 217–19
gnōmē 19, 66, 86, 88, 125, 132, 143, 150, 154, 164, 166
god(s) 62, 63, 71, 77, 82, 98, 102, 126, 127, 138, 159, 177, 178, 182, 193–4, 198, 204, 207
 in battle 58, 65, 66, 85, 119, 120, 180, 181, 184, 184, 224, 230
 as creator of women 92, 103
 as guardians of morality 73, 78, 147, 150–1, 221, 223, 224, 234
 inspiring poetry 59, 145, 152–3, 223
 power/will of 69, 87, 88, 111, 112, 113, 124, 135, 136, 148, 154, 155
 See also individual gods (Athena, *etc.*), anthropomorphism, cult, festivals, Muse(s), prayer, syncretism

Hades 81, 106, 155, 175, 197, 224
hair
 eastern style 11, 189
 as erotic image 79, 82, 85
 of goddesses 225
 as symbol of vanity 71, 72, 100, 191
hapax legomenon 94, 95, 97, 98, 180, 199, 200, 210, 211, 218
helots 12, 113, 114, 115, 227
Hephaestus 93, 125, 126, 127, 152
Hera 74, 80, 81, 198, 223, 224
Hermann's Bridge 172, 183
Hermes 5, 92, 195, 196, 197–9, 204–6, 207, 212, 217, 225
hero-cult 57, 131, 221, 226, 228
hetaireia 5, 65, 74, 129, 132, 170, 216
hiatus 63, 125, 130, 155, 168, 175
homoeroticism, homosexuality 1, 4, 13, 60, 81, 87, 90, 123, 132, 156, 164, 165, 174, 176, 221
 See also gender ideology
hoplites 142, 233
hybris 136, 137, 138, 140, 143, 147, 148, 149, 150, 154, 183, 221
hymn 3, 7, 80, 140, 192, 194, 196, 198, 220, 221, 223, 226, 228
hypallage 175
hyperbaton 152

iambus
 ancient and modern definitions 2, 3–4
 and cult 5
 language of 15–17
 metres of 3–4, 17, 72, 80, 194, 196, 198, 207, 213
 (re)performance of 5, 6, 7, 18, 87
 variety of 4–5, 7, 57, 69, 86, 158
imagery 17, 73, 105, 135, 215
 animal 70, 73, 84, 88, 90–103, 162, 163, 169, 171, 215
 epic 15, 142, 162
 natural 13, 80, 81, 82, 83, 84, 91, 93, 95, 96, 97, 102, 122, 124, 125, 126, 135, 140, 144, 149, 150
 physical 62
impotence 15, 195, 209, 210
invective 2, 4–6, 17, 57, 68, 79, 80, 86, 195, 196, 212–13, 217
Ionia(n) 1, 8, 12, 14, 71, 110, 129, 134, 190, 195, 200, 233

lacuna 106, 107, 128, 135, 137, 140, 157, 181, 200, 204, 227, 232, 236
lament 2, 62, 63, 64, 219
luxury 99, 100, 101, 189, 206, 209

rejection of 11, 68, 69, 99, 137, 180, 189–91
Lydia 11, 12, 57, 68, 69, 121, 128, 129, 131, 189–91, 195, 198, 200, 209, 220, 221
  language of 196, 198, 199, 205, 209, 210
lyric, Greek
  canonical poets of 6
  choral 219
  classification of 1, 18
  definition of 9
  erotic 91
  language of 4, 14, 15
  (re)performance of 3, 18

masculinity 13, 92, 116, 155, 157, 236
masturbation 85, 200
medicine (and medical language) 63, 153, 155, 206
metaphor 15, 17, 64, 69, 78, 82, 88, 102, 107, 108, 109, 119, 131, 138, 140, 143, 159, 161, 167, 174, 184, 203, 226, 234
metre 3–4, 16–17, 19, 71, 80, 87, 89, 97, 100, 103, 104, 105, 106, 115, 160, 187, 190, 191, 194, 196, 198, 207, 213, 217
  See also caesura, elegy, elision, Hermann's Bridge, hiatus, iambus, synecphonesis, synizesis
metronymic 204
misogyny 14, 90, 91, 92, 103, 105, 208
morality 148, 150, 164, 166, 181, 182
  animal and human 75–8
  affirmation of 4, 10, 19, 20, 73, 79
  rejection of 60, 74, 184, 185
moralizing 4, 16, 17, 66, 86, 107, 147, 151, 154, 164, 183
Muse(s) 58, 59, 121, 128, 146, 147, 148 164, 175, 176, 221, 223, 225, 226
music 5, 7, 10, 16, 110, 181

narrative 10, 64, 65, 199, 223, 227, 231
  erotic 80, 86
  in elegy 3, 121, 220
  in iambus 5, 10
  mythological 1, 2, 7, 64, 66, 121
  Near East 12, 68, 73, 150, 205
  See also Lydia, Persia
neologism 134, 210

oaths 159
  breaking of 5, 73, 74, 196, 212, 213, 215
  importance of 4, 10
obscenity 3, 4, 15, 195, 196, 203, 209
old age 1, 7, 13, 88, 120, 121–5, 155, 156
onomatopoeia (and other sound effects) 15, 63, 165, 201, 204, 211, 215
oracles 111, 112, 177, 178
oxymoron 63, 90

Panhellenism 7, 8, 110, 185, 186, 221, 223, 224, 225, 235
papyri 19, 79, 111, 141, 195, 212, 213, 214, 215, 220, 230
particles 87, 104, 105, 107, 122, 124, 126, 134, 136, 145, 150, 154, 169, 173, 179, 181
patriarchy 14, 79, 91, 92, 94, 103, 105, 236
  See also gender ideology
patronymic 164, 169, 170, 218
performance (and reperformance) 1–8, 9, 18, 60, 65, 73, 87, 92, 106, 110, 114, 121, 126, 132, 133, 136, 139, 146, 164, 167, 173, 176, 180, 183, 188, 197, 205, 221
  See also elegy, festival, iambus, *symposion*
periphrasis 59, 70, 98, 139, 151, 152, 154, 170, 186, 200, 222, 226
Persia
  knowledge of 115, 231
  praise of 227
  ruled by 180, 190, 191
  victory over 12, 190, 219–22, 229, 230, 232, 233, 234
persona (speaker, lyric 'I') 1, 5, 9–11, 15, 17, 57, 60, 62, 71, 79, 86, 87, 89, 131, 132, 133, 139, 145, 163, 164, 167, 170, 195, 197, 205, 206, 207, 208, 212, 225, 226
personification 76, 103, 122, 135, 138, 139, 151, 159, 182, 207
phalanx warfare 13, 72, 116, 119
  See also hoplites
pharmakos 210, 219
  See also cult, ritual
philosophy 2, 4, 9, 12, 16, 17, 161, 173, 180, 187, 194
  parody of 191–3
pleonasm 84, 109, 122, 161, 174

political poetry 1, 2, 4, 5, 7, 8, 11,
    12–13, 17, 58, 131–2, 158, 164
  See also aristocracy, civil war,
    democracy
polyptoton 77, 90, 155, 219
Poseidon 87, 96, 224
prayer 76, 77, 78, 79, 120, 146, 147,
    176, 177, 183, 200, 204, 206,
    213, 226, 234
parody of 195, 196, 200, 204, 206,
    213, 218
priamel 16, 116, 120, 144, 186, 188
proem 121, 128, 218, 223, 227
promiscuity 17, 79, 84, 94, 102, 104,
    202
  See also gender ideology
prostitutes 13, 70, 101, 181
proverb 16, 74, 77, 84, 87, 89, 91, 93,
    96, 98, 101, 117, 146, 151, 165,
    169, 179, 183, 189, 214, 236
pun 200, 210, 212

revenge 4, 57, 73, 76, 77, 78, 79, 163,
    176–7, 186, 197, 199, 202, 215
riddle 125, 126, 127
ring composition 16, 88, 105, 112,
    128, 140, 150, 154, 158, 162,
    167, 168

seduction 57, 73, 79–80, 81
Seven Sages 131
sex 4, 13–14, 69, 70, 79–85, 86, 90,
    98, 103, 104, 122, 123, 173, 176,
    199, 202, 203, 209
  See also ejaculation, fellatio,
    genitalia, homoeroticism,
    obscenity
simile 15, 70, 96, 97, 115, 124, 131,
    149, 158, 162, 169, 173, 178,
    211, 223
sources of texts edited here 18–19,
    111, 113, 114, 131, 141, 196
  See also transmission
symposion 2, 3, 6–8, 18, 60, 70, 73, 87,
    92, 106–7, 110, 126, 132, 133,
    139, 164, 166, 174, 180–5, 197,
    201–2, 218, 221

syncretism 198–9
synecphonesis 191
synizesis 89, 160
synonym 93, 102, 170

tmesis 63, 77, 81, 100
tragedy 9, 182, 200
transmission 1, 5, 18–20, 163, 174
  See also papyri, written texts
Trojan War, Troy 64, 67, 77, 105, 106,
    109, 150, 176, 220–6
tyranny 12, 69, 99, 100, 132, 143, 144,
    145, 146, 161, 163, 167, 168,
    176, 190, 229

values 6, 73, 79, 164, 165, 166, 174,
    195–6
communal 13, 106, 132
egalitarian 7
heroic 58, 60
militaristic 113
sexist 92
  See also aristocracy, democracy,
    gender ideology, morality
virginity 79, 80, 83, 84

wealth 5, 7, 12, 15, 88, 92, 99, 100,
    101, 116, 117, 142, 152, 165,
    172, 177, 195, 205, 206, 207
dangers of 7, 131, 135, 136, 137,
    138, 143, 146, 154, 189, 191
god of 207
rejection of 68, 69, 136, 137, 147,
    148, 149, 155, 173
  See also hybris
wine 59, 70, 181–4, 206
women 8, 14, 64, 70, 79, 81, 82, 86,
    90–106, 122, 123, 208, 209, 225
  See also domestic violence, gender
    ideology, misogyny
written texts 18–19, 164, 174

Zeus 64, 72, 74, 76, 77, 78, 80, 81,
    87, 92, 93, 95, 96, 101, 103, 105,
    108, 111, 117, 123, 125, 126,
    136, 138, 140, 146–51, 154, 155,
    159, 165, 176, 184, 186, 196,
    198, 204, 207, 224, 228, 232, 234

Printed by Printforce, the Netherlands